From Property to Family

FROM PROPERTY TO FAMILY

*American Dog Rescue and
the Discourse of Compassion*

Andrei S. Markovits
University of Michigan

and

Katherine N. Crosby
University of South Carolina

The University of Michigan Press
Ann Arbor

Published in the United States of America by
The University of Michigan Press
Manufactured in the United States of America
⊗ Printed on acid-free paper

2017   2016   2015   2014   4   3   2   1

A CIP catalog record for this book is available from the British Library.

ISBN 978-0-472-07246-0 (hardcover)
ISBN 978-0-472-05246-2 (paper)
ISBN 978-0-472-12076-5 (e-book)

Contents

Conclusion   297

Preface and Acknowledgments

Successful book projects have multiple origins. They meander for years, are dormant for lengthy periods, shelved for other endeavors, only to reappear much later in contexts that, in hindsight, were unimaginable at the outset. This book is no exception. There is no doubt that the germinal for this book happened in the late 1980s with two markedly distinct events: the first entailed my girlfriend and my purchase of a Golden Retriever puppy from an advertisement in the *Boston Globe* at some point in 1987. Over the previous year or two, I had fallen in love with the spunky Golden Retriever named Sascha that belonged to one of my colleagues at the Center for European Studies at Harvard University. I had never had a dog in my life, nor did I grow up in a family to whom dogs or any animals were particularly close or important. It had never crossed my mind that I wanted to have a dog. Moreover, my life at this time was so peripatetic that being a dog's guardian would have been completely irresponsible. And yet, I could not dismiss my feelings for Sascha. Every day when I saw him at the office, I laughed and delighted in petting him. I came to spend more and more time with him, walking him around campus. I simply wanted him. Without any research, any further thought, any real preparation, I convinced my girlfriend that we needed to buy a puppy. So we did, from some person who placed an ad in the newspaper. We had no knowledge whatsoever about puppy mills, breeders, anything relating to dogs beyond the childlike wish to "own" a Golden Retriever puppy. We picked up this puppy on a Saturday afternoon before planning to go to a movie that night. We named him Jascha—the closest we could come to Sascha and because my girlfriend and I adored the divine sound produced by the violin virtuoso Jascha Heifetz—and on the way home, we decided to forgo our going to the movie, which in retrospect was my first vaguely responsible act in this sorry affair.

Contrast this to the second event that happened barely two years later when upon the end of our relationship and my girlfriend's departure for her residency, Jascha exited from my life. It was at this juncture—in the fall of 1989—that I first encountered the term "rescue" in the context of dogs when, upon hearing from me that I wanted an adult dog, Jascha's veterinarian mentioned something called Yankee Golden Retriever Rescue to me. He, too, knew very little about this organization and referred me to one of its flyers that he had hanging in his clinic's waiting room. I read this and could not believe my eyes. One needed to fill out a lengthy application; then had to wait to be approved based on the content of this application not to receive a dog but to be accorded an onsite home visit to ascertain whether the premises were to the group's liking and then perhaps be considered a worthy recipient of a rescue dog. If approved—which was by no means certain—one then had to travel to a kennel in New Hampshire to meet the dog that the organization believed to be the best fit for the applicant. Making things even stranger, one could only visit this kennel—a two-hour drive from Boston—on Saturday mornings because the Golden Retriever breeder solely by the grace of her heart, homed these rescue dogs and could only accommodate potential rescue adopters on that day. But I persevered and eventually passed the arduous audition. The length of time involved and the obvious seriousness of the application process not only helped the organization get a good idea about who I was but also forced me to engage with the changes that this new relationship was to bring to my life. Above all, it helped me prepare for my new partner. I purchased the best leash, the snazziest bowls, the best food that the local convenience store carried. (It would be years before I came to steadily improve this low-grade fare leading to the healthy and high-quality home-cooked diet that our dogs have received in the meantime. But I did not know any better then.) I read about dogs, Golden Retrievers in particular; I even hired a canine specialist to advise me as to what I should and should not do with an adult dog who was going to share its life with me. This then led to Dovi entering my life who, as Brandi, had been an eight-year-old "owner turn in" (OTI) from Connecticut. He was the organization's 548th rescue.

The completely different mindset with which I approached the Jascha from the Dovi situation forms the core of this book. In barely two years, my relationship to animals had changed profoundly. I had acquired Jascha to be my dog. I adopted Dovi to become my family member. Dovi accompanied me everywhere, including to Austria in 1996 where I had a Fulbright professorship at the University of Innsbruck. He flew across the Atlantic sitting next to me on the Concorde for which I gladly used nearly half of my salary. In addition to this prestigious academic appointment, Dovi and I had another reason to travel to Austria, which was to spend six months with Kiki, then still living in Vienna, with whom I had enjoyed a singularly gratifying relationship since 1991 and who was to become my wife in 1997. My love for Kiki has been boundless, my admiration for her equally strong. Her limitless commitment to and love for animals are merely two of her many qualities. I have dedicated a number of my books to Kiki because her very being has made my life infinitely better and richer, allowing me the succor and comfort to write such things. But no book's very topic remains so inextricably linked to Kiki's very being as this one. Simply put, this book would never have happened without Kiki's love for animals and dogs. After Dovi's passing in 1996, Kiki and I presented each other with a wedding gift in the fall of 1997 in the form of our adopting Kelly from the Yankee Golden Retriever Rescue. Kelly, too, accompanied us everywhere and she, too, flew on the Concorde in 1998 and 1999 when I was honored to be a fellow at the Institute for Advanced Study Berlin where Kelly became a beloved presence for our ten-month stay. It was one rainy afternoon in my office, with Kelly slumbering at my feet, that I somehow came to discuss animals and their changed role in society with none other than the legendary Jürgen Habermas. He will surely not remember this, but I certainly have never forgotten it.

Following my stay in Berlin, we returned to the United States where I assumed my position at the University of Michigan, which has become my beloved home ever since. Among the very first people whom we met in our first days in Ann Arbor was Dr. Betty Jean Harper, the Visiting Vet. We encountered her name and telephone number in some handbook devoted to helpful tips for traveling with dogs, from dog-friendly hotels and accommodations, to food, health, and safety. Fifteen years later, Dr. Harper remains our trusted vet who, beginning with Kelly, has wondrously and lovingly nurtured three of her successors. In the process, Betty has become a close personal friend whom all members of our family love and admire. This book owes Betty a lot. Ditto with our dear friend Paulette Lerman, who has been a mainstay of Golden Retriever Rescue of Michigan through which we came to adopt two Golden Retrievers, Stormi and Cleo Rose. Perhaps no other person than Paulette has been able to convey to me what being engaged in a breed specific rescue really means, the kind of commitment it demands, the love for animals it presumes. Paulette's name does not appear in the text of the book. Nor is it listed in Appendix D among our sixty interviewees. But Paulette's conceptual markers and intellectual imprint on this book remain indelible. I owe her immense gratitude for her help and even greater admiration for her commitment to rescue. I am equally admiring of Mackenzie's Animal Sanctuary in Lake Odessa, Michigan, from where we adopted our Cody, as I am of Yankee Golden Retriever Rescue and Golden Retriever Rescue of Michigan that entrusted us with two dogs each who deeply enriched our lives. In particular, I thank Tommie Foote warmly for her dedication to give countless dogs a better home with good meals, a comfortable bed, safety, love, and dignity. I know that Cody will remain forever grateful to her.

My fifteen years on the faculty of the University of Michigan have been nothing short of unbridled joy. Without a doubt, they constitute, on the research and publication side as well as in teaching, far and away the most productive period of my academic career. The oft-repeated mantra of the beneficial symbiosis of teaching and research has actually been reality for me. Most of my publications of the past decade have involved co-authorships either with colleagues or with students, both graduate and undergraduate. This book is a solid case in point. In the course of wonderful discussions about the ins and outs of Swiss German in notable contrast to its Viennese variant, as well as about the dubbing of American films into German, I discovered that my colleague Robin Queen was, if anything, an even greater dog lover than I. Deeply devoted to and knowledgeable of all dogs, Border Collies in particular, a number of whom she includes in her family, Robin mutated from a fine scholar in linguistics to a colleague who knew an equal amount about dogs. In the course of our relationship, we began to discuss breed specific rescue, which, eventually, led to the publication of our research in the fine scholarly journal *Society and Animals*. My work with Robin remained germane to this book. Indeed, it represents a good portion of Chapter 2 of which Robin—as indicated at the beginning of the chapter—is a full-fledged co-author. My work with Robin as well as quite a bit of background reading that found its way, directly as well as indirectly, into this book, happened during my yearlong fellowship at the Center for Advanced Study in the Behavioral Sciences of Stanford University in 2008–2009. I thank the Center for providing me the opportunity to complete work that came to full fruition a number of years later in this book. In terms of benefiting from the cooperation with wonderful students, I would like to mention in particular Greg Cairns, Maya Kalman, Mark Rozny, and David Watnick. All helped immensely on various aspects of the book. I owe them much gratitude. Scott Cederbaum deserves praise all his own because in the summer of 2009, when I began the first round of interviews on this project beyond the ones that Robin and I had conducted for our article, he was there with me every step of the way, from helping me to conceptualize the questions to beginning the arduous transcription process of these documents that came to form the backbone of our study. Over the past three years, Joseph Klaver became an integral part of my scholarly life. We not only published a small book on the thirtieth anniversary of the German Greens' entrance into the Bundestag that appeared in English, German, and Georgian, but I also benefited immensely from Joe's input to this project. Indeed, his research for Chapter 3 was so decisive that we gave Joe full co-authorship of that part of the book. Lastly, of course, I owe the most profound thanks to Katie Crosby, this book's co-author. Katie was one of those rare students who come along once in a while in a professor's life and by their very presence affirm the joy and validity of the professor's career choice. Katie took two of my classes, one on German politics in the twentieth century, the other on the German and European Left. It was in the context of the latter that I mentioned the discourse of empathy and of compassion with some frequency and even a rudimentary conceptual clarity though with no connection to the human–animal relationship whatsoever. It was at one of Katie's visits during my office hours that we began to ruminate in the direction that was to become the core idea of this book. Working with Katie on this project was sheer pleasure. I owe her much gratitude and immense thanks.

The University of Michigan has not only provided me excellent colleagues and students but also financial assistance, for which I am deeply grateful. First and foremost, I am truly honored to have two name chairs, both of which come with a small research budget that helped greatly in the production of this book. Moreover, I want to thank the Department of Political Science, the Department of Germanic Languages and Literatures, and the Office of the Vice President for Research who each contributed funds to this project that led to its successful completion. Lastly, to remain within the confines of the University of Michigan, I am really delighted that this book will be published by the University of Michigan Press. I owe many thanks to its superb editor Aaron McCollough who acquired the manuscript, chaperoned it skillfully through the treacherous roads that comprise the production process, and—most important to me—really stood by this book's topic with his heart and soul. I am also grateful to the fine help that Marcia LaBrenz and Renee Tambeau accorded me with their expertise at the Press. Nicholle Lutz from BookComp, Inc. deserves a special shout-out for her helping me so kindly with the occasionally frustrating technicalities of copy editing. Thanks for the comments offered us by the two anonymous reviewers of our manuscript. They have markedly improved the final product.

Last but most certainly not least, I thank all our interviewees and all the rescuers who are the subjects of this book. I remain not only a multiple beneficiary of their dedicated work and incredible commitment, but, perhaps more important than that, I continue to remain their fan and admirer. This book is nothing more than an ephemeral footnote compared to the daily work that they produce. I still hope that they will enjoy reading it. Above all, I want them to regard this work as a loving tribute to them personally as well as to their priceless project of rescue. I owe these people nothing but gratitude and respect for sharing their world with us.

Although I have dedicated a number of my books to the Golden Retrievers that enriched my life when these books were published, I have yet to do so featuring all the Goldens who have smiled at me for a quarter of a century. I cannot think of a more appropriate book for such an occasion than this one. So here it is: To Jascha, Dovi, Kelly, Stormi, Cleo Rose, and Cody! Thank you so much for everything!

Andrei S. Markovits
Ann Arbor, Michigan
May 2014

✦   ✦   ✦

I would like to start by thanking my family. Without your love, help, encouragement, and sometimes even browbeating, none of this would have been possible. Thank you for pushing me and believing in me. I love you.

I must also thank my co-author, Andy Markovits. What started as the seed of an idea has bloomed into a wonderful project, and for that, I would like to give you my sincerest appreciation. Words cannot convey my gratitude for having had this opportunity to work with you.

For all the animal rescues, thank you for sharing your world with us and letting us work with you on this project. Thank you for your participation, your suggestions, and your advice. Thank you for doing the work that you do. Your rescues are testaments to the strength of your passion for saving animals, and for that, I thank you from the bottom of my heart.

For all of the dogs in my life, past and present, thank you India, Bailey, Roxie, Cali, and Stella, for being the silly, wonderful, loving, and amazing creatures that you are.

Katherine N. Crosby
Columbia, South Carolina
May 2014

Introduction

> We call all our committed and dedicated employees "soldiers of compassion" who fight what we call the "war of love" in an "army of compassion." We are winning, but make no mistake, evil is a formidable opponent.
>
> —Tanya Hilgendorf
> President and CEO of the Humane Society of Huron Valley
> In a speech at a fundraiser for the Society in Ann Arbor, Michigan,
> June 20, 2013

In his magnum opus *The Better Angels of Our Nature: Why Violence Has Declined*, Steven Pinker confesses to us that as a sophomore holding a summer assistant job in an animal research laboratory in 1975, he inadvertently killed a rat by doing what the professor asked him to—"throw the rat in the box, start the timers, and go home for the night." Instead of finding a fully conditioned rat per the experiment's expectations, upon his return to the lab the next morning, Pinker, to his horror, happened upon a deformed animal that would soon die in visibly excruciating pain. "I had tortured an animal to death," Pinker writes with horror and remorse. And nobody thought anything of it. This was par for the course, totally the norm in 1975 across the land and all comparable Western liberal democracies, let alone elsewhere in the world. By 1980, "indifference to the welfare of animals among scientists had become unthinkable, indeed illegal."[1]

Although it might appear provocative and downright grotesque to start a book about compassion toward animals by depicting the inadvertent torturing of a rat to death, even by the noted Steven Pinker, we believe that this incident well illustrates in a nutshell the massive shift in acceptable attitudes and behavior toward animals that lies at the core of this book. In the late 1960s and early 1970s, something fundamental had altered how Americans came to relate to animals. It is this something that this book tries to capture. Although we are unsure whether we are equipped to explain the major tenets of this immense cultural change to a degree that will convince our readers of its unique transformational powers, we are even less sure about offering proper explanations as to the reasons for this change. We do know for certain that without this "culture turn"—something that in our case and for our topic deserves the sobriquet "animal turn"—breed specific canine rescue, the topic of this book, would never have happened.

Pinker's optimistic story forms the context wherein we squarely place our topic. He argues cogently and with vast empirical material that, viewed in the long run, the process of civilization has tamed humans and consistently rendered them substantially less violent than they had been. Although the current world is far from perfect, Pinker demonstrates convincingly that on the whole we torture less, we engage in fewer acts of cruel punishments, we have fewer frivolous executions, we have less slavery, we rape less, we stage fewer wars in which there is total disregard for human losses—in short, we are less brutal, callous, and cruel than at any previous stages of human history. Moreover, if—and alas when—we still commit these acts, they are widely viewed as moral transgressions that possess less legitimacy than ever before in human history. Above all, something additional and historically novel entered human culture and behavior on a large scale in Western liberal democracies almost exclusively in the decade of the 1970s, though commencing in the 1960s, that opened the floodgates for subsequent huge changes in public attitudes and behavior. This shift in attitude and behavior featured the consistently growing compassion for the disempowered; an increased empathy with the weak; the widening inclusion of the excluded; a palpable primacy of decency, support, and care; an unmistakable fronting of altruism; a genuine desire and commitment to relieve suffering; and the restoring to all hitherto disempowered their robbed or never-granted dignity, thereby also granting them clear voices and solid agency.

At the beginning of the third book of his magisterial *Democracy in America*, Alexis de Tocqueville offered a fine conceptual precursor for our argument about the growth of the discourse of compassion in liberal democracies. Pursuant to the title of Chapter 1 in his book, which reads "That Manners Are Softened as Social Conditions Become More Equal," Tocqueville submits that equality in social conditions and a better acquaintance with formerly distant groups lead to a growing civility in manners.[2] Originally, one has compassion for and empathy toward members of one's inner circle, one's immediate environment. But once one's horizon expands by virtue of economic and political development, one realizes a commonality with others that one never thought one had. One comes to regard them as equals, which means that one empathizes with their fate. "When each nation has its distinct opinions, belief, laws and customs, it looks upon itself as the whole of mankind, and is moved by no sorrows but its own. Should war break out between two nations animated by this feeling, it is sure to be waged with great cruelty. . . . On the contrary, in proportion as nations become more like each other, they become reciprocally more compassionate, and the law of nations is mitigated."[3]

We argue in this book that Tocqueville's insight about the "softening" of norms, which he very much perceived as one of the beneficial, because inclusive, dimensions created by democracy, has come to extend beyond humans and includes animals as worthy of the heightened discourse of compassion and empathy that, as of the late 1960s and early 1970s, became common, even expected, discourse and behavior in the liberal democracies of the advanced industrial world. Empathy and compassion, at their core, center on respect for others, on according them full agency, dignity and autonomy by admitting wrongs that one has committed against them.

One of the powerful early symbols of this new discourse of collective contrition and active apology was German Chancellor Willy Brandt's unplanned and spontaneous dropping to his knees on December 7, 1970, in Warsaw before the monument of the Warsaw Ghetto uprising in 1943. To be sure, the Federal Republic of Germany had commenced various restitution payments and other acts of "reparation" to some, although certainly not all, victims of National Socialism as early as the 1950s. Moreover, the Frankfurt Auschwitz trials of 1963–1965 spearheaded several other public events that signaled the beginning of a process that would confront Germans with the singularity of their crimes. But no official decrees, laws, speeches, and payments came close to having the power and symbolic value of Brandt's gesture of genuine contrition and heartfelt apology. Typically, statesmen, whose role has always been to uphold their governments' honor and, of course, to project their countries' power when traveling abroad, did not do such things. This, after all, was the chancellor of the Federal Republic of Germany, one of Europe's most powerful and stable countries, kneeling in a foreign capital to express personal contrition for the crimes that were committed in his country's name by a regime that had been thoroughly defeated and completely discredited a quarter of a century before. Needless to say, Brandt was heavily criticized back home for his gesture. Still, a hitherto unknown tone in international politics and public affairs had entered the stage.

As Elazar Barkan demonstrates in his superb *The Guilt of Nations: Restitution and Negotiating Historical Injustices*, the German case found its parallel in many other liberal democracies. Commencing in the 1970s and coming to fruition in the 1990s and the 2000s, we can witness a number of instances in which heads of state or government acknowledge (in some cases even atone for) crimes that their peoples committed in their countries' names. These acts of collective contrition assume many forms alone or in combination, ranging from the issuance of wholesale apologies for the past wrongdoings to the distribution of monetary reparations; from the much more tempered and qualified measures of acknowledging some malfeasance to the offering of various nonmonetary restitutions. Here are a few illustrations (from Barkan's book and beyond) of the collective contrition by a country toward the victims of its crimes: Japan's financial restitution for enslaving Korean "comfort women" for the sexual pleasures of its troops during World War II; Switzerland's admittance to having profited from not only being Nazi Germany's major source of foreign currency during the war but also having been the safe haven to which treasures amounting to many billion dollars were sent, often by Jews who sought this country's neutrality as their last resort of safety or by non-Jews depositing riches obtained from killed Jews. Known as the "Nazi Gold" phenomenon, the Swiss case attained such prominence that it spawned similar introspections by other European countries' comparable behavior during World War II, most notably Sweden, another neutral country like Switzerland. Under the rubric "'first nations' renaissance," Barkan discusses this phenomenon's proliferation well beyond the legacies of the crimes committed by World War II's Axis powers, demonstrating that in the past few decades this discourse has engulfed much of the developed world and its postcolonial legacies in Asia, Africa, and, of course the Americas.[4]

That the crux of this new discourse of sensitivity and contrition has little to do with the compensation for lost material resources and everything to do with the restoration of dignity and the restitution of authenticity and sovereignty is best underlined in Barkan's section tellingly titled "Bones," in which he demonstrates how such jewels of global culture and repositories of knowledge like the British Museum and the Vatican Museum have come under increasing pressure to return the remains of native peoples that were removed from their proper resting places by the European colonizers. "Many of the world's grand museums are hearing increasing demands for the return of human remains from former colonies or conquered peoples," writes Doreen Carvajal in an article in the *New York Times* featuring the conundrum facing Berlin's Museum of Medical History. "In many ways the German [Museums] Association is drawing on the experiences of museums in Britain and the United States, which started facing claims for the repatriation of human remains decades ago."[5]

In an op ed piece in the *New York Times* appropriately labeled "Atoning for the Sins of the Empire," the British historian David M. Anderson informs us that in a "historic decision last week, the British government agreed to compensate 5,228 Kenyans who were tortured and abused while detained during the Mau Mau rebellion of the 1950s. Each claimant will receive around £2,670 (about $4,000). The money is paltry. But the principle it establishes, and the history it rewrites, are both profound."[6] This decision by the British government, we learn, follows Britain's formal apology in 2010 "for its army's conduct in the infamous 'Bloody Sunday' killings in Northern Ireland in 1972," with the British Prime Minster David Cameron using a visit in 2013 to Amritsar, India, the site of a 1919 massacre, "to express 'regret for the loss of life.'"[7]

It would take us beyond the purview of this book to describe the controversies—even resistance—that each of these acts of contrition faced and continues to confront in all affected societies. Though very different from case to case, and country to country, all opposition to such acts of contrition had much less to do with money than with that elusive but immensely potent force called honor. On the whole, opponents of apologies, contrition, and atonement on the part of the perpetrators for wrongs they committed against the formerly disempowered felt that admitting past transgressions had less to do with compassion and empathy toward the former victims (national or international) as it did with a desire for self-denigration and needless guilt that had become so common in the wake of what we in this book have come to call the discourse of compassion. This, so its critics point out, celebrates weakness, absolves responsibility, and glorifies victims.

What about the United States? The parallels are solid and show that in this case, too, the discourse of empathy and compassion that had commenced in the 1970s came to fruition in the course of the ensuing decades. Under the aegis of President Bill Clinton's presidency in the 1990s, the United States came to issue important apologies to victims of its brutal ways. Although President Clinton may well be a man of great personal kindness and compassion, we doubt that these important acts of collective contrition were due to the president's fine qualities. Instead, they emanated from a completely altered zeitgeist that featured a fundamental change in the dominant attitudes and behavior toward the disempowered. Thus, for example, on October 1, 1993, President Clinton signed an "apology letter accompanying federal reparations checks" that were sent to Japanese American internees during World War II. The president wrote: "Today, on behalf of your fellow Americans, I offer a sincere apology to you for the actions that unfairly denied Japanese Americans and their families fundamental liberties during World War II."[8] In the very same year, President Clinton signed legislation that apologized to Native Hawaiians for the United States' role in overthrowing the Hawaiian monarchy.[9] Five years later, during a state visit to a number of African nations, President Clinton offered two apologies: In Uganda for the slave trade; and in Rwanda for the United States' and other Western nations' passivity (thus implied complicity) in the face of what has come to be known as the "Rwandan Genocide," in which approximately 600,000 Tutsis and moderate Hutus were slaughtered in the spring of 1994.

President Barack Obama signed the Native American Apology Resolution into law on December 19, 2009. Buried in the Defense Appropriations Act to which Senator Sam Brownback (Republican from Kansas) and Congressman Dan Boren (Democrat from Oklahoma) successfully added this resolution, the document "apologizes on behalf of the people of the United States to all Native Peoples for the many instances of violence, maltreatment, and neglect inflicted on Native Peoples by citizens of the United States" and "urges the President to acknowledge the wrongs of the United States against Indian tribes in the history of the United States in order to bring healing to this land."[10] This legislation represents merely the governmental tip of a huge societal and cultural iceberg that commenced its formation in the late 1960s and early 1970s, having the restoration of a modicum of dignity to the Native peoples as its sole mission.

Nothing manifests this culture turn more emphatically than the Native American mascot controversies that began to beset sports teams across the country in all sports and on all levels of play, from peewee through high school and college to the professionals. Many changed their nicknames and mascots; Stanford University—tellingly due to student pressure—dropped its "Indian" symbol in 1972, assuming the nickname "Cardinals" until 1981, which then mutated to the singular "Cardinal." Some maintained their previous Native American–related names and symbols only after getting the explicit consent and approval of the represented tribe, as has been the case with the Seminoles of Florida State University. Alas, some egregiously offensive chants and team names remain. That the National

Football League's team situated in our nation's capital is still called the Redskins in 2014 remains an especially painful reminder of the ubiquity of insensitive language that was perfectly acceptable in American public life before the advent of the cultural changes that began in the late 1960s and escalated throughout the 1970s and beyond, of which the discourse of compassion is an integral part.[11]

As to our nation's most acute violation of human beings—the enslavement of Africans on American soil—there have been a few tepid steps worthy of mention, all, of course, in the wake of the rising legitimacy of the discourse of empathy and compassion starting in the late 1960s and early 1970s: Five states have issued apologies for slavery; the Senate expressed regret in 2005 for having failed to pass antilynching laws; the same body voted in June 2009 to approve an apology for slavery though with a solid disclaimer for any reparations; and eleven months before this, the House of Representatives "issued an unprecedented apology to black Americans for the wrongs committed against them and their ancestors who suffered under slavery and Jim Crow segregation laws."[12] Though far from any apology, one needs to regard one of affirmative action's main reasons and purposes as a compensatory measure to rectify current inequalities that have been the result of past iniquities. Among other measures of distributive justice, affirmative action represents governmental policies that stand for contemporary steps of reparation and restitution for currently disadvantaged collectives largely on account of their mistreatment in the past.

Clearly, this immense culture turn did not drop from the sky. Instead, it was the result of bitter political struggles that are far from over and that continue to dominate American domestic politics quite divisibly and acrimoniously to this day. Pinker rightly labels this transformation "the rights revolutions" in that their thrust has been to extend full rights that the ruling strata had possessed for centuries to particular groups devoid of them. Needless to say, the sparks in this fierce encounter have been flying incessantly since the late 1960s and early 1970s with no signs of abatement. Pinker presents the following convincing stories backed by a bevy of data in his rightfully optimistic account of this pervasive struggle that remains far from being victorious: civil rights and the decline of lynching and racial pogroms; women's rights and the decline of rape and battering; children's rights and the decline of infanticide, spanking, child abuse, and bullying; gay rights and the decline of gay-bashing, and the decriminalization of homosexuality; and, lastly, animal rights and the decline of cruelty to animals. This list, of course, is not exhaustive. Indeed, the point of the whole story is that it constitutes a never-ending emancipatory process in which the formerly excluded and disdained finally attain their voice, face, and history. Just think of Charles Glass's wonderful book about the nearly 50,000 deserters from the American armed forces during World War II, in other words the outcasts of the much-ballyhooed and de facto sanctified "Greatest Generation" who now, many decades later, may be accorded some understanding if certainly no dignity or honor.[13]

And recall how mindful we have become of granting disempowered groups some of their dignity by dropping all assignations that they deemed demeaning to themselves but which were totally common and not seen as particularly offensive by society as a whole until the beginning of the 1970s. Indeed, the terms that in the meantime have become unacceptable were decidedly not the pejorative appellations that existed in quotidian language and—alas—continue to flourish unabated though beyond the pale of the acceptable. We went from "Indians" to "Native Americans"[14]; from "Negroes" to "Blacks" and—better still—"African Americans"; from "gypsies" to "Sinti and Roma"; from "girls" to "women"; from "cripples" to "disabled" and "physically challenged" or often "physically different"; from "retarded" to "mentally challenged" or "mentally different"; from "prostitutes" to "sex workers." Moreover, just think of the burgeoning lexicon relating to a new and much more sensitive—as well as decidedly less sexist—manner to characterize gender and sexual orientation (cisgendered, gender-questioning, transgendered, and many others).

Among Pinker's many convincing data demonstrating an undeniable growth in civility affected by the culture turn, he devotes a fascinating section of his book to a discussion of "empathy." He writes:

> We live in an age of empathy. So announces a manifesto by the eminent primatologist Frans de Waal, one of a spate of books that have championed this human capability at the end of the first decade of the new millennium. Here is a sample of titles and subtitles that have appeared in just the past two years: *The Age of Empathy*, *Why Empathy Matters*, *The Social Neuroscience of Empathy*, *The Science of Empathy*, *The Empathy Gap*, *Why Empathy Is Essential (and Endangered)*, *Empathy in the Global World*, and *How Companies Prosper When They Create Widespread Empathy*.[15]

Although we agree with Pinker that all these rights revolutions emerged during the decade of the 1970s and came to fruition in the subsequent era of the 1980s, and particularly in the 1990s, we would like to anchor the germinal for most, if not all, of them in the antinomian challenges to the "establishment" that occurred in the 1960s. The campus rebellions at Berkeley, Columbia, the Sorbonne, and the Free University of Berlin spawned such a hiatus between the new and the old, the countercultural and the established, that this phenomenon has earned its very own generational sobriquet most certainly in German with *achtundsechziger* and French with *soixanthuitards* with its English equivalent of "sixty-eighters" less used but also known. Although it would be foolish to deny some of the infelicitous legacies that emerged from this international movement's cultural thrust, there exists little doubt that this also included the culture turn and value change that Pinker rightly celebrates as the transformative rights revolutions, which have improved the human condition and enhanced our democratic order and outlook in that they proved inclusive of the formerly excluded, respectful of the formerly disrespected, and compassionate to the formerly abused.

The gaining of all these rights would have been unthinkable without a good dosage of empathy on all players' parts, including those belonging to the hegemonic group of the privileged and powerful. After all, no successes would have been possible had there not been some ability on the part of the dominant and included "to understand and share the feelings of another," in this case the subordinate and excluded.[16] The civil rights movement might possibly have not been successful had many white males—including many of the Freedom Riders, some of whom were brutally slain by Klansmen—not joined the cause in good part because they felt empathy with disenfranchised blacks. Even as distant outsiders, these white men had the ability to "understand and share the feelings" of African Americans who led much less fortunate lives than they did. Much social and cultural change emanates from outside the established order, from "below," so to speak; but none can claim meaningful and lasting success without significant contribution by established forces, from "above."

We argue that the driving force for the betterment of the conditions for animals was much less driven by empathy than it was by compassion, which the *American Heritage Dictionary of the English Language* defines as "the deep feeling of sharing the suffering of another in the inclination to give aid or support, or to show mercy."[17] Although we have ample compassion for dogs, cats, elephants, penguins, seals, wolves, dolphins, and even snail darters, it is hard to argue that our helping them emanates from our understanding and sharing these creatures' feelings and thoughts. Rather, our striving to better their conditions arises at the very least from our compassion for their precarious predicament but more often from our compassion for their outright suffering and the very endangerment of their lives.

Thus, we would group the movement toward the improvement of the lives of animals—that Pinker calls animal rights—in a slightly separate category from all the other emancipatory movements. By dint of the primacy of compassion instead of empathy as its motor, we group the animal rights movement with the environmental movement. After all, in this case, too, we feel compassion rather than empathy for a depleted forest or a polluted river. But the most important difference lies in the fact that in neither case—the environment or the animals—did either of these initiate their own struggle for their respective rights. Whereas African Americans had their Selma, Montgomery, and March on Washington; gays their Stonewall riots; women their marches and heroes from the first women's movement of the late nineteenth and early twentieth centuries plus their demonstrations and feminist writers of the late 1960s and early 1970s; the environment and animals could not assume any agency for their own cause. They never became the subjects of history as did all other emancipatory movements that changed our hegemonic culture since the late 1960s and early 1970s. Instead, just like children, animals and the environment had to rely completely on the compassion of benevolent and sympathetic human adults. But unlike children for whom adults can—and do—have lots of empathy if only because all of them were children themselves, the human bond with and advocacy for animals and the environment are completely one sided and unidirectional: from us to them. They only have our compassion as their advocates and allies, no one else.

The Animal Turn of the 1970s

Any regular watching of the television series *Mad Men* will reveal what a totally different country the United States of the 1950s and 1960s was from its counterpart four decades later. If taming (even conquest) of nature bespoke progressive politics and defined liberal culture from the era of the French and American revolutions of the late eighteenth century (arguably since the Enlightenment) until the late 1960s, a complete reversal occurred in barely a decade in which the task emerged to tame and conquer all human propensities that proved detrimental to and destructive of nature. If well-intentioned public mega projects like the federally owned Tennessee Valley Authority embodied the essence of progressivism in the 1930s, their counterparts of the 1970s quickly became perceived as reactionary behemoths that, because of their alleged environmental destruction and disregard of nature, had to be stopped virtually at all cost. Nothing defines this waning of the red (i.e., social democratic and communist) left and the concomitant birth of its green variant more emphatically than the iconic Tellico Dam controversy in which the aforementioned Tennessee Valley Authority, formerly progressivism's shining light, was taken to court for violating the Endangered Species Act of 1969 and its amended version of 1973 by threatening the habitat of the snail darter fish in the Tennessee River with the Authority's plan to construct the dam. Plaintiffs argued that the building of the dam would destroy the critical habitat and endanger the population of snail darters. With a six to three vote, the Supreme Court of the United States ruled in favor of plaintiffs "and granted an injunction stating that there would be a conflict between Tellico Dam operation and the explicit provisions of Section 7 of the Endangered Species Act."[18] Whereas protecting snail darters from encroachment by humans was nothing short of revolutionary in the 1970s, moving the launching pad for fireworks in suburban Seattle sufficiently far from bald eagle babies so they would not be scared by the noise had become par for the course of American morality and behavior toward animals by Independence Day of 2013.[19] Developments in the four decades separating these events made it completely natural that the comfort and safety of bald eagle babies be taken into consideration in the planning of the traditional July 4th fireworks.

In the United States, as in most comparable advanced industrial societies governed by liberal democracies, one of the most essential pillars of being progressive starting in the 1970s centered on an altered view of humans' relationship to nature, which mutated from the former unquestioned domination of it to one of preservation of and compassion for it. The decade of the 1970s was, by no coincidence, the one that spawned the birth and growth of green political movements and parties all over the industrial world that came to define progress very differently from its red predecessor. Again, not by chance, women and animals—the former both as subjects and objects, the latter still mainly as objects—were to assume pride of place in this new social, political, and cultural compact.

Rallying on behalf of the snail darter underlines the solid commitment expressed by the "animal turn" to protect and improve the lives of creatures way beyond the warm, fuzzy, furry, cuddly, and cute. Here is some additional evidence of the universal nature of this commitment: In contrast to 1970, when only three states had anything resembling felony animal cruelty provisions, interestingly all hailing from the nineteenth century (Massachusetts, 1804; Oklahoma, 1887; and Rhode Island, 1896)[20]; and to 1993, when just seven states had such statutes on their books; by 2013, there were only four states in the union without a felony animal cruelty law. Statutes that categorize animal cruelty as a misdemeanor exist in all fifty states.

To be sure, "these laws do not afford animals legal rights, but rather serve as the primary legal protection for animals in our legal system. It should be noted that there is no overarching federal anti-cruelty law; rather, all fifty states have individual anti-cruelty laws."[21] The closest legislation on the federal level features the Humane Slaughter Act of 1958 and the Animal Welfare Act of 1966, which—due to the time of its passage—was still quite circumspect and meek concerning the statutory protection it offered to animals. The law concerned itself primarily with dogs and cats and "was restrictive in regards to its coverage of the types of animals and regulated facilities. Research facilities only had to register if they received government funding and the dogs and cats had to have crossed state lines."[22] However, not surprisingly and confirming the gist of our argument, with each subsequent amendment of this act (1970, 1976, 1990, 2002, and 2007), the federal government's parameters in the treatment of animals became increasingly more humane, even if the actual punishment of cruelty against animals continues to remain in the purview of the fifty individual states. Again, bespeaking the salience of this concern, animal cruelty laws have become among the fastest growing laws of any in the United States.[23] But demonstrating these laws' circumspect nature is that virtually all of them punish random and wanton acts of cruelty without addressing the institutional kind totally common in any form of factory farming. Although in that case, too, some improvements (though far from sufficient) have happened on account of the changed nature of our moral attitudes vis-à-vis the disempowered, which, as a matter of course, now always include animals.

An increasing number of Americans—just like citizens of other advanced industrial societies—have come to view the conventional treatment of farm animals as cruel in some fashion.

> Though Americans oppose bans on hunting or on the use of animals in medical research and product testing, 62 percent support "strict laws concerning the treatment of farm animals." And when given the opportunity, they translate their opinions into votes. Livestock rights have been written into laws of Arizona, Colorado, Florida, Maine, Michigan, Ohio, and Oregon, and in 2008, 63 percent of California voters approved the Prevention of Farm Animal Cruelty Act, which bans veal crates, poultry cages, and sow gestation crates that prevent the animal from moving around. There is a cliché in American politics: as California goes, so goes the country.[24]

To be sure, none of these laws exacting crucial improvements in the daily lives of millions of animals accord these creatures the legal standing of humans. Instead, rather than according animals complete legal and moral equality with humans, thus giving them comprehensive rights comparable to those enjoyed by humans, these laws' very essence consists of protecting the weak and having compassion for the disempowered. As such, animals continue to be the objects of humans' wishes and actions instead of being the subjects of their very own fate. Still, the changes in substance as well as form are nothing short of massive when compared with the common view and quotidian treatment of animals that governed the morality of the pre-1970s era.

Indeed, the entirely new discipline of "animal law" emerged in the course of this culture turn. Befitting the spirit of the two pioneering explorers that gave the university its name, it is perhaps not by chance that Lewis and Clark University in the greenly progressive state of Oregon was the very first U.S.-based institution of higher education to establish an animal law program in 1992. It is also no coincidence that it was the same university's Law School that in 1970 inaugurated the very first program in environmental law in the United States. "Animal law is where environmental law was 20 years ago. It's in its infancy, but growing," said Pamela Frasch, who heads the National Center for Animal Law at Lewis and Clark Law School in Portland where she has been an adjunct professor for ten years.[25] Lewis and Clark opened the first Animal Legal Defense Fund chapter in 1992. Today, it has branches at more than 115 law schools in the United States and Canada. In 2000, nine law schools had animal law studies. In 2013, about one hundred did. "The reason it [animal law] is getting taught is student demand," said David Favre, who teaches animal law at Michigan State University College of Law and is a top authority in the field. "It's not because tenured professors wanted to teach it, it's that students want to take it."[26] The centrality of animal rights in the law has progressed to the point that in early December 2013, Steven M. Wise of the Nonhuman Rights Project "filed a classic writ of habeas corpus, that revered staple of American and English law and tired cliché of detective fiction—not for a person held unlawfully, but for Tommy, a chimpanzee in Gloversville, N.Y. . . . The use of habeas corpus actions is a time-honored legal strategy for addressing unlawful imprisonment of human beings. Mr. Wise argues in a 70-plus-page memo rich with legal, scientific and philosophical references that being human is not essential to having rights. He argues that captive chimps are, in fact, enslaved, and that the same principles apply to them as to humans who were enslaved."[27] Laurence H. Tribe, the renowned legal scholar at Harvard University, responded to the reporter's inquiries about this case that "'the classic writ of habeas corpus is as good a place to begin as any'" in seeking rights for nonhuman animals.[28] In a feature story of the *New York Times Magazine*, Charles Siebert argued persuasively how, by having Tommy sue his captors, Wise and his team have come to raise "profound questions about how we define personhood."[29] At the time of this writing, Tommy lost his case in the Montgomery County courthouse in Fonda, New York. But far from being a priori dismissive of the whole issue, Justice Joseph M. Sise took the case seriously and engaged the profound moral and philosophical questions addressed by it with great care, thus clearly conveying to Wise and the world that this was not a frivolous matter but quite possibly the forerunner of a whole new aspect of law and its accompanying morality. Justice Sise concluded the case by telling Wise: "'I'm sorry I can't sign the order, but I hope you continue. As an animal lover, I appreciate your work.'"[30] Confirming our placing the origins of this entirely new discourse in the late 1960s and early 1970s, Wise's commitment to animal rights hails from his becoming involved in the anti-Vietnam War movement.

This novel approach of according certain animals equal rights to humans in the eyes of the law, of giving them full agency as it were, rests not only on the unquestioned growth in many humans' compassion toward the disempowered over the past forty years, but also in concomitant scientific advances that demonstrate how certain animals—elephants, chimpanzees, dolphins, and other cetaceans—possess definitive abilities of self-awareness like recognizing themselves in mirrors or planning for the future. This, in essence, means that these animals have a clear sense of identity and autonomy, meaning that they have "'a very basic capacity to be aware of yourself, your circumstances and your future.'"[31]

In addition to law, animal studies have experienced a parallel academic proliferation in other disciplines. In 1992, the periodical *Society & Animals* commenced its existence as a much-respected scholarly journal devoted to the publishing of inter- and cross-disciplinary work in animal studies and the human–animal interaction broadly construed. Ten years later, "the American Sociological Association recognized a section devoted to Animals and Society, which meant that several hundred sociologists had indicated their interest in the topic by joining the section in formation. . . . A critical mass of sociologists has decided that the social world does not consist only of humans."[32]

We all have seen various statements in the rolling credits at the end of motion pictures assuring us that none of the animals in the film were harmed in any way during the film's production. Pinker took the trouble to research this very point further since it centrally confirms the gist of his book's argument. And sure enough, the data speak volumes. The American Humane Association, which attests to the proper treatment of all animals in motion pictures, issues a 131-page *Guidelines for the Safe Use of Animals in Filmed Media* that it first compiled in 1988 and updates regularly. Its definition of "animal" includes "any sentient creature, including birds, fish, reptiles and insects." Moreover, this organization only speaks of "animal actors" precisely because it insists that "animals are not props,"[33] thus according them the same sort of dignity given to Native peoples with the spurning of using their likeness as mascots, as sports props so to speak. Pinker also assembled the American Humane Association's compilation of motion pictures between 1972 and 2010 in which animals were harmed. His graph reveals that there were thirteen or fourteen such films annually between 1972 and 1980, when the number dropped precipitously to around three or four, where it stayed on an annual basis until 1989 when it decreased to one or fewer, which remains the norm.[34]

No dinner invitation in contemporary urban America can be extended without the proper query concerning the guests' dietary restrictions. All transportation venues, convention meals—let alone restaurants—offer some vegetarian food option as a matter of course. And an increasing number of eateries and stores assure their clientele that their meat products hail from animals that had been treated humanely until their inevitable murder. "Free-range" chickens have become a veritable marker of morality. What exactly such notations actually mean and what their claims to an alleged improvement in these animals' lives constitute in reality remain contested topics that are well beyond the confines of this book. Instead, what matters to the atmospheric framework of this project—to its very setting—is the fact that an increasing number of establishments, institutions, and organizations feel the moral need and financial necessity to display the benevolent treatment of animals even if in actuality this still might not be the case. Quite simply, the culture turn of the 1970s has created an animal turn that has rendered any mistreatment of animals morally unacceptable in the United States and comparable democracies of the advanced industrial world. This, alas, does not mean that such mistreatment—just think of industrial farming—does not happen constantly and as part of regular quotidian life. But what matters for our purposes is the fact that human domination and abuse of animals has now become illegitimate and fully contested in our contemporary culture.

For no animals is this massive change in attitudes and perception more pervasive and relevant than for cats and dogs. More than any other animals, cats and dogs have become an indispensable part of the modern American family. Indeed, the era under consideration in this book, meaning 1970 to the present, witnessed a major quantitative shift that is testimony to an equally important qualitative one in terms of popular attitudes toward these animals. "The U.S. has come a long way over the last few decades in increasing pet ownership and decreasing euthanasia," writes the Humane Society of the United States. "From 1970 to 2010, the number of dogs and cats in homes has increased from 67 million to 164 million. The annual number of dogs and cats euthanized in shelters has also decreased from 12–20 million to 3–4 million."[35]

Furthermore, it may well be argued that among all animals, dogs' relations—even more than cats'—with humans have attained the most powerful, explicit, and lasting change in the wake of the "animal turn." One well-documented marker of this shift is the upgrading of many dogs' social standing from the former companion animal to full-fledged family member. Many humans see and call themselves as "moms" and "dads" in their relationship with their dogs; people refer to dogs as the siblings of their human children; quite often people know dogs' names before (and instead of) the names of the dogs' human companions. Multiple studies have also documented the degree to which humans speak to their pets, using features of child-directed speech (also sometimes called "baby talk") and use their pets as a means of mediating family disputes and disagreements.[36] Moreover, like with all major shifts in social mores and attitudes, in this case, too, the acceptable nomenclature and language have changed. Thus, increasingly one does not speak of dog "owners" but of "caretakers," "parents," and "companions," connoting a clear shift in the bestowing of agency and dignity, if not yet total equality, to these creatures. Studies have also shown, particularly among women, the existence of a greater affiliation with dogs than with human family members.

Indeed, a well-known survey in 2006 by the respectable Pew Research Center in Washington, D.C., revealed the following "family intimacy standings" in terms of how "close" Americans felt to their pets and immediate family members: "dog" led by 94 percent followed by "mom" with 87 percent with "cat" garnering 84 percent and "dad" trailing last with 74 percent. The Center concluded: "Dogs edge both parents, as well as cats, in the [American] human intimacy sweepstake."[37]

The intimacy between humans and dogs is nothing new, of course. The bond that these two species have established over millennia is quite unique in its geographic, social, and cultural width, as well as in its emotional depth. The moving bond between Argos and Odysseus, who recognize each other instantly after ten long years of separation and express their deep love for each other silently lest the latter's identity be revealed to his enemies swarming his house, is merely one of many such cross-cultural instances that demonstrate this special relationship upon which—for good reason—the English language has bestowed the fitting sobriquet of "man's best friend." Countless books, letters, poems, paintings, and musical pieces have offered paeans to this special relationship over millennia. Mark Derr's superb book offers a fine account of dogs' ubiquity in all facets of American history and their constant presence in virtually every imaginable human activity on this vast continent, from war to peace; from work to leisure; from the public to the private.[38] Like no other animal, dogs have simply become an indispensable and integral part of the human condition.

If anything, the animal turn of the 1970s lent this relationship—at least from the human side—a new dimension of intensity and a novel level of intimacy that for millions of people has changed the very concept of "dog." Although various forms of anthropomorphizing of dogs have existed for centuries, and while dogs have been integral members of human families for the same time, they remained—though beloved, adored, needed, and wanted—for most people, dogs in their essence and being, meaning clearly different creatures from humans. For reasons having to do with many factors, some of which we will mention in this book, dogs in urban, middle-class, relatively affluent, and largely, though far from exclusively, blue-state America mutated from the beloved family pet to a de facto member of the family with a possible de jure status very much in the works. This constituted a huge cultural step that not only altered fundamentally the traditional relationship between humans and dogs but that—as we argue—provides the very crux of the rise of the breed specific canine rescue movement that is the subject of this book.

Here are some helpful data placing this relationship into its proper context: According to the Humane Society of the United States, Americans had nearly 79 million dogs as companions in 2012; 46 percent of U.S. households had at least one dog; 60 percent of American caretakers of dogs had one dog as their companion with 29 percent having two; and 12 percent took care of three or more dogs. The average number of dogs per household amounted to 1.7. Twenty-one percent of dogs living with Americans emanated from animal shelters. The average annual amount spent by dog parents on routine veterinary visits came to $278. Seventy-eight percent of parented dogs were spayed or neutered.[39]

Giving prima facie evidence to the importance of the shift in cultural and moral attitudes toward dogs has been the magnitude of this relationship's commercialization. In 1994, consumer spending on pets amounted to $17 billion. By 2012, this sum had ballooned to nearly $54 billion. To place this into proper perspective, eminent sports economist Andrew Zimbalist estimates that the entire annual revenue of the Big Four North American team sports of football, baseball, basketball, and hockey comes to around $15 billion.[40] In the most sports-crazed country in the world, people spend more than three times as much on their companion animals than they do on their beloved sports.

To be sure, much of this spending has been fueled by a vast increase in sales of improved nutrition, specialty products, and medical care.[41] But the pampering of dogs has also attained hitherto unknown dimensions that have become the norm. Dog boutiques continue to sprout all over the country, with Ann Arbor—a town of 113,000 year-round inhabitants—boasting three such stores, all of which seem to be doing very well. High-end international fashion houses such as Gucci, Louis Vuitton, and Burberry have rolled out specialty dog products in recent years, as have mainstream retailers like Target Corporation. Dog spas featuring aroma therapy, among other luxurious treatments, have proliferated well into the country's heartland from more exotic places like Beverly Hills and New York City's Upper East Side on the two coasts. Doggie day care has become a booming business as have sleep-over camps for dogs, exercise regimes for overweight dogs, Prozac-popping pooches and many such indulgences that would have either been unthinkable or completely objectionable (by virtue of their inappropriate opulence) barely two decades ago but have now all been accepted, even feted, as helpful to the overall improvement of dogs' lives. Regardless of their actual merit to dogs, these measures attest to the increasing entry of dogs into the human world that go much further than the manner in which people always used to anthropomorphize dogs.

The new moral regime features quotidian dimensions that extend way beyond crude commercialization. Indeed, the comfort and dignity of these animals are at least as important a factor in driving this change as are profits. Here are some random but relevant examples: One article in the *Los Angeles Times* describes at length how "creature comforts" drive architecture, art, and décor decisions for houses and apartments from coast to coast, all driven by the overarching imperative to make the human home as welcoming and comfortable to dogs as possible.[42] Another, published in the *New York Times* just a few days before discusses how a newly passed law in Maine shields animals in domestic violence cases because of growing evidence that there exists a statistically significant overlap between the violence committed against women by their disaffected and angry male partners and the harm that these men inflict on the pets whom they identify as the women's main source of emotional solace and support.[43] Almost daily, the market features a bevy of new products that are designed to enhance these dogs' comfort and well-being, which reaches way beyond the conventional fulfilling of their appetites and includes heartfelt attempts to enhance these dogs' mental stimulation and psychic well-being. Thus, there exist tick-tack-toe puzzles to encourage dogs' problem-solving abilities, as well as apps on tablets that foster dogs' doodling abilities and even the possibilities of taking selfies. Regular bowls have been replaced by "interactive feeding products like Dog Twister (imported from Sweden, no less for around $50), with rotating hidden compartments that make dogs reason their way to kibbles."[44]

The sophistication in canine (and feline) surgery has attained hitherto unimaginable dimensions both in their rapid proliferation as well as in their accepted normalcy in today's American culture. The commensurate growth in medical expenses does not appear to be a deterrent for an ever-increasing number of humans for whom the welfare of their four-legged family member is of unmatched significance, thus reaching the realm of what economists call "price inelastic," meaning that the size of expenses for helping companion animals enhance or restore or preserve their quality of life has become all but irrelevant to their caring guardians.

> Pets like [Mischa] are undergoing reconstructive surgeries as sophisticated as anything in human medicine: joint replacements, skin and bone grafts, ligament repairs, even therapeutic eyelifts for ingrown lashes and, yes, nose jobs—the last resort for snuffling, short-nosed breeds like pugs and Persian cats. That more and more pets are going under the knife stems partly from technological advances and the increasing presence of specialists in general practices. It also is a consequence of the fact that pets are living longer. Reaching 70, even in dog years, raises the odds of cancer and other ailments that call for surgical treatment. *But veterinarians say the biggest driver is demand by pet owners. Most now view their furry charges as members of the family—and are willing to spend accordingly.*[45]

An increasing number of companion animals routinely receive prosthetic devices. Dogs and horses—even lamas—enjoy renewed quality of life by having prosthetic legs restore their former ability to walk and run. "A pig with deformed rear legs has been fitted with a sort of hind-end wheelchair. . . . A swan that has had its beak mangled, presumably by a snapping turtle, is shown being fitted with a molded alternative."[46]

Lastly, nothing illustrates greater compassion than the hospice movement, which, after all, only has one purpose: to give a particularly needy and vulnerable group—the dying—a space of comfort, succor, and dignity. And by 2009, this movement had reached the canine world. "The International Association for Animal Hospice and Palliative Care, a group started in 2009, now has 200 members, mostly vets, but also several family therapists, lawyers and an animal sanctuary in Northern California that takes in and provides holistic healing and hospice for terminally ill and elderly pets."[47] Having proliferated throughout the country in this short period of time (from 2009 until the time of this writing in 2014), these institutions—together with in-home euthanasia—have emerged for the sole purpose of making the dying process for dogs less alienating, cold, and inhumane. "Dr. Amir Shanan, a vet in Chicago, who started the International Association for Animal Hospice, described the movement as growing, but still not mainstream; veterinary schools are only now embracing the idea. 'There are skeptics out there,' he said. 'But 20 years ago, there was almost no one other than skeptics, and that's changing rapidly.'"[48] These are but a few ways in the rapidly changing whole in which humans have come to insist on a more humane treatment of dogs.

Indeed, there are almost daily accounts of public sympathies shifting from humans to canines as victims, such as the case in Princeton, New Jersey, in which a landscaper was mauled by a German Shepherd, with a majority of the community rallying on behalf of the dog and not the person.[49] There has emerged a steady stream of accounts across the country in the past few years in which military service and police dogs have received burials with the same full honor given to humans. Instances such as the U.S. Air Force holding a memorial in Ohio for a deceased service dog with all due honors accorded a human appear increasingly normal to the American public.[50] "In 2013, Lackland Air Force Base in San Antonio unveiled a national monument that honors the service and sacrifice of military working dogs. The bronze sculpture features the four main breeds employed since World War II: the Labrador Retriever, the Belgian Malinois, the German Shepherd, and the Doberman Pinscher."[51] The U.S. Army has also come to engage in the bestowing of honors to dogs that had previously been reserved only for humans. Thus, Mina, a bomb-sniffing war dog, who served nine tours of duty in the U.S. Army, received a military burial with full honors in Oakland County, Michigan.[52]

Police departments preceded the military in giving their fallen dogs such human honors. Cade (a police dog) received an officer's funeral with full police honors, which has become the norm in the United States and comparable countries.[53] Indeed, Norway has granted its police dogs the full status of civil servants commensurate to what the force's human officers receive. And as of the early summer of 2014, a French law has reclassified dogs and cats as "living and feeling beings," departing from the 1804 Napoleonic civil code in which they were categorized as pieces of property like furniture. Most likely, acts of this nature would have not only been impossible, indeed unthinkable, before the animal turn; but, had they occurred, they would have been viewed as disrespectful of humans, indeed downright blasphemous.

Lastly, the salience of every aspect of the Michael Vick case of arranged animal fighting of the most cruel and callous variety—from the national headline news surrounding the discovery of the gruesome deed to the National Football League's prompt reaction, to the length of Vick's prison sentence—cannot be explained without an understanding of the fundamentally changed nature of the human–animal discourse in contemporary America and the advanced industrial world. In his book *Citizen Canine: Our Evolving Relationship with Cats and Dogs*, David Grimm offers the most complete account of the massive changes that have altered virtually every aspect of human–animal relations since the onset of the animal turn, commencing in the late 1960s and becoming part of acceptable public discourse by the mid-1970s.[54]

All major social movements that have led to substantial changes in societal attitudes, mores, and values have been associated with iconic statements of some kind. Often authored well before the full-blown emergence of such movements, thus constituting their conceptual germinal as it were, or attaining their importance as these movements were about to unfold, intellectual statements matter immensely in shaping such movements' very identities by giving them ideas and materials for further debate and development. Most of all, they lend all these movements a certain intellectual gravitas that gives them recognition and subsequent legitimation and proliferation in larger society and culture.

Thus, one will never be able to imagine any red movements—be they social democratic or communist—featuring the working class as subject of history and advocating policies in its favor without the power and presence of *The Communist Manifesto* (originally titled *Manifesto of the Communist Party*) written by Karl Marx and Friedrich Engels and published in 1848. In terms of comparable publications that attained iconic stature for the green movements centered on the environment, Rachel Carson's *Silent Spring* published in 1962 and The Club of Rome's book *The Limits to Growth* authored by Donella H. Meadows, Dennis L. Meadows, Jorgen Randers, and William W. Behrens III and published in 1972 most certainly take pride of place. Betty Friedan's *The Feminine Mystique* published in 1963 and the Boston Women's Health Collective's *Our Bodies, Ourselves* first published in 1971 with a subsequent eight new editions became iconic texts for the beginning and successful expansion of what has come to be known as second-wave feminism in the United States and well beyond. The civil rights movement is unthinkable without Martin Luther King Jr.'s "Letter from Birmingham Jail" published in 1963 and *The Autobiography of Malcolm X* (authored by Malcolm X and Alex Haley) published in 1965. Of almost equal importance for the civil rights movement and all its related rights movements and revolutions has been the "Port Huron Statement" of 1962 and Mario Savio's famous speech of 1964 on the steps of Sproul Hall of the University of California, Berkeley, forming the core of the "free speech movement." Both of these documents featured words and concepts that came to constitute the core credo and essential manifesto of the burgeoning student movement and the New Left.

So, too, the animal rights movement could claim an equivalent counterpart to all of the above: Peter Singer's *Animal Liberation* published in 1975. Arguably one of the most influential philosophers of the latter part of the twentieth century and an immensely respected member of Princeton University's faculty, it is virtually impossible to imagine the modern animal rights movement without Singer's work. In addition to exposing the chilling realities of factory farming as well as medical research among other regular abuses that humans all over the world had come to inflict on animals with total impunity and as a matter of widely accepted and practiced norms, Singer's book follows Jeremy Bentham's well-known view that argues emphatically that animals are humans' complete moral equals by virtue of sharing one crucial commonality: the ability to feel pain, to suffer. Thus to Bentham the issue about the moral equivalence of humans and animals amounted to one simple question that was not "Can they [animals] *reason*? Nor can they *talk*? But can they *suffer*?"[55] As Steven Best writes:

> Cutting through the tangled web of human prejudices against animals, and the Western idea that reason forms the human essence, Singer argues that the ability of animals to feel pain and pleasure puts them on a plane of moral equivalence with us. Whether or not animals can author treatises on mathematics, they, like us, feel pain, and we therefore have an obligation not to cause them needless suffering. Uncovering irrational prejudices akin to sexism and racism, Singer denounces all forms of what he calls "speciesism" whereby human beings believe they can exploit animals merely because they do not belong to the species homo sapiens.[56]

Just as was the case with all the other iconic works previously mentioned, in Singer's as well, the far-reaching importance of his book lies not so much in the unquestioned admiration that it spawned but rather in the immense controversy that it generated. We mention but two that we deem particularly influential in raising crucial points beyond Singer's thesis: Tom Regan's *The Case for Animal Rights* first published in 1983, which goes beyond Singer's utilitarian interpretation of pleasure and pain that humans and animals enjoy or suffer by claiming that animals possess an inherent moral worth beyond or apart from humans; and Matthew Scully's *Dominion: The Power of Man, the Suffering of Animals, and the Call to Mercy* published in 2002, in which the author argues powerfully that the central issue is not so much whether animals have rights and are thus our equals, but that precisely because they do not, thus making them our dependents, we owe them even more care and protection. "Animals are more than ever a test of our character, of mankind's capacity for empathy and for decent, honorable conduct and faithful stewardship. We are called to treat them with kindness, not because they have rights or power or some claim to equality, but in a sense because they don't; because they all stand unequal and powerless before us."[57]

As we argued previously, we believe that the term *compassion* rather than *empathy* better reflects the sentiments that Scully describes precisely because in the former, agency remains solely the domain as well as responsibility of humans, as opposed to empathy, in which human action is not only called upon to protect but also to share and indulge. Regardless, as we all can observe, it is patently obvious that the underlying motivation and commitment on the part of most activists comprising the breed specific canine rescue world owe their powerful presence to the sentiment of compassion to protect and help these needy animals rather than a desire to render them equal to humans by extending to them all the rights and privileges that we enjoy. Although adherents to the discourse of compassion and to rights comprise the big—and growing—tent of human activism in favor of animals, one could possibly call adherents to the former "moderates" while categorizing the latter as "radicals" with the concepts "minimalists" and "maximalists," "reformers" and "revolutionaries," or "realists" and "fundamentalists" that informed the very being of the German green movement and party also being apt characterizations of what we mean. Needless to say, both wings represent absolutely essential constituencies to any and all social, political, and cultural movements, as does the constant animosity and rivalry between them. In the eyes of the radicals, maximalists, revolutionaries, and fundamentalists, the moderates, minimalists, reformers, and realists will always be cowards, compromisers, indeed traitors of the cause, whereas to the latter, the former are dreamers, and quite often irresponsible actors who, with their unreasonable demands and egregious (often criminal) behavior threaten the very cause they purport to support. Of course, in all movements for social and cultural change, one cannot exist without the other!

A very similar continuum informs the demographic characteristic shared by a large majority of active members comprising the world of animal rights and welfare: women! One of the most obvious phenomena of any aspects pertaining to the human–animal relationship—including, as our research shows, breed specific canine rescue—is the preponderance of women in all facets of this world: its initiators, leaders, foot soldiers, activists, supporters, sympathizers. Without attempting to give any reasons for it, this fact alone speaks volumes as to the presence of compassion, empathy, understanding, and many other emotions and actions characterizing solidarity with the disempowered in the animal rights and welfare movement. Women are disproportionate ideological supporters of the welfare state, of policies favoring distributive justice, and of virtually all measures in the human world that emphasize cooperation, understanding, sharing, and help. Furthermore, by virtue of their disproportionate presence in the service and assistance professions, women are also disproportionate participants in the actual implementation of these policies on a daily basis. It would be beyond the purview of this book—not to mention our scholarly expertise—to debate the intricacies of the nature versus nurture complex as to the reasons for women's disproportionate presence as humanity's civilizing agents and its tamers in its continued aggressive encroachment against nature, including animals. But the numbers are overwhelming. Women have consistently expressed greater commitment to and interest in preserving nature than men. Of the 7.3 million Americans following a vegetarian-based diet in 2013, 59 percent were female and 41 percent male.[58] Whether, as the Dalai Lama has argued, women would make better political leaders because of their compassion than men and whether his ensuing hopes and predictions that because of such qualities, the next Dalai Lama should be a woman, is beyond our concern.[59] Rather, we give two symbiotic and confluent reasons for the preponderance of women in the struggle for animal rights and welfare and, more specifically, canine rescue.

The first is historical. "The great majority of activists in the nineteenth-century antivivisection and anticruelty movements were women, as today, it is estimated, 70 to 80 percent of animal rights movement adherents are women," write Carol J. Adams and Josephine Donovan in the introduction to their well-known and influential anthology *Animals & Women: Feminist Theoretical Explorations.*[60] The overlap between the women's movement, the environmental movement, and the animal rights movement has existed not only by virtue of their epistemological proximity and normative preferences but also because women have furnished the bulk of activists in all three. "Women make up some 75 percent of activists for animals, and it's not surprising that they've carried over language and lessons from the women's movement."[61] As historical feminist writers from Mary Wollstonecraft, to Susan B. Anthony, to Elizabeth Cady Stanton, all the way to contemporary scholars such as Josephine Donovan and others have persuasively argued, there are clear parallels between man's domination of nonhuman animals and man's domination of women.[62]

Indeed, the Society for the Prevention of Cruelty to Animals founded in 1824 in Britain and rendered "Royal" in 1840 when young Queen Victoria "took the organization under the sponsorship of the Crown,"[63] just as its cousins in the United States such as the New York Society for the Prevention of Cruelty to Animals (SPCA) established in 1866 followed by the Massachusetts SPCA two years later and the American Humane Association in 1877 combined their support for animals with campaigns to protect women and children.[64] In Victorian England "the majority of those who joined the major [anti-vivisection] societies were women."[65] Even a cursory reading of the relevant literature makes it amply clear that throughout eighteenth- and nineteenth-century Britain and the United States—and we have no reason to believe that this was any different in the countries on the European continent—the following patterns were common[66]: the vilest cruelty against animals such as public beatings, killings, and torture was completely common, with men being its preponderant (though not exclusive) perpetrators; men were disproportionately engaged in various blood sports that, too, were common in Britain and the United States at this time, from bull and bear baiting to dog and cock fighting among other forms of animal torture. There existed a clear link between male violence against women and animals; this violence, though quotidian and pervasive, became even more pronounced under the influence of alcohol. Not surprisingly, women became disproportionate protectors of and advocates for animals (and children) by—in essence—trying to tame men on all these abusive fronts, which men, predictably, disliked and disdained to the point that they often came to see a direct link between women and animals on many dimensions, from the meek and compliant to the threatening and tantalizing. Thus the gender disparity in both attitude and behavior toward animals is not new. The link between animals and women as disenfranchised beings in man's abusive relationship to nature has a long history.

The second reason for the preponderance of women in today's animal rights, welfare, and rescue world is strongly linked to the gains that the second-wave women's rights movement of the 1970s has attained. Concretely, there can be no doubt that the vast expansion of choices that women have today has increased their presence and importance in many movements, including that of animal rights, welfare, and rescue. Moreover, by being much better educated than their sisters of previous generations, today's women have all the necessary tools to excel at complex organizational tasks and leadership positions that they have assumed in these movements. Also, by being much less tied to the home and fully expected to enter the public sphere, women are no longer stigmatized if they find intellectual pursuits and institutional engagements outside the house.

Some, of course, have argued that women's growing commitment to animals is not so much a testimony to the liberating and progressive forces of the rights revolutions of the 1970s but rather the consequences of those very forces' disruptive and individualizing tendencies that have increased divorce, created instability in the workplace, and shattered the comforting bonds of family and friendship. People in general, and women in particular, according to this view, have come to rely increasingly on animals in general, dogs in particular, as their primary means of social and emotional support, often to the animals' and the dogs' own detriment. Rather than viewing the massive positive shift in human–animal relations as testimony to the constantly increasing humaneness of our existence, as does Pinker (as do we), authors such as Jon Katz see our increasing affection for and devotion to animals—dogs specifically—as clear signs of the deficiencies in our human institutions that have failed to offer the appropriate amount of humaneness that we crave and deserve.[67] In Katz's view, we therefore harness dogs—possibly against their will, and most certainly not always to their benefit—as ersatz props to offer us intimacy and companionship that we are simply unable to form with one another anymore. Somehow, animals and dogs have become the substitutes and dragooned companions for our failures to create a genuine human intimacy that is lasting and comforting. We have rendered animals into the victims of our lonely and asocial lives. Katz explicitly connects this new human–animal, human–canine relationship to the larger societal construct that Robert Putnam delineated in his influential book *Bowling Alone: The Collapse and Revival of American Community* and other similarly important works of social science that purport to argue that the key aspects of modern American life are anomie, alienation, and an increasingly individualized existence in which we write checks for our preferred causes but do not join them with our physical presence.[68] In such a world of social void, animals hit the spot. For Katz, the epitome of this faux construct of excessive compassion is "dog rescue," which he calls "uniquely American." In describing Best Friends Animal Sanctuary's "Dogtown" in Kanab, Utah, Katz's words of barely disguised cynicism encapsulate his dire view of the rescue movement: "Maybe we [humans] can't build a perfect world for ourselves, but we can try like hell to create a perfect world for you [dogs]."[69] The main protagonists of this movement, according to Katz, are middle-class suburban and exurban women, which brings us to the last substantive point in this introduction: thoughts as to the reasons for the emergence of these enormously influential rights revolutions of the late 1960s and the decade of the 1970s in the United States and the advanced industrial world.

Entire libraries have been written about the causes and reasons that led to the cultural and social (though far fewer, if any, political) revolutions of the late 1960s, which came to their lasting institutional fruition via the movements of the 1970s. None of these forces arose in dictatorships, and none in poor countries, which is not to say that elements from both often became the objects of these movements' affection and admiration though, at least in our view, not to a favorable assessment of their moral judgments. It is clear that all these transformative developments arose in countries governed by liberal democratic regimes enjoying unprecedented economic growth and prosperity. And it is in these two major arrangements that we anchor our views for the reasons of these immense changes. Let us discuss each of these factors in turn.

Having defeated fascism and confronted Stalinism, the virtues of liberal democracy seemed unimpeachable. On the whole—and in comparison with all other political regimes—liberal democracy provided the rule of law; allowed freedom of the press and speech; held regular elections in which the opposition had a chance to win, and often did; fostered a modicum of political participation by allowing citizens to vote for their candidates of choice; and protected the individual and *his* rights (much less hers at this time) both vis-à-vis encroachments from forces in civil society as well as, of course, the state. Liberal democracy flourished by touting not only the freedom of the individual but also the equality of all under the law. Such was this governing system's upside, its pretty face, its friendly calling card. But, underneath the beauty of this formal—and in good part very real—facade, there lurked a darker side that somehow did not live up to the system's very characterization and essential legitimation. All citizens were formally equal, except many (women and minorities, for example) were anything but in practice and reality.

Although liberal democracies distinguished themselves with their comparatively humane rule at home, they did nothing of the sort abroad. Just think of the brutal colonial rule by Britain and France and the expansionist quasi-colonial behavior of the United States. Therefore, it is not by chance that opposition to America's Vietnam War constitutes one of the most essential and ubiquitous ingredients of the rise of all these rights movements across the world in good part because the United States—more than the colonial powers of Europe, indeed any other comparable country in the world—embodied the contradictions of liberal democracy: a system of formal freedom and equality like no other accompanied by shortcomings in its domestic and international reality that, too, were unparalleled at this time. Liberal democracy's hypocrisy or inherent contradiction hailed, of course, from the fact that it provided a political regime of formal equality and freedom for a capitalist economy that had neither and was thus by definition not democratic.

The movements of the 1970s wanted to resolve this contradiction not so much by changing capitalism (although some tried that, too), but by taking liberal democracy at its word and demanding that it live up to the most basic essence of democracy, which is to include the hitherto excluded; to give voice to the formally voiceless; to empower the disempowered; in essence to create real equality for all living beings in a polity and society by including them as full and equal participants in their own right, with their own voices and their full dignity and authenticity. Thus, it would not be erroneous to categorize all these movements as being progressive (or of the left) if one defines the essence of being progressive and of the left as an unending endeavor dedicated to the inclusion of the excluded. And precisely because these movements embodied the causes of the excluded in the 1960s and 1970s—of "new" groups—they became identified, among other reasons, as the New Left. Though its overall aim of creating equality and dignity for all did not differ from its predecessor, the Old Left, the social composition of its founders, activists, subjects and beneficiaries varied mightily, which brings us to our second point.

The Old Left's mission of liberating capitalism's workers by making them into citizens with all rights and privileges accorded them in the formal arrangements of liberal democracies lasted from the middle of the nineteenth century until the postwar boom years of the 1950s and 1960s. Although by no means successful in alleviating class differences and creating genuine economic equality among all citizens, the Old Left's political expressions of social democracy and, to a lesser degree, communism proved worthwhile forces in attaining a relatively high level of economic and social security, as well as a modicum of dignity and a moderately powerful political voice for the main client of this Left's century-long struggle: the male industrial worker. The inclusive nature of a successful capitalist economy governed by a liberal democratic welfare state should not be underestimated. Indeed, it was this very construct that created a world of relative economic security and political freedom that gave rise to a new force that was to unleash the rights revolutions of the New Left a decade later.

Even though it would be cynical to characterize these forces and their struggles as one of simple luxury and abundance, there can be no doubt that—unlike the Old Left's main agenda, which pivoted around increasing the material well-being and economic and social welfare of the working class—these new subjects forming the New Left emerged in the context of economic comfort and material security. Their aim was to extend liberal democracy's full promise to segments of the population (animals included) that had thus far not come to enjoy much, if any, of it. As such, the New Left and its ensuing rights revolutions hailed from a world that had seemingly resolved its material problems, which Abraham Maslow described as needs of physiology and safety, the two lowest rungs of his hierarchy of needs pyramid, and was in search for love and belonging, esteem, and self-actualization, the three higher rungs of Maslow's conceptual construct.[70] In due time, though, the subjects of these revolutions became very much interested in the fate of attributes belonging to the two lower rungs, like breathing, food, water, sex and sleep (physiology), and security of body, resources, morality, and family health (safety), which they found far from resolved as the Old Left and other established players of liberal democracy had claimed. Instead they perceived them as quite ruined and exploited by these very players, including the Old Left, and thus in need of urgent repair via the introduction of a whole new discourse of compassion, empathy and empowerment in all walks of life, including everything affecting animals.

This then is the historical framework and social context wherein we situate the topic of this book: the emergence and proliferation of breed specific canine rescue in the United States. We argue that this new phenomenon embodies an expression of the larger forces depicted in the preceding pages and that it—quite simply—could and would not have happened without them. Rescue may not express explicitly its identity and very existence as a consequence of these emancipatory movements that we presented. Indeed, as will be obvious to the reader, rescue's main actors and carriers reveal a striking "ordinariness" that places them far from challengers of the dominant social system with its conventional culture and accepted mores and norms. They neither use the language nor exhibit any actions that might lead one to see these activists as revolutionaries or system challengers of any kind. But, we argue, the way these people have come to reorganize their lives in the quest of helping needy dogs of their beloved breed, the manner in which they have come to feature their commitment in their very busy quotidian lives, would never have happened—would, in fact be well-nigh unimaginable—without the culture-changing power of the social movements of the late 1960s and the 1970s.

Here is the map of our book: In Chapter 1 we reveal the nature and history of breed specific canine rescue. Chapter 2 features a case study of rescue in the state of Michigan. Here we present the results of a survey of 255 respondents who worked with seventy-nine different rescue groups. Chapter 3 provides an overview of the topography of the canine population of the United States between 1960 and 2000 that offers a crucial background for an understanding of the world wherein rescues operate. Chapter 4 looks at the history of Golden Retriever rescue as a major representative of this particular organizational genre of the canine–human relationship. Chapter 5 highlights the immense regional differences that inform rescue all across the United States. Chapter 6 features the relations that rescues regularly entertain with the outside world from humane societies to shelters and from other rescues to the public. Chapter 7 looks at the means of communication that rescues have. In particular it features our analysis of the Internet as a complete game changer for these organizations and rescue as a whole. Chapter 8 provides a comparative analysis of Golden Retriever rescues with their Labrador Retriever counterparts and investigates the factors that render the former more successful than the latter. Chapter 9 looks at the rescue of greyhounds; and Chapter 10 analyzes the case of pit bull rescues featuring the special difficulties that each encounter. We end this book with a brief conclusion and provide four appendices in which we feature data from our survey of Michigan rescues (Appendix A), then present our detailed survey instrument (Appendix B), followed by our interview questionnaire (Appendix C), and an alphabetized list of our interview subjects (Appendix D).

Notes

1. Steven Pinker, *The Better Angels of our Nature: Why Violence Has Declined* (New York: Penguin Books, 2011), pp. 455, 456. Representing yet another of many milestones in the lengthy process that tamed us in our treatment of animals, in this case, like Pinker's, for medical experimentations, we have recently learned that the National Institutes of Health "has announced a plan to retire nearly 90 percent of

government-owned chimpanzees to sanctuary, and significantly decrease chimpanzee research grants. . . . The good news doesn't end there! Fifty government-owned chimpanzees have already been moved from New Iberia Research Center to Chimp Haven, The National Chimpanzee Sanctuary." "Monumental Victory for Chimps," https://mail.google.com/mail/u/0/?ui=2&ik=1e1f94e76a&view=pt&search =inbox&msg=13f865e161f49345 (accessed on June 27, 2013).

2. Alexis de Tocqueville, *Democracy in America* (New York: Schocken Books, 1961), p. 195.

3. Ibid., p. 200

4. Elazar Barkan, *The Guilt of Nations: Restitution and Negotiating Historical Injustices* (New York: Norton, 2000), pp. 159–168.

5. Doreen Carvajal, "Museums Confront the Skeletons in Their Closets," *New York Times*, May 25, 2013, pp. C1 and C2.

6. David M. Anderson, "Atoning for the Sins of the Empire," *New York Times*, June 13, 2013, p. A25.

7. Ibid.

8. "Apology Letter Accompanying Federal Reparations Checks," http://hillyard history.net/uploads/President_Bill_Clinton_-_Internment_Apology_Letter__text ____Oct._1__1993_.pdf (accessed on June 20, 2013).

9. United States Public Law 103-150, http://www.hawaii-nation.org/publawall .html (accessed on June 20, 2013).

10. "President Obama Signs Native American Apology Resolution," http://native votewa.wordpress.com/2009/12/31/president-obama-signs-native-american -apology-resolution (accessed on June 20, 2013).

11. What makes matters worse still is that at a valuation of $1.6 billion, this Washington, D.C., based NFL franchise is the League's third most valued entity following the Dallas Cowboys and the New England Patriots. This team ranks among the top ten most valued sports entities in the world.

12. "House Formally Apologizes for Slavery and Jim Crow," http://www .huffingtonpost.com/2008/07/29/house-formally-apologizes_n_115743.html (accessed on June 20, 2013)

13. Charles Glass, *A Hidden History of World War II* (New York: Penguin, 2013).

14. "Native American" is an interesting case as the term was originally used in the early nineteenth century by whites born in the United States to distinguish themselves from Irish and German immigrants. We are grateful to Joseph Klaver for alerting us to this fact.

15. Pinker, *The Better Angels of Our Nature*, p. 571.

16. "Empathy—Noun; The ability to understand and share the feelings of another." *American Heritage Dictionary of the English Language* (Boston: Houghton Mifflin Company, 1981), n.p.

17. Ibid.

18. See *Tennessee Valley Authority v. Hiram Hill et al.*, or *TVA v. Hill*, 437 US 153 (1978); full decision available at http://caselaw.lp.findlaw.com/scripts/getcase .pl?court=use&vol=437&invol=153 (accessed on June 27, 2013).

19. "Fourth of July fireworks Moved so Bald Eagle Babies Won't Get Scared," http://now.msn.com/fireworks-display-moved-so-baby-bald-eagles-wont-be -disturbed (accessed on June 30, 2013).

20. "U.S. Jurisdictions With and Without Felony Animal Cruelty Provisions," http://aldf.org/resources/advocating-for-animals/u-s-jurisdictions-with-and-without-felony-animal-cruelty-provisions (accessed on July 6, 2013).

21. "My neighbor leaves his dog outside when it's freezing without a dog house or other shelter. Is this animal cruelty?" http://www.animallaw.info/articles/ovusstate crueltylaws.htm (accessed on June 27, 2013).

22. Benjamin Adams and Jean Larson, "Legislative History of the Animal Welfare Act: Animal in Law in Ages Past," http://www.nal.usda.gov/awic/pubs/AWA2007 /intro.shtml (accessed on June 27, 2013).

23. "Animal Cruelty Laws among Fastest-Growing," http://www.nbcnews.com/id /29180079/ns/health-pet_health/t/animal-cruelty-laws-among-fastest-growing/# .Ub9IpvY9znE (accessed on June 27, 2013). Ronald Desnoyers conducted fascinating research on the role of such laws in the state of Rhode Island between 1980 and 2004. His findings demonstrate that in this 24-year period, dogs were more commonly victimized than cats and that the overwhelming majority of defendants charged with animal cruelty were young males with an average age of 32.7 years. See Ronald Desnoyers, "Animal Cruelty in the State of Rhode Island: A Twenty-Five Year Perspective" (paper presented at the 2008 American Sociological Association Meeting in Boston, Massachusetts).

24. Pinker, *The Better Angels of Our Nature*, pp. 472, 473.

25. Lewis & Clark Law School, Center for Animal Law Studies, "Curriculum," http://law.lclark.edu/centers/animal_law_studies/curriculum (accessed on June 28, 2013).

26. "Animal Cruelty Laws among Fastest Growing," http://www.nbcnews.com/id /29180079/ns/health-pet_health/t/animal-cruelty-laws-among-fastest-growing/# .UdCSMpyOl8s (accessed on June 30, 2013).

27. James Gorman, "Rights Group Is Seeking Status of 'Legal Person' for Captive Chimpanzee," *New York Times*, December 3, 2013, p. A13.

28. Ibid.

29. Charles Siebert, "The Rights of Man . . . and Beast," *New York Times Magazine*, April 27, 2014. The quotation occurs on the cover of the magazine.

30. Ibid., p. 50.

31. James Gorman, "The Humanity of Nonhumans," *New York Times*, December 10, 2013, p. D5.

32. Leslie Irvine, *If You Tame Me: Understanding Our Connection with Animals* (Philadelphia: Temple University Press, 2004), pp. 5, 6.

33. Pinker, *The Better Angels of Our Nature*, p. 468.

34. Ibid., p. 469.

35. "Pets by the Numbers," http://www.humanesociety.org/issues/pet_over population/facts/pet_ownership_statistics.html (accessed June 29, 2013).

36. Deborah Tannen, "Talking the Dog: Framing Pets as International Resources in Family Discourse," *Research on Language and Social Interaction* 37 no. 4 (2004): 399–420.

37. "Dad's Popular—but Dogs Are More So," http://www.pewresearch.org/daily -number/dads-popular-but-dogs-are-more-so (accessed on June 28, 2013).

38. Mark Derr, *A Dog's History of America: How Our Best Friend Explored, Conquered, and Settled a Continent* (New York: North Point Press, 2004).

39. "Pets by the Numbers."

40. Andrew Zimbalist, "Sports & Economics," *Sports in America* (Washington, DC: U.S. Department of State, 2007), pp. 51–55, here p. 52.

41. American Pet Products Manufacturers Association.

42. Bettijane Levine, "Wow! Home Design Now Makes a Bow to the Dogs," *Los Angeles Times*, April 15, 2006.

43. Pam Belluck, "Battered Wives' Pets Suffer Abuse, Too," *New York Times*, April 1, 2006.

44. David Hochman, "You'll Go Far, My Pet," *New York Times*, April 13, 2014, SundayStyles, pp. 1, 12.

45. Susan Freinkel, "Rebuilding Our Badly Broken Pets," *New York Times*, January 14, 2013, p. D3, emphasis added.

46. Neil Genzlinger, "The Lives of Animals, Disabled and Otherwise," *New York Times*, April 9, 2014, p. C1.

47. Matt Richtel, "All Dogs May Go to Heaven. These Days, Some Go to Hospice," *New York Times*, December 1, 2013, p. A1.

48. Ibid.

49. Sarah Kershaw, "A Landscaper Is Mauled, and an Outpouring of Sympathy Goes to the Dog," *New York Times*, November 30, 2007.

50. "Air Force Holds Ohio Memorial for Military Dog," http://www.cbsnews.com/8301-201_162-57403778/air-force-holds-ohio-memorial-for-military-dog (accessed on June 29, 2013).

51. Michiko Kakutani, "Cats and Dogs, Reigning," *New York Times*, April 18, 2014, p. C23.

52. "US Army Dog to Get Military Burial," http://www.theoaklandpress.com/articles/201301/news/local_news/doc51085bdc14e0b125047983.txt (accessed on June 29, 2013).

53. "Cade, Burton Police K9 killed in accident, buried with full police honors," http://www.minbcnews.com/news/story.aspx?id=657546#.Ub9T (accessed on June 29, 2013).

54. David Grimm, *Citizen Canine: Our Evolving Relationship with Cats and Dogs* (New York: PublicAffairs, 2014).

55. Jeremy Bentham, *Introduction to the Principles of Morals and Legislation*, 2nd ed., 1823, chapter 17 (emphasis in original).

56. Steven Best, "Philosophy Under Fire: The Peter Singer Controversy," http://www.drstevebest.org/PhilosophyUnderFire.htm (accessed on July 1, 2013).

57. Matthew Scully, *Dominion: The Power of Man, the Suffering of Animals, and the Call to Mercy* (New York: St. Martin's Press, 2002), pp. xi, xii.

58. "Vegetarianism in America," http://www.vegetariantimes.com/article/vegetarianism-in-america (accessed July 3, 2013).

59. "Dalai Lama: Women Better Leaders Because of Potential for Compassion; Next Dalai Lama May Be Female," http://www.huffingtonpost.com/2013/06/14/dalai-lama-women_n_3440583.html?utm_hp_ref=mostpopular (accessed on July 2, 2013).

60. Carol J. Adams and Josephine Donovan, eds., *Animals & Women: Feminist Theoretical Explorations* (Durham, NC: Duke University Press, 1995), p. 5. Two other anthologies edited by these feminist scholars are relevant: Josephine Donovan and

Carol J. Adams, eds. *Beyond Animal Rights: A Feminist Caring Ethic for the Treatment of Animals* (New York: Continuum International Publishing, 1996); and Josephine Donovan and Carol J. Adams, eds., *The Feminist Care Tradition in Animal Ethics* (New York: Columbia University Press, 2007).

61. David Walls, "Animal Rights Movement," http://sonoma.edu/users/w/wallsd /animal-rights-movement.shtml (accessed on July 3, 2013).

62. Josephine Donovan, "Animal Rights and Feminist Theory," *Signs* 15, no. 2 (Winter, 1990), pp. 350–375.

63. Kathryn Shevelow, *For the Love of Animals: The Rise of the Animal Protection Movement* (New York: Henry Holt, 2008), p. 11.

64. Derr, *A Dog's History of America*, pp. 167–169.

65. Elston, as quoted in Corwin R. Kruse, "Gender, Views of Nature, and Support for Animal Rights," *Society & Animals* 7, no. 3, 1999, p. 180.

66. In addition to the already listed works, we found Katherine C. Grier's book particularly helpful. See Katherine C. Grier, *Pets in America: A History* (Chapel Hill: University of North Carolina Press, 2006).

67. Jon Katz, *The New Work of Dogs: Tending to Life, Love, and Family* (New York: Villard Books, 2003).

68. In addition to Putnam's important work, Katz cites Theda Skocpol and Morris P. Fiorina's *Civic Engagement in American Democracy* (Washington, DC: Brookings Institution Press, 1999), in which, according to Katz, the authors claim that "millions of Americans are drawing back from involvement in politics and community affairs." He also mentions the introductory chapter authored by Robert D. Putnam, Susan J. Phar, and Russell J. Dalton in Susan J. Phar and Robert D. Putnan's edited volume *Disaffected Democracies: What's Troubling the Trilateral Countries* (Princeton, NJ: Princeton University Press, 2000), in which, again according to Katz, the authors write that "confidence in leaders and institutions in the United States and other democratic countries has sunk to an all-time low. . . . These attitudes [of alienation and disengagement], say Putnam, Phar and Dalton, grow more pronounced every year—one more reason, perhaps, why people turn elsewhere for connection, companionship, and a sense of well-being." Katz, *The New Work of Dogs*, pp. 11, 12.

69. Ibid., p. 71.

70. Abraham Maslow, *Motivation and Personality* (New York: Harper and Row, 1954).

CHAPTER I

What Is Breed Rescue?

If not you, then who? If not now, then when?
—Annie Kassler
Foster home and adoption coordinator of
Yankee Golden Retriever Rescue in
the late 1980s and early 1990s

The Rescue Group—A Basic Picture

What is a breed specific rescue group? The broadest definition encapsulates any individual or group that assists in the placement of homeless dogs of a particular breed. For the purposes of the Internal Revenue Service (IRS), a rescue group is a 501(c)(3) tax-exempt charitable organization, although not all rescue groups, particularly small and new entities, have or intend to obtain 501(c)(3) status. Although 501(c)(3) status is advantageous for rescue groups, it is not necessary. The IRS defines a 501(c)(3) organization as one that "must be organized and operated exclusively for exempt purposes set forth in section 501(c)(3), and none of its earnings may inure to any private shareholder or individual. In addition, it may not be an *action organization, i.e.*, it may not attempt to influence legislation as a substantial part of its activities and it may not participate in any campaign activity for or against political candidates."[1] Most rescue groups are further classified by the IRS with the activity code D20, which declares their purpose to be animal protection and welfare. Functionally, this provision renders these groups into charitable organizations that are tax exempt, meaning that donations to them are also tax exempt and can be deducted from individual and corporate taxes. In essence, these groups do not have to pay income taxes, resulting in more of their money being allocated toward their charitable activities, in this case the rehabilitation and rescue of homeless dogs of a particular breed. Carol Allen, president of Golden Retriever Rescue of Central New York (GRRCNY, Jamesville, New York), emphasized the importance of 501(c)(3) status for rescue groups when she stated: "At some point, I do believe it is a major benefit to separate a rescue committee from a breed club; mainly because you obtain the 501(c)(3) group status that is immensely advantageous to rescues."[2] Although early involvement in clubs can be beneficial for rescue groups, Allen feels that continued membership in a club can limit a group's ability to grow and flourish.

Why are rescues necessary? Pet homelessness is a massive and profound problem in the United States; according to the American Society for the Prevention of Cruelty to Animals (ASPCA), "approximately 5 million to 7 million companion animals enter animal shelters nationwide every year, and approximately 3 million to 4 million are euthanized (60 percent of dogs and 70 percent of cats)."[3] Puppy mills, which breed dogs commercially in inhumane conditions purely for profit, contribute significantly to the problem, flooding the market with a large number of poorly bred dogs, many of which have congenital or genetic diseases as a result of careless animal husbandry. These dogs are distributed to pet stores, where they are sold to a generally unsuspecting public for profit, perpetuating the cycle of canine overproduction and homelessness. Finally, a failure on the part of dog owners to spay or neuter their dogs can result in backyard breeding or accidental mixed-breed litters. If puppies born by this means are not sold or destroyed, they end up in animal shelters, where they remain until they are adopted or euthanized. The combination of puppy mills and irresponsible dog ownership has created the current crisis of pet homelessness. Animal welfare organizations have emerged to combat this alarming condition. The forms these organizations take and the goals they espouse determine how they attempt to reduce pet homelessness in the United States.

Needless to say, breed specific rescue groups constitute just one of many organizational variants that exist solely for the purpose of rescuing animals. Community animal control facilities are arguably the most basic forms of animal rescue and often the most overworked. Typically, these institutions operate an animal shelter and contract with a municipality, usually either a city or a county, to handle homeless animals (mainly cats and dogs, but certainly not exclusively) within their specified geographic area. These organizations attempt to find owners whenever possible but are often unable to do so. Thus, many maintain—as an option of last resort—policies that require animals to be euthanized after they have spent a specified amount of time in the shelter if a home for them does not materialize. Humane societies often provide animal rescue services, although they perceive the core of their raison d'être as preventing and opposing animal suffering. These societies generally try to avoid euthanasia unless absolutely necessary and can be contracted by a municipality to provide some or all animal control services.

Breed specific rescue as an organizational form of humans engaging in and committed to the welfare of dogs emerged essentially in the 1990s (with some important precursors in the 1980s, even as early as the 1970s), totally separate from, often complementary to, but also frequently in direct competition and conflict with humane societies and animal shelters. Activists in the latter have often perceived the breed rescuers as "elitists" who only care about the welfare of their favorite breed while neglecting the fate of other dogs in need of shelter and a home. Breed specific dog rescuers, in turn, regard shelters as ill-equipped, sometimes even uncaring, institutions that cannot provide the proper care that dogs deserve. Breed specific dog rescue organizations differ from humane societies and animal shelters primarily in the sense that dogs are housed in volunteer members' homes, taught some basic household manners (housetraining, in particular), and then placed into the care of new families, who have generally undergone a rigorous application and review process prior to taking ownership of the dog. Like the altered discourse about dogs generally, the discourse of dog rescue is full of the language commonly used in the context of abandoned or neglected human children. Dogs are "fostered" by "foster moms and dads" and "adopted" by new "forever" families hand selected by the foster family as being a particularly good match for the dog in question. Rescue organizations typically guarantee a lifelong commitment to the dog and will generally take the dog back into the organization, even after several years, if the placement fails for whatever reason.

In contrast to humane societies and shelters, breed rescue groups are composed of volunteers looking to supplement local animal control or humane society efforts. They generally operate as foster home networks, rather than being based in a particular physical facility. Breed specific rescue groups are more specialized forms of all-breed rescue groups, as they devote their resources to rescuing one particular breed of dog or cat, rather than all breeds in the area.

The main function of a breed rescue group is simply to rescue and re-home homeless dogs of a particular breed. To achieve this goal, rescue groups must progress through the following steps for each dog they intend to rescue. First, they obtain the dogs in need of rescue. Rescue dogs generally come from one of two sources, either a local animal shelter or control facility or through owner surrenders, often called owner turn-ins (OTIs), where the original owner of the dog surrenders, via contract, any and all rights of ownership for the dog and often gives a donation to the group as a condition of accepting the dog. Second, the group must then address any health or behavioral problems the dog is experiencing. Local veterinarians, often for reduced rates, examine the dogs and ascertain any health and behavioral problems, the curing of which then becomes the responsibility of experienced group members or, in extreme cases, animal trainers or behaviorists. Third, the group must temporarily house the dogs until they are adopted. Foster homes are the most popular housing arrangement. Here, a dog is placed with a volunteer who takes care of the dog in her or his own home until the dog is adopted. Other housing options include boarding kennels, which is not the preference of the rescue organizations because they can be expensive and lead to behavioral problems if the dogs need to stay in these kennels for a long time, and group-owned facilities, which are rare because of the rescue groups' inherent expenses in the purchase and upkeep of such properties.

In order to achieve their main—indeed sole—goal of rescuing breed specific dogs, all rescue groups must engage in two activities that are not technically rescue but make rescue possible: fundraising and maintaining positive external relationships. Fundraising is vital for rescue groups to be able to function because dog rescue is an expensive proposition. "Many of us in rescue will take dogs which will require thousands of dollars of veterinary care because we know that we can still produce quality of life for these dogs,"[4] stated Robin Adams, president of Delaware Valley Golden Retriever Rescue (DVGRR, Reinholds, Pennsylvania). Adams's attitude demonstrated an idealistic view of rescue, one which we will explore in greater detail later in this chapter. And Maureen Distler, a volunteer with Lowcountry Labrador Rescue (Charleston, South Carolina), elaborates in terms of explaining the daily costs of running such organizations:

> I don't think that people understand the whole concept about saving dogs and how expensive this is. I mean, like, heartworm medication for all these dogs every month, flea meds every month, food for all these dogs, you know. Sometimes we'll have thirty dogs, that's a lot of money. I mean, even just flea stuff once a month is about $10, that's $300 a month just for flea medication for thirty dogs.[5]

Add to these regular expenses the major outlays that become routine for every rescue, because dogs incur illnesses and injuries that, although not the norm for any particular dog, become just that for a collective of dogs, and these projects become very costly. Moreover, the very nature of these rescue organizations features a disproportionate amount of dogs in some kind of need, often, of course, physical and health related. Almost by definition rescue groups have a tendency to collect dogs that are injured, ill, seniors, or have behavioral problems that require a higher investment than healthy dogs. Phil Fisher of NORCAL Golden Retriever Rescue (Menlo Park, California) explains:

> And then we occasionally have dogs with serious problems, like dysplasia neglect issues, just all kinds of awful things and, you know, if I told you it would break your heart so I'm not going to tell you. So that's anywhere between $5,000 to $10,000 per dog and we have enough money that we'll do a few of these every year if there's good potential outcome for the dog. We have spent as much as $10,000 on a dog.[6]

Because of the high costs associated with rehabilitating dogs and preparing them for adoption, fundraising is of utmost importance for rescue groups; without the ability to secure funds for veterinary and other expenses, rescue would be impossible.

Every aspect of dog rescue has both monetary and opportunity costs that groups must meet to succeed, from obtaining dogs (shelters not infrequently charge rescue groups the very same adoption fee for dogs that they do for any other adopter), to veterinary care (which, in spite of the discounts offered by the majority of veterinarians, accounts for the single greatest expenditure for all breed rescue groups), to caring for the dogs while in the program (boarding dogs in a kennel costs the group money, as does feeding dogs and ensuring they have the necessary supplies such as collars, leashes, and preventative medicine for fleas and heartworm). Group fundraising activities can take a variety of shapes, from local dog washes, can drives, and raffles to national capital campaigns, the solicitation of corporate donations, and partnerships with organizations like the United Way. Larger groups tend to use more complex fundraising methods like capital campaigns, which, while potentially more labor intensive initially, yield far higher returns than are possible with more pedestrian methods such as bake sales, can drives, or raffles.

Also critical to well-functioning rescue groups are positive external relationships with other, nonrescue organizations and entities involved in the canine rescue world. Chapter 6 will explore this phenomenon further, but here a brief explanation will suffice. Rescue groups maintain relationships with the general public, local animal shelters, other local breed rescues, local breed clubs, and national breed clubs. Because the quality of these relationships determines the resources available to the rescue group and has a direct impact on its success in rescuing and providing new homes to its dogs, it is of paramount importance to each group's efficacy that its relationships with all these outsiders be as cordial and supportive as possible. Rescue groups therefore must devote part of their often meager and overstretched resources, including temporal and monetary, to maintain these positive relationships if they want to ensure that the resources available through these relationships remain accessible to them. Concrete examples of such costs include website design and hosting, booth rates at dog shows, and adoption costs at local shelters, among others. Maintaining positive external relationships constitutes perhaps one of the most important ingredients in any rescue group's overall success and forms a vital part of its core being.

Group Origins

Comprehending the manner in which breed rescue groups function is not possible without understanding their origin and formation. A breed rescue group, regardless of which breed it represents, can come into existence in one of three ways: either as part of a club, an independent startup, or as a split from another rescue group. The origin of a group has a large impact on the group's format, function, and capabilities and is therefore critical to a proper understanding of the group's subsequent existence and operation.

The most common type of a rescue group's origin is the independent group; 74 percent of rescue groups for the top-ten breeds were formed independently. There are two archetypes of the independent group: those formed unintentionally, what we would call the "single-dog" type, and those formed intentionally, what we call the "perceived-need" variant. The single-dog type commences with an individual rescuing a single dog, without having any intention of starting a rescue group. After the initial rescue, the individual gradually becomes more involved in rescue, rescuing more dogs and involving more individuals until a group is formed. These groups tend to be the earlier independent groups and seem to take longer to obtain their 501(c)(3) status. The perceived-need group, by contrast, is intentionally formed by an individual or group of people. These groups emerge to fill a perceived need for a rescue in their area and are typically the independent groups that commenced at a later date in terms of these organizations' institutional chronology. In sharp contrast to the single-dog groups that obtain their 501(c)(3) status much later in the group's existence, if at all, the perceived-need groups typically make it a point to receive their 501(c)(3) status early in their existence, often before they rescue their first dog. In other words, the latter groups approach their task with a much more professional mindset, which is likely to inform virtually all facets of their activities centered on the rescue of dogs in their geographic area.

Seventeen percent of rescue groups for the top-ten breeds start in clubs. Groups that have their origins in a club are, by definition, part of a larger organization. Their inclusion in the breed club profoundly shapes the rescue group as a whole. Rather than being a separate organization, these groups are typically committees in the club, meaning that they are answerable to the club, rather than the leader of their rescue group. The club has a variety of interests and activities and is not solely focused on rescuing dogs. Rescue groups of this kind tend not to have 501(c)(3) charity status, but there are exceptions to this rule, as there are to all rules. Moreover, rescue groups emanating from clubs are on the whole less active in their rescue activities than groups that were formed independently or as a split from another group or a club. Clearly, this is mainly due to the diverse interests of the club, among which rescue is but one.

Another origin of rescue groups hails from intragroup schisms that result in splits and departures by members and the formation of new groups. There are two common reasons for such splits: personal issues and geography. Pertaining to the former, most splits occur either because of disagreements about group policy, preferences, aims, or operational modalities, on the one hand, or personal dislikes and intrigues, on the other hand. To be sure, rather than being mutually exclusive, these two personal categories overlap considerably to a point where it is virtually impossible to disentangle purely personal antipathies from genuine policy differences and organizational preferences. As with any human interaction in virtually all organizations, these two causes for tension and eventual dissention are mutually reinforcing rather than exclusive. Although there may be genuine differences in beliefs as to what constitutes the best way to rescue dogs in general or even in specific contexts particular to the group's environment, such contested policy issues may very well receive an added dimension of incompatibility due to personal grudges and antipathies that have absolutely nothing to do with the issues at hand.

Given that the people engaged in rescue activity care deeply about their avocation, which they perceive more like a calling than a chore and for which the rewards are almost never monetary but exclusively the immense joy in having improved the existence of downtrodden and helpless creatures; and given that all engagement is completely voluntary, lines of hierarchy that are typical for organizations remain blurry. The fluidity of authority structures means that if disagreements arise for whatever reason, maintaining "voice" and "loyalty" options in terms of sticking with the organization and trying one's best to make it all work become costly and "exit" options very facile. With regards to the Golden Retriever rescue situation in Arizona, for example, Barbara Elk of Rescue a Golden of Arizona (Phoenix) describes how personality problems cause group splits as follows: "And it was about that time that I found out that the organization was formed in 1998 and that it had split about one year after it had been formed. . . . because the people could not get along, and here we were, they were going to be splitting again because the new people could not get along either."[7] When personalities clash in a rescue group, it can cause a rift within the group that ultimately results in the formation of a new group, because members decide they want to continue rescuing dogs, but not with the group to which they currently belong.

Depending on the particular acrimony that leads to such splits and schisms, future cooperation among such groups, while most certainly of paramount importance for needy dogs, may on occasion not be the smoothest. The consequences of a split are many: In addition to the negative emotional toll that an acrimonious division causes, members who leave the established rescue group are forced to start from scratch organizationally (write a new charter, find new members, and build a new network and reputation, among other things) and financially (fundraising and financial planning). These groups have to overcome such problems and the negative residues caused by such schisms if they wish to cooperate successfully on the matter that forms the sole reasons for their existence: the improvement of the lives of suffering dogs.

Geographic splits, on the other hand, are much more prosaic affairs and hail almost exclusively from the problem of having the original (or parent) group covering a geographic area that—for myriad reasons—became too cumbersome, too taxing, or simply too inefficient for servicing the quantity of needy dogs that these members try to accommodate. Because these divisions lack the animosity and tension that accompany schisms from the previous category, groups caused by geographic splits tend to avoid networking problems with other groups, which could have impeded the efficacy of their work. With no contentious issues of any kind causing the split and thus the formation of the new entity from the old, harmonious continuity prevails much more in this case of new group creation than in the instances in which tensions related to personality or policy disagreements constitute the genesis of the new organization.

Group Networking

Rescue group interactions with other organizations, including shelters, local breed clubs, the national breed club, and other rescue groups, profoundly influence the ways in which these groups rescue dogs. Positive communication with these organizations can help groups with all aspects of rescue, from information, to sharing material resources, to helping dogs in need of rescue. When communication between these groups is rocky, breaks down, or has been nonexistent, groups are less effective at rescuing dogs.

Group interactions with shelters are critical to the function of rescue groups. Most rescue groups obtain their dogs from a combination of animal shelters and OTIs. Having a good working relationship with shelters is therefore critical to the group's function, as it ensures that it can rescue the dogs that are in shelters that might otherwise be euthanized. When groups do not have good relationships with the shelters in their area, it can lead to the unnecessary euthanasia of dogs as well as potential harm to the reputation of the rescue group. If the rescue group and the shelter are seen as being at odds, it decreases the rescue group's apparent legitimacy, which could have a negative impact on the donations it receives or the effectiveness of its adoptions. Most groups therefore cultivate positive relationships with their area shelters.

Rescue group interaction with breed clubs is also a critical component of rescue group function and effectiveness. Positive interactions between rescue groups and breed clubs can lead to greater financial support (some clubs actively fundraise for local breed rescues) and exposure to potential adopters and volunteers who already love the breed. Such good relations also facilitate opportunities to educate the public about the breed in particular (but also dogs in general) at club-sponsored events such as breed shows. Negative relationships with breed clubs can actually hurt rescue groups, as they lose potential funds, adopters, and volunteers. If rescue groups have neutral relationships with breed clubs, they might fail to take advantage of the resources that these clubs represent. The bottom line is, having a positive relationship with local breed clubs constitutes a key benefit for all breed rescue groups. We will demonstrate the importance of this resource by using the institutional topography of organizations devoted to Golden Retrievers as a case study in Chapter 4.

The national breed club is another organization that benefits rescue groups when they are in contact with one another. We will expand on this in greater detail subsequently as well, but the impact of the Golden Retriever Club of America's National Rescue Committee (GRCA-NRC) cannot be overstated. The GRCA-NRC coordinates efforts among rescue groups, provides information and assistance to groups at all levels of development, and, in conjunction with the National Rescue Foundation, helps fund the rescue efforts of individual groups in need. Groups that are not in contact with the GRCA-NRC do not receive these benefits, leaving them at a distinct disadvantage when compared with groups that work with the GRCA-NRC.

The most profound network that a rescue group can establish is that with other rescue groups. Rescue groups can help one another in a variety of ways. They can provide information, furnish forms, discuss and showcase policies and procedures, offer transportation help, share resources, and take dogs in need when other groups' facilities and capabilities are full. Rescue groups can help one another on every level. Perhaps more important still, they understand how to help one another in ways that nonrescue group organizations may not. Negative relationships among rescue groups reduce the help that such groups are willing to provide one another in terms of sharing support and offering information; thus they may yield to the most dreaded and undesired consequence of fewer dogs being rescued than possible. Consequently, rescue groups that maintain good relationships with other rescue groups are more successful in their overall mission of helping needy dogs.

Differing Philosophies and Guiding Principles

Although there are many conceptual and ethical approaches to which rescue groups subscribe as their guiding principles to rescue as many dogs as they possibly can, we categorize, at the risk of simplicity, these approaches into two contrasting types: pragmatic and idealistic. Pragmatic rescues tend to focus on local dogs and pursue decidedly realistic and short-term goals. They are interested in working with the American Kennel Club (AKC) and tend to have positive relationships with the club that represents the breed they are rescuing. Pragmatic rescues are populated by what one could term "dog" people, or people who see dog rescue as the responsibility of ethical dog enthusiasts who, on the whole, enjoy participating in club-sponsored activities such as show, field, and agility.

Dog people could be described as the traditionalists of the canine world. They see dogs primarily as property, although not exclusively so. Indeed, some dog people view their animals as members of the family, but this is not the norm. As some of our interviewees have noted, dog people want to do dog things with their dogs: show them for their strong and impeccable breeding, compete on their training ability, contest in agility competitions, and use them for hunting and tracking (field) activities. It should be noted, however, that although dog people see their dogs as dogs rather than as furry children or members of the human family, they typically allow their dogs to live in the house and are extremely unlikely to kennel their own dogs outside on a regular basis. Indeed, we would conjecture that doing so would be seen as abuse by a dog person. Dog people have no problem kenneling rescue animals for months at a time. Indeed, this process of segregating rescue dogs from their own often constitutes a dog person's essential relationship to rescue. Central to this world is the view that dog breeding is not only a common practice, but it is also absolutely essential to the continuation of the breed's existence. Thus, to a dog person, the contentious issue is not the existence of breeding, but that it occur in a "responsible" way. This means that a breeder needs to make every effort to create genetically healthy offspring and that he or she never overproduces. Furthermore, the breeder must try her or his most to place a dog with a responsible family who will take care of it, thus ensuring as much as humanly possible that the dog not be surrendered for any capricious or frivolous reasons. Finally, the dog person's concept of responsible breeding typically involves an expectation that the breeder take the dog back unconditionally in the event that the adopting family no longer has the ability to care for the dog.

In the world of rescue, dog people could be considered as constituting the conservative side of the spectrum. They see rescue as a necessity in a world with irresponsible breeders and a manifestation of their very own obligation and responsibility as enthusiasts of the breed to help rescue some of its members who, through no fault of their own, have met with an adverse fate. The term *enthusiast* is crucial, as *love* is generally too strong a term for many people who fit under the dog person umbrella. Consider these people as *compassionate conservatives*,[8] fiscally responsible individuals who want to help needy members of their breed, but also have clear limits in doing so. "I think the rescue activity just starts out of compassion," stated

Jeannette Poling, president of the Golden Retriever Club of San Diego County (San Diego, California). She continued:

> We get dogs when people go on vacation; we get dogs at Christmas because people are having company come. And it's cheaper to get rid of the dog than board it. Pretty disgusting comment on humans. . . . Doing dog rescue is a way for me to give back to all the dogs who have brought immense pleasure to my life, but it does not define me. It simply does not, and I think maybe that's the difference about our rescue: we do what we can do but we do not believe that we can help every dog.[9]

Thus, while being clearly committed to helping needy, neglected, and abused dogs, dog people do not let rescue define their view of the entire canine world, let alone the human–canine relationship. Compassion rather than passion constitutes the primary emotion of their commitment.

Dog people see it as prudent policy to set some limits as to how much they will invest to cure a dog, not because they are cheap or uncaring but because they hold that not all dogs are salvageable and that given limited resources in the world, such triage is not only ethically acceptable but indeed preferable. For dog people, euthanasia represents a perfectly legitimate solution to dogs that are too sick, injured, or exhibit severe behavioral problems. Indeed, one of the discriminating factors of a dog person from a pet person (whom we will discuss below) is that dog people believe that "bad" or incorrigible dogs do in fact exist and that it is best for all concerned that such dogs be euthanized.

The pragmatism of dog people is particularly evident in the rescue's intake procedures in which sick or problematic dogs are treated as liabilities and will not be accepted into the program unless there is a lull in the adoption of "normal" dogs, thus providing the rare luxury of open space and resources in the rescue. Indeed, rescue organizations that are run by dog people seem to have a greater selectivity for the type of dogs they are willing to accept, are less likely to take mixes (and most likely averse to doing so), and find groups that are less selective to be irresponsible, if not "crazy." We encountered a number of dog people who, in our interviews with them, referred to such—in their view mindless and counterproductive—attitudes and behaviors as belonging to "bleeding-hearts." Indeed, some rescuers of the dog people variety did not shy away from labeling the actions by bleeding-hearts as tantamount to animal abuse. One additional factor delineating a dog person is that he or she is rarely, if ever, willing to adopt a rescued dog, as such an animal is unable to fit into the world of dog activities (primarily competition and tracking) in which dog people engage their canine companions. Most rescued dogs are unable to be used in breeding activities, as they tend to lack AKC papers.

In summation, dog people view rescue activities as a noble and necessary obligation as well as responsibility, but seem rather baffled by the fact that people exist in the world that actually devote major parts of their lives to rescuing dogs. Dog people's instrumental and practical view of dog rescue hinges ultimately on their pragmatic perception of dogs, whom they regard as wonderful companions worthy of all respect, comfort, and dignity. However, the strict boundaries of dogs and humans generally never blur for dog people. As a rule, dog people form rescue groups that continue to be part of local AKC clubs or once belonged to such. These groups tend to follow a pragmatic philosophy in their rescue of dogs belonging to their preferred breed.

This approach contrasts sharply with what we have termed *idealistic* rescue. Organizations subscribing to this worldview have lofty, long-term goals that are, in essence, to end any and all pet homelessness, not only in their own geographic location but globally as well. These groups tend to attract what we have come to call "pet" people, meaning individuals who see dogs as beloved pets or "fur-children" and who treat them as true and completely integral members of their family. Idealistic rescue groups often disdain clubs that include breeders as part of the problem of canine overpopulation. Although not outright hostile, these rescues' relationship with the AKC remains often quite tepid and guarded.

For individuals in such idealistic groups, rescue constitutes an all-consuming passion. Unlike dog people, the individuals who fall under the pet people categorization do not care about showing their pets or using them for traditional tracking activities. This has not been an interest and will likely never become an interest for these individuals. Indeed, considering the fact that most pet people have some level of antipathy for breeders, it is highly unlikely that a pet person will ever purchase a dog from a breeder.[10] For the pet person, taking care of the dog, spending time with the animal, and having its companionship are simply enough. Because the dog is a member of the family, pet people are more likely to invest large sums of money into its medical treatment. Though individuals on either pole are unlikely to see their dogs as replaceable, a pet person is more likely to invest a greater percentage of her or his temporal and financial resources in saving her or his dog's life than a dog person would. It is this passion for each individual animal that filters so strongly into a pet person's rescue activities.

Breed rescue activities are typically the only collective measures in which pet people engage under the breed umbrella. Unlike their dog person counterparts, who choose—indeed want—to balance their dog time between rescue and showing, pet people devote all their efforts to rescue. For them, this is their primary responsibility, and they want to place dogs in good homes. This passion typically translates into a highly devoted participation in rescue, willing to go to great lengths to save dogs. Most will have driven hundreds of miles to save one dog, fostered many in their own households, and invested huge amounts of time and money to ensure that in the end a dog emerges healthy and happy in its new forever home. Indeed, some will invest many thousands of dollars in curing a dog of physical ailments. Pet people rarely believe that a dog can be bad and view negative canine behavior as a product of the environment in which the dog was raised. This assessment typically creates a divide among pet people, with some seeing euthanasia for behaviorally challenged dogs as a dreaded but necessary must, while others regard it as an unacceptable course of action that should be avoided under any and all circumstances. Pet people not only devote huge amounts of their time to rescue organizations, but they fully enjoy doing so.

On the whole, pet people see themselves as advocates in favor of more humane animal treatment, including the once-and-for-all cessation of pet overpopulation. Idealists involved in canine rescue perceive their activity as part of a larger worldview that focuses on the improvement of the living conditions for all animals of which the particular canine breed they are committed to rescuing offers but one representative. For idealists, canine breed rescue assumes a much greater emotional and ideological salience than it does for pragmatists. The terms *activist* and *movement* pertain to the former; whereas the latter invokes concepts such as *volunteer* and *interest group*.

The vast majority of rescuers consists neither of purely idealistic pet people nor of purely pragmatic dog people. Instead, most rescuers occupy a variety of positions along a complex spectrum of philosophical attitudes toward rescue, bookended by these two ideal–typical extremes. In other words, most rescuers are solid "centrists" who incorporate aspects of both visions to varying degrees depending on the particular demands of each situation. Though overarching ideologies informing the human–canine relationship most certainly matter in defining the identities of these breed specific rescuers, it is the offering of concrete and immediate solutions to the daily demands of particular dogs in specific situations that guides these people's everyday lives. Thus, there are many committed rescuers who own and even breed AKC-approved dogs and who adopt rescued dogs that they love on the very same level as their well-bred pets. Many rescuers work well with breeders and do not despise or disdain them, even though they fully understand and even condone the concerns that render pet people hostile toward breeders. Perhaps one crucial difference between the adherents of the two approaches to dog rescue lies in the fact that, as a rule, pet people are willing to devote almost all their time to breed rescue, while dog people choose to devote time and effort to other dog activities, thus making their commitment to breed rescue apparently less encompassing. Understanding the philosophy that a group might favor and thus pursue as its overall operational strategy can provide key insight into the group's behavior and policies, particularly when it comes to evaluating the types of dogs a group will accept, as pragmatic groups tend to be more restrictive than idealistic groups and less interested in handling dogs with serious illnesses or behavioral problems.

Leadership Categories

Again, at the risk of oversimplification, we categorize the leadership running rescue groups into the following two ideal–typical polar opposites: On one end of the spectrum resides the single leader who, often as the group's founder and certainly among its most active participants, exerts a leadership style and presides over the organization that one could best call personalistic. As such, this person's authority conforms closely to what Max Weber so aptly characterized as "charismatic." On the other end, we have observed the collective leadership of a multiperson board, which, usually, represents a kind of authority that Weber categorized as "legal-rational."

Although not always the case, rescue groups with a single charismatic leader tend to be smaller. This leader is almost always the founder of the group, and all decisions, from routine, day-to-day affairs to large-scale policy-setting agendas, emanate from this leader or—at a minimum—must enjoy her or his approval and support. All other group members help the leader as necessary, and if the group possesses a board, its functions are more or less auxiliary to the leader's agenda and supportive of her or his decisions and activities.

Groups governed by boards, however, exhibit much more rule-driven and regularized authority structures that guide the collective's policies, strategies, and actions. Thus, for example, groups of this kind feature transparent mechanisms of office seeking and office holding with clearly delineated procedures for any changes in the incumbency of all of the group's positions, from the lowest (usually at-large board members) to the highest (usually the president). Board members may be elected by the general rescue group population or they may be appointed by the current members of the board on an as-needed basis. Whatever the specific rules governing each particular organization may be, rescues adhering to the legal-rational modus operandi exhibit a management structure in which the organization's overall governance permits individual board members a degree of autonomy in responsibility for actions and measures that they themselves have reached via consensus of the board as a whole. Overall governance thus constitutes not only the organization's agreed-upon formal rules but also, perhaps more important still, its informal cultural consensus. To be sure, in these legal-rational organizations, too, plenty of ad hoc matters arise that require the formal consensus of the entire board. In groups beholden to the charismatic style of leadership, board members do not enjoy such autonomy, because virtually all authority for the organization's actions and policies rests with the charismatic leader.

As has been the norm in the case of all new beginnings—be they the automobile industry or its computer counterpart or religions or political movements—the world of dog rescue also commenced with innovators who, by definition, created an authority regime that perfectly fit Weber's definition of the charismatic. Following their hearts, their passion, and their conviction and seeing the societal need to have their desires and hopes realized, these strong-willed and idealistic individuals set out to create a whole new world that we have come to know as dog rescue. We were fortunate to interview some of the pioneers of this world who clearly fall under the rubric of Weber's charismatic form of leadership. It was by their sheer will, vision, dedication, and hard work that their particular rescues became reality. Again, very much pursuant to the characteristics of Weber's charismatic form of authority, these individuals came to embody these new organizations and governed their every nook and cranny. In addition to having had the initiative of starting these new organizations, these individuals' leadership authority was further enhanced by the tireless constancy of their commitment to these new entities and their mission. These charismatic leaders not only invented these organizations' new policies and strategies but they also implemented and lived them with their smallest details, from driving hundreds of miles to rescue a dog in dire need, to taking it to the vet, nurturing it to health, setting it up for fostering, and many other crucial steps all necessary for the single purpose of having this dog attain a loving forever home.

With a few exceptions emanating most notably from organizations that originated by splitting from another, most of the rescue groups we encountered in our research commenced with a charismatic leader. Furthermore, apart from very few cases in which such founding leaders were a husband and wife team, the vast majority of these innovators and initiators were women. Perhaps none were more typical—and original—than the late Norma Gurinskas who commenced rescuing Dobermans in the 1970s in New Hampshire and Maine and who—without a doubt—was one of the true pioneers of the rescue world. Typical for the beginnings and the charismatic stage of most rescue organizations, Norma started everything by herself, making up steps and procedures on the fly.

> People would call, and they'd be looking for a Doberman, and I would send them an application form which I made up and they would return the form, and I would check it over to see if I wanted these people as part of my organization and if I wanted to place a dog with them. The same thing happened when people wanted to get rid of a dog. I'd send out a different kind of form, and they would fill that in, and bring it to me and the dog's medical records and the dog and we would go from there. I don't think that I ever refused any dog that I can remember, but for me to take the dog, they'd have to have this form.[11]

It is clear that for Norma the forms were at best merely auxiliary items, seemingly legal-rational window dressing for a purely emotional and inclusive transaction. She told us that she never turned a dog away in her decades of rescue, yet she invented these forms that in their completed version became a seemingly impersonal bureaucratic part of this highly personalistic transaction. Norma started her rescue as a one-woman operation but—quite untypical for much of the rescue world—she also ended it more or less alone. Thus, Norma's rescue never outgrew its original charismatic and personalistic stage by mutating into a larger organization beholden to a legal-rational modus operandi and overall character.

One need not be a stubborn believer in the correctness of the dialectical method to realize that it was precisely by virtue of the immense success of these charismatic individuals' overall work that eventually their authority and position in these organizations came to be challenged. For as Weber and his contemporary Robert Michels taught us so well, as soon as these new, largely personalistic, entities experience success, they attract follow-ers. This, of course, means that these organizations commence to grow to the point that authority in them cannot be efficiently exercised by one person, no matter how devoted, dedicated, and charismatic, thus necessi-tating some rule-driven, bureaucratic construct, the governance of which requires a completely different logic from its earlier, person-dependent predecessor. Weber calls this difficult—but inevitable—organizational transition the "routinization of charisma." As soon as any of these rescue groups attain a certain size, which, of course, they have done by virtue of being successful, they come to be governed by boards and rules and regu-lations that replace the authority of one individual, regardless of the quality and commitment of her involvement and charisma. This is not to say that in a legal-rational framework and more bureaucratically structured organi-zation the role of individuals and their personal engagement on the group's behalf do not matter. Far from it! Dog rescue—particularly because it still is almost exclusively a purely voluntary and nonremunerated activity—will always depend on the deep emotional involvement and affective action on the part of individuals committed to improving these dogs' lives.

But as in the case of any other entity that is crowned by success and popularity, there comes a point for dog rescue as well in which the initial stage of charismatic authority structure is superseded by its legal-rational successor. This transition usually occurs when the charismatic leader either retires or is asked to depart from the group, leaving leadership in the hands of the next generation of committed rescuers. This development is clearly more prevalent in larger groups than smaller ones that often remain such precisely to maintain the charismatic leader's incumbency. As is evident, change in leadership is never an easy issue for any entity. This is true in the rescue world too, where one can witness many organizational splits and lots of discord and personal animosities related to this transition. Whatever the case may be, it is vital to the long-term survival of the rescue group that it transform itself from its charismatic organizational origins to a legal rational one because no charismatic leader lives forever.

Just beneath either style of group leadership, organizations structure themselves as their needs require. Large groups tend to divide assign-ments according to tasks necessary for the group to function: they create committees and coordinators for dog intake, dog placement, fundraising, administration, and outreach, among others, and assign volunteers to one or more of these committees. Individuals therefore have a clear chain of command and structure in which they pursue their tasks. After all, rescue by large organizations requires complex operations in diverse areas that need careful supervision of an army of volunteers who may be deeply committed to the cause but who still need guidance to perform their assignment optimally. Jane Nygaard, founder of Retrieve a Golden of Minnesota (RAGOM) (Minnetonka, MN), described this in the following manner:

> Large, institutionalized rescues have a broad volunteer base that is engaged in very different things. All of these need instruction and training. Each person that is going to foster will need to go through a training session. You need support from others. There's people that have mentors. . . . We have volunteers that just go and answer the mailboxes. We have volunteers that just do the website. A person that just does thank-you notes.[12]

As the number of volunteers in a rescue group increases, the organization of the rescue becomes more complex, with volunteers having to master greater degrees of specialization with increasing complexity.

The chance is high that all of these diverse and often complex tasks will be performed very well because two crucial components for the production of good work exist in abundance in these organizations: first, the commitment of the workforce could not be higher because virtually all of it consists of volunteers who truly love what they are doing and believe in the virtue and value of their cause; and second, the skill and educational level of many participants is often quite high. This is how Jacky Eckard of Safe Harbor Lab Rescue (Golden, CO) describes her team of a Labrador rescue:

> Well, on our board, I'm the president and I have an MBA and my field of emphasis when I did that years ago was nonprofit management, but now I work part time as a school librarian. On our board we also have a CPA, we have . . . an attorney, so, you know, we have folks like that. We have a marketing manager, a marketing director . . . and then people that are retired that have a variety of skills, like executives in the insurance industry, we have a small-business owner, we have someone who's an environmental scientist, so I mean, we have people like that on our board.[13]

In contrast to larger groups, their smaller counterparts tend to be unstructured, as the small number of volunteers requires that each perform multiple types of tasks, such as a volunteer doing both intake and fundraising. The group does not perceive a need to subdivide alongside various tasks, as its informal communication and reporting structures are sufficient to fulfill properly the group's organizational needs. As groups grow in size, they tend to become more hierarchical, and volunteers in larger groups tend to specialize more than those in smaller groups. Regardless of group size, however, there exists one constant that informs the character of virtually all rescues' workforce: a deep dedication to the cause based on little more than true compassion for the dogs in need.

Rescue Group Sizes

Breed rescue groups can vary in size from one person rescuing dogs out of her or his own home to bureaucratized institutions with hundreds of volunteers and rescuing hundreds of dogs annually. Homeward Bound Golden Retriever Rescue & Sanctuary in Elverta, California, is the largest Golden Retriever rescue group in the United States. In 2009, it had 200 volunteers and rescued 854 dogs. On the other end of the spectrum is With a Golden Spirit in Irwin, Pennsylvania, which is one of the smallest Golden Retriever rescue groups in the country. With only one foster home and four members on its board, this organization rescued thirteen dogs in 2009. The vast difference in size between these two groups demonstrates the organizational breadth that rescue has in which little is shared, with one paramount exception: the goal to rescue needy dogs belonging to the specific breed, which all the participants in these most varied organizations have come to love.

The size of a rescue group determines its expected behavior concerning every aspect of its activities. As is often the case, in the world of breed specific rescue, too, quantity has major qualitative ramifications. Fundamentally, the number of dogs a rescue group is capable of rescuing in a year is determined by the number of volunteers in the rescue group. Countrywide, only three Golden Retriever rescue groups with fewer than fifty volunteers accepted more than 200 dogs in 2009. With more volunteers at their disposal, large rescue groups can have volunteers specialize in activities other than rescuing dogs, thus allowing the rescue group to diversify its activities by having volunteers specialize in activities that, in turn, enhance the group's efficacy in its rescue efforts. The two most crucial of such activities are fundraising and public relations. But group size also affects a variety of other dimensions essential to the rescue mission. Thus, for example, a larger group can engage in a greater variety of fundraising activities on a more frequent basis than a smaller group can. The former have the organizational resources to run sophisticated capital fundraising campaigns, while the latter's fundraising efforts, by necessity, remain confined to activities such as dog washes or silent auctions. Big groups have the resources to accept dogs with behavioral problems and health issues that— as a rule—smaller groups most often cannot. The former have the money and quite often the requisite expertise as well as the luxury of time to treat such dogs and rehabilitate them. In contrast, the smaller groups simply lack such resources and thus by necessity have to confine their intake to healthy dogs that will be adopted much more readily and speedily. In short, the sheer size of a rescue group has a major impact on the behavior and policies that determine the group's engagement in rescue.

Rescue group size is also important because it reflects the resources available to the group. Rescue groups with more volunteers have greater pooled resources than those with only a few volunteers. A larger volunteer base is more likely to include a variety of professions, from lawyers to public relations managers to accountants, all of whose skills can be donated to the group and thus enhance its efficacy in the rescue mission. A larger number of volunteers in a group also increases its visibility and outreach with the general public, as the collective networking power of the rescue group multiplies with every volunteer it adds to its base. Sheer numbers have a snowball effect in that every volunteer has friends and relatives and circles in which the group and its activities become known by virtue of this volunteer's engagement. Needless to say, such grassroots anchoring then translates into the group's enhanced visibility in its immediate community, which in turn leads to its gaining greater legitimacy and then results in enhanced successes in the all-important realm of fundraising.

Finally, a rescue group's size can give partial but useful insight into the collective's goals and preferences as well as to those of its individual leaders. In the following presentation, we will discern three sizes of rescue organizations, which shape the very nature of these organizations' approach to and preference for breed specific canine rescue.

Microgroups

Groups that have fewer than twenty-five volunteers can well be labeled microgroups. Because virtually all rescue organizations are small at their inception, we discern two categories of microgroups: those that choose to remain small on purpose by virtue of its members' preferences or contextual circumstances, and groups that are too recent to have grown. The former encompass a variety of ages and are best exemplified by the Golden

Retriever Club of San Diego County Rescue Service [GRCSDCRS] (San Diego, California). The club has a rescue committee that it created in the early 1980s. As of 2009, the group had four volunteers and an intake of thirty-two dogs. The committee has had the time to accrue the resources necessary for it to leave the club and create its own 501(c)(3) rescue group but has chosen not to pursue this path. In fact, the club president, Jeannette Poling, informed us that there was a greater likelihood of the club folding than the rescue splitting from the club and becoming independent from it.[14] GRCSDCR, which was founded in 1980 and has had thirty-four years to make any changes it wished in terms of defining the goals and ways of its program, chose to remain a microgroup on the rescue side. It pursued this course of action because the rescue's activists continued to view its mission as part of a service to the Golden Retriever breed as a whole whose main guardians, according to this viewpoint, remained the breed clubs.

Typically, microgroups are led by one or two people, though some may have small boards as well. These groups are the only rescues for whom obtaining a 501(c)(3) status and insurance are not considered an absolute must for their existence and operation. The decision to abstain from procuring a group's 501(c)(3) status is not without controversy, but some microgroups, particularly those that consist of a single person or a married couple, feel that the paperwork necessary to obtain the tax-exempt status unnecessarily diverts energy and resources from rescuing dogs. One example of this is Trish Richardson from Southwest Virginia Lab Rescue. The group consists of herself, her husband, and four foster homes. Trish informed us that the group does not adopt enough dogs to need a 501(c)(3) status, and that obtaining such a status would entail more work than is feasible and necessary for the group's mission to rescue needy Labrador Retrievers and place them into loving forever homes.[15] Although groups that do not apply for a 501(c)(3) status are ineligible for tax exemption, their leaders feel that attaining such a financial advantage might not be worth the effort of an application, particularly if the decision of remaining small is such groups' preferred policy. Pertaining to a very similar logic, such microgroups often refrain from purchasing insurance of any kind. The rationale for declining to obtain insurance for the group is much the same as the decision not to pursue tax exemption: a cost–benefit assessment in which the costs of the application seem to outweigh the benefits of the results that it might yield. In the case of insurance, there is, of course, the added dimension of expensive premiums that would consume a large proportion of such microgroups' meager budgets and thus diminish the already constrained resources needed for their desired purpose of dog rescue. Forgoing both tax exemption and insurance remain completely predicated on the low volume of rescue, which remains the modus operandi for these microgroups.

Midsized Groups

With the wide range of having 26 to 149 volunteers, midsized groups possess the greatest variation of the three group categories. Not as small as microgroups, yet not as large as megagroups, these midsized groups are the most frequent in the contemporary rescue world. Both charismatic and board-governed leadership styles exist in groups of this size, each with their advantages and disadvantages. Unlike their smaller counterparts, midsized groups characteristically possess both tax exemption by having a 501(c)(3) status and insurance covering group activities. But unlike megagroups, midsized groups do not to have their own facilities or paid employees. The leadership of many midsized groups remains content to continue operations at their current size, while others are eager to grow and thus join the ranks of the megagroups.

Megagroups

Yankee Golden Retriever Rescue (YGRR) furnishes perhaps the ideal–typical megagroup. Occupying the exact opposite of the organizational spectrum from the microgroups, YGRR emerged from being part of a Golden Retriever breed club from which it departed and commenced its rescue as an independent organization. The group grew from three people in 1985 to an organization that had 350 volunteers in 2009 and had an intake of 135 dogs in that year.[16] The largest of the three sizes, the megagroups feature 150 or more volunteers. Another megagroup, very similar in development and trajectory to YGRR, has been RAGOM, which started with two volunteers, Hank and Jane Nygaard, in 1985. By 2009, that number had ballooned to 280. Megagroups of this kind are led almost exclusively through board governance, although a few charismatic leaders manage to shepherd their groups into megagroup territory. As a rule, however, smoothly running megagroups require the delegation and specialization of leadership positions that is not possible or efficient in a charismatic leadership situation. What further sets these megagroups apart, however, is that several of them own their own shelters and have paid employees managing their kennels. These facilities are solid, physical structures that represent the culmination of breed rescue group organization. These groups, in essence, operate with the professionalism of small businesses and represent the immense transformation that breed specific rescue has undergone since its marginalized beginnings of the 1980s to its institutional presence in the completely changed topography of contemporary America's human–animal relations.

The trajectories of newly formed groups are hard to predict because changes in leadership often result in accompanying changes in strategies and policies, which in turn lead to changes in size and behavior. When they are new, rescue groups operate by necessity like microgroups, but as they age, they exhibit traits and characteristics that indicate their intention to either remain small or to expand.

Comparing Sizes

Comparisons among the three rescue sizes provide important context for the differing behaviors in which these organizations engage. In particular, we found the following factors in these comparisons quite illuminating for a proper assessment of these rescues' attitudes, policies, and behavior: their institutional longevity; their average income in relation to the volunteers who work in these groups and the number of dogs admitted to their respective programs; and their fundraising activities.

The average start year of the three different group sizes shows the effect that time and opportunity can have on rescue groups. Microgroups active in Golden Retriever rescue featured 1997 as their average start date; but this is somewhat misleading because of the presence in this calculation of older groups like the Golden Retriever Club of San Diego Rescue Service, Southern Indiana Golden Retriever Club (Evansville, Indiana),[17] and Dirk's Fund (Pacific, Missouri),[18] which remained small by explicit choice and policy preference on the part of their respective leaders. Thus, apart from these three organizations, the average start date for microgroups shifts to 2001, which reflects their relatively recent institutional presence in the larger world of breed specific rescue. Midsized groups have an average start year of 1999, earlier than the adjusted average start year of the microgroups but later than that of the megagroups, which was 1994. The fact that larger groups, on average, are older than smaller groups is self-evident, as the larger groups have had a longer amount of time to accrue the resources necessary to grow to their current size. It is telling that the decade of the 1990s became the starting date for all three of our size categories, demonstrating that it was at this time that breed specific canine rescue came to be truly accepted in the world of human–animal relations in the United States.

Although the number of volunteers in a group can generally be used to predict the number of dogs a rescue will take into its program, the rate at which this increase occurs is surprising. As would be expected with groups of their size, microgroups do not have large intake numbers. In 2009, microgroups accepted seventy-three dogs on average. This means that, as a rule, there were five dogs accepted into a rescue for every volunteer serving in a microgroup. With midsized groups, the average number of dogs admitted to the rescue groups in 2009 was 135, or slightly less than double the average number of dogs admitted to the microgroups; the average number of dogs per volunteer dropped, however, from five dogs per volunteer with microgroups to two dogs per volunteer with midsized groups. This trend continues into megagroups, where the average number of dogs admitted in 2009 was 280 (or slightly more than double that of the midsized groups), with the number of dogs per volunteer dropping to one. In other words, the "productivity" of volunteers as measured by the intake—thus rescue—of dogs, which, after all, embodies the very raison d'être of these organizations, has been much higher among those working in the smallest groups and decreases progressively with the increase of the group's size.

This obvious productivity drop, witnessed in the decreasing proportion of rescued dogs to volunteers as rescue group size increases, is generally attributable to volunteer specialization, which in turn accompanies any process of organizational growth and modernization. If we compare two hypothetical groups, one with 10 volunteers and one with 175 volunteers, we will see why volunteer specialization has to occur by the logic of structural differentiation that characterizes the complexity of any large organization.

In a group of ten volunteers, the ability to delegate responsibilities is severely limited, as all ten volunteers must assume the multitude of tasks necessary to run a functioning rescue. This situation is further complicated by the fact that groups of this size often feature the group's leader as being solely responsible for approving all of the group's intake, placement, administrative, and fundraising activities. Typical for such small organizations, all other volunteers are frequently relegated to subordinate positions as providers of foster homes or expected to check in with the group leader before performing any other actions for the group. This means that most of the volunteers in a small organization are foster parents who, on occasion, may assume other ad hoc duties as necessary. The absence of structural differentiation and the paucity of any luxury in terms of staffing mean that volunteers in such microgroups have to be jacks-of-all-trades in order to accomplish the organizations' very mission. Needless to say, this impressive productivity can only be attained by each and every single volunteer's immense commitment to the cause. Thus, it should come as no surprise that a greater propensity of personalistic rule and charismatic authority presides in microgroups than in their larger counterparts. There is a clear interaction, on multiple levels, between being numerically and organizationally small—often as the result of a definitive choice on the part of the committed activists—and following a personalized form of authority.

In a group with 175 volunteers, however, not all of them need to be foster parents for the rescue group to function. Volunteers are in fact encouraged to specialize, often in activities that support rescue but do not involve actual fostering of dogs, such as coordinating intake and placement, running a website, planning fundraisers, or managing the books. Thus, megagroups rescue more net dogs than their microgroup counterparts, but have a smaller proportion of their volunteer base directly involved in fostering.

The average income and fundraising efforts of a rescue group also depend on the size of the rescue group and show similar patterns that we discerned in the case of volunteer specialization. Microgroups have an average annual income of $47,571. The fundraising efforts of microgroups are typified by short-term, small-return activities such as dog washes, raffles, and bake sales. Indeed, some microgroups do not engage in any fundraising activities at all. This is not to say that these groups will decline donations, but rather they do not attempt to solicit them from others in part because they lack the time and resources to engage in any activity beyond the actual rescuing of dogs. Such absence of fundraising is most prevalent in groups with five or fewer volunteers.

Midsized groups have an average annual income of $89,415. In contrast to the microgroups' fundraising efforts, those pursued by the midsized groups involve slightly more complex and creative activities that require greater planning and networking. Still, such activities typically only involve one-day events featuring silent auctions, sponsored walks, and wine tastings.

With an average annual income of $334,667, the megagroups, by necessity and by definition, have to be much more sophisticated fundraisers, as is demonstrated by their penchant for capital campaigns, solicitation of corporate donations (from companies such as Purina, Eukanuba, and PetSmart), partnerships with organizations like the United Way, and cultivated donor lists within their region. Coordinating and executing these fundraising activities are immensely labor intensive for these rescue groups, but the rewards are equally substantial. Volunteer specialization works in favor of the megagroups, as they can recruit volunteers whose sole purpose is to fundraise for the group. Such volunteers are typically not asked to foster or transport dogs, manage the group's website, or engage in any activity other than that of garnering funds for the group. Joy Viola, a former volunteer for Yankee Golden Retriever Rescue, best describes the contrast in commitment to fundraising between micro- and midsized groups on the one hand and megagroups on the other when she states:

> A lot of these groups got started with simple fundraising things like dog washes and little events, and maybe their auctions, their membership fee or a little raffle, etc. They don't know what it is to really do a professional job of fundraising, to look for major donors, to cultivate those donors and steward them, keep them interested in your organization, and to write letters to donors and to make them feel like a part of the organization.[19]

The volunteers' decision to devote all of the hours they are donating to the group solely to fundraising means that megagroups spend more hours planning fundraising activities than the other groups. This, in turn, means that megagroups can constantly increase the sophistication of their fundraising tools, which helps their cause immensely.

The rules governing the behavior of a rescue group based on the number of volunteers within the group are not immune to outliers. One microgroup, Dirk's Fund, is an excellent example of this case. Dirk's Fund had twenty-five volunteers in 2009, but admitted 200 dogs into its program, nearly triple that of the average for typical microgroups. This particular rescue group was started in 1980, making it significantly older than the majority of the other microgroups. Most interestingly and exceptionally for such a small group, Dirk's Fund rents a sheltering facility for its own exclusive use. Dirk's Fund represents an interesting hybrid: Though it shares many traits, most notably the immense number of its intakes, with megagroups, it maintains the volunteer base of a microgroup.

This dichotomy is the result of the unique history of Golden Retriever rescue in St. Louis, Missouri. Whereas Dirk's Fund was the first such group in the St. Louis area, it was followed by two others that spread the potential Golden Retriever volunteer pool in this area while allowing the continuation of Dirk's Fund's exclusivity. Unlike in the case with most of the rest of the country (with Texas furnishing an interesting exception that we will discuss in a subsequent chapter), where there exists only one breed specific rescue group per geographic area, in St. Louis there have been three, giving potential volunteers options as to where they would like to pursue their passion. Thus Dirk's Fund has had the luxury of remaining small, while it could also assume the benefits of a megagroup by virtue of one particular donor's consistent financial generosity. Dirk's Fund garnered the experience and efficiency that larger groups possess, but without adding substantially to its volunteer base. Enjoying the best of both worlds—a small group's personalistic style and atmosphere and a large group's resources and facilities— Dirk's Fund owes much, if not all, of its financial largesse and spirit of generosity to Bob Tillay, one of the Fund's founders.

Conclusion

The purpose of a breed specific rescue group is to alleviate homelessness among dogs of a particular breed within a geographic location that the group has designated as the purview of its operations. Rescue groups attain this goal by admitting dogs to their program, vetting them for health and behavior and placing them with new "forever homes." To be able to rescue dogs, rescue groups must also perform administrative tasks that support their rescue operation. Among the most important of these are fundraising and maintaining positive external relationships with a bevy of organizations crucial to the rescue's successful work. The size of a rescue (be it a micro-rescue, a midsized rescue, or a megarescue) determines the ways in which a rescue group will behave and the policies it will pursue with respect to the activities just mentioned. In particular, a larger quantity of volunteers offers greater opportunities and resources for a rescue group through the possibility of volunteer specialization. Size is therefore a critical component to understand how breed rescue groups function. Chapter 2 presents a detailed look at a dog rescue's overall gestalt and its activists' sociological profile by featuring the State of Michigan as a representative case study. Above all, the chapter will highlight dog rescue's most pervasive characteristic: the massive prevalence, indeed uncontested dominance, of women.

Notes

1. Internal Revenue Service. "Exemption Requirements—Section 501(c)(3) Organizations." http://www.irs.gov/Charities-&-Non-Profits/Charitable-Organizations/Exemption-Requirements-Section-501(c)(3)-Organizations (accessed on April 23, 2014). Emphasis in original.

2. Carol Allen. Interviewed by Andrei Markovits. Telephone Interview. July 7, 2009.

3. American Society for the Prevention of Cruelty to Animals. "Pet Statistics." Last modified 2013. http://www.aspca.org/about-us/faq/pet-statistics (accessed on June 2, 2013).

4. Robin Adams. Interviewed by Andrei Markovits. Telephone Interview. July 7, 2009.

5. Maureen Distler. Interviewed by Katherine Crosby. Telephone Interview. July 28, 2010.

6. Phil Fisher. Interviewed by Andrei Markovits. Telephone Interview. July 30, 2009.

7. Barbara Elk. Interviewed by Andrei Markovits. Telephone Interview. August 19, 2010.

8. We use the term *compassionate conservative* in the common sense. It is related to the evolving discourse of compassion, but is a weaker form thereof.

9. Jeannette Poling. Interviewed by Andrei Markovits. Telephone Interview. June 22, 2009.

10. It should be noted that although many pet people purchase their first (few) dog(s) from breeders, many will never do so. Pet people oftentimes adopt their first dogs from animal shelters or breed rescue organizations and from that point forward will only adopt rescued dogs.

11. Norma Gurinskas. Interviewed by Andrei Markovits. Telephone Interview. August 17, 2009.

12. Jane Nygaard. Interviewed by Andrei Markovits. Telephone Interview. August 6, 2009.

13. Jacky Eckard. Interviewed by Katherine Crosby. Telephone Interview. July 29, 2010.

14. Jeannette Poling. Interviewed by Andrei Markovits. Telephone Interview. June 22, 2009.

15. Trish Richardson. Interviewed by Katherine Crosby. Telephone Interview. August 9, 2010.

16. We are using Golden Retriever rescues for the bulk of our information because the GRCA-NRC undertakes and publishes an annual survey with regard to intake, veterinary expenses, and volunteers that the majority of Golden Retriever rescue groups respond to, and it is difficult to obtain similar data for the other canine breeds.

17. Southern Indiana Golden Retriever Club refers to its rescue committee as FLASH, or Finding Loving and Secure Homes.

18. Dirk's Fund represents an outlier that we will explore in greater detail below.

19. Joy Viola. Interviewed by Andrei Markovits. Telephone Interview. July 16, 2009.

CHAPTER 2

The Overwhelming Predominance of Women in the World of Dog Rescue

The State of Michigan as a Representative Case Study Enhanced by Relevant Interview Data from Rescuers Elsewhere[1]

with Robin Queen

Women are so much more sensitive and caring than men. Then, again, they just might have more time. But they sure as heck are much better organizers and know what needs to be done. Most important, they actually go out and do things without pontificating and grandstanding about them.

—The late Norma Gurinskas
Founder of the New Hampshire Doberman Rescue League

Without any question, women are the predominant participants in dog rescue. A quick perusal of the gender of the sixty individuals listed in Appendix D who have been long-standing dog rescue workers whom we interviewed for our study reveals the huge overrepresentation of women among this group. Although we in no way argue that our work represents a statistically significant sample of the breed specific rescue population that began in the United States in the 1980s and proliferated throughout the 1990s, we are reasonably certain that the preponderance of women in this field not only constitutes a solid fact but it also indeed marks one of its major characteristics. Dog rescue, like virtually all other aspects of human assistance to and care of animals, has become a heavily feminized world in contemporary America.

Here are some cursory data that we encountered in our work supporting the pervasive nature of this phenomenon: Of the ninety-five officially registered Golden Retriever rescue organizations in the United States in 2005, only five had a male president and nine others listed a male–female combination as copresidents, most often a married couple. Of the sixty-plus Golden Retriever clubs registered in the United States in the same year, only two had male presidents. The feminization of this world goes well beyond the presidencies of these organizations. In 2007, Yankee Golden Retriever Rescue, which was founded in 1985 and is one of the oldest of any dog rescues in the country, had twenty-two women among its officers, board of directors, and professional staff, with only one man being listed as having any leadership role in the organization. Until 2011, Golden Retriever Rescue of Michigan, founded in 2000, had no men in any leadership roles, something that was true of all but one of the rescue organizations represented by the thirty-seven dog rescue workers whom we interviewed for the Michigan-based aspect of our project and who formed a subset of a larger group of rescue workers that completed a comprehensive survey about dog rescue work for us. (See Appendix B for our survey instrument.)

This convincing overrepresentation of women in the canine rescue world merely mirrors the virtually identical situation in many other aspects of the human–canine relationship. Although women were among the main proponents of the humane treatment of animals throughout the nineteenth century,[2] the proportion of women involved in animal-related professions radically shifted beginning in the 1970s with a massive upturn in the 1980s and 1990s. For instance, in 2005 women authored 85 percent of the books published concerning dog training and social aspects of dogs, as compared with 30 percent in 1970 (this is in addition to the substantial overall rise in the number of such books published, from 50 in 1970 to 287 in 2007). Similarly, according to the 2007 edition of the American Veterinary Medical Association's *United States Pet Ownership & Demographics Sourcebook*, women had the primary responsibility for the care of their dogs in 74.2 percent of households that included a dog.[3]

A shift in the gender of veterinarians over the past four decades reveals a comparable trend. In 1972, women accounted for 9.4 percent of the veterinary school graduates in the United States. By 2002, the figure had grown to 71.5 percent.[4] Anne E. Lincoln shows that the shift in gender composition of veterinarians is particularly prevalent in small animal practice, which is also the most rapidly growing subfield in veterinary medicine.[5]

Lincoln's findings underline the changing gender composition of veterinary medicine when compared with other female-dominated fields in selected health professions. In a comparison of first-year student enrollment in six schools of selected health professions, Lincoln shows that veterinary medicine boasted a 71.5 percent female enrollment in 1999, with optometry at 55 percent and osteopathy at 42.2 percent. The gender shift in veterinary medicine also commenced much earlier than in the other two professions: For the former, female students comprised 10.1 percent of first-year vet school students in 1990; for the latter two categories the comparable numbers were 3.7 percent in optometry and 2.7 percent in osteopathy.[6] Lastly, women's numerical dominance in the rescue world may be an artifact of their much greater presence in virtually all aspects of nonprofit charitable work. Joy Viola, one of the rescue world's most successful professional fundraisers, stated her belief regarding this issue: "I think that there is a preponderance of women in rescue in the same way that there is in the nonprofit charitable world. . . . Women are more socially conscious and caring than men . . . and they have more time and a greater inclination to put these virtues into practice.[7]

Data Collection for Our Michigan Study

In conducting our analysis of dog rescue workers in the State of Michigan, we used a mixed approach, incorporating both survey and interview methods. The survey instrument was administered online using proprietary polling software developed at the University of Michigan. Survey respondents were solicited by using petfinder.com (a sort of "one-stop shopping" website for people interested in placing or adopting a rescued animal). We gathered information from all the rescue organizations listed as operating in Michigan, of which we found 411. We then eliminated any organizations that were not primarily focused on dogs, leaving us with 217 or 53 percent of them. We subsequently excluded any organization that did not have any dogs for adoption as of May 15, 2007, that did not have e-mail contact information, or those that were all-breed rescue groups that had fewer than ten dogs listed. We then sent the survey information via e-mail to 105 contact e-mail addresses on May 25. The survey was "live" until

June 22. We asked the contact people to forward our e-mail solicitation to the volunteers in their respective rescue group. We received 283 completed surveys: 37 additional people started the survey but did not finish it and thus were excluded from our analysis, and 28 completed surveys were omitted from final analysis because the respondents did not answer 20 percent or more of the survey questions, even though they completed the survey itself. Thus, our statistical analysis is based on 255 respondents. Our respondents worked with seventy-nine different rescue groups, and of those, sixty-four were rescue groups that had been included in the original solicitation e-mail. This yields a 61 percent response rate from at least one person affiliated with a group that received a solicitation. Fourteen percent of the rescue organizations represented by our respondents did not receive a solicitation e-mail directly from us, and eleven respondents reported they did not work for a specific organization and thus must have received the solicitation from a source other than us.

Following the closing of the survey, we proceeded to the interview stage of the project: 211 of our 283 respondents indicated on the survey that they would be willing to be interviewed. Of these 211, we selected all respondents who identified themselves as having been presidents or vice presidents of rescue organizations. This comprised twenty-four individuals. Then we randomly selected thirty-six additional respondents to be interviewed. We contacted these sixty people in early July, approximately two weeks after the completion of our survey, and asked if they were still interested in being interviewed. Forty-four people responded affirmatively. We did not re-contact anyone who did not respond to our earlier messages. Three people contacted us asking to be interviewed, so we included them as well. In total, we assigned forty-seven interviews to three interviewers (or a combination of interviewers). Of the original forty-seven, nine people did not respond to requests to set up the interview and one person did not appear for her interview. In the end, we interviewed a total of thirty-seven people, which amounts to 13 percent of our original survey respondents. The interview data were analyzed using traditional discourse analysis.

The survey instrument contained ninety-three different questions and provided both categorical data, which were analyzed using chi-square analyses, and Likert scale data (7-point scale), which were analyzed using analysis of variance. (Please consult the survey instrument in Appendix B.) We constructed a separate class index based on a variety of questions concerning household income, house location, and similar categories. We then used this index for linear regression modeling. The survey consisted of three parts. The first part comprised largely personal demographic and belief questions; the second part featured questions related to the respondents as dog owners; and the third part concentrated on questions about canine rescue generally and the rescue organization with which the respondent worked specifically.

For our present purposes, we report on two primary sets of survey results. First, we present the responses to the survey based on the gender of the respondent, showing specific differences in the ways in which male and female respondents approached some questions. Second, we highlight differences in the ways respondents answered questions concerning the involvement of women in rescue work as a function of other independent variables (such as income level, political affiliation, among others). We then supplemented both of these analyses with comments concerning the role of women in the world of rescue that were found in our interviews.

Independent Variable: Gender

Two hundred thirty-five of our respondents defined themselves as female; twenty identified as male. This fact alone underlined our initial hypothesis, our reading of the relevant literature, and our own informal and anecdotal observations that women assume an overwhelming presence in virtually all aspects of dog rescue work. Mary Jane Shervais, one of the founding pioneers of the Golden Retriever rescue world, confirmed this near-total female presence from her own experience by saying: "We were not quite 100 percent female but nearly so. We had many more female participants at every rung of the ladder than male."[8] Although males furnished a small percentage of our sample data, their inclusion in our analyses was methodologically feasible and we modeled gender as an independent variable using an independent samples t-test on all of our noncategorical survey data. We used 0.05 as the level of significance and cases where the results were significant at the 0.05 to 0.09 levels are reported as "trends."

Thus, on a 7-point Likert scale, men reported their general fitness and activities levels higher than did women. The only other demographic difference between male and female survey respondents was in terms of political affiliation (chi square = 26.308, df = 1, p <.000), where fewer men reported having no political affiliation or being Democrats than the statistical model predicts and more men reported being Independents, Libertarians, or Republicans than the model predicts. The female respondents more or less follow what the statistical model predicts except that more women reported having no political affiliation than would be predicted by chance.

Women were more likely than men to agree strongly with the idea that animals have the same basic rights as people and were also more likely to concur with the proposition that they regularly chose to spend time with their dogs rather than their spouses or significant others. Women were also more likely to agree that their friends with dogs spent as much time with their dogs as they (the respondents) did with theirs. Overall, then, this cluster of questions suggests that women see themselves as spending more time with their dogs and preferring to spend time with their dogs than did the male respondents.

Whereas we found no statistically significant differences between men and women in terms of the benefits they derive from rescue work, we did find fascinating (and statistically meaningful) differences in how women and men assess the costs of being involved in dog rescue. Women consistently gauged their involvement with rescue to have greater costs to their lives than did men. Female respondents were more likely to agree with the statement "I do not have enough time for other things I want to do" than were male respondents. Similarly, women were more likely than men to agree that rescue work impinged on their ability to get their paid work completed and that they spent too much time on the computer as a result of their rescue work. Perhaps the most interesting responses that highlighted gender differences pertained to a cluster of questions that featured putative reasons why women might be more involved in rescue work than men. For instance, men were more likely to agree that more women were so deeply involved in rescue compared with men because women had more time and fewer responsibilities than men. In notable contrast, women were more likely to agree that more women were involved in rescue than men because they deemed women to be more caring and nurturing, more interested in animal well-being, and more willing to deal with problems than men.

An interpretation of this cluster of responses leads us to the conclusion that—at least in this instance—women had a much more essentialist interpretation of the reasons for their increased involvement in dog rescue than did the men. To men, women seemed to be primarily involved in dog rescue because they had more time and fewer responsibilities; in other words, the reasons were purely instrumental and technical. But to the female respondents, the more important reasons for women's involvement with rescue were their perception of women being more caring and nurturing, more interested in animal welfare, and generally more willing to deal with problems. All of these bespeak the fronting of conventionally held cultural characteristics that have traditionally been ascribed to women as opposed to men. (Consult Appendix A for a tabular presentation on these results.)

These survey findings were amply corroborated by our interviews. The most frequent response given by women interviewees as to the reasons for women's overwhelming presence in dog rescue was their commonly perceived sentimental, loving, sensitive, maternal, and emotional nature. Other answers varied from women being more talented than men at multitasking to women's role in society as "the givers." Some interviewees argued that women were more prone than men to volunteer in general. If this is the case, and if dog rescue contributes directly to an increase of women's activities in public life, and if such activities in general foster a more inclusive and democratic polity and a more caring and participatory culture, then the growth of rescue organizations over the past two to three decades might indeed be beneficial way beyond the many thousands of dogs that it has helped.

Some of our interviewees voiced other conventional gender traits. Thus, one person argued that the emotional involvement of women in dog rescue also leads to lots of infighting and "cattiness," and if men were more involved, there would be less of both and work in rescue would be more productive. Others said that men preferred not to deal with all the drama that accompanies many aspects of dog rescue and thus chose to stay away. Some believed that much of such drama was caused—essentially—by women being women and that a greater presence of men would reduce such behavior. Men's presence in dog rescue—while appreciated—was also subject to a traditional perception of gender roles: Men's contribution was perceived as being helpful in various "manly" activities such as lifting, driving, and performing information-technology–related work. Only one respondent stated flat out that men's involvement in rescue would not be helpful at all.

A traditional view of "masculinity" constituted the most important reason for our interviewees' interpretation for the low presence of men in rescue. Because dogs are perceived as "cute," so the reasoning went, men tend not to associate themselves with them, because men do not want to be associated with the signifier "cute." When men do associate themselves with dogs, respondents opine, it will be for hunting, police training, or other "manly" purposes, but certainly not rescue. A frequently heard comment was the lack of competitiveness in rescue. If there were more competition in rescue, or if it looked less like "doing laundry," then maybe more men would be involved. Others stated that men simply had "better things to do" than get involved in rescue. Moreover, interviewees also addressed the importance of money. Men were described as more "money driven" than women and more concerned with being involved in matters related to property owning. The conditions to make dog rescue more appealing to men would have to feature more manly activities such as increased competition and money-related involvement.

We addressed the paucity of men in dog rescue with a number of our interviewees who gave us many interesting insights on this topic. Here, for example, is Beryl Board's view:

> At our rescue organization we had some strategic planning sessions around this topic that by far and wide margins the majority of participants we have are women. We have tried to recruit men for our board of directors. We have tried recruiting men for our director positions. . . . I joke all the time about the time I spent down there after Hurricane Katrina. . . . The only people that I saw down there that were men were people in front of the camera or guys that were there to support their wives. . . . There is very little power to be had in rescue. And men like to seek those power positions. . . . And if you're in a group of women, that power is generally distributed very evenly. We women do not seek power for power's sake. . . . Too bad because men are actually very good at rescue. They're very helpful, very supportive, but they rarely do things on their own. They need women to prod them. . . . And the men that we do have in our group prefer to work behind the scenes.[9]

We also asked our rare male interviewees for their views on the topic. In addressing this issue, Gene Fitzpatrick raised many of the often-mentioned reasons that we encountered as explanations for the paucity of men in the rescue world, ranging from women's allegedly greater genetic or inherent propensity for nurturing and caring to men's lack of time for such activities on account of their work lives: "I think that more women have the time for rescue. Our organization has several housewives that are volunteers and devote a lot of their time to rescue. I just think women have that nourishing gene, so to speak, and a lot of guys, they're just too busy with their work. My work is flexible where I can take off to do this and that, you know, all those different things."[10] And then Gene—completely unselfconsciously— contradicted his earlier views about women's "nourishing genes" being the main reason for their disproportionate presence in rescue by stating, "I actually think that the women's participation has more to do with socialization than any genetic factor, but that's just me."[11]

Married interviewees or those in a stable relationship seemed to believe that although men tended to stay away from being involved in dog

rescue on their own, they were very supportive of their wives' and partners' engagement with rescue, even though they at times bemoaned the
great amount of time exacted by rescue work. Annie Kassler from Yankee
Golden Retriever Rescue detailed her standard adoption interview proce-
dure, merely one of the many activities in which she engaged routinely as
an active rescuer:

> I would get their name and number and hear that they are interested
> in a two-year old female ('cause isn't everybody) and so I would give
> them a call and follow this up by sending them a whole form with
> tons of questions such as "Do you have a fenced-in yard? How many
> hours are you away from home? Is your dog allowed to live inside
> the house?" Our form has many questions of this sort. Then I would
> follow up with a visit once I received their completed form. All the
> family members will have to be there when I go for my visit, includ-
> ing the kids. And I want to see the whole house and the whole yard
> and I want to see any or all other dogs or pets that might live there.
> I would want to make sure that these folks really understood every-
> thing about dog care and that this involves a lot of attention and
> cuddling and walking and paying vet bills and food bills and the
> whole thing . . . and if I found things that were not to my liking I
> would ask them to fix it and then I would come back and see whether
> they did in fact fix it, like a leaky fence. . . . And by the time I was
> adoption coordinator, and I want to say this lovingly because I loved
> doing all of these things, I will tell you that it took over my life. I
> mean it was forty, fifty, sixty hours a week with no break. Nothing
> else, you couldn't do anything else in your life.[12]

Many of our interviewees used almost identical language to Annie's in
describing the time-demanding, attention-exacting, indeed all-consuming
nature of their involvement in rescue. From a Labrador Retriever rescue,
Julie Jones told us that:

> I would then go out and basically check the fencing, make sure that
> the family was ready for a dog, what kind of Labrador they were
> looking for, such as seniors or puppies. We would always try to get
> a feel for what the family was capable of and what it was willing to
> do with the dog, what it had energy for, what it was willing to put
> up with, and be willing to work with. Basically, we wanted to see the
> family's commitment level.[13]

Rescuers routinely commit huge amounts of time as well as emotional energy to rescue, in the hopes that such efforts will be rewarded with the lasting, successful placement of dogs.

After understanding the inordinate time commitment, rigor, and effort that rescue work demands of its activists, all for the sole purpose of optimizing the benefits for the dogs, it is perhaps not surprising to hear this sentiment as recounted to us by Joan Puglia of Yankee Golden Retriever Rescue: "This is what that lady from DSS [Department of Social Services] said to me, 'I adopted my last three kids much easier than I have adopted a dog from you people.'"[14]

Respondents noted that those men who were actually actively involved in rescue were superb foster parents. Perhaps tellingly, they were also characterized as being more "feminine" types of men. Our only male interviewee among the Michigan rescue groups seemed to attribute the preponderance of women and the paucity of men in dog rescue to women's greater work ethic. Contrary to accepted beliefs that were so prevalently voiced by a vast majority of our respondents and interviewees, this man also opined that men were actually more sensitive than women and could thus not handle giving up the dogs they fostered. This interviewee informed us that men would rather keep the dogs than surrender them because they were actually more emotionally attached to them than were women. Priscilla Skare, for example, told us how she experienced men using at least as much baby talk with the dogs as did women, and men fawned over the dogs just as warmly and emphatically as women, though she also said: "Maybe women tend to be more nurturing than men. . . . I could say something on this topic that might offend you as a guy [speaking to Markovits]."[15] And our interviewing Joanna Mackie who, with her husband, Rob, has been active in a Canadian Golden Retriever rescue for many years, led to the following view on men's involvement with dog rescue:

> I did know of men, I'll call them the gentle soul men, including one of them sitting next to me right now [referring to her husband, Rob] that adopt Golden Retrievers. So when we have gone and volunteered at different fairs and things, where we set up a booth to educate people and we take our three dogs and we go, there are always quite a few men who come to talk with us and who genuinely care about these animals and are very gentle with them and also will adopt them and give them a wonderful new home. It's just that men are somehow not involved in the actual leadership of these organizations, at least that I have seen.[16]

Mackie's opinions of men in rescue seem to be widely shared throughout the dog rescue world.

Other Independent Variables and Responses to Why Women Are More Involved

In addition to comparing how female and male respondents answered the survey questions, we also examined a wide variety of other independent variables. Among them were education level, marital status, political orientation, religious affiliation, income level, and type of employment. We briefly report on differences among these various categories in relation to the cluster of questions we asked concerning women's involvement in rescue work in order to round out our exploration as to why women are more involved in dog rescue. For the most part, there were few main effects and no interactions among factors.

Beginning with age, women in the age groups of twenty-six to thirty-five, thirty-six to forty-five, and forty-six to fifty-five reported working in rescue organizations where at least 90 percent of the leadership positions were held by women. This finding differs significantly from what our statistical model predicted. In effect, our finding shows that women in their prime working years play, or are perceived to play, a disproportionately prominent role in leading these organizations. Respondents in the thirty-six to forty-five age group were more likely than other age groups to agree that women are involved in this endeavor because "women are more interested in looking good by doing good"; because "women are more willing to deal with problems"; and lastly, because such work is "more likely to give them emotional and social support."

In terms of class, two trends are worthy of mention: first, the higher the respondent's class scale, the more likely it is that she will agree with the following statements: first, that rescue work is less valued than other types of volunteer work; and second, that women seem to make better rescue workers than men. Very similar results are found when we modeled income alone: There is a statistically significant positive correlation between income level and seeing rescue work as being less valued than other kinds of volunteering. Additionally, as income level increased, respondents were more likely to agree with the statement that women have fewer responsibilities, which allows them to partake in dog rescue activities.

In terms of education, those with some college experience, as well as respondents with completed associate's, bachelor's, master's, professional, and doctoral degrees feel quite strongly that women are active in dog rescue because they derive emotional and social support from such work. Though to a lesser extent, level of education also seems to be a significant variable in gauging women to be better rescue workers than men.

As to the marital status of our respondents, the only instance where we discovered any statistical significance relating to the cluster of questions pertaining to why women's presence dominates in dog rescue was the issue of women being more caring and nurturing. For this item, respondents who were currently married and never divorced differed from all other groups in expressing less agreement with the statement that women are involved in dog rescue because they are more caring and nurturing.

Interestingly, although religious influence revealed some significant findings pertaining to matters such as holistic care of the dogs and the use of food treats as a training tool for one's dog—where, with the exception of the one Buddhist in our sample and the three neo-pagans, all respondents clocked in at a high 6-plus point range, with the six Jews marking this item at a perfect 7 points—it seems not to have played any role in terms of emphasizing possible reasons for women's involvement in dog rescue.

This was not quite the case with the political orientation of our respondents. Here, all groups—Independents, Democrats, Republicans, Greens, Libertarians, and "Other"—felt quite emphatically that women were more caring and nurturing than men; however, the Libertarians and the Independents had lower mean scores (as determined in post hoc testing) than the other groups. Similarly (and interestingly), the Libertarians also had higher mean ratings for the statement that women were involved in rescue because they were more interested in looking good by doing good.

The number of years someone was involved with rescue, the number of years someone had fostered dogs, and whether someone had held a leadership position in the rescue group also demonstrated main effects with two items in the battery of our questions as to why women are involved in rescue. Pertaining to the assertion that women make better rescue workers than men, being in a leadership position and the longevity with which a person has been involved in rescue correlate with stronger agreement that women make better rescue workers than men as opposed to the assertion that women's advantages as rescue workers hail from their possessing inherently more caring and nurturing characteristics than men.

Conclusion

At the risk of oversimplification, we present a profile of the prototypical breed specific canine rescuer in contemporary America.

The average rescuer is a white, heterosexual female between the ages of thirty-six and sixty-five. She is married and has never been divorced and lives with no children under 18.[17] She holds a bachelor's degree. She is a Democrat and politics are reasonably important to her. She is a fairly liberal Protestant and religion is of middle importance to her. She eats most types of food and marks a 4 on a 7-point scale for physical fitness and physical activity.

She owns her own home in the suburbs and the home is a detached, single-family home with two or three bedrooms, two bathrooms, and a formal dining room. The yard is fully fenced and is less than half an acre. Her household income is between $70,000 and $100,000 and she is employed full time, spending an average of forty-one to fifty weekly hours outside the home. She devotes one to three hours a week to reading dog-oriented materials but does not subscribe to any publications.

She definitely sees herself at a minimum as a dog person, although quite frequently as a pet person.[18] She believes that there are no bad dogs, only bad dog owners. She generally prefers dogs to people and feels that people quite frequently do not understand her relationship to dogs. She believes that animals have the same basic rights as people. She occasionally chooses to spend time with her dogs over her spouse or best friend; many of her friends spend as much time with their dogs as she does with hers and she thinks she would have about the same number of friends whether or not she had dogs. The majority (60 to 80 percent) of the people whom she knows who spend a lot of time with their dogs are women.

She has two dogs and no other animals. Her dogs sleep in bed with her, and she believes it is very important for dogs to live in the house. Her dogs spend between one and four hours alone during the day but would not be left in the house alone overnight. When she travels, she takes the dogs to a friend's house. She feeds the dogs a premium dry dog food, takes them on daily walks, and they play daily in a fully-fenced backyard. She uses traditional vet care and has no personal experience with veterinary medicine. She believes that the two most important commands to teach a dog are "come" and "stay" for the sole purpose of enhancing the dog's safety. She is primarily a positive reinforcement–based trainer.

She has been involved in dog rescue for one to four years and became active after adopting a dog from the group with which she now volunteers. She spends about two hours a week on rescue work. She sees the following as important benefits of rescue work: spending time with the people in the group; talking to people on the phone or via e-mail; solving problems; feeling valued and needed by her rescue work; hearing new ideas; and taking her mind off the stresses of life. She also likes raising awareness of the breed she rescues and finding people the dog of their dreams. The only major cost of rescue work for her—and it is a big one—is her awareness that there will always be dogs that cannot be saved.

The rescue organization for which she works has no paid employees and more than thirty volunteers. She does not now hold and has never held a position of leadership. Women hold 90 percent of the leadership positions in the group in which she volunteers. She has fostered dogs for one to four years and has fostered more than twelve dogs in that time. She had no foster dogs at the time of the survey. She believes it is important to try to save all dogs.

She thinks that women are more involved in rescue than men because they are more caring and nurturing, reasonably more interested in animal well-being, more willing to deal with problems, and more likely to get emotional and social support from rescue work. She does not believe that women make better rescue workers than men or that women care more about their companion animals than men do.

Above all, she is most assuredly not an activist of any kind, least of all for animal rights, let alone animal liberation. She fully rejects the assignation "activist," which she finds objectionable and in sharp contrast to what she sees as her work on behalf of animals. As Jessica Greenebaum's research on canine rescuers—precisely our study's subjects—amply demonstrates, most of the participants in her study disdain animal rights or liberation activists as too crass, too "in your face," too political, too provocative.[19] Instead, rescuers much prefer working behind the scenes, eschewing publicity and any form of extremism, which they find counterproductive for the only task at hand: rescuing needy dogs in the here and now without couching any such activity in complex ideological debates best left for philosophers and academics. Just like Greenebaum, our study also found the women comprising the breed specific canine rescue world to be perfectly content in their normalcy, with no ambitions to alter the grand schemes of global politics, society, and culture, totally happy merely to improve the world for the well-defined clientele of needy dogs belonging to the breed for which each particular rescuer developed a passion often hailing from her childhood.

Our study demonstrates quite clearly that the relatively new world of dog rescue is an overwhelmingly female one. Women dominate all of its facets, from its leaders to its foot soldiers. They do so—on the whole—with verve, enthusiasm, commitment, and with the perceived and experienced benefits of this activity much outweighing its costs. Our study also reveals that these women—far from being social misfits or loners in search of a meaningful involvement that might fulfill their purportedly empty existence—are leading active lives, are married or partnered, and are, by all measures, "normal" citizens who happen to love dogs on whose behalf they assume many tasks and obligations, which they, however, do not, as a rule, experience as burdensome. Our study also reveals that most of our respondents view their activity in dog rescue as a form of creating and fostering social capital that they clearly treasure. Although the form of this capital is obviously more of the "bonding" rather than the "bridging" kind—unless one categorizes interbreed rescues as an expression of the latter—it is nonetheless a clear means of a social involvement that bespeaks civic commitment. If indeed there is a compellingly evident relationship between the way people regard and treat animals, dogs in particular in our case, and the way they view and treat humans, as many studies in different disciplines have demonstrated, the argument might not be too far-fetched that these women's passionate commitment to dog rescue might indeed contain a humanizing and civilizing force in our society.[20]

Our data also reveal that an overwhelming majority of our respondents are well aware of the preponderance of women in the world of dog rescue. Perhaps one of our most interesting findings features the different reasons that men and women attributed to this phenomenon. Whereas the former saw this largely as a function of women having more time and being less taxed in their work lives than men, the latter reasoned much more emphatically in terms of women's more caring and nurturing nature, which furnished a much greater compatibility with the world of dog rescue than men's allegedly more aloof emotional inclination and psychological constitution. Although in contrast to some of our interviewees the quantitative data presented in this chapter were obtained from only one state in the United States, we are reasonably certain that our findings would not differ too much on a nationwide scale. Indeed, many of the traits defining our subjects are also prevalent among dog owners in the United States, well beyond the specific world of dog rescue, as reported by the 2005–2006 National Pet Owners Survey conducted by the American Pet Products Manufacturers Association.

In order to understand the context of the canine landscape wherein these rescues emerged and have continued to operate, the next chapter presents the topography of the numeric existence of canine breeds in the United States between 1960 and 2009. It will reveal the considerable fluctuations in the popularity of canine breeds that have clearly had important implications for the world of breed specific rescue.

Notes

1. This chapter is an abbreviated and adapted version of "Women and the World of Dog Rescue: A Case Study of the State of Michigan" published by Andrei S. Markovits and Robin Queen in *Society and Animals* 17, no. 4 (2009), pp. 325–342.

2. Emily Gaarder, "Risk & Reward: The Impact of Animal Rights Activism on Women," *Society and Animals* 16, no. 1 (2008), pp. 1–22.

3. American Veterinary Medical Association, *United States Ownership & Demographics Sourcebook*. Schaumburg, IL: American Veterinary Medical Association, 2007.

4. Commission on Professionals in Science and Technology. http://www.cpst .org (accessed on July 1, 2008).

5. Anne E. Lincoln, "A Supply-Side Approach to Occupational Feminization: Veterinary Medicine in the United States, 1976–1999." Unpublished doctoral dissertation, Washington State University-Pullman, 2004.

6. Ibid.; Ben Gose, "The Feminization of Veterinary Medicine," *Chronicle of Higher Education*, April 24, 1998.

7. Joy Viola. Interviewed by Andrei Markovits. Telephone Interview. July 16, 2009.

8. Mary Jane Shervais. Interviewed by Andrei Markovits. Telephone Interview. August 17, 2009.

9. Beryl Board. Interviewed by Andrei Markovits. Telephone Interview. July 29, 2009.

10. Gene Fitzpatrick. Interviewed by Andrei Markovits. Telephone Interview. August 17, 2009.

11. Ibid.

12. Annie Kassler. Interviewed by Andrei Markovits. Telephone Interview. July 9, 2009.

13. Julie Jones. Interviewed by Katherine Crosby. Telephone Interview. July 29, 2010.

14. Joan Puglia. Interviewed by Andrei Markovits. Telephone Interview. June 30, 2009.

15. Priscilla Skare. Interviewed by Andrei Markovits. Telephone Interview. August 19, 2010.

16. Joanna Mackie. Interviewed by Andrei Markovits. Telephone Interview. June 29, 2010.

17. The lack of children in the household is almost certainly an artifact of the number of people over forty-five who responded to the survey. For survey respondents in the eighteen to thirty-five age ranges, there is a higher number of children in the household than would be predicted by chance.

18. Please note our differentiation between "dog people" and "pet people" introduced in chapter 1 and throughout this book.

19. Jessica Greenebaum, "'I'm Not an Activist!' Animal Rights vs. Animal Welfare in the Purebred Dog Rescue Movement." *Society and Animals* 17, no. 4 (2009), pp. 289–304.

20. For just two articles presenting arguments and citing further studies corroborating the fact that empathy toward animals correlates positively with empathy toward humans, see David A. Nibert, "Animal Rights and Human Social Issues," *Society & Animals* 2, no. 2 (1993), pp. 115–124; and William F. Vitulli, "Attitudes toward Empathy in Domestic Dogs and Cats," *Psychological Reports* 99, no. 3 (2006), pp. 981–991.

CHAPTER 3

The Topography of Breed Specific Dog Registrations from 1960 to 2009

An Important Contextual Framework for Rescue

with Joseph Klaver

Help control the pet population. Have your pets spayed or neutered.

—Bob Barker
Television game show host of *The Price Is Right*

Clearly, the phenomenon of breed specific canine rescue commenced in a particular context. People choosing dogs as pets—including those whom they obtain through rescue—does not happen randomly or in a vacuum. Whereas we delineated the human dimension of rescue in this book's introduction and its first two chapters, we also need to shed light on its canine context, which we do in this chapter primarily by using extensive annual American Kennel Club (AKC) registration data.

As we will present in greater detail in Chapter 10, we need to mention here as well that AKC registration is not an accurate predictor of the actual number of dogs of a particular breed present in the United States at a given time. Not all dogs are registered with the AKC, and the owners of some breeds are more likely to register their dogs than owners of others. As is quite evident, this important fact relates closely to the owners' economic class, social status, and cultural milieu, which in turn correlate substantially with the expenses such owners will incur for their dogs, including footing the bill for their proper registration.[1] Nonetheless, we believe that the annual new AKC registrations, which we use throughout the remainder of this chapter, illustrate quite helpfully the changing trends in dog breed popularity in the United States over a substantial period of time. Point in fact: The Humane Society of the United States has found a clear link between the top-ten AKC-registered breeds, on the one hand, and the breeds most likely to be produced by puppy mills, on the other hand.[2] We therefore believe that in spite of all the caveats associated with this method, the use of AKC data constitutes an appropriate approach to analyze broad trends of dog popularity in the United States. In particular, we will present the landscape of dog breeds that attained popularity in the United States between 1960 and 2009. We will do so by decade to demonstrate the rise and decline in the popularity of breeds, which we believe furnishes a crucial framework wherein to contextualize breed rescue. In each decade we include all breeds that were in the top ten for at least one year.

The 1960s

The 1960s were a time of rapid growth for breed specific dogs. By the end of the decade, the AKC was registering over 900,000 dogs per year, more than twice the approximately 440,000 per year that the organization had registered at the beginning of the decade. Growth in the registration rate peaked in the middle of the decade, when it rose above 12 percent in 1964 and again in 1965.

The 1960s saw fourteen different dogs enter the top-ten spots of the AKC's registry. These included Poodles, German Shepherds, Dachshunds, Beagles, Miniature Schnauzers, Chihuahuas, Pekingese, Collies, Labrador Retrievers, Cocker Spaniels, Basset Hounds, Pomeranians, Boston Terriers and Boxers.[3]

The Poodle breed took the top spot in 1960, passing Beagles, who had held that title for most of the previous decade. Registering over 73,000 dogs in 1960, Poodles held a more than 20,000 dog advantage over the second-place breed, a numerical edge they would maintain for the next twenty-two years.

German Shepherds also made very large registration gains in this decade. In 1960 the AKC registered 33,701 German Shepherds. By 1967 more than 100,000 German Shepherds were being registered yearly and the breed had risen to the second spot among the top-ten most registered breeds.

TABLE 3.1. The Top Fifteen Canine Breeds in the United States per AKC Registration in the 1960s

POODLE		GERMAN SHEPHERD		DACHSHUND	
Year	Registrations	Year	Registrations	Year	Registrations
1960	73291	1960	33701	1960	42727
1961	99256	1961	40412	1961	46185
1962	123865	1962	44541	1962	44491
1963	147055	1963	52769	1963	46993
1964	178401	1964	63163	1964	48569
1965	207393	1965	78241	1965	49316
1966	235536	1966	93046	1966	53022
1967	255862	1967	107936	1967	57133
1968	263700	1968	104127	1968	57460
1969	274145	1969	102081	1969	60453

BEAGLE		MINIATURE SCHNAUZER		CHIHUAHUA	
Year	Registrations	Year	Registrations	Year	Registrations
1960	54170	1960	5758	1960	44600
1961	53069	1961	7212	1961	46089
1962	47961	1962	8681	1962	45965
1963	49769	1963	10890	1963	42659
1964	53353	1964	13593	1964	40966
1965	56128	1965	17172	1965	41086
1966	58953	1966	21020	1966	39329
1967	61568	1967	26001	1967	37324
1968	56940	1968	30868	1968	33686
1969	60221	1969	36233	1969	28801

PEKINGESE		COLLIE		LABRADOR RETRIEVER	
Year	Registrations	Year	Registrations	Year	Registrations
1960	19209	1960	16132	1960	6549
1961	21076	1961	16842	1961	7576
1962	22070	1962	16062	1962	7685
1963	22538	1963	16918	1963	9125
1964	23989	1964	18424	1964	10340
1965	25599	1965	21032	1965	12370
1966	26712	1966	22748	1966	13686
1967	27242	1967	24325	1967	16710
1968	26278	1968	24200	1968	18492
1969	24856	1969	24822	1969	21611

TABLE 3.1. *(Continued)*

COCKER SPANIEL		BASSET HOUND		POMERANIAN	
Year	Registrations	Year	Registrations	Year	Registrations
1960	17044	1960	8782	1960	11893
1961	15864	1961	10218	1961	12840
1962	14509	1962	9978	1962	13187
1963	14791	1963	11763	1963	13659
1964	15632	1964	13716	1964	13960
1965	16308	1965	14686	1965	14692
1966	17433	1966	16140	1966	15247
1967	18525	1967	17595	1967	15425
1968	18443	1968	17452	1968	15047
1969	20123	1969	19319	1969	14232

BOSTON TERRIER		BOXER		GOLDEN RETRIEVER	
Year	Registrations	Year	Registrations	Year	Registrations
1960	12209	1960	14228	1960	2445
1961	12840	1961	12549	1961	2867
1962	12372	1962	9941	1962	2800
1963	12233	1963	9319	1963	3467
1964	12231	1964	8872	1964	3993
1965	12698	1965	8993	1965	4703
1966	12662	1966	9082	1966	5644
1967	12579	1967	9570	1967	6789
1968	12406	1968	9450	1968	7607
1969	11830	1969	10025	1969	9535

Although Miniature Schnauzers, Labrador Retrievers, Basset Hounds, and Golden Retrievers began the decade with significantly lower registration numbers than Poodles and German Shepherds, they also experienced great growth in this decade. All of these breeds witnessed growth greater than 100 percent in this period, with yearly Basset Hound registrations increasing by approximately 120 percent, Labrador Retriever registrations growing by approximately 230 percent, Golden Retriever registrations increasing by almost 300 percent, and Miniature Schnauzer registrations growing by over 500 percent in the course of these ten years.

The only breed to experience a significant contraction in registrations during this decade was the Chihuahua, which started the decade by having over 40,000 dogs registered per year but ended it by registering fewer than 30,000 dogs per year. These data are presented in Table 3.1 and Figure 3.1.

Year	Total Dogs Registered
1960	442875
1961	493300
1962	516800
1963	568300
1964	640300
1965	722800
1966	804400
1967	885800
1968	909300
1969	973100

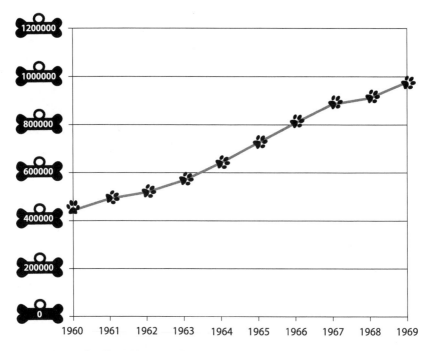

Figure 3.1. Total Number of Dogs Registered by the AKC in the 1960s

The 1970s

Following the brisk growth in registrations in the 1960s, the 1970s were a decade of gradual decline. After registering just over 1,129,000 dogs in 1971, registrations fell by approximately 14 percent to 965,250 in 1979. The 1971 peak was the high water mark of registrations in the postwar time period, which would not be surpassed until the late 1980s.

Between 1970 and 1979, fifteen different dog breeds were among the ten most popular for at least one year. These dogs included Poodles, Dobermans, Cocker Spaniels, German Shepherds, Labrador Retrievers, Golden Retrievers, Beagles, Dachshunds, Miniature Schnauzers, Shetland Sheepdogs, Irish Setters, Chihuahuas, Pekingese, Collies, and St. Bernards.

Poodles continued their reign as the country's most popular dog, which they had throughout the 1960s, by registering an average of over 150,000 dogs per year. Although maintaining their status as top dog, by the end of the decade their registrations had been more than halved, from 265,879[4] in 1970 to 94,950 in 1979.

Doberman Pinschers experienced an explosion of growth during the 1970s: by 1979, only Poodles registered more new dogs per year. Between 1970 and 1979, Doberman registration increased more than fourfold, from 18,636 in 1970 to 80,363 in 1979.

Although not quite as striking as the growth in Doberman registrations, the 1970s were also a time of significant growth for America's top two Retriever-class dogs, as well as the Cocker Spaniel. All three breeds grew mightily in this decade, substantially increasing their registrations over this ten-year period. In 1970, 11,437 Golden Retrievers and 25,667 Labrador Retrievers were registered. By 1979, those numbers had increased to 38,060 and 46,007, respectively. Cocker Spaniel registrations grew at a similarly brisk clip, increasing from 21,811 in 1970 to 65,685 in 1979. Although Labrador Retrievers registered more new dogs in absolute numbers than did Golden Retrievers and Cocker Spaniels, the latter two breeds' registration growth exceeded the formers' as a percentage of their total from the beginning of the decade. Indeed, Goldens and Cockers more than tripled their registrations over the course of the decade, whereas Labrador Retrievers increased by just under 100 percent.

In addition to the significant losses suffered by Poodles, German Shepherds, Beagles, and Dachshunds, Chihuahuas also experienced significant contractions in their registrations in the course of this decade. Excluding Poodles, the actual numerical registrations of German Shepherds decreased the most during this period, falling by more than 50,000

TABLE 3.2. The Top Fifteen Canine Breeds in the United States per AKC Registration in the 1970s

POODLE		DOBERMAN		COCKER SPANIEL	
Year	Registrations	Year	Registrations	Year	Registrations
1970	265879	1970	18636	1970	21811
1971	256491	1971	23413	1971	24846
1972	218899	1972	27767	1972	27355
1973	193400	1973	34169	1973	31158
1974	171550	1974	45110	1974	35492
1975	139750	1975	57336	1975	39064
1976	126799	1976	73615	1976	46862
1977	112300	1977	79254	1977	52955
1978	101100	1978	81964	1978	58719
1979	94950	1979	80363	1979	65685

GERMAN SHEPHERD		LABRADOR RETRIEVER		GOLDEN RETRIEVER	
Year	Registrations	Year	Registrations	Year	Registrations
1970	109198	1970	25667	1970	11437
1971	111355	1971	30170	1971	13589
1972	101399	1972	32251	1972	15476
1973	90907	1973	33575	1973	17635
1974	86014	1974	36689	1974	20933
1975	76235	1975	36565	1975	22636
1976	74723	1976	39929	1976	27612
1977	67072	1977	41275	1977	30263
1978	61783	1978	43500	1978	34249
1979	57683	1979	46007	1979	38060

BEAGLE		DACHSHUND		MINIATURE SCHNAUZER	
Year	Registrations	Year	Registrations	Year	Registrations
1970	61007	1970	61042	1970	41647
1971	61247	1971	60954	1971	45305
1972	57050	1972	55149	1972	43280
1973	54125	1973	51000	1973	41745
1974	51777	1974	47581	1974	41392
1975	45210	1975	40617	1975	37786
1976	44156	1976	38927	1976	36816
1977	40850	1977	35087	1977	35072
1978	36920	1978	33660	1978	33534
1979	35374	1979	32777	1979	32666

TABLE 3.2. (*Continued*)

SHETLAND SHEEPDOG		IRISH SETTER		CHIHUAHUA	
Year	Registrations	Year	Registrations	Year	Registrations
1970	16423	1970	23357	1970	28833
1971	18478	1971	33516	1971	26878
1972	19673	1972	43707	1972	23969
1973	21845	1973	54211	1973	22253
1974	22944	1974	61549	1974	20639
1975	22715	1975	58622	1975	16494
1976	23950	1976	54917	1976	16478
1977	24464	1977	43367	1977	15841
1978	24668	1978	30839	1978	15206
1979	25943	1979	20912	1979	15512

PEKINGESE		COLLIE		ST. BERNARD	
Year	Registrations	Year	Registrations	Year	Registrations
1970	27190	1970	26979	1970	27297
1971	27717	1971	28772	1971	35320
1972	26062	1972	28459	1972	35559
1973	24926	1973	28573	1973	35397
1974	23631	1974	28068	1974	31161
1975	20150	1975	24464	1975	22430
1976	20400	1976	25161	1976	17537
1977	19891	1977	23386	1977	13186
1978	18892	1978	22032	1978	9727
1979	17992	1979	21210	1979	7444

dogs over the course of the decade. By continuing to tally approximately 50,000 new registrations per year, German Shepherds retained a more than respectable rank among America's most popular dogs. By seeing their yearly registrations halved, Beagles, Dachshunds, and Chihuahuas also lost a similar percentage of their yearly AKC-registered populations as did German Shepherds.

Visible in Table 3.2 are two breeds that experienced a brief popularity stint during the 1970s before plunging once again out of the top-ten registry spots: Irish Setters and St. Bernards were the "fad dogs" of this decade. The popularity of Irish Setters peaked in 1974, when over 60,000 new Setters were registered, making them the third most popular dog in the country. The St. Bernard trend began in the late 1960s and peaked in the early 1970s, when between 1971 and 1974 well over 30,000 new St.

Year	Total Dogs Registered
1970	1056225
1971	1129200
1972	1101943
1973	1099850
1974	1103249
1975	1022849
1976	1048648
1977	1013650
1978	980299
1979	965250

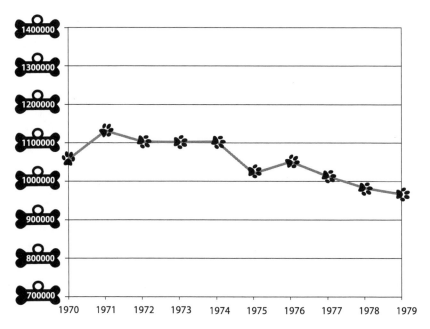

Figure 3.2. Total Number of Dogs Registered by the AKC in the 1970s

Bernards were registered (Table 3.2). Registrations for both breeds diminished rapidly over the second half of the decade, with both breeds registering significantly fewer dogs per year and falling out of the top-ten most popular dogs by the decade's end.

The 1980s

Gradual increases in dog registration in the 1980s followed its steady decline in the 1970s. Only in 1984 did registrations drop in this decade. However, even this dip was by the nearly negligible amount of slightly more than 1 percent. Although gradual, the gains in the 1980s were sufficient to offset the losses of the previous decade. Between 1980 and 1989, total registrations increased by just over 24 percent.

In the 1980s, fourteen different dog breeds entered the top ten for at least one year: Miniature Schnauzers, Beagles, Dachshunds, Chow Chows, Rottweilers, German Shepherds, Golden Retrievers, Poodles, Labrador Retrievers, Cocker Spaniels, Shetland Sheepdogs, Dobermans, Pomeranians, and Yorkshire Terriers.

The multidecade reign of Poodles as America's top dog ended in the early part of this decade. Despite significant losses, the rate at which poodle registrations diminished also leveled off by the end of this ten-year period. Still, by 1989 Poodles had been passed by both Cocker Spaniels and Labrador Retrievers as America's most popular dogs. And even having relinquished the leading position Poodles enjoyed for several decades, they still clocked in at the respectable number of nearly 80,000 registered dogs per year.

Although the contraction in Poodle registration occurred gradually, a similar development afflicted the Dobermans much more dramatically. In 1980, just shy of 80,000 Dobermans were registered. By 1989, that number had been reduced to 21,782, a decrease of over 70 percent. Although somewhat longer lasting in their preeminence than other fad dogs, such as Irish Setters and St. Bernards of the previous decade, the speed with which Dobermans gained and lost popularity is nonetheless remarkable.

Just like they did in the 1970s, Cocker Spaniels, Labrador Retrievers, and Golden Retrievers experienced significant gains in their registration numbers. Increasing their registration by over 70 percent, Labrador Retrievers scored the largest growth in the 1980s. The registration of

TABLE 3.3. The Top Thirteen Canine Breeds in the United States per AKC Registration in the 1980s

POODLE Year	Registrations	COCKER SPANIEL Year	Registrations	MINIATURE SCHNAUZER Year	Registrations
1980	95250	1980	76113	1980	34962
1981	93050	1981	83504	1981	35912
1982	88650	1982	87218	1982	36502
1983	90250	1983	92836	1983	37820
1984	87750	1984	94803	1984	37694
1985	87250	1985	96396	1985	38134
1986	85500	1986	98330	1986	38961
1987	85400	1987	105236	1987	41462
1988	82600	1988	108720	1988	41558
1989	78600	1989	111636	1989	42175

BEAGLE Year	Registrations	DACHSHUND Year	Registrations	CHOW CHOW Year	Registrations
1980	35091	1980	33881	1980	14589
1981	35655	1981	33560	1981	18511
1982	35548	1982	32835	1982	22623
1983	39992	1983	33514	1983	27815
1984	40052	1984	33068	1984	32777
1985	40803	1985	33903	1985	39167
1986	39849	1986	35537	1986	43026
1987	41972	1987	40031	1987	49096
1988	41983	1988	41921	1988	50781
1989	43314	1989	44305	1989	50150

ROTTWEILER Year	Registrations	GERMAN SHEPHERD Year	Registrations	GOLDEN RETRIEVER Year	Registrations
1980	4701	1980	58865	1980	44100
1981	6524	1981	60976	1981	48473
1982	9269	1982	60445	1982	51045
1983	13265	1983	65073	1983	52525
1984	17193	1984	59450	1984	54490
1985	22886	1985	57598	1985	56131
1986	28257	1986	55958	1986	59057
1987	36162	1987	57612	1987	60936
1988	42748	1988	57139	1988	62950
1989	51291	1989	58422	1989	64269

TABLE 3.3. *(Continued)*

LABRADOR RETRIEVER		SHETLAND SHEEPDOG	
Year	Registrations	Year	Registrations
1980	52398	1980	28325
1981	58569	1981	29481
1982	62465	1982	30512
1983	67389	1983	33375
1984	71235	1984	33164
1985	74271	1985	34350
1986	77371	1986	35064
1987	81987	1987	37616
1988	86446	1988	38730
1989	91107	1989	39665

DOBERMAN		POMERANIAN	
Year	Registrations	Year	Registrations
1980	79908	1980	17341
1981	77387	1981	17926
1982	73180	1982	18456
1983	66184	1983	19691
1984	51414	1984	21207
1985	41532	1985	22962
1986	33442	1986	25056
1987	28783	1987	27911
1988	23928	1988	30516
1989	21782	1989	32109

Cocker Spaniels and Golden Retrievers grew by approximately 45 percent in the course of this decade, going from 76,113 and 44,100 respectively in 1980 to 111,636 and 64,269 in 1989.

Chow Chows and Rottweilers make their first appearance in the top ten during this decade. Chow Chow registration increased from 14,589 in 1980 to 50,150 in 1989, having peaked the previous year at 50,781. This increase of nearly 40,000 registered dogs per year represents a jump of over 240 percent. Rottweilers also accreted a vast number of new dogs, increasing their registration by nearly 1,000 percent during the 1980s, going from under 5,000 newly registered dogs per year in the beginning of the decade to just over 50,000 in its last year. These data are presented in Table 3.3 as well as Figure 3.3.

Year	Total Dogs Registered
1980	1011799
1981	1033849
1982	1037149
1983	1085248
1984	1071299
1985	1089149
1986	1106399
1987	1187400
1988	1220500
1989	1257700

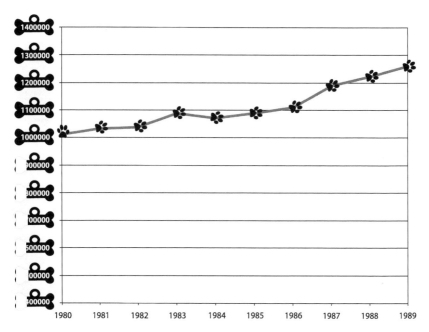

Figure 3.3. Total Number of Dogs Registered by the AKC in the 1980s

The 1990s

The gradual yet steady growth of the 1980s in overall dog registration continued throughout the country for a few years into the 1990s. However, as this decade concluded, registrations began to decrease quite considerably. Over the course of the decade as a whole, overall registrations declined by a hair over 10 percent, falling from 1,253,214 in 1990 to 1,119,620 in 1999. Indeed, ten of the sixteen breeds that appeared in the top ten for this decade registered fewer dogs at the end of the decade than they did at its beginning. Registration peaked at 1,442,690 in 1992; this sum also represents the most dogs ever registered in one year in the history of the United States. After 1992, the decade experienced gradual decreases, ranging from just over 1 percent to just over 8 percent, with the exception of a 4.2 percent increase in 1996.

A total of sixteen different dog breeds made appearances in the top ten during the 1990s. These included Labrador Retrievers, Golden Retrievers, German Shepherds, Dachshunds, Beagles, Poodles, Yorkshire Terriers, Chihuahuas, Boxers, Rottweilers, Pomeranians, Cocker Spaniels, Dalmatians, Shetland Sheepdogs, Chow Chows, and Miniature Schnauzers.

The first two years of positive registration growth, and the year of such in the middle of the decade (1996), can best be explained by the continued blistering growth in the Labrador Retriever breed. Following their already vigorous growth in the previous decade, Labradors again achieved huge gains, increasing their yearly registration by more than 60 percent, from 95,768 in 1990 to 154,897 in 1999. This growth was especially fast in 1991, 1992, and 1995.

Even though the growth in Rottweiler registrations had eased by 1993, the Rottweiler fad of the 1980s continued into the 1990s, stoking the overall growth in dog registrations during the early part of this decade. The peak in Rottweiler registrations in 1993 preceded a steep decline of nearly 60 percent in the second half of the decade, from which the breed never quite recovered. Rottweilers would not rejoin the top-ten ranks of America's most popular dogs in the following decade, with their registration continuing its decline.

Similar to the Rottweilers' trajectory, the Chow Chow fad also collapsed in the 1990s, albeit without the first few years of massive increases in the Rottweilers' case. In 1999, Chow Chow registration had decreased by 90 percent since the beginning of the decade, falling from 45,271 dogs in 1990 to only 4,342 in 1999. Just like Rottweilers, Chow Chows, too, would fail to enter the top ten in the coming decade.

TABLE 3.4. The Top Sixteen Canine Breeds in the United States per AKC Registration in the 1990s

	LABRADOR RETRIEVER		GOLDEN RETRIEVER		GERMAN SHEPHERD
Year	**Registrations**	**Year**	**Registrations**	**Year**	**Registrations**
1990	95768	1990	64848	1990	59556
1991	105876	1991	67284	1991	68844
1992	120879	1992	69850	1992	76941
1993	124899	1993	68125	1993	79936
1994	126393	1994	64322	1994	78999
1995	132051	1995	64107	1995	78088
1996	149505	1996	68993	1996	79076
1997	158366	1997	70158	1997	75177
1998	157936	1998	65681	1998	65326
1999	154897	1999	62652	1999	57256

	DACHSHUND		BEAGLE		POODLE
Year	**Registrations**	**Year**	**Registrations**	**Year**	**Registrations**
1990	44470	1990	42499	1990	71757
1991	48713	1991	56956	1991	77709
1992	50046	1992	60661	1992	73449
1993	48573	1993	61051	1993	67850
1994	46129	1994	59215	1994	61775
1995	44680	1995	57063	1995	54784
1996	48426	1996	56946	1996	56803
1997	51904	1997	54470	1997	54773
1998	53896	1998	53322	1998	51935
1999	50772	1999	49080	1999	45852

	YORKSHIRE TERRIER		CHIHUAHUA		BOXER
Year	**Registrations**	**Year**	**Registrations**	**Year**	**Registrations**
1990	36033	1990	24593	1990	23659
1991	39772	1991	29860	1991	26722
1992	39904	1992	31301	1992	30123
1993	39827	1993	32435	1993	30757
1994	38626	1994	32705	1994	30629
1995	36881	1995	33542	1995	31894
1996	40216	1996	36562	1996	36398
1997	41283	1997	38926	1997	38047
1998	42900	1998	43468	1998	36345
1999	40684	1999	42013	1999	34998

TABLE 3.4. (*Continued*)

ROTTWEILER		POMERANIAN		COCKER SPANIEL	
Year	Registrations	Year	Registrations	Year	Registrations
1990	60471	1990	34475	1990	105642
1991	76889	1991	41034	1991	98937
1992	95445	1992	42488	1992	91925
1993	104160	1993	40805	1993	75882
1994	102596	1994	39947	1994	60888
1995	93656	1995	37894	1995	48065
1996	89867	1996	39712	1996	45305
1997	75489	1997	39357	1997	41439
1998	55009	1998	38540	1998	34632
1999	41776	1999	33584	1999	29958

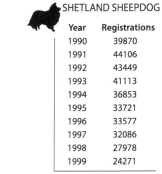

DALMATIAN		SHETLAND SHEEPDOG	
Year	Registrations	Year	Registrations
1990	21603	1990	39870
1991	30225	1991	44106
1992	38927	1992	43449
1993	42816	1993	41113
1994	42621	1994	36853
1995	36714	1995	33721
1996	32972	1996	33577
1997	22726	1997	32086
1998	9722	1998	27978
1999	4652	1999	24271

CHOW CHOW		MINIATURE SCHNAUZER	
Year	Registrations	Year	Registrations
1990	45271	1990	39910
1991	45131	1991	42404
1992	42670	1992	41058
1993	33824	1993	37267
1994	25415	1994	33344
1995	17722	1995	30256
1996	13587	1996	31834
1997	9536	1997	32351
1998	6241	1998	31063
1999	4342	1999	28649

Year	Total Dogs Registered
1990	1253214
1991	1379544
1992	1442690
1993	1422559
1994	1345941
1995	1277039
1996	1333568
1997	1307362
1998	1220951
1999	1119620

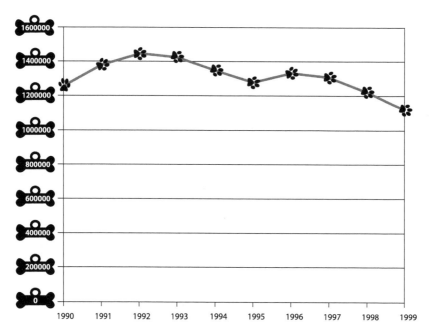

Figure 3.4. Total Number of Dogs Registered by the AKC in the 1990s

The most popular dog from 1983 until 1990, the Cocker Spaniel, witnessed its registration collapse over the course of the last decade of the twentieth century, decreasing from over 105,000 dogs in 1990 to just shy of 30,000 in 1999, which constitutes a decrease of over 70 percent.

Dalmatians entered the top ten for the first time in the 1990s, topping 42,000 registrations in 1993 and 1994. However, this surge in popularity was short lived, with Dalmatian registration falling by just over 89 percent between 1994 and 1999, from 42,621 in 1994 to 4,652 in 1999.

Unlike their Labrador brethren, Golden Retrievers did not experience profound growth in the 1990s. Instead, Golden Retriever registrations decreased by about 2,000 dogs over this period. However, despite this slight decrease, Golden Retrievers moved into the second spot in the top ten due to significant overall decreases in the German Shepherd[5] and Rottweiler populations that far outpaced Golden Retriever losses over the course of the same decade. These data are presented in Table 3.4 and Figure 3.4.

The 2000s

The first decade of the new millennium saw a tremendous and unparalleled downturn in breed specific dog registration. At the beginning of this period, more than 1 million new dogs were registered per year; by 2009, this had shrunk to under 650,000. This constitutes a decrease of more than 40 percent. Importantly, this drop in registration affected every breed fairly evenly with each of the top ten registering fewer dogs at the end of the decade than at its beginning, with the lone exception of Bulldogs.

Between 2000 and 2009, the following dog breeds appeared in the top ten most registered for at least one year: Labrador Retrievers, Golden Retrievers, German Shepherds, Dachshunds, Beagles, Yorkshire Terriers, Poodles, Boxers, Chihuahua, Shih Tzu, Miniature Schnauzers, and Bulldogs.

For both Bulldogs and Shih Tzus, the 2000s marked their first inclusion in the top ten. Shih Tzus had been on the outskirts of the top ten for several years before moving up in the ranks, mostly on account of a decline at a slower rate than other breeds, very much paralleling the development for the Golden Retrievers during the 1990s. Bulldogs were in a similar situation regarding their position outside the top ten in the 1990s. However, they also represented the only breed among the top ten to have more dogs registered at the end of the 2000s than at the beginning, increasing from 17,446 in 2000 to 23,248 in 2009.

TABLE 3.5. The Top Twelve Canine Breeds in the United States per AKC Registration in the 2000s

LABRADOR RETRIEVER

Year	Registrations
2000	172841
2001	165970
2002	154616
2003	144896
2004	146714
2005	137867
2006	123760
2007	114113
2008	100736
2009	89599

GOLDEN RETRIEVER

Year	Registrations
2000	66300
2001	62497
2002	56124
2003	52520
2004	52560
2005	48509
2006	42962
2007	39659
2008	34485
2009	30735

GERMAN SHEPHERD

Year	Registrations
2000	57660
2001	51625
2002	46963
2003	43950
2004	46054
2005	45014
2006	43575
2007	43376
2008	40909
2009	40938

DACHSHUND

Year	Registrations
2000	54773
2001	50478
2002	42571
2003	39468
2004	40774
2005	38566
2006	36033
2007	32598
2008	26075
2009	21089

BEAGLE

Year	Registrations
2000	52026
2001	50419
2002	44610
2003	45021
2004	44557
2005	42592
2006	39484
2007	37021
2008	33722
2009	30672

YORKSHIRE TERRIER

Year	Registrations
2000	43574
2001	42025
2002	37277
2003	38256
2004	43522
2005	47238
2006	48346
2007	47850
2008	41914
2009	37778

TABLE 3.5. *(Continued)*

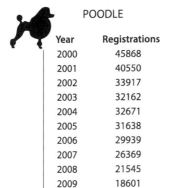

POODLE

Year	Registrations
2000	45868
2001	40550
2002	33917
2003	32162
2004	32671
2005	31638
2006	29939
2007	26369
2008	21545
2009	18601

BOXER

Year	Registrations
2000	38803
2001	37035
2002	34340
2003	34130
2004	37741
2005	37268
2006	35388
2007	33548
2008	29705
2009	25472

CHIHUAHUA

Year	Registrations
2000	43096
2001	36627
2002	28466
2003	24930
2004	24850
2005	23575
2006	22562
2007	19801
2008	15985
2009	14018

SHIH TZUS

Year	Registrations
2000	37599
2001	33240
2002	28294
2003	26926
2004	28960
2005	28087
2006	27282
2007	24951
2008	20219
2009	17314

MINIATURE SCHNAUZER

Year	Registrations
2000	30472
2001	27587
2002	23926
2003	22282
2004	24083
2005	24144
2006	22920
2007	20747
2008	17040
2009	14263

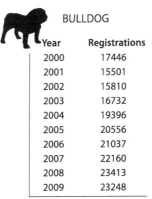

BULLDOG

Year	Registrations
2000	17446
2001	15501
2002	15810
2003	16732
2004	19396
2005	20556
2006	21037
2007	22160
2008	23413
2009	23248

Year	Total Dogs Registered
2000	1175473
2001	1081335
2002	958800
2003	915441
2004	958641
2005	920804
2006	870192
2007	812452
2008	716195
2009	649677

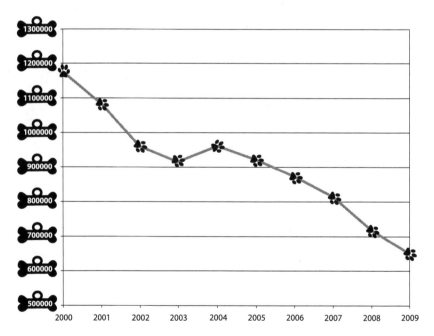

Figure 3.5. Total Number of Dogs Registered by the AKC in the 2000s

Despite significant year-to-year registration losses, Labrador Retrievers held on to their place at the top of the registry throughout the 2000s. In these ten years, Labrador Retriever registration decreased by approximately 48 percent, dropping from 172,841 in 2000 to 89,599 in 2009. Prior to 2009, 1990 was the last year Labs had registered fewer than 100,000 dogs in a year.

Golden Retrievers began the 2000s occupying the second highest spot in the registry. After a decade of declines that beset just about all of the breeds in the top ten, Goldens had fallen to the fourth spot by 2009, barely registering a few dozen more dogs that year than the fifth-place Beagles.

Most remarkable about this time period is the uniformity with which the various breed registrations decreased. Even with Bulldogs' small gains, registrations of the other top-ten breeds decreased by an average of just over 40 percent. The uniformity of these decreases throughout the first decade of the new millennium is visible in the data presented in Table 3.5 as well as in Figure 3.5.

Conclusion

Several forces drive the relative popularity of any particular dog breed at any given time. The first we would like to categorize a impetuousness, meaning that the particular breed's popularity is driven by short-term trends and fads. Typically, these arise mainly by blatant imitation of celebrities, politicians, and other media figures. In short, this force emanates from the power of popular culture.

These celebrity-induced fads have influenced the popularity of dogs way before the time periods that we examined in this chapter. Thus, for example, the popularity of German Shepherds in the wake of Rin Tin Tin's success in the film *Man from Hell's River* (1922) drove this breed's registration for quite some time in the first half of the twentieth century, including their stint as the most popular dog from 1925 to 1928. Lassie, the prototypical Collie, starred in her first movie in 1943 and, once again, Hollywood stardom corresponded with rising popularity. According to the AKC, "the Collie's popularity began to rise until ranking third in the nation from 1947-1949. In 2005 the Collie ranked 36th."[6] This pattern of short-term canine popularity, driven essentially by celebrity status, has continued to the present day.

Several prominent examples confirmed this very phenomenon in the 1990s, when both the St. Bernard and Dalmatian breeds achieved significant gains before once again declining in popularity. First, with the re-release of Disney's animated classic *101 Dalmatians* in 1991—not to be confused with the Glenn Close live-action remake released in 1996—Dalmatian registrations increased significantly, from 21,603 in 1990 to 42,816 in 1993, an average increase of approximately 25 percent per year. (It bears noting that this growth in Dalmatians' popularity began in 1987 when their registration increased by 38 percent.) Even if the popularity of the movie did not precipitate the initial increase in this breed's registration, it certainly seems to have helped sustain it.

Bucking the general downward trend of the 1990s, St. Bernards also underwent a certain renaissance by increasing their registration over 9 percent on average between 1992 and 1997. The former date was particularly significant because it witnessed the release of the motion picture *Beethoven*, starring a lovably large St. Bernard. It seems likely that the growth in this breed's registration had some connection to the popularity of this movie's main character, because prior to the film's release, the St. Bernard had experienced a steady decline in popularity throughout the 1980s and the very early 1990s, only to see this downward trend reversed after the movie's release in 1992.

Politicians' dogs can also achieve a great deal of prominence and serve as trendsetters. The Obama family's choice of Bo, a Portuguese Water Dog, has had an impact on AKC registration statistics. In 2002, Portuguese Water Dogs were the seventy-third most registered dog in the country. By 2012, these dogs were the fifty-fifth most registered. It is hard to discount the prominence of Bo Obama in contributing to this trend.

Trends in dog registration are also inconsistent across geographic regions, both intra- as well as internationally. In addition to its national registry, the AKC maintains records that differentiate breed registration by metropolitan regions. Of the fifty cities that the organization tracks, only Knoxville, Tennessee's top ten matches the national top ten.[7] There are also numerous breeds that occur in multiple local top-ten lists but fail to appear in the national top ten. Among these are the Cavalier King Charles Spaniel, Cocker Spaniel, German Shorthaired Pointer, Shetland Sheepdog, Maltese, English Springer Spaniel, and Boston Terrier.[8]

In addition to these interesting regional variations within the United States, there also exist significant variations in registration trends across countries. For instance, the Staffordshire Bull Terrier, the fifth most popular dog in the United Kingdom, is only the eighty-fourth most popular dog in the United States. Conversely, the Beagle is routinely among the ten most popular breeds in the United States, while it is currently only the twenty-ninth most popular dog in the United Kingdom.[9] Similar contrasts can be observed between certain breed registrations in Canada when compared with those in the United States. Thus, for example, the Bernese Mountain Dog is the twelfth most registered dog in Canada, while in the United States it is merely in forty-seventh place.

The second factor that we detect in terms of influencing the popularity of a dog breed could best be termed structural in that it revolves around less fleeting factors like trends and tastes and centers more on substantial matters like breeding stock, litter size, and other items related to the breed's overall ecology. It is mainly these factors that truly define the findings presented in this chapter. The various population trends that appear in the 1960s through the 2000s provide a valuable context for the development and institutionalization of breed rescue over the same time period. Two sequential epochs appear to hold particular relevance regarding the development of this relatively novel institutional manifestation of the human–animal relationship. Specifically, the emergence of the discourse of compassion, starting in the late 1960s and continuing through the 1970s, forms a crucial backdrop for the development of the earliest rescues and their institutionalization several decades later. It is our contention that the proliferation of the discourse of compassion at the end of the 1960s was instrumental in shaping human–animal relations and prompted significant changes in society's collective attitude toward animals in general, paving the way for the development of breed rescue in particular. So it follows that many of the earliest breed specific rescues would be devoted to dogs that gained popularity around the same time the societal attitudes about dogs were shifting.

The upsurge in the popularity of the Golden Retrievers in the late 1960s and early 1970s, combined with their continuing popularity in the following decades, was vital to the early development and institutionalization of their dedicated rescues. However, the emergence of this popularity of Golden Retrievers in the late 1960s and early 1970s constituted only part of the story. After all, there were numerous other dog breeds that became quite popular at the very same time as did the Golden Retrievers. And yet, most of these breeds' rescues did not become nearly as successful as did the Goldens', be it in the quantity of their presence or the quality of their mission.

The other piece of the puzzle lies in the 1990s. By the arrival of that decade, the generational cohort that was so influenced by the events of the late 1960s and its discourse of compassion had firmly reached middle age, carrying with it the attitudes that its members had picked up earlier in their lives. The 1990s were, after all, the first full decade in which we encountered a vast proliferation of rescue groups, on the one hand, as well as the beginning of the institutionalization and bureaucratization of this new entity as a whole, on the other hand. The fact that Golden Retrievers maintained their popularity during this decade became a crucial reason for the continued organizational excellence of many rescues devoted to this breed. Put differently, Golden Retrievers benefited a great deal from the mere fact that they became *and* stayed popular at crucial times in the development of breed rescue. Let's contrast the fortuitous confluence of Golden Retrievers and their rescues with two less auspicious cases, that of Dobermans and Labrador Retrievers.

Like Golden Retrievers, Dobermans' popularity grew tremendously in the 1970s. Indeed, the latter's popularity far outpaced the former's. Recall that one of the earliest examples of these breed specific rescue organizations was the New Hampshire Doberman Rescue League started by Norma Gurinskas. The temporal coincidence of Dobermans'—as well as other breeds'—popularity with the beginning stages of the societal proliferation of the discourse of compassion seemed to have led to the establishment of various early protorescue organizations in the late 1970s and early 1980s. However, in notable contrast to Goldens, Dobermans began suffering from an unwarranted "bad breed" reputation, and Doberman registration diminished significantly in the course of the 1980s. Because of the decline in this breed's popularity, coinciding with a crucial juncture of growth in the rescue movement, Doberman rescues missed out on the expansionary opportunities and gradual bureaucratization and successful institutionalization of the rescues in the 1990s. This is not to state that there were no highly successful and modern Doberman rescues by the closing of the twentieth century. Rather, it is merely to say that in a comparative context, Golden Retriever rescues benefited from auspicious—even contingent—opportunities much more than their counterparts in the Doberman world. Differently put, history contributed mightily to Golden Retriever rescues being more prolific than Doberman rescues.

Labrador Retrievers present an interesting case, as on the surface their postwar popularity seems to mirror that of Goldens. Both Golden Retrievers and Labrador Retrievers gained a large number of new registrations in the late 1960s and early 1970s.[10] They maintained their popularity in the 1980s and 1990s. But here is the major contrast between the rescues of these two related breeds. Although, just like Golden Retrievers, Labrador Retrievers attained their early popularity precisely at the juncture when breed specific rescues emerged on the landscape of human–animal relations in the

United States, the growth in popularity of Labrador Retrievers attained such dimensions in the 1990s that the sheer numbers of Labs rendered the efficient and effective establishment of their rescues well-nigh impossible, certainly much more complex and taxing than the successful institutionalization of Golden Retriever rescues in this crucial period. Labrador growth was so dramatic as to create a seemingly insurmountable organizational problem that severely frustrated rescue efforts. Due to the extraordinary number of Labs that enter shelters, it became very difficult for nascent Lab rescues to attain any sort of foothold that any movement in its formative stages desperately needs to become successful as a lasting institution. Despite the great similarities between Labs and Goldens, it is clear why, on the whole, Golden Retriever rescues emerged as better equipped to serve their breed more efficiently than have Labrador Retriever rescues. We will devote Chapter 8 in this book precisely to a comparative analysis of the respective rescues devoted to these two very similar dog breeds.

AKC registrations have steadily decreased since the 1990s. Part of the reason for this decline surely lies in the American people's cultural transition from dog people to pet people. As dogs increasingly became members of the family, the prestige associated with having a dog of a particular breed registered with the AKC assumed diminishing importance. Indeed, such increasingly antiquated views of dogs came to be construed, at least in part, as being possibly quite contrary to the principles that lead people to view their dogs as family members. The affection one bestows on a family member hinges little on the approval of racial purity decreed by a distant agent of accreditation. At the bottom line, compassion, as we argue throughout this book, constitutes an important democratizing factor, emphasizing inclusion over distinction meaning that the emotional currency of "mutts" increased significantly during these decades with the value of pure breeds losing some of their importance in American society as a whole. Thus, the changing discourse of compassion in the United States not only influenced the popularity of particular breeds of dogs but more importantly also gave rise to a movement that countered the negative aspects of such popularity by creating the new institution and movement of breed specific canine rescues. In former times, breeders were so convinced of the absolute value and impeccable worth of their breeds that they simply could not imagine that anybody would surrender such a dog or that any abuse might befall it. In such a perfect world there simply was no place for breed specific rescue. The growth of the discourse of compassion came to demonstrate without any reasonable doubt that such a world simply did not exist and that all kinds of adversity befell breed specific dogs who needed help in spite of their alleged perfection. Lastly, the growth of this discourse also influenced the decision of whether to register a dog with the AKC. With purity becoming less important to the American public combined with a simultaneous growth in compassion for the weak, AKC registration came to lose some of its former cachet. Chapter 4 will present a detailed history of Golden Retriever rescue, which we find not only interesting and telling on its own, but, more important for our project, a valuable prototype, a case study, for breed specific rescue as a whole.

Notes

1. Additionally, crossbreed "designer dogs" such as "Labradoodles" (Labrador Retriever/Poodle Mix) and "Puggles" (Pug/Beagle Mixes), which have had a recent surge in popularity, are not recognized by the AKC because they are not purebred.

2. Humane Society of the United States, "AKC's Most Popular Breeds Found in Puppy Mills," May 1, 2013, http://www.humanesociety.org/issues/puppy_mills/facts/akc_breeds_puppy_mills.html (accessed on April 23, 2014).

3. Despite the fact that they would not enter the top ten until the 1970s, we have included the registration statistics for Golden Retrievers in the figures for this decade as well.

4. This number is already significantly lower than the postwar peak in Poodle registration that occurred in 1969, when 274,145 were registered.

5. German Shepherds experienced modest gains in the early 1990s before succumbing to the general trend of decreasing registrations in the second half of the decade.

6. American Kennel Club, "AKC Registration Statistics: Fact Sheet." http://classic.akc.org/pdfs/press_center/popular_pooches.pdf (accessed on April 23, 1014).

7. Ibid.

8. Ibid.

9. Ibid.

10. Although Labs were more popular during the 1970s, Goldens were growing at a faster rate.

CHAPTER 4

The History of Golden Retriever Rescue as a Case Study of Breed Specific Rescue

The only goal that we have is that we will never let a Golden Retriever die in a shelter

—Lauren Genkinger
Adopt a Golden, Atlanta, Georgia

A person looking for a Golden Retriever rescue in 1979 would have discovered that such a thing simply did not exist in the United States. Thirty-five years later, there are over one hundred such groups in the country, covering all fifty states, not infrequently featuring multiple rescues located in the same city. The evolution of Golden Retriever rescues is a product of the discourse of compassion that emerged in the United States (as well as other liberal democracies) in the 1970s. Understanding how these groups function today requires a detailed examination of their history and the factors affecting their creation, growth, and function. The sections that follow present a timeline of the history of Golden Retriever rescue.

1980: The Accidental Rescues

As is the case with most new things, the first Golden Retriever rescues emerged completely ad hoc, haphazardly, and with very different perspectives than they came to assume barely a decade later. These organizations appeared because of needs that existing ones failed to address for one reason or another. These new entities shared a few unifying characteristics: they emerged completely locally with no ambitions beyond helping needy dogs in their immediate purview; they addressed urgent needs without placing these into a larger regional, let alone national, context; and they were invariably the creation of one or two committed individuals who, perhaps surrounded by a few like-minded friends volunteering their helpful services on occasion for different reasons and adhering to very different views of dogs, animals, and many social issues, found the pursuit of this particular matter of such importance that they chose to create until then unknown structures. Even though we see the very creation of these first rescues as haphazard, informal, even accidental events, we very much view the individuals creating them as fitting the Weberian mode of charismatic authority and legitimacy. It is quite simple: Without the determined initiatives and concrete actions on the part of these individuals, these organizations would not have happened. This section gives a brief account of two Golden Retriever rescue groups—the Golden Retriever Club of San Diego (San Diego, California) and Dirk's Fund (St. Louis, Missouri)—that we were able to identify as being among the very first—if not indeed *the* very first—such organizations in the United States. In doing so, it will be clear how, from the very beginning of this new institutional creation, very different organizational paths and divergent conceptual preferences and philosophical visions informed the world of Golden Retriever rescue. In spite of these differences, however, rescue groups united under the umbrella of one sole purpose: the improvement of the lives of needy Golden Retrievers.

The Golden Retriever Club of San Diego's Rescue Service (GRCSDRS) was informally, perhaps even accidentally, started in 1980 by some club members and a well-intentioned booklet that underlined the participants' still-maintained beliefs that their task was not only to help indigent dogs but also, by doing just that, to uphold the breed's high standards by buying back well-bred dogs that had stumbled on hard times through no fault of their own. Jeannette Poling provides a description of this important moment in the history of breed specific canine rescue in the United States, which went well beyond its immediate intent of rescuing indigent Golden Retrievers:

> Here was our club; there were probably four or five of us, and we typed up, I mean really typed up on a typewriter this little book

and we thought we were being snazzy, and we entitled it "Better Goldens" and we advertised it in the Pets for Sale section of the newspapers . . . I'd write articles about dog rescue or what the club was doing, or what the club functions were. And we gave our little booklet, our 44-page booklet "Better Goldens," to the Golden Retriever Club of America, who had people who were like me or smarter than me or had more time than I did, and they turned this booklet into a 96-page version called "Acquiring a Golden Retriever," which is still available in print.[1]

Poling, along with several other members of the club, noticed that there was a high incidence of poorly bred dogs with genetic problems in the late 1970s. These concerned people also posted notices in classifieds stating, "Before you buy or breed a Golden, call us."[2] People in the area started to call them, "not about our book, but telling us that they wanted to give us their dogs."[3] Rather than allow these dogs to go to animal shelters, Poling and her fellow club members decided to take and re-home these needy dogs, describing these humble but auspicious beginnings in the following way: "We did eight dogs in 1980 from August to the end of December, and we thought that we were like running the IBM Company or something and that we were rocking and that we really had a system going. And then it was more and more dogs."[4] From these small initial steps, Poling and her colleagues' rescue efforts grew until their organizational endeavor became a full-fledged committee of the club. The club's reasoning behind taking the rescue of Golden Retrievers into its own hands, rather than allowing shelters to re-home dogs, was: "We did think that we were elitist in a good way, in that we could quickly screen people for a home for these dogs much better than any shelter."[5]

Poling described her group's philosophy in detail:

> Our rescue was never about saving every Golden Retriever that is born in this county or in the State of California or in this world. That was not it. Our thought initially was that we are a breed club that is composed of people . . . and then, we wanted to help dogs. We do not consider ourselves dog guardians, we are dog owners. It was never about dogs' rights; it was always about dogs that we can care for.[6]

Poling elaborated eloquently on the different philosophies present in rescue when she said that "there is a big faction [in breed specific rescue] of a kind of elitism which believes that if you really are a genuine and committed rescuer, then you do not buy dogs or show dogs, or work with them, or have any fun with the fancy AKC [American Kennel Club] and dog shows."[7] Poling here addresses the major divide and distinction between what we termed *dog people* versus *pet people*, with the former comprising animal rescuers, like Poling herself, who feel participation in AKC events and organizations is not only ethically permissible but also the best course of action to help needy dogs. In contrast, pet people feel that engaging with and condoning the AKC's activities and its very being are counterproductive to the mission of animal rescue to the point of negating the legitimacy of being a bona fide rescuer if one approves of dog breeding. Note also how the term *elitist*, unless explicitly stated to be used positively as Poling did when she invoked her organization's obvious expertise with all things Golden Retriever that was useful in terms of screening prospective adopters, has assumed a negative, even pejorative, connotation in common parlance in contemporary America. Poling perceives pet people's animal-rights–leaning rejection of dog breeding and dog showing as elitist, whereas the latter view the institutions and conventions dear to Poling's heart as also elitist.

When asked if Poling believed that her highly organized and deeply committed rescue operation would ever split from the club, she stated emphatically, "No, it probably never will—I think there's a greater likelihood of the club folding than the rescue splitting from it or dying."[8] Poling expounded on this by explaining that "the power brokers in the club wouldn't allow such a defection. The power brokers in the club, which would be me, and my girlfriend, and a couple of other women and the husbands are all very proactive."[9] Poling thus characterized her rescue committee as being fully dedicated to staying in the club. This commitment has rendered her rescue and club quite exceptional in terms of their mutual relations when compared with other rescues that start in clubs, as most choose to split from these clubs if only for financial reasons such as being able to obtain a tax-exempt status as a 501(c)(3) entity. In addition to such pragmatic considerations for splits between club and rescue, there often develop substantial philosophical differences between the two over policies, strategies, and the very goals that each entity sees as central for the reasons of its existence and identity. Given the latter point, it should not come as a surprise if a number of such splits occur in less than amicable circumstances.

Another rescue model, which, like Poling's operation in San Diego, was one of the very first breed rescue organizations in the United States is Dirk's Fund in St. Louis. It all began in 1980 when Bob and Ona Tillay rescued Dirk, a Great Pyrenees. As Golden Retriever owners, they were frequently contacted after rescuing Dirk to help rescue Golden Retrievers as well. Bob stated:

> People started, you know, giving us Golden Retrievers saying, "I can't take care of this, I can't take care of that, can you help?" And it grew from being a nice guy helping here, helping there, to becoming, I guess, a major operation in which we saved about 210 Golden Retrievers last year. We've probably rescued more than 3,000 of them since we began way back in 1980.[10]

When Bob discussed what he was doing in the early 1980s, he stated that "I didn't know about rescue. I mean it wasn't that I was trying to rescue dogs, Goldens in particular, I was just trying to help the dogs."[11] In essence, Bob said that he did not consciously set out to start a rescue, but rather tried to help one dog at a time, which then gradually led to the major operation that he currently runs. Bob described the state of the breed rescue world in the 1980s:

> There might have been some rescues, to be sure, but they were like me: we were just kinda doing it. There was no network, there were no guidelines, no blueprints, no contacts, nothing national. It all happened completely isolated and local because there was nobody to talk to and ask "What's going on?" Some of the big shelters here knew me and my wife, and if somebody came in with a Golden or something the shelter folks thought was extra-special, and because the shelters were all full then like they are now, they would call us and ask us if we'd help them.[12]

The Tillays had a reputation for rescuing Golden Retrievers, and local shelters knew they could be counted on to take sick, injured, or behaviorally challenging Golden Retrievers. The rescue then began to grow by word of mouth and reputation with people bringing their unwanted Goldens to the Tillays and leaving them there instead of the much more impersonal shelters. Moreover, "then friends, or people that heard about us or people we adopted dogs to, came to us and said, 'How can we help?'"[13] What is interesting about Dirk's Fund as a rescue is that it is one of the oldest organizations in the Golden Retriever—indeed breed specific canine—rescue world, and yet the organization has networked very little when compared with many of the other rescues; this is likely because, at the time of Dirk Fund's inception, there were very few breed rescues in the country.

Moreover, the Tillays' initial and then continued determination to confine their rescue efforts strictly to the local meant that networking with the outside world of other rescues and organizations could be kept to a minimum. Bob stated, regarding this matter:

> We're a very large, we're probably like one of the largest, top five Golden Retriever adoption organizations in the country, but we're just not well known. The reason is, when we started, me and my wife funded it all. We didn't think that we'd need to do anything like networking or fundraising or any such things. In the last four or five years, we've realized we need help from people to fund our operation and we've started to promote things. We now get 2,000 hits a day on our website. Nobody that I know of gets that many hits, it's just unbelievable.[14]

And to make matters more interesting—and impressive—still, Dirk's Fund has attained undeniable stature and recognition in the greater St. Louis area as attested to by Bob's being invited to throw out the first pitch at a St. Louis Cardinals game. Anybody even a tad knowledgeable about that city's culture knows that nothing comes close to the reverence that the Cardinals have enjoyed there for over 130 years. And had it not been for some transportation snafus that scuttled two very particular adoptions, Oprah Winfrey and Ellen DeGeneres would have each become the forever homes of two Dirk Fund's Golden Retrievers.[15]

These then are perhaps the two oldest Golden Retriever rescue efforts in the country. Both started very small, both almost haphazardly, both led by committed and competent individuals who only had one goal: to help Golden Retrievers in distress. They assumed very different organizational tracks divided by more than 2,000 miles completely unconnected to each other and—really—to any other organizations of their kind, which simply did not exist at this time. And yet these two organizations' almost simultaneous emergence bespoke a zeitgeist that had come to disseminate values that were indeed shared and known in California as much as in the Midwest. A prominent facet of these values was the discourse of compassion.

1984: The Early Golden Retriever Rescue Period

Four Golden Retriever rescue groups were created in 1984. Two of them, Midlands Golden Retriever Rescue located in Columbia, South Carolina, and Gateway Golden Retriever Rescue situated in St. Louis, Missouri, were independently created. Two organizations, DFW Metro Golden Retriever Rescue in Dallas, Texas, and NORCAL Golden Retriever Rescue in Menlo Park, California, started as committees within their area breed clubs. Of these four, Gateway Golden Retriever Rescue and NORCAL Golden Retriever Rescue emerged with very particular intentions and explicit strategies. Unlike the rescues formed in 1980 and also dissimilar to Midlands Golden Retriever Rescue and DFW Metro Golden Retriever Rescue, these two rescues did not commence with any rescue activities until their organizational structures had been completely established. Thus, their beginnings were quite different from that of others who began to rescue dogs first and then proceeded to establish commensurate organizations. In a matter of a very few years, systematic forethought and careful planning had entered the world of Golden Retriever rescue. The premeditation with which Gateway Golden Retriever Rescue and NORCAL Golden Retriever Rescue were created contrasted sharply with the ad hoc learning-by-doing method pursued by GRCSDR and Dirk's Fund. This marked a pivotal moment in the world of Golden Retriever rescue as it indicated the clear awareness on the committed rescuers' part that organizational savvy and planning had to accompany their good intentions and compassion to guarantee the overall mission's sustained success. As is the case in the development of all new structures, organizational innovations in the breed specific canine rescue world do not displace earlier methods of operation. Instead, they complement and coexist with them for quite some time, never fully jettisoning the personalistic nature of the founding era in a realm like dog rescue, which, of course, continues to be propelled purely by the voluntary dedication of people who remain emotionally committed to the task at hand.

Midlands Golden Retriever Rescue originated, like others, notably Dirk's Fund, by virtue of one dog's tragedy and eventual triumph. In Midland's case, the catalyst was a dog that had been shot and almost killed by its owner. This incident mobilized Mary Williams, the founder of the group, who was soon joined by like-minded individuals and evolved into this rescue organization's members. This organization appears to have a solid dog people philosophy, which renders it quite similar in its approach to rescue as pursued by the Golden Retriever Club of San Diego County. Thus, Mary Williams stated, "I cannot save them [Golden Retrievers] all nor do I intend to 'collect' dogs. If you pity too much and do not keep your perspective, you do a disservice to the Goldens in need."[16] Midlands Golden Retriever Rescue has a typical origin story for rescue groups of the accidental persuasion. The group also provides a useful example of a compassionate individual's discovery of a dog in need and how such an event catalyzed the creation of a rescue group under this individual's lasting leadership. Midlands Golden Retriever Rescue thus represents a fine case of what we have come to categorize as our charismatically organized rescue group.

DFW Metro Golden Retriever Rescue started in the local breed club, the DFW Metro Golden Retriever Club. Unlike the Golden Retriever Club of San Diego Rescue Service, however, this rescue eventually separated from the club, becoming a standalone group in 1988 and obtaining its 501(c)(3) tax-exempt status in 1995. The reasons for separating from or staying with the club seem entirely situational and depend largely on a combination of the following considerations: Some rescues stay within the club for personal reasons or because they rescue so few dogs that it is impractical to separate from the club, while others choose to become their own organization in order to obtain their 501(c)(3) status or to focus entirely on rescue, rather than splitting their attention between rescue and club activities such as shows. Each of the paths has its advantages and disadvantages, and it is critical for rescues in clubs to determine which option makes the most sense for them. As presented earlier, in the case of the San Diego situation, the rescuers decided to remain firmly ensconced in their original breed club; in the DFW instance, the rescuers opted to depart from the club and found their own organization.

Gateway Golden Retriever Rescue represents another first in the Golden Retriever rescue world; joining Dirk's Fund in St. Louis, it became the first Golden Retriever rescue to establish itself in a city—St. Louis, in this case—where a Golden Retriever rescue had already existed. The group's website describes its beginnings:

> Golden Retriever Rescue of Greater St. Louis (GRR-GSL) was established January 1, 1984 by two individuals who loved and trained Goldens. The organization quickly grew into a well-staffed and trained group of volunteers. In November of 1999 we adopted the name Gateway Golden Retriever Rescue (GGRR) to reflect the geography and breed we serve. The word "gateway" not only symbolizes the St. Louis area, but also our role in providing a gateway for Goldens in finding permanent, loving homes.[17]

There are two complementary, but also competing, interpretations of why Gateway Golden Retriever Rescue established itself in St. Louis when another group, Dirk's Fund, was already present. It is clear to us that Bob Tillay of Dirk's Fund was well known in the animal shelter world at this juncture; what is less clear is whether he had appeared on the radar of the local Golden Retriever Club world as well as that of the local dog owners. One possibility is that Tillay was not well known to the local club and among local owners, and therefore the individuals from these worlds that wanted to rescue Goldens did not know of him, thus feeling compelled to start their own rescue group. The other possibility is that Tillay was known to individuals from the club and owner worlds, but that the rescue needs in St. Louis at the time required more than the Tillays could provide or that at this early stage of rescue its purpose remained somewhat murky to the established club world and local Golden Retriever owners. Suffice it to say that St. Louis appears to be the very first metropolitan area in the United States that featured two rescue organizations for the same breed at this very nascent stage of the rescue movement.

NORCAL Golden Retriever Rescue started as an idea by several members of the breed club. Phil Fisher, president of the rescue in 2008 and 2009, described the circumstances surrounding the organization's beginning:

> There were people who belonged to the Golden Retriever Club that were not breeding dogs at the time or had retired, but were still active and said, "You know this is 1984 we really need to start a rescue group." So rescue started out as sort of an informal, ad hoc arrangement, but then people realized, you know, if we're going to raise money to be a successful rescue, then we have to have an IRS [Internal Revenue Service] nonprofit approval.[18]

Fisher went on to say that in the beginning the group "started out pretty small just in the Bay Area using cookie and bake sales to raise money. And then we gradually moved so that we're from Fresno to the Oregon border now, we don't have people everywhere but we're pretty much active in twenty-five of thirty-five counties, with about 200 volunteers."[19] The size of the area NORCAL currently covers demonstrates the impressive growth it has experienced as an organization from its formation in 1984 to the present.

1985: The Year of Influential Rescues

In 1985 we saw the birth of three rescues that have remained crucial in their importance and centrality to the Golden Retriever rescue world until the present. Yankee Golden Retriever Rescue (YGRR) has had an unparalleled influence on the development of the Golden Retriever rescue community across the United States and even into Canada. Retrieve a Golden of Minnesota (RAGOM) assumed a similar function in that state as well as adjacent ones, spurring the creation of another large group in the region, which in turn created several other local groups. Finally, there is the Golden Retriever Rescue Club of Charlotte, North Carolina, which is quite rare in the rescue world in that its rescue activities completely transformed its organizational origin as a club into that of a rescue.

YGRR is considered one of the most influential rescue groups in the country. As the oldest of the three large rescues in existence today (we will discuss the other two later), YGRR has had a tremendous effect on the growth of the Golden Retriever rescue world through its commitment to sharing information and helping other groups succeed. In our research we regularly encountered comments that especially praised YGRR in its concerted effort to help groups at the all-important beginning stages of their organization by readily sharing with them the necessary steps to apply for 501(c)(3) status, by furnishing models for application forms, and by providing information about fostering options, to name just a few crucial components in the rescue process. Many of our interlocutors attested to YGRR's model-like leadership position in the Golden Retriever rescue world. Here is just one example of this phenomenon, as voiced by the late Bob Bornstein of Sooner Golden Retriever Rescue:

> I chose to pattern our organization after another Golden Retriever rescue, Yankee Golden Retriever Rescue, in New England. I actually talked to the two cofounders of Yankee in 1986 and asked them about what they did and how they did it, because they had been in existence for about three or four years by then, I believe, and seemed to be successful. So we patterned our organization after theirs, meaning, among others, that all our officers and board members are appointed whereas there are quite a few Golden Retriever rescues now where these folks are elected by the general membership. But we have never done that. There are advantages and disadvantages to each system, I've discovered.[20]

And YGRR's reputation and influence reached beyond the United States. Thus, for example, Barb Demetrick from the Canadian Retriever Adoption Service, Inc., in Barrie, Ontario, which calls itself appropriately by the short and generic "Golden Rescue" that it has copyrighted, had this to say about YGRR: "We knew all about Riverview, YGRR's famed facility, and how it got started, and all the different steps that Yankee Rescue went through to get to where they are today. It's an incredible role model. . . . I also went down and spent two days at Yankee to visit their impressive operation."[21] YGRR's leadership within the Golden Retriever rescue community provided other Golden Retriever rescues with invaluable information and assistance, facilitating rescue group start-ups. There can be no doubt that YGRR has served as a powerful pioneer for the breed specific rescue community beyond the world of Golden Retrievers.

YGRR was founded by Joan Puglia and Susan Foster. Both were members of Yankee Golden Retriever Club, which was the local breed club for Golden Retrievers. When deciding how best to commence with their rescue mission, Puglia and Foster initially thought to have it as part of the club. Puglia stated:

> The breed club said that they really didn't feel that rescue was in their mission statement. They could not take it on. This was not a negative attitude towards rescue at all. But the club just didn't feel that rescue activity was why the breed club was developed and feared that something like rescue could be a complete drain on both the energy and the money that was there for something totally different.[22]

Puglia and Foster therefore decided that the club and the rescue needed to become and remain separate, but chose the name Yankee to reflect that "we're kind of all in this together, and we all care about the dogs, and that is what motivates all of us."[23] Although Puglia and Foster had assumed at the beginning that there would not be too many dogs to help, they soon discovered otherwise; Puglia described to us the early years:

> We went forward and sort of designed things as we went along, completely on the fly, improvising all the way. And we soon found that the demand for rescuing dogs was really pretty large. It was like holding a tornado by the tail type of thing. It was an all-encompassing commitment for the first few years especially. Rescue started out just with the two of us, and then what we would do is go back to the breed club and ask for as well as receive help from it for certain things like transportation, because these were skilled people who we knew had suitable crates and knew how to handle dogs.[24]

In her interview with us, Puglia's description of her experiences in the early years of YGRR emphasized the nascent cultural shifts of the time that led to broader society's recognition of the need for breed specific rescue. Although many in the club saw Puglia and Foster's efforts as a tad strange, and certainly beyond the club's purview, mission, and capabilities, the two women also detected a growing respect by club members for this novel endeavor. Above all, many realized that far from being superfluous, perhaps even detrimental, to the fine reputation of the Golden Retriever breed, which—so the conventional assumption—did not need rescue beyond what all reputable clubs already offered anyway, concerted rescue efforts that Puglia and Foster began to establish were indeed needed and thus appreciated.

Essentially, Puglia and Foster developed YGRR as an organization completely from scratch and by trial and error, keeping policies and procedures they liked and that they deemed successful, discarding ones they found less useful, and being ever willing to try new measures when and where they felt improvement was needed. Puglia explained this process: "The whole thing was evolving, you know, gradually and unplanned, but we learned. And every time we learned something we passed it on."[25] The group flourished, providing an example for the rest of the country to follow. Puglia elaborated on YGRR's dedication to helping other groups: "We organized many seminars, I can't tell you how many hundreds of packets we sent out to organizations all over the country, and the organization continues to send stuff out today as well . . . but now with the Internet. Believe me, that has made such a tremendous difference. It is so much easier today than when we did this."[26] Although YGRR started, like most other rescues, with very rudimentary fundraising efforts, the group realized quite early in its existence that to attain greater success in terms of placing an ever-mounting number of dogs, professionally more advanced methods to obtain the needed money were called for. Enter Joy Viola, who joined YGRR with immense experience as a fundraiser in the nonprofit sector and who quickly put her skills to good use for the organization. She described to us how YGRR came to professionalize its fundraising efforts quite early in its organizational existence and how it still stands apart from many other Golden Retriever rescue groups:

A lot of these groups, probably all of them, got started with simple fundraising things like dog washes and little events, and maybe their auctions, their membership fee or a little raffle, or something or other. YGRR was no different, of course. But we also raised money by identifying potential donors, like wealthy or influential people in the community who had Goldens or who we knew liked Goldens and dogs. The little fundraising things will always remain. But the big things have to emerge to really push things forward. The only ones that have ever broken out of the small things are Yankee, Delaware Valley, and Homeward Bound.[27]

Although YGRR may have started in a manner similar to most rescues, the group soon evolved beyond pursuing only rather rudimentary methods for the procurement of funds, thereby assuming yet another pioneering role in the world of Golden Retriever rescue.

Annie Kassler, a former member of the group, told us "I think that all these innovations emerged because of Joan and Susan. In a sense, theirs became the model to do rescue well. And I think that this model spread through the US and Canada, too."[28] Her comment underlined the influence that YGRR has had on the rest of the Golden Retriever rescue world. YGRR further solidified its model-like character in rescue by purchasing its very own kennel facility, Riverview in Hudson, Massachusetts; YGRR was the first major rescue to do so, and only two other groups currently own their own facility: Delaware Valley Golden Retriever Rescue in Reinholds, Pennsylvania, and Homeward Bound Golden Retriever Rescue & Sanctuary in Elverta, California, the two other groups mentioned by Joy Viola in her singling out the importance of professional fundraising methods for the growth of rescues. Even with Puglia and Foster now retired from YGRR, this organization continues to be a leader in the Golden Retriever rescue world.

To their credit, Puglia and Foster realized that YGRR's continued success lay in their establishment of the sound foundation for a transformation from YGRR's early charismatic stage of organizational structure and leadership to an institution governed by impersonal legal-rational rules. This crucial step commenced with the funding of a paid position. Puglia stated it this way:

> We felt if we really love our program, and we want to see it be successful, then we needed to make it so that, if we were to drop dead or whatever, that everybody would get an extra biscuit that night, and put the flag down for one day, and the whole thing would go on like there were no differences at all. So in this spirit, we developed a paid executive director position.[29]

One could not articulate the transition from charismatic to legal-rational form of any institutional governance better than Puglia did. Moreover, this governance has reached way beyond the purview of YGRR's actual organization in that this rescue's structure became the model for so many others in the country. Making matters more impressive still is that this imitation has occurred stealthily. Puglia stated on this issue: "The people in rescue groups have grown and changed so tremendously over the years, so the paperwork that they are using to run these organizations, a lot of it is from us, but they don't know that."[30] There can be no better evidence for an organization's relevance and influence than widespread imitation of its daily modus operandi.

RAGOM, located in Minnetonka, Minnesota, is also an influential group in the world of Golden Retriever rescue. Jane Nygaard, one of RAGOM's founders, describes the organization's beginnings with the story of the first dog she rescued:

> All over the area we kept hearing about people that didn't want their dogs. I mean, why wouldn't anybody want a Golden Retriever? So when we got a phone call from one of our friends, I was just getting ready to leave the house, and she said she was looking for a cat with her friend and there was a little Golden Retriever, still actually about nine months old at the shelter, could we take it in? And I was like, "Yeah! We can take it in!" . . . We took it out to the vet we had been going to with our dogs and had her spayed and had her shots all done. And the vet himself phoned us days later and said, "Do you still have the little girl?" And I said, "Yeah, we still have her." The vet then said: "We have a client whose dog died, we just put her to sleep so they didn't want a puppy; could we come and keep your little girl?"[31]

From these humble beginnings, the group grew into one of the largest in the country. RAGOM, too, profited a good deal in its early days from YGRR's model-like existence as well as generosity in terms of sharing its organizational knowledge. Nygaard stated:

> Yankee had a lot of forms and everything where they had gone through all the legal counsel and such. So, when we were starting and getting our 501(c)(3), they said that we could have all their forms and they would assist us so a RAGOM volunteer and I went out to Yankee's group and they showed us their facilities and gave us all the forms and just showed us what they did.[32]

Soon thereafter, RAGOM commenced its impressive growth. Nygaard explained that she was convinced that in good part, this growth was due to technology, as "once the Internet got out there, then it was really a whole different deal, everybody wanted to help."[33] RAGOM continued to grow, gaining a reputation as a group that would help out in any way it could; its rescue work during Hurricane Katrina exemplified the group's attitude of assisting others. Beryl Board, a RAGOM member during Hurricane Katrina, described to us the group's dedication to assisting Golden Retrievers when she told the story of how she came to be involved in rescue during that awful disaster. Board recounted her initial work with RAGOM:

> I've always been very passionate about Golden Retrievers.... I've always been very impressed with the breed.... I realized what a good organization RAGOM was ... from the people that I had met to the processing they had in place, to the website they maintained.... It just seemed like such a better experience than I had had with the sort of corporate type humane society.[34]

She joined the group but it was during Hurricane Katrina that Board's involvement assumed a completely new and different dimension:

> The biggest leap into what became a driving force that sort of pushed me up the executive ladder of RAGOM was when Hurricane Katrina occurred.... So at the time, I had called the president of RAGOM and I said, "Here's what I'm going to do. If I could get Golden Retrievers out of the disaster area, will RAGOM take them? So I was christened RAGOM's representative and given the green light on the spot, with no hesitation whatsoever. They told me, "Of course. You know, whatever needs help, if you can get it here, we'll take it in, we'll do whatever needs to be done to save it and give it another fine chance."[35]

Thus, RAGOM was in the forefront of rescuing hundreds of dogs from the ravages of Katrina and probable death following periods of certain misery.

On a subsequent occasion, RAGOM helped with a puppy mill closure in South Dakota that resulted in eighty Golden Retrievers requiring foster care and rehabilitation before being put up for adoption. "RAGOM was contacted by the U.S. Department of Agriculture for a puppy mill that they were closing down due to animal abuse.... 'We have eighty Golden Retrievers, can you take them?'," Board told us.[36] She continued: "We did not have eighty fosters. We did not have the funds to take in eighty dogs, but these dogs were in horrible condition. Many had died, frozen to death on the property. And we just knew that we could not say no because we just didn't know where they would go if we didn't take them."[37] Board credited

RAGOM's impeccable local reputation for much of its success, arguing that without the organization's standing in the region, finding volunteers and funds during these immensely urgent situations would have been much more difficult if not impossible. Board continued:

> I believe that the reason that RAGOM is successful, at least in our community, is the fact that the leadership, at least when I was in leadership and our current leadership, and probably past leadership too, we resist the temptation to become elitist. [Note again how the term *elitist* assumes a negative connotation.] We're not the best. We don't know the only way. We make mistakes, but our integrity and desire to help these needy creatures is unquestioned. Folks reward such dedication and humility with lots of resources, not least of which are money, time, and effort.[38]

Well beyond the Golden Retriever world, RAGOM has become an important regional player in the rescue community by helping many rescues with their development and day-to-day operations. "I've been contacted by the Rottweiler Rescue, the Pit Bull Rescue, the Minnesota Spay/Neuter project," said Board. "They are all really astounded not only with the volume of volunteers we have but also their dedication and excellent work." Concerning RAGOM's reach well beyond its immediate geographic area and its networking with many rescues far and wide, Board stated:

> We transport dogs between rescues now. We also do intakes for rescues that do not have enough foster homes or cannot afford the medical cost on dogs. We just took in seven dogs from Oklahoma. Sooner Rescue just had a huge influx of Golden Retrievers into their program and they're a relatively small rescue. . . . So we worked out a deal with Bob Bornstein, the president of Sooner, to take in these seven dogs. I think we'll probably be doing this again before winter, maybe sometime in September or October.[39]

RAGOM's dedication to helping other Golden Retriever rescue groups demonstrates the devotion its members feel to the breed but also to dogs in general. The group's ability to assist other rescue groups and to step forward when crises such as Hurricane Katrina and puppy mill closures happen is possible only because of the RAGOM volunteers' desire and commitment to do so. And even though, just like in YGRR's case, RAGOM, too, has successfully transitioned from its early charismatic stages to a much more bureaucratized organization, Nygaard's and Board's engagement and dedication—just like Puglia and Foster's in YGRR's case—created an institutional ethic that has rendered RAGOM into the respected and influential megagroup that it is today.

The Golden Retriever Rescue Club of Charlotte based in Charlotte, North Carolina, is quite exceptional in the Golden Retriever rescue world in that it is—at least to our knowledge—the only rescue that started as a club and then mutated completely into a rescue instead of continuing as a smaller part of the club or splitting from the club entirely. Gene Fitzpatrick, president of the group, stated that while the group commenced purely as a local breed club:

> What happened was members had begun to get calls, and were told that somebody was moving and then they said, "Are you interested in helping their dog?" So people would then adopt, and it got to the point where they just said, "Hey, you know, we need to do something to help these dogs more systematically," and they became a semi-rescue group.[40]

The group continued to increase its involvement in rescue until 1991, when its members decided to transition completely from a club to a rescue. The group briefly had a facility that was owned by a member, but she retired from rescuing dogs, forcing the group to transition yet again, this time from a facility-based rescue organization to a foster-based one.

Gauging from the group's continued success in rescue, the rare transformation from club to rescue does not seem to have hurt its efficacy. Indeed, this organization has flourished as an integral member of Golden Retriever rescue on the national level. Gene Fitzpatrick stated on this topic:

> We are a member of the NRC, which is the National Rescue Committee, of the Golden Retriever Club of America. If you go to their website, they have a list of all the rescue groups in the country, and we are listed among them. We are on all the e-mail distribution lists with all the presidents. There is a distribution list for all the presidents, there is a distribution list for all the rescue adoption coordinators, there is a distribution list for all the intake coordinators. And, of course, I get copies on each one of these as president, so I am well aware of what's going on nationally. We get warnings about various scams, like fake donations, and we get updates about the raiding of puppy mills.[41]

The Golden Retriever Rescue Club of Charlotte represents a fine case that highlights the profoundly symbiotic, if not quite interchangeable, nature of club and rescue. After all the real and purported differences between these two structures have been said and done, the unifying bottom line between the two is quite evident: The very essence of club and rescue lies in the overall betterment of the lives of their beloved Golden Retriever breed.

1986: Sooner Golden Retriever Rescue and Golden Retriever Rescue, Education and Training

In notable contrast to the just-presented organizations, Sooner Golden Retriever Rescue, based in Oklahoma City, Oklahoma, emerged completely unaided by the local breed club. Indeed, the latter actively opposed the creation of the former. The late Bob Bornstein, one of the founding members of the rescue group, was a member of the breed club when he and his wife heard about this new phenomenon known as Golden Retriever rescue. Immediately recognizing its importance and taking an instant liking to this new concept in the human–canine relationship, the couple proceeded to create their own local Golden Retriever rescue group. As mentioned earlier, the Bornsteins availed themselves of YGRR's early expertise and adopted YGRR's organizational structure as the best option for Sooner Golden Retriever Rescue's approach to this novel task. Although several members of this fledgling group were also members of the club, Bornstein states that "the folks in this breed club were actually opposed to the idea of our starting a rescue and have never really gotten on board. To be sure, there are individual members that work with us, but the club as a whole and the club leadership doesn't work with us at all."[42] Bornstein attributed this issue to personality differences between the club and rescue leadership, stating that he would have preferred to cooperate with the club if possible.

Sooner Golden Retriever Rescue has pursued a controversial policy pertaining to puppy mill dogs: The organization buys breeding dogs at puppy mill owner auctions rather than allowing such dogs to be bought by another breeder and then being forced to continue producing litters of puppies. Although this policy supports mill owners by putting money in their pockets, it also saves the dogs in question and prevents future litters emerging from such purchased dogs. Bornstein told us about this rather unconventional, even controversial, rescue method:

I think one of the really nice things about Golden rescue nationally is that there are two viewpoints on this issue, and we have all pretty much agreed to disagree and just move on down the road and respect the other person's viewpoint, because there are rescues out there that will not send any money to our puppy mill auction fund to get the dogs out of the mill; they are just absolutely opposed to that. But they are more than ready to take the dogs that we get and find homes for them, and then we've got other organizations who can't take any dogs because of what their situation is, but are more than willing to send money to us to purchase these dogs from puppy mills, so it's worked out very well. I think the Golden rescue community has handled this very well.[43]

Sooner's ability to work with other groups nationally, in spite of philosophical differences, has had a profound impact on its ability to rescue Goldens, as its open-mindedness toward potentially contentious policies and its catholicity to various approaches increases the number of Golden Retrievers the group has rescued. The controversy of purchasing puppy mill dogs is one that divides the Golden Retriever rescue world, but, as Sooner Golden Retriever Rescue demonstrates, disagreement about this issue does not have to impede cooperation among rescue groups. This conflict mirrors a parallel controversy in the Greyhound rescue world focused on Greyhound racing. But unlike the Greyhound racing controversy, which we will explore in greater detail in Chapter 9, the puppy mill issue never came to consume the Golden Retriever rescue world. Though extant and often tense, philosophical differences on this subject—as well as others, for that matter—never undermined the collaborative effort among Golden Retriever rescues to the detriment of the dogs in need.

Golden Retriever Rescue, Education and Training (GRREAT) from Merrifield, Virginia, shares similarities in its history with YGRR. GRREAT's founder, Mary Jane Shervais, was a member of the Potomac Valley Golden Retriever Club. She worked in a veterinary hospital when she became involved in rescue. After rescuing for a while, Shervais realized that Golden Retriever rescue was a task that required more than one person. She approached her club for help. Three members agreed to furnish it. Together they formed GRREAT, which they developed by "trial and error. We just sort of had to jump into the fire, and realize what we needed."[44] Like YGRR, GRREAT "stayed aligned with the Potomac Valley Golden Retriever Club, but was not part of it and we kept that separation from the very beginning and I think that was probably a very wise way to go and I think that this separation might have been one of the reasons why we succeeded and became as strong of an organization as we did."[45] And as in the case of so many Golden Retriever rescues, in this case, too, YGRR played an important role in GRREAT's early days: "Yankee helped us a lot," said Shervais. She continued: "For example, if there was a dog that Yankee had found out about in our area, Yankee would make us aware of it and we would provide the collection, foster and care of it. . . . I mean, we were not alone in our early efforts and we were certainly aware of other groups, especially like Yankee, and we were more than willing and pleased to work with them and learn from them." GRREAT has grown substantially since its inception in 1986, spawning three spin-off groups for geographical reasons: Southeastern Virginia Golden Retriever Rescue, Education, and Training (SEVA GRREAT) in Yorktown, Virginia; Goldheart Golden Retriever Rescue in Owings Mills, Maryland; and Almost Heaven Golden Retriever Rescue in Delray, West Virginia.

Perhaps the most striking factor of this development was the smoothness with which a successful transition in leadership from the founders of the original group to the second generation of rescuers in these organizations was institutionalized. Shervais explains:

By the time I left Virginia, which was in December of 2000, for probably the last two years of the time I was there, we had people in that organization who didn't even know who I was. And that to me was a great thing because it made clear to me that the organization had moved so far beyond the initial founding thing and had successfully created a leadership of its own that knew what it was doing and did not have any hang-ups about the founders, and there were no conflicts in any of this, which often plagues these organizations. I think that this was a hugely positive situation.[46]

Essentially, GRREAT accomplished what few groups have attained with such success: not only surviving a transition from the stage of its charismatic founder generation to that of its legal-rational successor, but also thriving under the new regime and flourishing in this newly institutionalized and much less personalized authority structure and organizational framework. Few rescues can claim such a successful routinization of charisma as GRREAT had accomplished.

The histories of Sooner Golden Retriever Rescue and GRREAT both provide important insights into the world of Golden Retriever rescue. Sooner was created in spite of opposition from the local Golden Retriever club. It has continued to court controversy through its policy of purchasing puppy mill breeding dogs to prevent their continued dog production. GRREAT has successfully completed its transition from a charismatic leader to a more institutionalized style of leadership, and did so relatively painlessly, as Shervais explained in her interview. The common thread between these two groups is their status as outliers within the world of Golden Retriever rescue; their stories are a bit uncommon and demonstrate the extant and feasible diversity among rescues of a particular breed.

1989–1992: New Frontiers in the Golden Retriever Rescue World—The First Golden Retriever Rescue Boom

The period from 1989 to 1992 witnessed the creation of Golden Retriever rescues in seven states where such organizations had not existed before. In 1989, Companion Golden Retriever Rescue emerged in West Jordan, Utah, with Golden Bond Rescue of Oregon in Portland, Oregon, commencing operations one year later. Golden Retriever Rescue of Mid-Florida in Goldenrod, Florida, Golden Retriever Rescue of Atlanta in Atlanta, Georgia, and Golden Retriever Rescue of Michigan in Auburn Hills, Michigan, began in 1991 and came to represent their respective states in this new organizational construct of the human–canine relationship. Low Country Golden Retriever Rescue, located in Johns Island, South Carolina, was also founded in 1991, thus becoming the second Golden Retriever rescue in that state. In 1992, Golden Retriever Rescue in Nebraska in Boys Town, Nebraska, became the first Golden Retriever rescue in the Cornhusker State; and Golden Retrievers in Need Rescue Service in Cleveland, Ohio, emerged as the first Ohio-based Golden Retriever rescue. The expansion of the Golden Retriever rescue world to include Utah, Oregon, Florida, Georgia, Michigan, Nebraska, and Ohio furnished an important moment in the development of Golden Retriever rescue if merely for doubling the number of states with Golden Retriever rescue groups in the space of four years. This development demonstrated emphatically that breed specific rescue emerged in the span of barely a decade as an integral ingredient and legitimate organizational framework in the larger context of supporting and protecting animals from human neglect and abuse. The rapid proliferation of Golden Retriever rescues proved that the breed specific method of canine rescue enjoyed success and was here to stay.

Few things better bespeak the established presence of any new institution than the imitations and splits that it spawns. After all, imitations and splits offer prima facie evidence that the issue underlying and causing either or both is of sufficient significance to people that it warrants their efforts to imitate or putatively to improve upon the original construct, thus causing disagreements concerning the best way to implement measures that lead to the desired goals. Some want to imitate the tried and true strategies and structures; others want to implement new steps. Passions run high and splits occur. Both imitations and splits are testimony to a cause's great importance to a growing number of people, otherwise neither would occur. Splits, of course, also happen when things expand geographically or when a cause's popularity grows. And sure enough, it was at this juncture that the first split-start rescues emerged reflecting both reasons: the need and desire for geographic expansion as well as the consequences of differences in opinion concerning operational procedures, organizational policies, and overall philosophies.

The first schism in the Golden Retriever rescue world came from GRREAT and produced SEVA GRREAT. The group states on its website that it was "established in the Hampton Roads area in 1990 to serve the Tidewater area from the North Carolina/Virginia state line to the greater Richmond area."[47] GRREAT, the parent group, lists the new group as a partner to the south, indicating that the two groups have continued to collaborate in the rescue of Golden Retrievers in their respective areas, proving that splits, far from impeding cooperative and cordial relationships, can also serve as testimony to the positive proliferation of a new construct. This first split—more of a spawn, really—proved that the new entity of "Golden Retriever rescue" had matured to such a degree that it was to the cause's benefit and the movement's interest for a well-run organization to help generate another in order to maximize logistical efficacy and best serve the needs of a steadily growing clientele of dogs requiring rescue. As with all institutional successes, the growth in supply and demand emerges in congruity and reinforces both in a mutually beneficial manner. Thus, with the increasing presence and visibility of these breed specific rescue organizations, people's growing awareness of such entities led them to see these rescues as new, perhaps even preferable, options to parting with their animals than had been previously the case with shelters and humane societies. The period from 1989 to 1992 was an important era in the Golden Retriever rescue world. Doubling the number of rescues in four short years, these developments constituted what one could describe as the first boom in the Golden Retriever rescue community. At least in the world of Golden Retrievers, rescue had departed from its initial existence on this world's fringes and came to emerge as one of its established institutions.

1993–1994: The Beginning of Another Rescue Powerhouse

Delaware Valley Golden Retriever Rescue (DVGRR) from Reinholds, Pennsylvania, holds a very prominent position in the Golden Retriever rescue world. Robin Adams and Kathy Irvine founded DVGRR in 1993. By 2000, the organization had grown so much in stature that the purchase of its own rescue facility had become warranted. After a mere seven-year existence, DVGRR thus became the second Golden Retriever rescue group in the country to obtain its own facility, a feat that took YGRR eleven years. DVGRR's growth has been nothing short of remarkable, as it now—just like YGRR—employs paid full-time staff who care for the well-being of the dogs. Adams described her beginning with Golden Retriever rescue:

> [While at dog shows] I would put a sign on the back of my chair indicating that I knew of a Golden Retriever who needed a new home. And at this time, I was doing it by referral. People would call me and tell me that they had a dog available for adoption. And then I would just circulate the news and we would find the dog a home. I was then asked to join another group that wanted to get organized and that was in New Jersey and I went with that group and I drew up the necessary paperwork and I formalized the program, but at that point, we had a couple of volunteers who were sort of independent and preferred not to follow the rules and regulations. And they were placing dogs with biting histories.[48]

These policies and other issues informing this group[49] were not to Adams's liking so she departed from it. "And shortly thereafter, a friend, Kathy Irvine, left that group as well, and she contacted me and said that we needed to set up a new rescue group in Pennsylvania and follow the rules and routines that we had successfully established and experienced. So, we started Delaware Valley Golden Retriever Rescue . . . which was incorporated in 1994."[50] This was among the first splits in the Golden Retriever rescue world that can be attributed to a disagreement over policies, rather than the more prosaic case of a split simply due to geographic circumstances.

Adams then explained to us the organization's initial set up, stating, "At that time we had no money, and the first funds that we obtained by successfully placing our first dog at DVGRR we used to pay for the next dog's veterinary care. And slowly, we built a treasury. And we were boarding dogs at a local kennel, because we didn't have a foster network at the time."[51] Upon seeing one of the group's dogs being poorly treated at the local kennel where it was being kept, Adams and her colleagues resolved to purchase their own facility, where such incidents could be prevented. In 2000, the group had a meeting during which the decision was made to commence a fund with the sole desire to purchase a building. Adams explained:

> So in 2000 when we had our reunion, we announced that we were starting a building fund so that we could build our kennel. And we saw this as five to ten years down the road. Immediately, someone handed us a $100 check and the next thing that was handed to me was the real estate brochure for a boarding kennel that was for sale and it happened to be six miles from my house. We never thought that we could afford anything like this, but my husband said "let's drive past and take a look at it," and the minute I saw it I knew this was where we had to be. We offered the gentleman who owned the property $10,000 to take it off the market for ninety days and to give us ninety days to raise the money for the mortgage and down payment. Our deal with him was: if we cannot raise the money, you keep the $10,000; if we can raise the money, the $10,000 goes towards the purchase price. Governor [Ed] Rendell adopted two dogs from us, and we asked him to be our honorary chair, and Mandy, his dog, to be our honorary chair-dog. And the governor agreed immediately and with delight. So we began our capital campaign, and it was very intense. We had phone-a-thons, we took one person from each class adoption from 1994, and the 1995 alumni, and so on and so forth, and we asked them to call every adopter that year and ask them for a pledge. . . . We were about $100,000 short, when Governor Rendell asked Pete Musser, a well-known Philadelphia philanthropist, who had Golden Retrievers all his life . . . his office wall was decorated with pictures of him and a Golden, to help us. So anyway, Pete donated $100,000 and we got our mortgage.[52]

Having a politician of Ed Rendell's national stature—two-term mayor of Philadelphia and two-term governor of Pennsylvania, as well as a key player in the national Democratic Party who, among other important positions, was one of Hillary Clinton's main advisers and aids in her quest for the nomination for president in 2008—surely helps. But it in no way diminishes the immense accomplishment that Adams and her colleagues had achieved with their determination, commitment, and hard work.

In addition to claiming this success story, DVGRR has consistently been committed to helping other groups, as Adams explained: "if we get a group that needs help, we'll send them our policies and procedures manual, our constitution and bylaws, we help them in every possible manner."[53] It is safe to say that over the course of the past two decades, DVGRR has become a leader and model for other Golden Retriever rescues, joining YGRR at the top of the Golden Retriever rescue world. As we will discuss later in this chapter, Adams's personal initiative beyond her own organization led to crucially important innovations in Golden Retriever rescue on the national level that have accorded this movement a quantum leap in terms of its wide-ranging efficacy and success.

1994–1995: The Last of the Pre-Internet Groups and a Fascinating Precursor

The brief period between 1994 and 1995 witnessed the establishment of the last of the pre-Internet groups. The Southern Indiana Golden Retriever Club based in Evansville, Indiana, and the Autumn Valley Golden Retriever Club in Vestal, New York, started their rescue committees in 1994. Both of these did not mutate into independent rescues, choosing to remain in their respective clubs where they performed excellent rescue work, albeit of relatively small programs. In 1995, Golden Endings Golden Retriever Rescue in Columbus, Ohio, and Rag Tag Golden Retriever Rescue in Waterbury Center, Vermont, emerged.

The outlier of the five rescue groups formed in 1994 and 1995, however, was Golden Retrievers in Cyberspace. An online rescue ahead of its time, this group, formed by the late Helen Redlus, was the forerunner of all rescue groups on the Internet today. Utilizing the then rapidly growing but still socially niched Internet, Redlus and the members of this group focused on all things Golden Retriever way beyond rescue but also coordinated rescuing dogs via the website. Redlus's goal was to have her own facility eventually where the dogs could stay, but she died before her dream was realized.

Redlus's group was an inspiration to many others, including Deb Haggerty of Homeward Bound Golden Retriever Rescue & Sanctuary, an organization we will discuss later. Redlus's pioneering personality and relentless engagement gave rise to two game-changing networking legacies in the Golden Retriever rescue world: first, informal but important annual gatherings called Gold Stock and Camp Lucy, bringing together rescuers—and their dogs, of course—from all over the country for a weekend of fun and socializing (which we will revisit briefly toward the end of this chapter when we discuss Golden Retriever rescue's national structures); and second, the rise of the Internet as the all-important new medium and forum for all things Golden Retriever rescue. There can be no doubt that by innovatively and passionately employing a totally new and different technology, Redlus assumed a pioneering role in the world of canine breed specific rescue, which, most likely, has far surpassed her own expectations and imagination. In a matter of a few years, the Internet was to become a real game changer in most aspects of American life, canine breed specific rescue fully included.

1996–1999: The Popularization of the Internet and the Beginning of the Second Golden Retriever Rescue Boom

Prior to 1995, the Internet was used largely for academic purposes, and its commercialization was prohibited by the National Science Foundation Network's (NSFNET's) "Acceptable Use Policy."[54] This changed when NSFNET, the system the Internet had employed, was dismantled in 1995.[55] Rapid commercialization occurred, revolutionizing the ways in which communication and commerce was to happen in the very near future. This revolution in the means and methods of communication inspired Betsy and Jared Saul, a New Jersey couple, to start a website that would help shelters adopt pets. Created in 1996, this website became Petfinder.com, the oldest and largest pet adoption website in existence.[56] Petfinder.com, and the pet adoption websites that followed, revolutionized the ways in which people in the United States have come to adopt pets; instead of relying on individuals coming into shelters to look at pets, a virtual countrywide shelter emerged that greatly expanded the number of potential adopters, thereby substantially increasing the number of adoptions.

The rise and commercialization of the Internet has had a truly profound impact on breed specific rescue as it exists today. Its rapid proliferation fundamentally altered not only virtually every aspect of dog rescue's modes of operation, but it also changed the whole project's very scope, creating new options and horizons that were simply unimaginable before. It would not be too much of an exaggeration to characterize the advent of the Internet as a fundamentally new force that transformed dog rescue's very structure and thus character. The Internet facilitated networking and communications among until then completely disparate organizations, as e-mail listings and Yahoo! groups became areas where rescuers could discuss problems and share solutions. Fundraising was taken to an entirely new level, as growth in exposure led to increased donations, particularly through the advent of PayPal's online donation capabilities, which replaced the mailing of checks with a mouse click. Adoptions increased, as people became more aware of rescues through accessing their websites, looking at pictures of available dogs and reading about their personalities. The Internet has, in short, revolutionized the function of rescue groups, creating a new world in which these organizations could grow and interact. One would be hard put to exaggerate the enormity of the changes the Internet has brought to the world of canine rescue. Indeed, any rescue today is simply unthinkable without the Internet.

During the sixteen-year period between 1980 and 1995, twenty-six Golden Retriever rescue groups emerged in the country; in the four-year span from 1996 to 1999, a total of twenty-one Golden Retriever rescue groups were created.[57] The number of Golden Retriever rescues in existence in the late 1990s practically doubled in one-quarter of the time. These groups had origins of every possible type (club, independent, split), and added seven new states to the twenty already represented in the previous sixteen years. With increased communication and networking possible among groups, it became significantly easier to start a rescue during this period than any previous one. Moreover, the Internet also rendered the acquisition of all requisite expertise much more facile and speedier than ever before, meaning that newly established rescues hit the ground running much more easily and completely than their predecessors from the pre-Internet period. We will devote a good deal more attention to the Internet as an existence-altering phenomenon in Chapter 7, where we will focus on the centrality of social media for rescue.

Golden Retriever Rescue of Central New York (GRRCNY) located in Jamesville, New York, was formed in 1998 as a committee of the local breed club, the Golden Retriever Club of Central New York. The founder of the rescue committee was Carol Allen, who would prove to be a critical—arguably the most important nodal—figure in the world of Golden Retriever rescue across the United States. When describing her rescue's early beginnings, she stated:

> From 1995 until 1998, we were a committee of the Golden Retriever club. That allowed us to get started, and most importantly, it allowed us to be covered by the club's insurance, which early on would have been prohibitive in terms of affording it. We always had a separate treasury and separate membership lists, so we didn't blend ourselves completely into the club—we did maintain those particular distinctions.[58]

In terms of learning the ropes of rescue, Allen could not have picked a better mentor: "I went out and spent a weekend with Robin Adams and learned everything I possibly could."[59] Here we see the importance of mentorship for the creation of successful new organizations and leadership in Golden Retriever rescue. By networking with a more experienced rescue, GRRCNY's founder was able to ensure that her own rescue group could benefit from the knowledge gained by DVGRR, and would later be able to act as a mentor for other Golden Retriever rescue groups herself.

Allen felt that, while being a committee of the club was a beneficial place to start for the rescue, the club did not constitute an appropriate organizational location in which the rescue should stay permanently. "At some point, I do believe it is a benefit to separate a rescue committee from a breed club; if only to obtain the 501(c)(3) charitable status. There is a lot of value in saying to someone that your donation will be income tax deductible. I think every program has seen its contributions shoot up after obtaining 501(c)(3) status."[60] Once the club had served its purpose of providing much-needed incubational capital for the fledgling rescue, the latter's goals and purpose, so Allen believes, are best achieved as a separate organization. Despite the rescue's complete organizational independence affirmed by its 501(c)(3) status, GRRCNY continues to maintain cordial relations with its parent club to the mutual benefit of both. After all, Allen should know best, having remained active in both: "I have been a trophy chair for a long time, helping out in the club's field events and serving as president of the Golden Retriever club for ten years . . . the club members know that I have their interest at heart . . . I work hard for rescue but their club as well."[61] There can be no question that Allen was a critical player in the development of her rescue. Indeed, Allen also assumed a central role in the countrywide world of Golden Retriever rescue by becoming a major figure in the Golden Retriever Club of America National Rescue Committee, a decisive structure in the institutionalization of Golden Retriever rescue in the United States, which we will describe shortly.

Middle Tennessee Golden Retriever Rescue in Franklin, Tennessee, provides an excellent example of a typical organization that commenced as a spinoff from another group during this period. Burt Augst and the rest of the new group's founders were initially members of Tennessee Valley Golden Retriever Rescue (TVGRR), but decided to split from this organization for geographic regions. Augst described this step by saying that a group of volunteers in the Nashville area had become a satellite outfit of the main rescue in Knoxville. But due to logistical reasons, the Nashville area group decided to depart and create an organization of its own.[62] Explaining the new group's initial policies, Augst stated that "it was '98 when our group came together and of course TVGRR was already having foster homes. So yeah, that was in like '97, '98. But from the time we started, as an independent entity in '98, that's the way we did it."[63] This exemplifies how split groups of the time maintained many of the same procedures as those of their parent group. In describing the way his group developed, Augst informed us that "the truth is really that we just kind of evolved. I theoretically am the one who knows the most about how we evolved, even the women say that, but I don't necessarily. We just grew."[64] Middle Tennessee Golden Retriever Rescue has, from its split in 1998 from TVGRR, grown extensively and functions well today.

Rescue a Golden of Arizona (RAGAZ) in Phoenix, Arizona, presents an interesting case. Founded in 1998, RAGAZ was the first Golden Retriever rescue group to establish itself in Arizona. Since that date, three groups split from RAGAZ, two of which still exist. Barbara Elk, president of the rescue group in the period of our research, said that while some of these splits may have occurred under circumstances that were not ideal, the RAGAZ board decided to maintain a professional relationship with all the departed groups, which she affirmed "created calm relations"[65] among all of the Golden Retriever rescues in Arizona. RAGAZ's relationships with other groups demonstrate the increased interorganizational networking that Golden Retriever rescue groups currently enjoy. Thus, for example, Elk informed us that in RAGAZ's effort to rewrite its bylaws she relied on the help of other Arizona-based rescues and had "been in contact with so many people through the national group that have the same type of organization that we do, where the officers are elected as opposed to being appointed, and I've made use of that, I've called them, and they've sent me copies of their bylaws."[66] Rather than reinventing the wheel, these groups have been able to rely on one another for all kinds of help and advice, with RAGAZ, for example, saving lots of time, labor, and money by relying on the adoption and adaptation of already extant bylaws in creating new ones for its own purposes.

The Internet's profound effect on a small rescue group's creation and its proper continued function is well represented by With a Golden Spirit (WAGS) from Irwin, Pennsylvania. This organization was founded in 1998, after Mike and Sharon Davin took to the Internet in an effort to help their son in California find his lost Golden Retriever (whom he later located safely). While desperately seeking this lost animal, the couple discovered the phenomenon of Golden Retriever rescue and decided to become involved by creating their own group. The remarkable story of one of their dogs, Pappy, demonstrates how the Internet can link rescues to people who, pre-Internet, would likely never have connected. The Davins explained to us that Pappy was a fifteen-year-old dog in their rescue program in Pennsylvania. Individuals and rescues from as far away as British Columbia had seen Pappy's profile on the WAGS website and contacted them with the impression that Pappy could have previously belonged to them.[67] Although this was not the case, the frequency with which rescue organizations strewn all over the North American continent contacted the Davins demonstrates the Internet's power. Pappy died at the age of seventeen in the care of the Davins. The affection they provided Pappy in his last years in the rescue are a testament to the Davins's pet people notion of rescue, as they worked to make Pappy as comfortable as possible during his final years.[68] WAGS, which consists of the Davins and a few other board members, garnered international attention through the use of the Internet, which simply would not have happened in the pre-Internet era.

Peppertree Rescue, formed in 1999 in Albany, New York, provides a special case because even though the organization primarily rescues Golden Retrievers, it can and does rescue other breeds as well. The president of Peppertree Rescue, Kevin Wilcox, stated that "we handle all kinds of breeds. The way we choose the breeds we help depends on our volunteers. A lot of people are attracted to our group who do different types of dog rescue, or have done so in the past, and they bring that expertise with them."[69] Although some Golden Retriever rescue groups may occasionally handle dogs that can be mistaken for Golden Retrievers, such as Great Pyrenees, Labrador Retrievers, and Flat-Coated Retrievers, Peppertree Rescue is unique in that, though specializing in the rescue of Golden Retrievers, it also has rescued American Pit Bull Terriers and Shih Tzus among dogs belonging to many other breeds. This group's more liberal and inclusive intake policy makes Peppertree unusual in the Golden Retriever rescue world.

Due to the nature of its multibreed involvement, Peppertree furnishes a valuable source for the comparative efficacy of different breed rescues in the United States. By necessity, Peppertree has established regular contacts with many organizations representing different breed rescues. When asked about his assessment of the effectiveness of different breed rescues, Wilcox responded:

> It seems that Golden Retriever rescues are better organized nationally than rescues of other breeds. I would also guess that since Goldens have been a popular breed for so long, and there are so many people who are Golden advocates, it seems to me that people who love Goldens are the breed's staunch advocates and have succeeded in translating their passion into organizational effectiveness.

Of course, every breed has its devoted following, every breed has its passionate advocates, but I think because of the sheer number of Goldens and their immense popularity, Golden rescues perhaps started earlier than others. Whatever the case may be, I think that Golden rescues have, at least for the time being, ended up as better rescues than those of other breeds.[70]

Peppertree Rescue's existence as a different kind of Golden Retriever rescue group gives it a unique and valuable perspective on the larger world of canine breed rescue.

To fill a void in rescue group coverage, Cape Fear Golden Retriever Rescue was formed in 1999 in Wilmington, North Carolina. Priscilla Skare, one of the group's founders, was originally interested in joining another rescue in North Carolina, but discovered that this group was not as focused on her area as she wanted it to be. Deciding to take matters into her own hands, she and another local woman founded Cape Fear Golden Retriever Rescue, modeling much of their organization on Neuse River Golden Retriever Rescue, which is located in Raleigh, North Carolina. Skare described the intergroup dynamics by saying, "We help each other a lot more now, especially us and Neuse River."[71] She stated that, although Cape Fear Golden Retriever Rescue was in an area that used to be Neuse River territory, the groups do not compete with each other, choosing to collaborate instead. The relationship between these two groups demonstrates that the prevailing—though certainly not exclusively extant—attitude among Golden Retriever rescues is one of cooperation and collaboration, rather than competition.

2000–2006: Rescue in the New Millennium

Rescue in the new millennium benefited in many of its activities from further technological innovations. This period witnessed the birth of social media: MySpace was founded in 2003, Facebook in 2004, and Twitter in 2006. We will devote a much more detailed assessment of these media's effect on rescue in Chapter 7. For introductory purposes here, the popularization of these new forms of communication was highly advantageous to rescue groups, who found them useful for volunteer recruitment, fundraising, event planning, and coordination of daily activities, all in one place, and all for free. The advent of social media has had a profound impact on the function and behavior of groups today. These new fora of mass communication gave groups another outlet to gain exposure, further simplifying the rescue group formation process; during this period, forty-one Golden Retriever rescue groups commenced, indicating that the explosion of the Internet was beneficial to the new rescue groups that emerged during this period.

Golden Retriever Rescue of Wisconsin (GRROW) began in Port Washington, Wisconsin, in 2000 when it split from the aforementioned Minnesota-based RAGOM to focus solely on Wisconsin. The split was amicable, with RAGOM helping GRROW establish itself in the area. GRROW became successful and began to cover other regions, such as northern Illinois, which placed a strain on the organization. Debbie Lukasik, president of the group, explained:

> GRROW at one point used to cover Illinois as well. GRROW helped As Good as Gold start up, just like RAGOM helped GRROW. There was a need for northern Illinois to have its own rescue, but we used to cover that area. We used to do between two and three hundred dogs a year in GRROW which covered that area. We helped them get set up and gave them that entire area with blessings and then some.[72]

The advantages that GRROW and As Good as Gold Golden Retriever Rescue based in Woodridge, Illinois, enjoyed by being the products of geographic splits are substantial: both organizations shared the good experience of older groups' helping them start with policies and procedures, which they in turn borrowed and tailored to their own needs; and both developed relationships with these older groups that have ensured both will be assisted with any problems they may face in the future.

Homeward Bound Golden Retriever Rescue and Sanctuary, located in Elverta, California, is currently the largest of the three Golden Retriever rescues that own their own shelters (the others being Yankee Golden Retriever Rescue and Delaware Valley Golden Retriever Rescue). It is also the most recent of these and quite possibly the largest Golden Retriever rescue in the country. Indeed, Homeward Bound might very well be among the largest rescues of any breed. Its founders, Mike and Jody Jones, decided to become involved in Golden Retriever rescue while their Golden Retriever was recovering from being hit by a car. They initially joined NORCAL but left due to differences of opinion with the leadership of that rescue organization. They decided to found Homeward Bound in 2000. Initially, the couple started small; Jody Jones says that "we would have volunteers come on Saturday, and we built a bathtub out of a horse trough, and we would roll it out of the garage on wheels into the driveway, and volunteers would help bathe the dogs we were fostering."[73] Limits placed on the number of dogs they could have in their home forced Mike and Jody to seek an alternative location for their rescue. Jones describes the situation: "I needed to move, and I needed to be someplace where there was room for us to have some dogs, so that I could build a kennel. . . . And then one night, my girlfriend, who had adopted several Goldens, called me to say, 'You know, my mom's got this place that's way out in Elverta. There's eight acres.'"[74] This was the beginning of Homeward Bound's sanctuary at its facility in Elverta not far from Sacramento, California's capital. Deb Haggerty, a volunteer for the group, had worked with Helen Redlus of Golden Retrievers in Cyberspace before. Haggerty described her involvement in the initial stages of Homeward Bound: "A number of us who had worked with Helen from the very beginning realized that what Jody and Mike had created here was exactly what Helen was trying to do."[75] Homeward Bound has since expanded its purview of adoptions from the Sacramento and Bay Area region of California to include pretty much the entire state, having area coordinators as far away as Redding, Fresno, and Bakersfield.

Love a Golden Rescue from St. Louis, Missouri, emerged in 2001. The organization was founded by members of a group based in Kansas City who decided to split from it to form an organization that could cover rural Missouri and Illinois. President and founding member of the new group Jan Knoche informed us that she and her colleagues borrowed their bylaws from the original group they had left.[76] In the meantime, Love a Golden Rescue became so successful that it regularly engages in networking with other rescue groups, St. Louis-based Dirk's Fund included, and helps them with all aspects of rescue. Knoche discussed the group's networking with local rescues of other breeds through the St. Louis Pet Lovers Coalition, and with other Golden Retriever rescues through the GRCA-NRC, saying, "there's respect among groups in this area, which I feel is good, and because of GRCA and NRC, its rescue division, Golden rescue here and in general, I think, is very well organized and has a very good support base because of GRCA and Carol [Allen],"[77] which not only helps Goldens but rescues of other breeds as well.

Adopt a Golden Atlanta (Atlanta, Georgia) furnishes a rare case in that it emanated from a split that was neither personal nor geographic. Instead, the reason for the organizational departure hailed from some members' expressing a desire to emphasize rescuing owner turn-ins rather than shelter dogs. Lauren Genkinger, one of the founders of Adopt a Golden Atlanta, had joined the original Golden Retriever Rescue of Atlanta (GRRA) after turning in her own dog, at which point she noticed that GRRA was focused primarily on rescuing Golden Retrievers from shelters, rather than owner turn-ins. Genkinger, along with several other GRRA members, decided to form their own rescue with a focus on owner turn-ins, with the belief that:

> If we took dogs from owners who needed to turn in their dogs, we would have the dogs' behavior history, we would have their vet history, unlike what you get at shelters. And if we had all that, then we thought that we could probably do a quicker turn around on adoptions, because families with young children would shy away from shelter rescues because they don't know the dog's history.[78]

The group has grown dramatically, working well with GRRA and Golden Retriever rescues in nearby states. Like other Golden Retriever rescues, Adopt a Golden Atlanta has actually helped create a rescue group for a breed other than Golden Retrievers. Genkinger explained that "a few years ago we had a huge need in this area to help Great Pyrenees, because farms in the state's north were being shut down on account of a severe drought that hit Georgia then. So we started helping that breed, and last year we were successful in finding people to start the Great Pyrenees Rescue of Atlanta."[79] The group's willingness to help establish a rescue for a breed that is not its own is a fact that shows the health of the group, as this indicates that it enjoyed sufficient security on all important dimensions to expend valuable resources of money and human labor on organizing the rescue of another breed.

Great Lakes Golden Retriever Rescue (GLGRR) of Grand Rapids, Michigan, was formed in 2003 as a result of a split from the Golden Retriever Rescue of Michigan (GRROM) due to differences of opinion over policy choices. Allie Medendorp, one of the founders of GLGRR, describes the group's beginnings:

> We had absolutely nothing. We all chipped in together to pay the registration fee, and up until a year and a half ago, maybe almost two years now, we were still barely scraping by . . . and it was tough, because we had to make a lot of decisions where we couldn't take heartworm-positive dogs or dogs that required a lot of surgeries because we just didn't have the funds.[80]

Medendorp paints a picture of a group that initially struggled but has finally begun to feel measures of stability and success. The initial struggles

GLGRR overcame likely parallel those of other groups splitting from a parent group during this period. Although by the early to mid-2000s the founding members had come to attain the necessary knowledge to form a rescue, acquiring the requisite resources to implement their knowledge provided a challenge that was difficult to surmount at the outset.

Shore Hearts Golden Retriever Rescue from Lanoka Harbor, New Jersey, is distinct from other groups because of the nature of its partnership with Golden Recovery Retrieving Retrievers Rescue Midwest (GRRRRM), which is situated in Blue Springs, Missouri. Shore Hearts founder Lana Winters initially worked with GRRRRM as a foster, even though the rescue organization was located in Missouri and she lived in New Jersey. Winters expanded her involvement to create a satellite group in New Jersey, where she found like-minded rescuers who then formed Shore Hearts in 2003. What makes the relationship between these two groups special is the fact that GRRRRM is the only parent organization to have created a spinoff group in a state that was not contiguous to its own. This demonstrates technology's growing influence on rescue, as it shows that Winters, at least until she formed her own group, was able to be a valuable part of an organization that only shared actual physical links between its two locations when transporting dogs from one place to the other. Even with Winters's creating her own independent organization, the two groups maintain very close ties.

Formed in 2003 in Houston, Texas, Golden Retriever Rescue of Houston emerged from a split from Golden Beginnings Golden Retriever Rescue, which, too, was a Houston-based rescue group. The idea behind forming a new group in the area was solely driven by the constantly growing volume of Golden Retrievers needing rescue in the Houston metropolitan area.[81] Tom Whitson, president of the Golden Retriever Rescue of Houston, describes the group's current rescue situation:

> We have had a synergistic relationship with Gold Ribbon Retriever Rescue, which is the Golden Retriever rescue of Austin. For some reason, the demographics or markets are such that most families that want to adopt an older dog are in Austin, whereas in Houston, we have a lot of interest in dogs of all ages, especially young dogs, so we have often taken their [Gold Ribbon's] puppies or young dogs.[82]

In the case of these two rescues, they recognized that the demographics of their respective cities are looking for a particular age range for Golden Retrievers, making the two organizations enter into a partnership thus ensuring that they are each able to place their respective Golden Retrievers in suitable homes. This partnership appears to be quite exceptional in the Golden Retriever rescue world because its sole driving force seems to be a productive division of labor centered on the respective rescue dogs' age and their being matched with adopters of commensurate ages, thus ensuring that the demographic harmony of humans and canines coincide thereby enhancing the chances for a more harmonious relationship between the two.

Wisconsin Adopt a Golden Retriever (WAAGR) from Brookfield, Wisconsin, was formed in 2004 and showcases a broad approach to rescue held by many of its sister organizations across the nation. The group formed to help rescue Golden Retrievers in its area, while having its members remain committed to assisting other rescues as well. Craig Cwiklowski, the president of the group, explains how the philosophy of helping other rescues has become a staple of the rescue world: "I just joined them [the NRC] this year, and I started getting on the e-mail list and getting the correspondence from these e-mails myself, and I'm opening myself up to taking that next step of getting involved on the national level as well as helping out on the local level as best I can. Folks are expanding their work and are spreading their experience."[83] The tenor in Cwiklowski's statement is obvious: By the mid-2000s—meaning twenty years after the very beginnings of the Golden Retriever rescue world and ten years after its real proliferation—this has become a highly interconnected network on a national level in which the organizational horizons of formerly almost exclusively local groups have changed. The statement also bespeaks a level of solid confidence in the overall achievements and successful institution building of this young movement in the larger context of human–animal relations. We will now turn to a short presentation of Golden Retriever rescue's organizations on the national level, which, we are convinced, have been absolutely indispensable in the successful transformation of this formerly marginal phenomenon into its current stature in the overall human–animal interaction of the contemporary United States.

Important Developments on the National Level

In 2002, a truly decisive player emerged in the Golden Retriever rescue world: the Golden Retriever Club of America–National Rescue Committee (GRCA-NRC). The Committee to Assist Rescue, a precursor to the GRCA-NRC, had started in the 1990s. It successfully implemented several far-reaching ideas, none perhaps more notable than the national survey distributed annually to all Golden Retriever rescues registered by the club. Robin Adams, founder of DVGRR, was involved in the creation and administration of this survey and described to us how it came to be. Initially, she met with lots of skepticism and doubt by club members pertaining to the very need for and idea of rescue. Although Adams had repeatedly informed GRCA members about the need for as well as institutional advances in rescue, she was often met with disbelief and resistance. In an effort to educate the members and show them the true nature of the problem, Adams told us that she:

> started a national survey, and with my own funds, I wrote to every rescue group in the country, and asked them to give me the statistics of the number of dogs they adopted, what they were spending on veterinary fees, how many dogs they euthanized, among other things. I broke it down into age categories of the dogs, from zero to one year, one year to four years, all the way up to ten and over and then I started to present these figures to the Golden Retriever Club of America.[84]

In other words, in order to confront the GRCA's establishment with the seriousness of rescue needs facing the very breed that they all so loved, Adams became a bona fide social scientist who developed compelling collective explanatory categories such as age of dogs, numbers adopted, and veterinary fees to highlight the existence of a real need to solve the concrete problem of a growing number of indigent Golden Retrievers across the nation. By clearly demonstrating to the GRCA that Golden Retrievers were homeless in large numbers across the country, Adams accomplished several important tasks simultaneously, none more prominent than opening lines of communication with rescue groups across the country and thereby paving the way for effective intergroup cooperation that would become the hallmark of contemporary Golden Retriever rescue. Additionally, and of equal importance for the long-range success of Golden Retriever rescue, Adams's efforts confronted the skepticism of the GRCA establishment and—as a testament of ultimate triumph—converted the initial doubts and resistance into a genuine dedication to alleviate the real problem of homeless Golden Retrievers in the United States.

Adams's systematic and steady empirical study of the plight of Golden Retrievers led to more than a mere attitudinal change within the GRCA leadership and membership. There also ensued an important institutional change that was to have far-reaching beneficial effects on the overall project of helping homeless Golden Retrievers via rescue in the United States The concrete result was, as Adams, explained to us, that the GRCA:

developed the Golden Retriever Foundation, which now funds through grants, moneys to Golden Retriever rescue groups all across the country to fund their infrastructure. . . . So a kind of GRCA arm was formed called the Committee to Assist Rescue and I was one of the founding members of this new thing. . . . One year we met in Denver, Colorado, to prepare a mission statement, to outline our goals as to what we would do for the rescue community, and how we would help it in going from a very loosely organized group to an organized functional group that could really do something for Golden Retrievers who were being displaced.[85]

The first organization of its kind, the GRCA's Committee to Assist Rescue was tasked with aiding Golden Retriever rescues in their quest to help homeless Golden Retrievers. Rather than establishing a GRCA national rescue group that was to somehow be involved with actual rescue—or its active coordination—on a national level, the GRCA decided instead to create an organization that was to become kind of an effective clearinghouse, a helpful traffic cop, a service organization on the national level facilitating Golden Retriever rescue and coordination among groups on the local level. Although this organization would ultimately be replaced by the NRC, the Committee to Assist Rescue provided an important nodal point in the nascent phase of the nationally interconnected Golden Retriever rescue world.

Over the ensuing years, the GRCA became increasingly involved in Golden Retriever rescue on many levels. Providing advice and support became a focal point for the GRCA, which developed into a genuinely helpful institution to any Golden Retriever rescue in the country that chose to avail itself of the GRCA's services and assistance. Adams stated:

I also wrote a manual called "How to Start and Manage a Rescue Organization," which was donated to the Golden Retriever Club of America. . . . So from nothing the Golden Retriever Club of America has really gotten behind the rescue groups after it realized that there is a real problem with our breed because of its popularity, and how disposable many of these poor dogs had become.[86]

The GRCA's decision to educate rescue groups and foster their growth has had a massive impact on the trajectory of the Golden Retriever rescue world. Many of our interviewees told us repeatedly that the GRCA's information and coordination proved vital in guiding their efforts during their organizations' early months and years. They mentioned to us how the GRCA's guidelines and its leadership's obvious willingness to assist as well as its cumulative expertise helped their groups avoid the pitfalls that often beset the formation of any such endeavors and how the GRCA's assistance contributed to the groups' initial survival and subsequent growth.

A fine case in point is the Golden Retriever Foundation (GRF). Created by the GRCA as an independent organization, the foundation has had a profound effect on the world of Golden Retriever rescue. It dispenses funds to Golden Retriever rescues to help them cover their expenses, most notably veterinary bills. As with any solid modern institution, the foundation has clearly delineated requirements and application processes that rescue groups must fulfill to receive funds for their purposes. Compliance with these requirements has also contributed to a certain shaping of the rescues' culture as modern organizations. Adams explained:

> We laid the groundwork of what we wanted to see in our rescue groups. In order to get a grant from the Golden Retriever Foundation, you need to be a nonprofit, registered 501(c)(3); you need to send them your financials of the year that closed; you need to participate in the annual survey; and you need to have a set of policies and procedures and constitution and bylaws. They placed these four parameters on the groups: if you want funding, you need to have these structures.[87]

The four requirements the GRF places on rescues create a uniform standard of behavior for Golden Retriever rescue groups that ultimately benefits their overall mission of saving as many homeless Golden Retrievers as possible. As we will explain in subsequent chapters, other breeds that lack an organization comparable to the GRF do not have the same financial incentives to engage in these uniform and unifying measures that create a certain common culture and organizational framework, which gives Golden Retriever rescues an edge in their overall mission when compared to comparable groups devoted to the rescue of other breeds.

The Club's Committee to Assist Rescue was eventually succeeded by the NRC. Carol Allen described the current state of the NRC:

> What they eventually did was to form the Golden Retriever Foundation, to be very independent, to make decisions of a financial nature without influence, without being concerned about local politics . . . and then they formed the National Rescue Committee to be able to network and talk with the programs without having to worry about revealing their shortcomings and worrying whether it would affect the next grant they apply for.[88]

Allen also affirmed how Robin Adams's original survey has become routinized by the NRC as an annual exercise in getting crucial information on the state of Golden Retriever rescues across the land:

> Each year we ask each program to answer several pages of questions, and we standardized the questions so that they are the same questions year after year, to allow the program to have an ongoing collection of data on such things as the number of dogs that have been spayed or neutered, the particular problems that arose that year. . . . We have such things as total finances, total vet bills . . . number of volunteers.[89]

Talk about successful routinized institutionalization! It is amply evident how high the degree of organizational sophistication attained by the institutions constituting Golden Retriever rescue in the United States has become barely three decades after its beginning.

By establishing separate funding and assistance organizations, the creators of these innovative new mechanisms allowed groups to avail themselves of their respective benefits without worries that applying for help from one might have adverse effects with the other. In addition to providing important assistance to Golden Retriever rescue groups by giving them information packets regarding all kinds of pertinent materials, including copies of policies and procedures, the NRC also offers two representatives in each area whose job is to facilitate any assistance that the national organization might possess that could prove helpful to rescues on the regional and local levels. Moreover, these NRC-led initiatives furnish an important vertical link between the grassroots level of Golden Retriever rescue and the national headquarters. By doing so, these measures have quite possibly had an even greater influence on the horizontal level by providing important conduits among Golden Retriever rescue groups themselves. Many of these have come to know and help one another via the institutions provided by the national organization, which has undoubtedly led to a greater number of dogs being helped in a more efficient and less costly manner.

Carol Allen has played a central role in the development of the NRC's outreach and institutional innovations. As its president, she heads the NRC's e-mail list for rescue group presidents and is known by name to most leaders of the Golden Retriever rescue groups in the country. Without her involvement in the NRC, it is likely that this institution would not enjoy the level of success in efficacy and legitimacy in the national community of Golden Retriever rescue that it does today. In researching this topic, we heard nothing but substantial—and completely unsolicited—praise for

Carol Allen on the part of many of our interviewees. Jody Jones of Homeward Bound said: "I think Carol Allen has done a superb job with the NRC to make breeders more aware of rescue, to make them more responsive to it and respectful of it . . . and when the Foundation was running a capital campaign, there was a very good response."[90] Allen's national networking and being crucially nodal player in the world of Golden Retriever rescue were also evident in her role right after Hurricane Katrina. Allen's engagement on the heels of that catastrophe left an institutional legacy that continues to this day. Jones talked about this event:

> In the wake of Hurricane Katrina, Carol was orchestrating 24/7, getting all the rescues contacted and talking to shelters in Alabama, Mississippi, and Louisiana and getting people together to organize transports to get the dogs out of there. . . . Her work has set up a network which now is functioning when there is a puppy mill closure which is happening more and more as the recession hits the puppy millers. Carol was simply tremendous. Her knowledge and commitment have really helped Golden rescue reach a whole new level.[91]

It is evident, of course, that the pre-Katrina existence of a well-ensconced countrywide Golden Retriever rescue structure that featured all these vertical and horizontal interorganizational networks helped Golden Retriever rescue to respond to this terrible disaster in such an effective and admirable manner. With the forethought, commitment, and hard work of individuals like Allen, Golden Retriever rescues had the mechanisms in place to be able to coordinate their efforts in the face of such an unexpected natural calamity. These institutional innovations have also proven beneficial in the battle against other adversities, most notably the presence of puppy mills.

Needless to say, not everybody was enthusiastic about the structures that Allen, Adams, and their colleagues established at the core of the Golden Retriever rescue world in the United States. We did hear some distanced, if not necessarily disappointed, voices such as that of Mike Davin:

> I do not want to say anything about the Golden Retriever Foundation, but it's large and we are involved with the Northeast chapter. And when I say involved, I mean we receive a questionnaire once a year from them but other than that, there is very little, if any, interaction. They never contact us, they know about us, I am quite sure of that, and from what I've been told, there's money available, but we've never asked for any help whatsoever.[92]

Involvement with organizations like the GRCA-NRC and the GRF is a choice with costs and benefits for rescue groups. Although interactions with such large organizations can prove beneficial to groups, the time needed to communicate with them may become too high an investment for smaller groups, forcing them to carefully consider whether the potential benefits outweigh the costs.

As already mentioned earlier, we wanted to refer to two additional items in the context of our brief discussion of various translocal developments in the establishment of all-important networks in the Golden Retriever rescue world: Gold Stock and Camp Lucy. Deb Haggerty, who spoke about both of these items prominently in our interview with her, referred to them in her mention of Helen Redlus with whom she worked. Haggerty provided details about these two national networking channels:

> Gold Stock started in 1999 and it was the idea that a number of people had to organize small get-togethers for Goldens. Gail Lustic owned a children's camp in Pennsylvania at the time and invited some folks to come there that first year and about fifty people showed up. . . . When Gold Stock was started, rescues were all very individual, and they didn't know other rescues, and they didn't work with other rescues. . . . The Gold Stock event still exists [in August 2009 when we interviewed Deb Haggerty]. . . . The Gold Stock fund, which was created as part of a 501(c)(3) coming out of the event, also attends the Gold Stock get-togethers. And we also have an event called Camp Lucy, which is an educational approach; it's a weekend of activities to promote the human–canine bond. This will be the second year of Camp Lucy, and it is on the weekend after the Gold Stock event which is on Labor Day, so Camp Lucy will happen on September 12th this year.[93]

Thus, in addition to the various formal and institutional networking opportunities provided by the national Golden Retriever establishment in the form of the club and its structures committed to rescue, there also exist these grassroots kind of networks like Gold Stock and Camp Lucy that enliven the interaction of Golden Retriever rescues all across the country.

Conclusion

The Golden Retriever rescue world continues to grow. Eleven new organizations emerged between 2007 and 2010, with nine more appearing by the summer of 2013. All signs are that this world is on solid footing and can proudly claim to have been resoundingly successful in accomplishing its sole mission: helping thousands upon thousands of dogs get a life of love, security, and dignity. Still, in order to survive long term, rescue groups require the routinization of charisma, or to put it differently, the transition from personalistic organizations run by charismatic leaders to institutionalized groups controlled by elected or appointed officials. Most, if not all groups, start as personalistic organizations. These groups tend to have a charismatic leader or group of leaders who oversee all aspects of the rescue group and successfully lead the group to new growth. Their success comes at a price, however, as they invest more of their personal time into the day-to-day activities of caring for the dogs than most individuals are able or willing to offer. As is the case with all innovators and first-generation leaders, the founding generation worries that it might have a hard time finding individuals with the same level of commitment that the founders had, and they rightly believe continues to be necessary for these organizations based purely on devotion and compassion to survive and remain effective in their mission of rescuing needy dogs. In order to ensure long-term survival, these groups must be able to survive the retirement of their founders. This requires the codification of rules, rather than having decisions being made at the discretion of the charismatic leader. It becomes necessary to pass the torch of leadership from the charisma of the founding generation of leaders to the organizational skill of the second generation's members who, while not necessarily charismatic in the Weberian sense, need to possess definitive leadership and delegation skills to run the group as a modern organization governed by legal-rational criteria. To date, many groups have successfully transitioned to institutionalized organizations, among them Yankee Golden Retriever Rescue and GRREAT. But such a transition has certainly not occurred ubiquitously. If groups that have yet to take this step intend to survive beyond their founders' participation, they must depart successfully from their initial charismatic and personalistic stage to a more legal-rational, bureaucratized, and depersonalized one. This is never easy precisely because charismatic people who commenced this whole endeavor achieved so much solely by virtue of their commitment, passion, skills, and also their timing in that they were the first, the founders. As such, they create an institutional aura that only enhances their charisma and makes their succession and routinization difficult for all: their successors, the organization, and—last but not least—themselves.

There can be no doubt that even if not unique in the breed specific canine rescue world, Golden Retriever rescue furnishes one of its most successful representatives. Over the past three decades, Golden Retriever rescue created a dense nationwide network of a decentralized system, with each rescue embodying a fully sovereign entity, but with national breed club support readily available if needed. The cooperative attitude of Golden Retriever rescue groups, which characteristically go out of their way to help others, including organizations rescuing different canine breeds, is exemplary of the rescue world. Particular groups like YGRR, RAGOM, DVGRR, Homeward Bound, and individuals like Joan Puglia,[94] Jane Nygaard, Robin Adams, Jody Jones, and Carol Allen—just to mention a few—have had a profound influence in shaping the very nature and existence of the Golden Retriever rescue world, providing models for other groups to aspire to and helping them every step of the way to reach their goals. Perhaps the single most distinct aspect of Golden Retriever rescue is its exceptional networking; for reasons analyzed later in this book, other breed rescues do not appear to network and communicate with one another the way Golden Retriever rescues do. This is particularly evident when Golden Retriever rescues are compared with the history of Labrador Retriever rescues; the two breeds share similar physical and behavioral characteristics, with the Labradors being the more popular of the two breeds, yet the Golden Retriever rescues appear to have greater longevity and networking capabilities than their Labrador Retriever counterparts, a phenomenon that will be explored in Chapter 8.

The next chapter will turn our attention to the pronounced regional differences in which dog rescues need to operate. The variations in these environments—from culture to climate—shape the surroundings, which in turn influence virtually every aspect of these rescues' being, from their financial resources to their adoption methods, from the medical services they need to provide their dogs to their ultimate goal: the placement of dogs in loving forever homes.

Notes

1. Jeannette Poling. Interviewed by Andrei Markovits. Telephone Interview. June 22, 2009.

2. Ibid.

3. Ibid.

4. Ibid.

5. Ibid.

6. Ibid.

7. Ibid.

8. Ibid.

9. Ibid.

10. Bob Tillay. Interviewed by Andrei Markovits. Telephone Interview. August 18, 2010.

11. Ibid.

12. Ibid.

13. Ibid.

14. Ibid.

15. Ibid.

16. Mary Williams, "News." Midlands Golden Retriever Rescue. n.d. http://midlandsgoldenrescue.org/AboutUs.html (accessed on September 26, 2011).

17. Gateway Golden Retriever Rescue. "About Us." n.d. http://www.goldenrescue stlouis.org/AboutUs.asp (accessed on September 26, 2011).

18. Phil Fisher. Interviewed by Andrei Markovits. Telephone Interview. July 30, 2009.

19. Ibid.

20. Bob Bornstein. Interviewed by Andrei Markovits. Telephone Interview. August 12, 2010.

21. Barb Demetrick. Interviewed by Andrei Markovits. Telephone Interview. June 23, 2009.

22. Joan Puglia. Interviewed by Andrei Markovits. Telephone Interview. June 30, 2009.

23. Ibid.

24. Ibid.

25. Ibid.

26. Ibid.

27. Joy Viola. Interviewed by Andrei Markovits. Telephone Interview. July 16, 2009.

28. Annie Kassler. Interviewed by Andrei Markovits. Telephone Interview. July 9, 2009.

29. Puglia interview.

30. Ibid.

31. Jane Nygaard. Interviewed by Andrei Markovits. Telephone Interview. August 6, 2009.

32. Ibid.

33. Ibid.

34. Beryl Board. Interviewed by Andrei Markovits. Telephone Interview. July 29, 2009.

35. Ibid.

36. Ibid.

37. Ibid.

38. Ibid.

39. Ibid.

40. Gene Fitzpatrick. Interviewed by Andrei Markovits. Telephone Interview. August 17, 2010.

41. Ibid.

42. Bornstein interview.

43. Ibid.

44. Mary Jane Shervais. Interviewed by Andrei Markovits. Telephone Interview. August 17, 2009.

45. Ibid.

46. Ibid.

47. Southeastern Virginia Golden Retriever Rescue, Education, and Training (SEVA GRREAT), "FAQ." n.d. http://www.sevagrreat.org/index.php?option=com _content&view=article&id=2&Itemid=3 (accessed on September 26, 2011).

48. Robin Adams. Interviewed by Andrei Markovits. Telephone Interview. July 7, 2009.

49. Although Adams mentioned this group's name in our interview, we felt it best not to reveal this information because we believe that publishing the group's name adds nothing to an understanding of Adams's important point.

50. Adams interview.

51. Ibid.

52. Ibid.

53. Ibid.

54. Janet Abbate, "Government, Business, and the Making of the Internet." *Business History Review* 75, no. 1 (April 1, 2001): pp. 147–176.

55. Ibid.

56. Petfinder. "The Petfinder Story." Last modified 2012. http://www.petfinder .com/birthday-petfinder-story/ (accessed on June 15, 2013).

57. 1996: Golden Retriever Rescue of the Rockies (Arvada, Colorado), Golden Retriever Rescue and Adoption of Needy Dogs (GRRAND, Louisville, Kentucky), Golden Retriever Rescue of North Texas (Dallas, Texas). 1997: Golden Retriever Rescue and Community Education (GRRACE, Plainfield, Indiana), Triad Golden Retriever Rescue (Greensboro, North Carolina), Golden Re-Triever Rescue Inc.– New Jersey (Oak Ridge, New Jersey), Tennessee Valley Golden Retriever Rescue (Knoxville, Tennessee), Golden Moments Golden Retriever Rescue (Casper, Wyoming), Long Island Golden Retriever Rescue (Plainview, New York). 1998: Neuse River Golden Retriever Rescue (Raleigh, North Carolina), Golden Retriever Rescue of Central New York (GRRCNY, Jamesville, New York), Heartland Golden Retriever Rescue (Knoxville, Tennessee), Middle Tennessee Golden Retriever Rescue (Franklin, Tennessee), Gold Ribbon Golden Retriever Rescue (Austin, Texas), Rescue a Golden of Arizona (Phoenix, Arizona), Retrievers and Friends of Southern California (Temecula, California), Golden Retriever Rescue of South Florida (Plantation, Florida). 1999: Peppertree Rescue (Albany, New York), GoldHeart Golden Retriever Rescue (Owings Mills, Maryland), Golden Beginnings Golden Retriever Rescue of Texas (Houston, Texas), Inland Empire Golden Retriever Rescue (Spokane, Washington).

58. Carol Allen. Interviewed by Andrei Markovits. Telephone Interview. July 7, 2009.

59. Ibid.

60. Ibid.

61. Ibid.

62. Burt Augst. Interviewed by Andrei Markovits. Telephone Interview. July 28, 2009.

63. Ibid.

64. Ibid.

65. Barbara Elk. Interviewed by Andrei Markovits. Telephone Interview. August 19, 2010.

66. Ibid.

67. Mike Davin. Interviewed by Katherine Crosby. Telephone Interview. August 23, 2010.

68. Petfinder. "Petfinder Adopted Dog | Golden Retriever | Irwin, PA | Pappy." Last modified 2012. http://www.petfinder.com/petdetail/12728691-Pappy-Golden Retriever-Dog-Irwin-PA (accessed on June 16, 2013).

69. Kevin Wilcox. Interviewed by Andrei Markovits. Telephone Interview. August 18, 2010.

70. Ibid.

71. Priscilla Skare. Interviewed by Andrei Markovits. Telephone Interview. August 19, 2010.

72. Debbie Lukasik. Interviewed by Andrei Markovits. Telephone Interview. August 12, 2010.

73. Jody Jones. Interviewed by Andrei Markovits. Personal Interview. Elverta, California. August 20, 2009.

74. Ibid.

75. Deb Haggerty. Interviewed by Andrei Markovits. Personal Interview. Elverta, California. August 20, 2009.

76. Jan Knoche did not indicate which group this was in her interview.

77. Jan Knoche. Interviewed by Katherine Crosby. Telephone Interview. August 9, 2010.

78. Lauren Genkinger. Interviewed by Katherine Crosby. Telephone Interview. August 18, 2010.

79. Ibid.

80. Allie Medendorp. Interviewed by Katherine Crosby. Telephone Interview. August 10, 2010.

81. Tom Whitson. Interviewed by Katherine Crosby. Telephone Interview. August 9, 2010.

82. Ibid.

83. Craig Cwiklowski. Interviewed by Andrei Markovits. Telephone Interview. August 20, 2010.

84. Adams interview.

85. Ibid.

86. Ibid.

87. Ibid.

88. Allen interview.

89. Ibid.

90. Jones interview.

91. Ibid.

92. Davin interview.

93. Haggerty interview.

94. That Joan Puglia's engagement on behalf of dogs and her commitment to their well-being has assumed a lifelong dimension that reaches well beyond her having

founded and led Yankee Golden Retriever Rescue can best be attested to by her having taken a leading role in the establishment of the Golden Retriever Senior Rescue
Sanctuary and Education Center (GRSRSEC). This organization's mission is "to
provide life-long care for senior rescue Goldens, especially those with special needs
including hospice care" (http://www.goldenretrieversanctuary.org/The_History
.html). Giving this project even more gravitas than Joan Puglia's involvement already
accords it is the fact that it is housed in and jointly administered by Delaware Valley Golden Retriever Rescue (DVGRR), led by Robin Adams and arguably one of
the Golden Retriever rescue world's most pedigreed, accomplished, and respected
organizations.

CHAPTER 5

Regionalism in the Breed Rescue World

Humane societies and rescues have a very wide definition depending on where you go in the United States.[1]

—Elena Pesavento
Labrador Friends of the South

Rescue groups are not created in a vacuum. The material conditions of the environment in which a rescue group is formed have a profound impact on the ways in which it will develop and behave. Investigations into regional variations are critical for determining the true differences among canine rescue groups, as comparisons of groups from different regions may not be appropriate without correcting for factors beyond the control of the rescue groups themselves and mainly attributable to their environmental condition. With this in mind, this chapter will quantify the regional conditions of rescue groups and study the effects that different regions have on the rescue world. To ensure a consistent analysis, we decided to use the category of the Standard Federal Regions created by the Office of Management and Budget. These regions are as follows.

- Region 1: Connecticut, Maine, Massachusetts, New Hampshire, Rhode Island, and Vermont
- Region 2: New Jersey and New York (Puerto Rico and the U.S. Virgin Islands are also in this region, but were not examined in our research)

- Region 3: Delaware, Maryland, Pennsylvania, Virginia, and West Virginia
- Region 4: Alabama, Florida, Georgia, Kentucky, Mississippi, North Carolina, South Carolina, and Tennessee
- Region 5: Illinois, Indiana, Michigan, Minnesota, Ohio, and Wisconsin
- Region 6: Arkansas, Louisiana, New Mexico, Oklahoma, and Texas
- Region 7: Iowa, Kansas, Missouri, and Nebraska
- Region 8: Colorado, Montana, North Dakota, South Dakota, Utah, and Wyoming
- Region 9: Arizona, California, Hawaii, and Nevada
- Region 10: Alaska, Idaho, Oregon, and Washington

Using these regions, we analyzed several variables to determine what effects these regions have had on rescue groups. With the help of such an analysis, we are more confident in the validity of our comparisons of groups in our study. Substantial regional variations in, among others, disease treatment costs, shelter and community spay and neuter laws, puppy mill laws, rescue networks, attitudes toward dogs and other animals, and dog breed populations, have had an immense effect on the very presence, let alone the identities, roles, and efficacy of breed rescues in the United States. These items will be discussed in this chapter.

Preventable Canine Diseases

The average cost to treat preventable canine diseases varies depending on the relative incidence of diseases and their costs. Some diseases, such as heartworm, demand special treatment and are expensive to implement. Other illnesses, such as Lyme disease, require only a course of antibiotics and are thus relatively inexpensive to treat. To calculate the average cost per dog, we compiled data on four common but preventable diseases: heartworm, Lyme disease, anaplasma, and Ehrlichia. Heartworm is transmitted by mosquitos, while Lyme disease, anaplasma, and Ehrlichia are all tick-borne diseases. Heartworm treatment costs vary by veterinary clinic and are difficult to estimate, but after much research we arrived at a reasonable figure of approximately $400 for treatment. For the other three diseases, a course of antibiotics is required, and the average cost for such a course of antibiotics at the recommended dosage was $43.20.

After ascertaining the average cost to treat these diseases, we found the incidence of each disease for all states from 2007 to 2011.[2] We then calculated the average treatment cost per dog for each state and compared the costs regionally. These data are shown in Figures 5.1 and 5.2.

The most expensive regions were 6 and 4. These states had a high incidence of heartworm and a very low incidence of the other three diseases. Many of the rescues in these regions would agree with the words of Lauren Genkinger, a rescuer with Adopt a Golden Atlanta: "In this part of the country [Georgia], we spend our money primarily on heartworm treatment. Twenty-five percent of all our dogs come in with heartworm, and it costs us $500 per dog, and we try desperately to teach people about heartworm prevention."[3] The least expensive were regions 1 and 2. These regions had high rates of Lyme disease but a very low incidence of heartworm.

The average cost per state for these four very common diseases computed at $328.96, with the highest incurred in Louisiana with an average cost of $378.79 and the lowest in Minnesota with an average cost of $49.83. Of course there are some outliers such as Utah, for example, which has expenses comparable to Louisiana's, amounting to more than $350 per dog

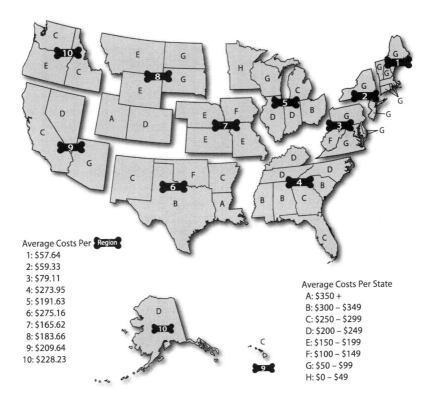

Average Costs Per Region
1: $57.64
2: $59.33
3: $79.11
4: $273.95
5: $191.63
6: $275.16
7: $165.62
8: $183.66
9: $209.64
10: $228.23

Average Costs Per State
A: $350 +
B: $300 – $349
C: $250 – $299
D: $200 – $249
E: $150 – $199
F: $100 – $149
G: $50 – $99
H: $0 – $49

Figure 5.1. Average Treatment Cost Per Dog by State

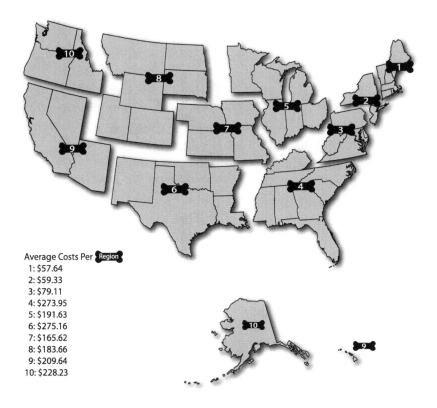

Average Costs Per Region
1: $57.64
2: $59.33
3: $79.11
4: $273.95
5: $191.63
6: $275.16
7: $165.62
8: $183.66
9: $209.64
10: $228.23

Figure 5.2. Average Treatment Cost Per Dog by Region

in a region where the average expense at $183.66 is slightly less than half that sum.

Here we present a brief discussion as to what these figures mean for breed rescues in these regions. The average cost to treat preventable diseases for rescues in region 1, the region with the lowest average expenses, is $57.64 per dog, while the average treatment cost in the region with the highest average expenses, region 6, is $275.16. This means that it is almost five times as expensive in region 6 to treat preventable diseases as it is in region 1. In effect, regions that have high incidents of heartworm, rather than Lyme disease, Ehrlichia, or anaplasma, are at a distinct disadvantage because the cost of treating heartworm is approximately ten times higher than the cost of treating the other three diseases. The more money groups are required to spend on veterinary care per dog, the fewer dogs they can rescue, potentially creating coverage gaps in rescue and jeopardizing their very mission. Moreover, this also means that rescues in regions with expensive treatment regimens need to devote many more valuable human resources to raise necessary funds than do organizations engaged in rescue in areas that demand less costly medical treatments.

Spay and Neuter Laws

Shelter and community spay and neuter laws represent an absolutely critical component in the overall rescue mission: Not only do these laws affect the respective state's dog population, but they also have a major influence on a group's potential expenses. If the state has a shelter spay and neuter law, it is likely that the rescue groups in this state would have a smaller percentage of unaltered dogs in their program that require spaying or neutering. Understanding laws regarding spaying and neutering, whether enforced by the state or by the community, is therefore important to make accurate comparisons among groups and assess their respective efficacy in rescue.

In order to compare the spay and neuter laws of all states, we compiled a list of extant spay and neuter laws. There seem to be two basic types of laws in effect: statewide statutes requiring shelters to spay or neuter pets before putting them up for adoption; and community-enforced laws requiring that all pets within city bounds be spayed or neutered.[4] In Figure 5.3 we thus discerned four options for each state: (A) both types of laws present; (B) only shelter spay/neuter laws present; (C) only community spay/neuter laws; or (D) no spay/neuter laws.

We could not detect clear patterns when examining these laws regionally with the possible exception of region 6, in which all states had at least shelter spay and neuter laws. Among these states, New Mexico, Texas, and Oklahoma had both types of spay and neuter laws. Most of the other regions, however, did not reveal any consistency in terms of spay and neuter laws. An analysis of the likelihood of spay and neuter laws in Democratic (Blue) versus Republican (Red) states, pursuant to the hypothesis that they would be frequent in the former and sparse in the latter, also failed to yield any significant findings. Of the twenty-five states with state-mandated spay and neuter laws, thirteen voted for Barack Obama in the 2008 presidential election (52 percent) and twelve voted for John McCain (48 percent). Sixteen states possess community-mandated spay and neuter laws, and of those twelve voted for Obama in the 2008 presidential election (75 percent) and four voted for McCain (25 percent).[5] In this case, a regional analysis is less useful than a state-by-state accounting for each group or comparisons among groups.

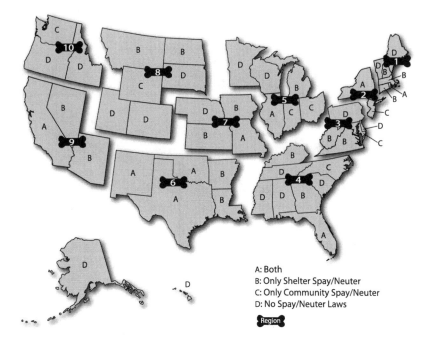

A: Both
B: Only Shelter Spay/Neuter
C: Only Community Spay/Neuter
D: No Spay/Neuter Laws

Region

Figure 5.3. Spay and Neuter Laws in the United States

The presence (or absence) of spay and neuter laws in some form plays a vital role in the environment in which rescue groups are formed and have to function. States without any spay and neuter laws are likely to have a higher proportion of unaltered dogs coming into rescue programs. Affected groups would then have to allot more money to spaying and neutering than rescue groups in states that have spay and neuter laws. This results in a higher rescue cost per dog for the former groups, reducing their available financial means for rescuing other dogs. Rescue groups that are formed in states with some kind of spay and neuter law need to have a smaller portion of their budget reserved for spaying and neutering dogs and are therefore able to spend their funds on other crucial items required for a successful rescue operation of indigent dogs.

Puppy Mills

Few factors can have a more decisive presence on a local breed rescue's very being than puppy mills. After all, it is these that have a major effect on the availability of a certain breed's dogs. Especially with the closing of such mills, there ensues a veritable flooding of the market with dogs belonging to that breed often suffering from physical deficiencies and exhibiting behavioral problems that require a significant investment of time and money to alleviate and render the dogs healthy for adoption. Puppy mills are such negative game changers for rescues and provide such taxing problems for them that Jeannette Poling's exasperation with their very existence makes sense: "I don't think that I'd even do rescue if I lived in a puppy mill state."[6] Restrictions on puppy mills affect the number of dogs for which a rescue group might have to provide care in the event of a mill closure, as states with such restrictions are less likely to have puppy mills. Using Michigan State University's Animal Law and History Web Center, we were able to determine which states did and which did not have laws regarding puppy mills. In Figure 5.4 we feature our map of the ten regions of the United States depicting the presence and absence of puppy mill laws.

The data reveal that the regions possessing more than one state without any puppy mill laws were region 4 (Kentucky, Mississippi, Alabama, Florida, and South Carolina), region 6 (New Mexico and Texas), region 8

Figure 5.4. The Presence and Absence of Puppy Mill Laws in the United States

(Montana, North Dakota, South Dakota, Wyoming, and Utah), and region 10 (Alaska and Idaho). We would therefore expect to see more puppy mills in these regions, particularly regions 4, 6, and 8, as one of region 10's states with no mill laws, Alaska, is unlikely to have puppy mills for reasons of geographic size, paucity of population, and harshness of climate.

States with restrictions on dog breeding are less likely to have large puppy mills. Moreover, the puppy mills that do operate in them tend to have at least somewhat better standards of care for their dogs than mills formed in states without puppy mill laws. When puppy mills are closed, the region surrounding the mill is flooded with poorly bred dogs with a variety of physical and behavioral problems that represent a significant drain on rescue group resources. In effect, states without puppy mill laws have a greater probability of rescuing puppy mill dogs, and the dogs they rescue are more likely to be deficient in their health than their counterparts in states with puppy mill laws. The number of potentially unadoptable dogs or those that require extensive rehabilitation before becoming viable candidates for adoption place a huge burden on rescue resources that could, under more auspicious circumstances, be utilized to ready more adoptable dogs for their much-deserved forever home. Needless to say, the latter are much more likely to take up much less space and time—both rare and much-desired resources for all rescues—than dogs with major health problems and serious damage caused by puppy mills. Regardless of the ethical implications of puppy mills, their very presence bears direct consequences for breed rescue.

Even in states with puppy mill laws, their scope and strictness vary significantly. This, of course, does not even address the huge discrepancy in the practice of enforcement, which is far from guaranteed. Pennsylvania, a state with dog breeding laws on the books, has long been home to the largest concentration of puppy mills in the United States. These mills, many of which are run by members of the Amish community of Lancaster County, often keep their dogs in inhumane conditions and skirt the laws meant to protect the dogs. This behavior results largely from the prevailing attitude in the area that dogs are purely a source of income rather than pets, let alone integral members of the family. Bill Smith, founder of Main Line Animal Rescue, a rescue in Pennsylvania that often handles puppy mill dogs, stated that "Dogs in this community are viewed as livestock—nothing more. Chickens or pigs or goats. It's just a source of income for them."[7] In Pennsylvania, the law establishes cutoffs for acceptable breeder behavior based on the number of dogs a breeder has at a particular facility: for example, if a kennel has fewer than sixty dogs, its owners may shoot and kill them. But if a kennel has more than sixty dogs, they cannot be shot and killed.[8] Thus, even states that have puppy mill laws could potentially have puppy mill issues if the laws in place are weak or rarely enforced.

Regional Rescue Networks

Regional rescue networks are associations of rescue groups covering a specified geographic area. Member groups often account for a variety of pet species from cats and dogs to fish and exotics like birds and lizards. Typically, networks include cities and their outlying suburbs, although some are large enough to operate statewide. As a rule, regional rescue networks form to help local groups cooperate with one another. These networks organize events and fundraisers that benefit all member groups; they share information about disreputable breeders and blacklisted adopters; and, through the network requirements, they publicize how groups behave regarding such key issues as spaying or neutering, for example, thus becoming a valuable clearinghouse, advocate, and supporter for these groups. These networks thus contribute to a group's "seal of approval," which is crucial for the legitimation of its overall standing in the community that its activities address and from which it draws its support and standing. A rescue group's membership and participation in a regional rescue network demonstrate the group's higher level of organization and more committed involvement in the rescue world.

Measuring a particular rescue group's participation in a regional rescue network depends on the number of potential networks a group has to join. There are three possible scenarios: (1) there are no regional rescue networks to join; (2) there is one regional rescue network that a group can join; and (3) two or more regional rescue networks exist from which a group chooses the one it perceives as its best fit. Of course, the group can also decide to join all available networks.

Scenario 1 is typically found in sparsely populated regions and states, such as Wyoming. If there are no rescue networks for a group to join, it is impossible to say whether groups would participate in such an arrangement given the opportunity. With scenarios 2 and 3, it is important to note that there are a variety of reasons why a group might not participate in a network, including being too new, having too few people, lacking interest in joining the network, and unawareness of the network's existence. Our research thus remains confined to information derived from groups that actually chose to join such networks, as opposed to such that did not. When scenario 2 occurs, a rescue group's decision regarding its participation in the single network available can reveal aspects of the rescue group's overall operation. For example, one can infer by that group's choosing to become involved in its sole regional network that there exists a high congruity and agreement between the two regarding such crucial issues for the rescue world as spay and neuter policies. Groups that join networks also tend to have matured in their development beyond their initial startup phase and have established themselves sufficiently to broaden their focus to include activities with other groups. Group participation in regional networks under scenario 3 also reveals telling aspects of the group's overall existence and standing. Specifically, groups that choose to participate in all available networks indicate that they are interested in being involved at an advanced level in the rescue world and that they have the organizational resources and financial stability to do so. A rescue group's decision to participate in regional rescue networks can illuminate aspects of its general behavior and overall attitude and approach to dog rescue. Networks have a major effect on a rescue group's overall ability and standing in the rescue world. Thus, this organizational dimension must be taken into account when attempting to compare rescue groups and analyze their function and activities.

The Rural (and Southern) Effect

Regional differences in how the general culture views animals can also affect the rescue capabilities of groups in the area. We want to emphasize that we do not mean to sound normative or appear to be passing judgment on such a sensitive issue in an academic culture in which the discourse of tolerance and compassion forbids any generalizations that could be construed as being negative toward any collective. It appears from our research that—on average and all things being equal—treatment of animals in rural and southern regions remains commensurate with the sensibilities and orientations that predate the era which we have come to associate with the rise of what we have termed the *discourse of compassion*, meaning that dogs on the whole continue to be viewed and treated as trusted companion animals but rarely as family members virtually on par with humans. The latter view of and approach toward dogs has become prevalent in America's urban and suburban areas largely as a consequence of the rise and proliferation of the discourse of compassion and the culture of inclusion.

Regions 1, 2, and 3 had population densities of over 200 people per square mile, regions 4, 5, and 9 had population densities of more than 100 and fewer than 200 people per square mile, and regions 6, 7, 8, and 10 had population densities of fewer than 100 people per square mile. Region 2 was the most densely populated, with 445 people per square mile, and region 10 was the least dense, with only 14 people per square mile.

Dog owners in southern states and rural areas tend to treat dogs like animals, rather than family members; dogs in these areas are often companion animals that still perform the jobs for which they were bred, such as herding, guarding, and hunting, as opposed to becoming family members whose sole role, really, is giving and receiving unconditional affection. Inhabitants of southern and rural areas are less likely to spend money on neutering their animals or giving them preventative care, are less likely to have community- or state-mandated spay and neuter laws, and are less likely to volunteer for animal rescue groups than their urban and suburban counterparts. Sparsely populated regions are more likely to feature dog owners that exhibit characteristics we attributed to a category we labeled as dog people, as opposed to those we associated with a group whose members we called pet people, who clearly are more prevalent in more densely populated regions.

Telling of the salience of this cultural divide and perception gap between basically two Americas as to what constitutes a dog's proper role and standing in our society was the fact that many of our interviewees raised this issue unprompted by us when describing their organization's larger context. Elena Pesavento, a rescuer with Labrador Friends of the South had this to say about Labrador rescue in the South:

> There's not really a super strong Labrador club in Georgia, but we are on the AKC [American Kennel Club] website. That's about it, they don't do much down here . . . there is definitely not a spay and neuter policy and culture, so that is the big long-term problem that you have in the South . . . and a lot of backyard breeding. . . . Humane societies and rescues in Georgia don't mean anything.[9]

Kevin Wilcox amplified this point by stating: "We also work with a lot of southern shelters. Down south, they're loaded with one- to two-year-old mixes, Golden mixes, wonderful dogs, but spay/neuter programs are not effective in the South."[10] Joy Viola commented: "Delaware Valley Golden Retriever Rescue struck up a relationship with Mid-Florida Golden Retriever rescue because there is a different mindset in the South about dogs."[11] This perceived cultural difference has an effect on the adoption process and burdens the communication between rescues and potential adopters. Bob Bornstein offered his thoughts on this matter:

So primarily those education efforts revolve around making sure that Goldens wind up in the right home and get into the proper environment, and as you would expect with an effort like that, especially living out here in good ol' boy country, there are some people who really don't appreciate our advice, but that's just fine, because we can choose not to place a dog with them and they can go somewhere else.[12]

States in the South have a reputation among animal rescuers for being a more hostile environment for rescues than that found in other parts of the country. Cultural differences between the South and the rest of the United States create a scenario wherein the interest in enforcing spay and neuter laws and improving the treatment of animals appears to lag in the former when compared with the latter.

This difference in perception and culture has had major tangible implications for rescues in that it spawned a veritable explosion of dogs being steadily transported from South to North, leading to a net outflow of dogs from one to the other. Tom Whitson told us "There is more of a demand and less of a supply of available Goldens and Labs in the North than in the South."[13] His group, Golden Retriever Rescue of Houston, regularly ships dogs to the North to family members of previous adopters. "We got dogs coming from as far away as Florida and Texas," said Jody Jones from California's Homeward Bound.[14] "I've got one coming from Florida tomorrow. . . . We hope that folks down there can do what they can for their dogs, but if not, we will always make it work at Homeward Bound."[15] And Renee Riegel informed us that "I have taken dogs from Georgia, Tennessee, Kentucky, yeah, I have been taking them steadily from the South."[16] And if the occasional eighteen wheeler is not available, Maureen Distler described to us other transportation modalities that these rescues have come to arrange as a matter of course: "Okay guys, I've got to get this Lab to a rescue up in New Jersey so I have volunteers up and down the East Coast who sign up for two-hour legs and they will take the dog and they will meet people at gas stations on the highway, give them the dog, and then these folks will drive two hours and hand over the dog to others—there is a whole well-established network like this going on, absolutely fascinating, and all through the Internet."[17]

The glut of dogs available in the South has even spurred new businesses to facilitate the evacuation of dogs from the South to other parts of the country. One such business involves professional transportation crews, which Cathy Mahle describes: "So I adopted this dog from Missouri and flew him to Connecticut. . . . We couldn't get people to drive that often from Tennessee to Maine or even further, so we started employing a professional transporter that brings Labs to us every week, mainly from the South, and we can save many more that way."[18] And Maureen Distler told us: "There's a couple of websites that will organize dogs from shelters in the South and they will give the dogs their vet check and will make them ready to go. The dogs will be delivered mainly by van. I mean there's this one eighteen wheeler that regularly runs up the East Coast dropping off dogs from the South to people that we have already approved as adopters."[19] Beryl Board and other interviewees recounted virtually identical methods of transporting rescued dogs over long distances across the land with the animals almost always departing from regions 4, 6, 7, and 8 bound for locations in states in regions 1, 2, some 3, some 5, and California with trips in the reverse direction quite rare.

To be sure, intraregional transportation often is available, like the Colorado Access Rescue Express or CARE that regularly ferries lots of rescue dogs along the I-70 corridor between Kansas City and Denver. Becky Hildebrand shared her thoughts on this topic: "Linda in the CARE group organizes all those transports servicing all sorts of rescues in Colorado, I don't know, twenty-five, thirty-five rescues, something like that, in any case, it's a lot . . . she also will organize transports for cats for different rescue groups . . . probably at least 50 percent of our dogs will come on a CARE transport."[20] Regional variance in dog overpopulation and in the perceptions of how regions treat dogs, most notably the South, have produced mechanisms to redistribute in effect dogs from the South to the rest of the country in order to ensure that as many dogs as possible are adopted into safe, loving homes.

Burt Augst's comments emphasize that this undeniable cultural gap in the perception of a dog's standing in contemporary America may not be so much a function of a North–South divide but rather of an urban–rural divide:

> I grew up in the country, and a lot of what they call "Southern" down here [in Tennessee], as far as I'm concerned, is really country. . . . I mean, I do not see much difference between how folks see dogs in rural Tennessee from rural Wisconsin. So I think that there is a different concept of Dog in the country compared to the city, maybe more so in the South. But I think that this view really extends into rural areas of the North as well.[21]

Augst's argument in favor of a rural–urban divide characterizing humans' perceptions of and behavior toward dogs does not necessarily contradict the parallel presence of the southern-exception hypothesis. After all, the regions which the South covers (i.e., region 4 and part of region 6) have lower population densities than several other regions in the country. The lower population density of these regions means that preceding the culture turn of the late 1960s and 1970s in which humans continue to view dogs may be attributable to the prevalent culture of the region, to its rural nature, or a combination of the two.

Dog Breed Populations

The number of dogs belonging to a particular breed constitutes yet another critical factor in the comparative assessment as to how regional differences influence the world of canine rescue. The average number of a particular breed's dogs in shelters varies by region; this variation is caused by a multiplicity of factors, among which the presence (or absence) of puppy mills, the number of shelters and rescues available to accommodate the dogs in need, and the regional popularity of the breed are perhaps the most salient. By comparing the regional concentrations of Golden Retrievers, Labrador Retrievers, and Pit Bulls, we demonstrate how such variation exists and what it means for rescue groups regionally.

Nationally, Golden Retrievers averaged 0.18 dogs per shelter in 2011. When broken down into regions, one region in particular stood out: region 8 had twice the number of Golden Retrievers, on average, than any of the other regions. This should be viewed in the context that this region had an average of 0.64 dogs per shelter, while the comparable figure for other regions was 0.30 dogs or fewer. Although the higher concentration of Golden Retrievers in region 8 was at least partially attributable to the region's sparse population, other factors also appeared to be likely contributors to this situation, most notably the presence of puppy mills in the region. Over the past decade, several puppy mills closed in North Dakota, adding a burden to rescues that, in conjunction with the decreased human population density in the region, dramatically increased the concentration of Golden Retrievers in the region. Perhaps most telling in this instance is that Retrieve a Golden of Minnesota, the rescue group handling all the fallout from these mill closures, hails from the neighboring State of Minnesota, which has a higher population density than North Dakota. Rescues in North Dakota were simply unable to handle crises of the magnitude of puppy mill seizures and closures and thus had to rely on groups outside the state, indeed, outside the region, to assist the dogs in need.[22] In practical

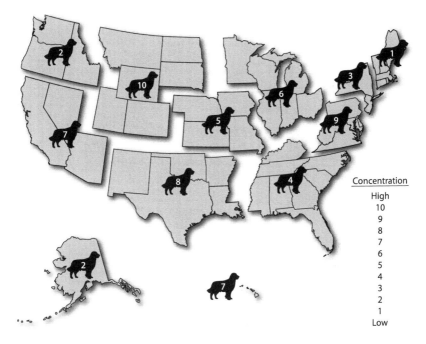

Figure 5.5. Golden Retrievers in U.S. Shelters in 2011

terms, this means that in 2011 Golden Retriever rescues in region 8 were more likely to have a greater number of dogs relative to their counterparts in other regions. These data are presented in Figure 5.5.

Nationally, an average of 2.97 Labrador Retrievers were present in shelters in 2011. Disaggregated by regions, however, it becomes evident that the population of Labrador Retrievers in America's shelters varied significantly among regions. Regions 6 (4.37 dogs per shelter), 7 (4.05 dogs per shelter), and 4 (3.63 dogs per shelter) had the highest concentrations of Labrador Retrievers in shelters, with all other regions sporting averages under three Labrador Retrievers per shelter. Regions 1 (1.35 dogs per shelter), 2 (1.54 dogs per shelter), and 8 (1.67 dogs per shelter) had the lowest concentrations of Labrador Retrievers in their shelters. Effectively this means that on average, shelters and rescue groups in region 6 had 3.27 times as many Labrador Retrievers to rescue as their counterparts in region 1, making rescue in region 6 considerably more costly than it was in region 1. These data are shown in Figure 5.6.

Pit Bulls have had an entirely different regional distribution than Golden Retrievers and Labrador Retrievers. The average concentration

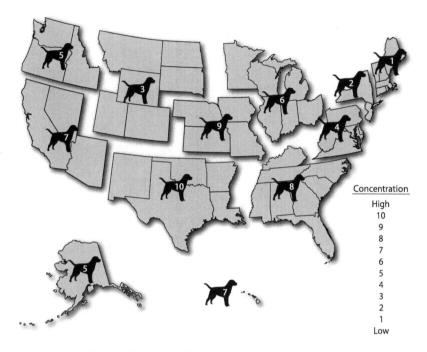

Figure 5.6. Labrador Retrievers in U.S. Shelters in 2011

of Pit Bulls nationally in 2011 was 2.54 dogs per shelter. Pit Bulls were most heavily concentrated in regions 9 (4.66 dogs per shelter), 10 (3.94 dogs per shelter), and 1 (3.05 dogs per shelter). Regions 6 (1.41 dogs per shelter), 7 (1.47 dogs per shelter), and 8 (1.54 dogs per shelter) had the lowest concentration of Pit Bulls. This distribution pattern means that Pit Bull rescues were particularly challenged in regions 9, 10, and 1 and had a comparatively easier time in regions 6, 7, and 8. It is also important to note that breed selective legislation (BSL) affects the distribution of dogs like Pit Bulls, as they are often targeted for restrictions based on their reputation. BSL is most often implemented on a county or city level and can range from registration and muzzling requirements to outright bans on the breed in the affected area.[23] Pit Bull bans like those in Denver, Colorado, Cincinnati, Ohio, and Miami-Dade County, Florida, prevent the legal ownership of Pit Bulls in these locations and therefore have an effect on the populations of Pit Bulls in these areas. But because these bans occur on the local rather than the state level, it is difficult to gauge whether their existence affects Pit Bull populations statewide.[24] These data are presented in Figure 5.7.

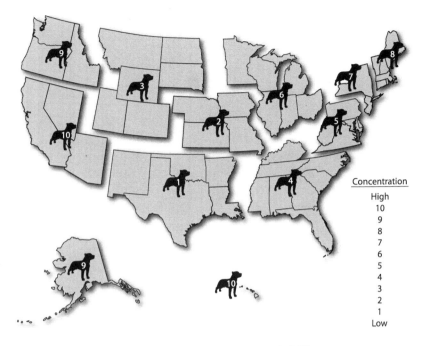

Figure 5.7. Pit Bulls in U.S. Shelters in 2011

The preceding paragraphs reveal that there existed significant variation in the population densities of Golden Retrievers, Labrador Retrievers, and Pit Bulls across the United States in 2011. We are reasonably certain that our findings reflect a similar situation in other years of the past decade. Comparing breed population densities for region 10, for example, demonstrates the vast disparities in the number of dogs per shelter for each breed. In region 10, there were approximately 0.04 Golden Retrievers per shelter, 2.54 Labrador Retrievers per shelter, and 3.94 Pit Bulls per shelter. This means that in shelters in region 10 there were approximately 63.5 times as many Labrador Retrievers as there were Golden Retrievers and 1.55 times as many Pit Bulls as Labrador Retrievers. So in region 10, the rescues that service each of these breeds have dramatically different numbers of dogs to assist, while each draws from the same population for volunteers. Rescues for Labrador Retrievers and Pit Bulls in region 10 have significantly larger burdens to bear than Golden Retriever rescues. In a sense then, the rescues devoted to these three different breeds operate in three different environments as measured by the outside burdens imposed on each. To conclude, breed specific rescue not only depends on cultural and geographic differences affecting humans, but also on the variance in the canine population in the United States.

Conclusion

What do all these numbers mean for rescues? First, breed of dog seems to be of paramount importance, as illustrated by our comparison of Golden Retrievers, Labrador Retrievers, and Pit Bulls. Second, geographic location is also important. In order to have an accurate comparison between two breeds in a specific region, one needs to control for the differing magnitude of population of these breeds in that region. To illustrate the necessity for a nuanced interregional analysis, we will briefly compare the regional factors affecting Alabama (region 4) and New York (region 1). The average cost to treat preventable canine diseases in Alabama is $335.80 with the average New York cost being $61.21. This means that on average rescues in Alabama spend 5.5 times more per dog than rescues in New York to cure preventable diseases in their dogs. Alabama does not have any legislation concerning puppy mills, while New York does have laws regulating their creation and operation; thus, rescues in Alabama have a higher likelihood of dealing with puppy mill dogs than their New York counterparts. Alabama has neither state-mandated nor community-mandated shelter spay and neuter laws, whereas New York has both; thus, Alabama rescue groups are more likely to have a higher proportion of dogs requiring neutering than those located in New York. With New York being a more densely populated state than Alabama, it is more likely to have a higher proportion of pet people within its population, and New York rescue groups are therefore more likely to have greater resources available to them than rescue groups in Alabama.

Using Labrador Retrievers as an example, we can see that the region in which Alabama is located has an average of 3.62 Labrador Retrievers per shelter, while New York's region has an average of 1.54 Labrador Retrievers per shelter, which amounts to less than half of the dogs requiring rescue in New York compared with Alabama. In short, rescue groups located in states like Alabama are at a distinct disadvantage when compared with rescues located in states like New York. Thus, comparing the efficacy, devotion, and commitment of rescue groups without correcting for the environment in which they exist will result in faulty conclusions.

In order to understand why groups function the way they do, it is critical to analyze the environment in which they operate. Factors such as high disease treatment costs, lack of state-enforced spay and neuter laws or state-enforced puppy mill laws, regional rescue networks, being in rural areas, and regional concentrations of dogs can have a drastic effect on the number of dogs a rescue group will need to accommodate and also a major effect on the group's overall efficacy. Of particular concern are regions 4 and 6, as they bear higher than average cost for the treatment of preventable diseases and have few puppy mill laws. A perfect storm exists in region 4, as it has high average treatment costs, few puppy mill laws, and fewer spay and neuter laws than region 6. This leads to a situation where there are many more potential dogs for groups to rescue and a higher average cost per dog to do so. In essence, groups that became established in regions 4 and 6 have had more obstacles to overcome than similar groups in regions with more advantageous conditions, like regions 1, 2, and 3. It is therefore important to compare rescue groups within regions, and in some cases within states, in order to have accurate analyses of how such groups function.

The next chapter will analyze another crucial aspect of the external environment that shapes the lives of these rescues. Departing from the physical, geographic, and climate-related aspects, which was the focus in this chapter, in Chapter 6 we will examine the rescues' organizational and institutional surroundings. In particular, we will look at their relations with humane societies and shelters and with other rescue organizations belonging to their breed as well as those serving other breeds. Lastly, we will also examine these rescue organizations' relations with breeders, AKC clubs, and their national organizations.

Notes

1. Elena Pesavento. Interviewed by Katherine Crosby. Telephone Interview. August 8, 2010.

2. DogsandTicks.com, "Map of Lyme Disease, Canine Ehrlichiosis, Heartworm, Anaplasma," 2012, http://www.dogsandticks.com/diseases_in_your_area.php (accessed on April 26, 2014).

3. Lauren Genkinger. Interviewed by Katherine Crosby. Telephone Interview. August 18, 2010.

4. Humane Society of America's website (http://www.americanhumane.org /animals/adoption-pet-care/caring-for-your-pet/spaying-neutering.html) does not address the issue of mandatory spay and neuter laws directly but does provide useful information on spaying and neutering in general. Michigan State University's Animal Law and History Web Center has two very useful links pertaining to spaying and neutering. The first link provides a survey of state spay and neuter laws (http://www.animallaw.info/articles/ddusspayneuter.htm). The second link offers a

map that shows which states have mandatory spay and neuter laws (http://www
.animallaw.info/articles/armpusspayneuter/htm).

5. "President Map." *New York Times*, December 09, 2008. http://elections.ny
times.com/2008/results/president/map.html (accessed on July 4, 2013).

6. Jeannette Poling. Interviewed by Andrei Markovits. Telephone Interview.
June 22, 2009.

7. "Puppies 'Viewed as Livestock' in Amish Community, Says Rescue Advocate,"
ABC News, March 31, 2009. http://abcnews.go.com/Business/story?id=7187712
&page=1 (accessed on April 26, 2014).

8. Ibid.

9. Pesavento interview.

10. Kevin Wilcox. Interviewed by Andrei Markovits. Telephone Interview.
August 18, 2010.

11. Joy Viola. Interviewed by Andrei Markovits. Telephone Interview. July 16,
2009.

12. Bob Bornstein. Interviewed by Andrei Markovits. Telephone Interview.
August 12, 2010.

13. Tom Whitson. Interviewed by Katherine Crosby. Telephone Interview.
August 9, 2010.

14. Jody Jones. Interviewed by Andrei Markovits. Personal Interview. Elverta,
California. August 20, 2010.

15. Ibid.

16. Renee Riegel. Interviewed by Katherine Crosby. Telephone Interview.
August 18, 2010.

17. Maureen Distler. Interviewed by Katherine Crosby. Telephone Interview.
July 28, 2010.

18. Cathy Mahle. Interviewed by Katherine Crosby. Telephone Interview.
August 3, 2010. This is confirmed by J. Courtney Sullivan's article "Adopt a Dog
With a Southern Drawl," published in the *New York Times*, May 26, 2014, in which
the author makes it clear that finding homes for pets in the north is imperative lest
they be euthanized in the south.

19. Distler interview.

20. Becky Hildebrand. Interviewed by Katherine Crosby. Telephone Interview.
July 29, 2010.

21. Burt Augst. Interviewed by Andrei Markovits. Telephone Interview. July 28,
2009.

22. Kare11.com, "Puppies Rescued from ND Puppy Mill Recovering." http://
www.kare11.com/news/article/904698/0/Puppies-rescued-from-ND-puppy-mill
-recovering (accessed April 26, 2014); TwinCities.com, "Recovering Retrievers."
http://www.twincities.com/ci_5520662 (accessed on April 26, 2014).

23. Linda Weiss, Animal Legal & Historical Center, "Breed Specific Legislation
in the U.S." http://www.animallaw.info/articles/aruslweiss2001.htm (accessed on
April 26, 2014).

24. Libby Sherrill, *Beyond the Myth*. Screen Media, 2012.

CHAPTER 6

Rescue Groups and
External Relationships

We try to get along with everybody and we do get along with everybody.

—Burt Augst
Middle Tennessee Golden Retriever Rescue

Like all organizations, breed specific rescue groups exist in a wider milieu. The act of rescuing necessarily involves obtaining dogs from individuals who are not rescue group members and placing them with other individuals who are also not members of the rescue group and often not even part of the larger world of animal rescue well beyond the rescue focused on one canine breed. Thus, the substance, tone, and mechanism informing the interactions between rescue groups and the rest of the human–animal world profoundly affect every aspect of the former's existence, from obtaining dogs for the program to funding the groups' rescue mission; from providing proper foster care for the rescued dogs while they are under the groups' supervision to the successful placement of them in loving forever homes, which, after all, is every rescue's ultimate goal, indeed its very raison d'être. Therefore, understanding the types of external relationships that every rescue group must establish and then cultivate and the impact that these relationships have on the group's actual functioning is critical to a proper contextualization of the breed specific canine rescue world's very identity.

First, we will enumerate the potential players with whom rescue groups are likely to interact. Any rescue group's largest relationship is with the general public, or those individuals and organizations that are unaffiliated with the rescue world per se, indeed often quite ignorant of its mission and existence. Then, this chapter examines the wide network of animal shelters and humane societies, because this complex comprises organizations that are most likely to be the first recipients of stray or unwanted dogs from which the rescues obtain their animals. Additionally, rescues establish relationships with other rescue groups in the area, whether or not they represent the same breed. Moreover, it is often to a rescue's benefit to establish relationships with local American Kennel Club (AKC) groups. Finally, national AKC groups and their rescue committees also constitute possible partners with many advantages for rescue groups. Each of these levels of interaction has a different effect on the rescue groups' activities, resources, and opportunities as well as, of course, their interlocutors on the other side. This chapter will describe each of these external relationships that are so essential to the very identity and operation of any breed specific canine rescue group.

Rescue Groups and the General Public

By far the largest potential partner for all rescue groups, the general public constitutes individuals and organizations that are unrelated to the world of rescue or often even to anything concerning animals. After all, it is ultimately the general public that represents the rescues' eventual consumers and clientele both in terms of the placement of dogs and in terms of creating a culture of greater compassion and responsibility for the growing canine presence in American family life. The methods by which rescue groups attempt to engage in dialogue with the general public offer advantages and disadvantages that can have lasting effects on the respective outcomes of such interactions, influencing the groups' financial resources, their reputation in the community, and other factors that could easily help or harm these groups' standing and modus operandi. It is therefore necessary to analyze both the methods these groups choose to interact with the public as well as the potential outcomes of such choices to understand how relationships between rescue groups and the general public affect the existence and behavior of the former.

Rescue Group Methods of Contacting the General Public

Rescue groups contact the public in a number of ways. Among them are newsletters, public outreach or educational events, and the Internet. The most important contribution of newsletters is to provide a steadily open channel of communication with members and previous adopters. This is crucial because this medium reminds the recipients of the organization's continued existence and its activities. Beyond that, it also triggers new donations and adoptions.

The importance of public outreach or educational events pertains mainly to the creation of new contacts in the rescue group's vicinity. For example, an event located in a park or a pet store will attract individuals with an interest in and love for dogs who might not have had exposure to the group in particular and rescue in general or might indeed be novices and first-timers in terms of wanting to incorporate a dog into their lives. As discussed previously, rescue is perhaps still the least known among the various extant institutions dedicated to improving the lives of needy dogs. After all, as we mentioned earlier, rescues—unlike shelters and humane societies—did not exist prior to the 1980s, actually the 1990s if looked at in terms of their wide societal proliferation. Institutionally speaking, rescues are a very recent phenomenon whose public outreach and educational efforts have undoubtedly contributed to raise the growingly receptive public's awareness about the paramount importance of animal health in general and spaying and neutering in particular.

Lastly, the Internet provides a multidimensional communication forum that facilitates the rescue groups' communication with the general public in just about every aspect—from fundraising to new member recruitment and from routine exchanges detailing the needs and activities of various dogs to all forms of emergency responses and crisis management. The centrality of social media in rescue groups' communication with the public has attained such importance over the past decade that we will devote Chapter 7 to present this case in its necessary detail.

Consequences of Rescue Group Relationships with the General Public

Newsletters, public outreach or education events, and social media are all methods rescue groups use to communicate with the general public. Each method, with its various advantages and disadvantages, affects the opportunities and resources available to the rescue groups. Those who use these communication methods effectively will have greater access to the resources the general public has to offer, as opposed to groups that either neglect or mismanage communications with the general public, thus forgoing an important reservoir of resources of which the following three are of particular importance: volunteers, donations, and owner turn-ins.

When used effectively, newsletters, public outreach or education events, and social media are all capable of mobilizing volunteers for rescue groups. Newsletters encourage previous adopters and donors to take a more active role in the rescue group. Public outreach or education events and social media can be used to locate and mobilize volunteers and donors who have not had previous experiences with the rescue group, as Maureen Distler emphasizes:

> [Rescue will] put pictures of dogs in shelters that [they] need foster homes for . . . when we're at the meet and greets in grocery stores and we go to these events where we set up a table and bring our dogs and talk to people, you know. We try to educate them on the need to spay and neuter and the need to rescue dogs from the local shelters. And, of course, we try to educate them about heartworm treatments and things like that 'cause the public really is totally not aware of all these things. The other place we do all these things is on Facebook.[1]

In addition, Distler's rescue organization receives positive responses from individuals who had not previously fostered for it. Thus, these particular methods used by Distler's group demonstrate that engagement of this kind yields positive results for her group. If rescue's ultimate goal is to reduce the number of needy dogs in the United States, then outreach becomes a necessary group activity, as it attempts to ensure the spread of the discourse of compassion to those who may not have been fully exposed to it previously. In so doing, these rescue groups modify the behavior of the general public, resulting in more spayed and neutered animals and healthier lives for animals in homes today, in addition to preventing the production of millions of homeless animals in the future.

Edith Bryan confirms the importance of educational outreach to the public in such grassroots and community-based events:

> The Puget Sound Labrador Retriever Association urges all of its members to be involved with public education. Seattle Purebred Dog Rescue has a booth virtually every weekend, certainly in the summer, at dog shows and events and fairs, and its volunteers set

up dozens and dozens of public education booths that try to tell the public what rescue is all about.[2]

Debbie Lukasik talked about her organization's outreach via its newsletter:

We do have a newsletter that's online, and we do have a newsletter that is hard copy. And the vets that we work with who give us significant discounts for their services and some who even give us free consults, get the hard copy version of our newsletter for their waiting rooms. And people can subscribe to our newsletter for $5 a year and they will get it mailed to their house. But we just send out an e-mail blast to all of our volunteers that the newest newsletter is on the website, and then it's out there for the public to see as well.[3]

Lastly, Phil Fisher furnished us with this information as to his organization's use of its newsletter:

We have an annual end-of-the-year Christmas donation letter that we send out to all of the people who have donated in the past and all of the people on our newsletter list, which now includes about 6,000 names and addresses. We receive quite a bit of money at the end of the year from these donations which would not be possible without our newsletter's reach.[4]

When rescue groups fail to communicate effectively with the general public, volunteers and donors who could be mobilized to join the groups remain uninvolved, leaving the valuable resources of people and their potential donations untapped. Absent such communication by the rescues, there remains a void in terms of spreading the discourse of compassion beyond their membership, and this failure prolongs the plight of homeless animals.

As to donations, the situation is obvious. The better known a rescue group is in its community—which, in this Internet-driven world might very well include much more than its geographic propinquity—the greater its success to raise much-needed money from it. In this case, rescue groups are not much different from any other charitable organization that depends in a considerable way on the goodwill and financial generosity of its environment.

Owner turn-in rates are also affected by the quality of the rescue groups' communication with the general public. Groups that communicate positively with the public through outreach or education events and social media have the opportunity to divert the flow of owner turn-ins from overburdened shelters to rescue groups. With an emphasis on education, some groups will work with potential owner turn-ins to see if they can fix the problem and prevent the dog from being surrendered in the first place. Susan Wells says that "if somebody contacts us to give up a dog and they're telling us they need to give up this dog because they can't get it housebroken, we will do a lot of individual education, we will go out and work with them to change their minds and keep the dog."[5] Rather than merely accepting the dog without attempting to ameliorate the situation, groups that behave in this proactive manner clearly reduce the number of owner turn-ins for preventable reasons like problems with housebreaking and engaging in destructive behavior.

Allie Medendorp explains that owners in her region will place dogs on Craigslist.org:

> [Our intake coordinator] talks to them and tells them the benefits of rescue. . . . [The intake coordinator] educates them on the kind of questions to ask and what to be careful about. There are people that will come and say they're going to take good care of [the] dog, and then sell it to research. We will give them a copy of our application policy so that this can help [the owner] to find a good home for their dog, and nine out of ten people get so overwhelmed by how many people call and want their dog that they just end up giving the dog to our organization.[6]

When owners are determined to surrender their dogs, rescue groups in possession of effective communication skills with the general public can ensure that the dog in question is placed properly, instead of winding up in a research facility or euthanized in an overcrowded shelter. Precisely to prevent such occurrences, many rescue organizations have banded together to keep questionable adopters from getting possession of the dogs. There exist various blacklists and other similar screening measures. Tami Stanley from the Dallas–Fort Worth region talked about the collaboration of a large number of rescues in this area precisely on the matter of safety for the dogs that rescues would like to have adopted:

> For sure, there is a main blacklist on the Dallas–Fort Worth CARES [Canine Rescues] roster which includes every breed. There is a master file which lists, among others, such things as this person wants to keep the dog outside, these folks gave up their dogs, they didn't

keep their dog on heartworm prevention, whatever other bad things people do to dogs for whatever reasons. . . . Rescue groups will not tell potential rescuers who get rejected the reasons for the rejection because they fear that folks will re-apply with another rescue group and simply lie about the factors that previously disqualified them.[7]

By communicating effectively with the general public and with other rescues, rescue groups can reduce the return rate of dogs into their programs. They can also diminish the likelihood that a dog is adopted into an inappropriate home or a dangerous situation.

Rescue groups that fail to engage in these proactive and positive methods with the general public are much more likely to have negative and frustrating experiences with owner turn-ins than those that try to communicate and work with members of the general public who are attempting to contact them. Thus, by utilizing newsletters, public outreach or education events, and social media to communicate with the general population, rescue groups can increase their volunteers and donations and effectively decrease the owner turn-ins the group experiences. Of course, good relations with the public also enhance a group's chances of obtaining more financial support for its work. In sum, rescue groups that communicate successfully with the general public experience much better all-round conditions in which to conduct their activities than those groups that do not.

Rescue Groups and Local Shelters

Relationships between rescue groups on the one hand and shelters or humane societies on the other are complex. They range from amicable and cooperative through business-like and sober to hostile and antagonistic. What lies in the balance, of course, is the welfare of the dogs, which can be substantially enhanced when the relationship between these two entities is cordial and cooperative but can also be considerably diminished when the relationship is fraught with animosity. As is always the case in any interorganizational relationships, many factors influence the quality of the tone and substance in the interaction between rescue groups and their local shelters.

Although certainly not all inclusive, our observations point to three dimensions that we deem especially salient in this relationship: first and foremost, the particular personalities involved in each case. With both of these institutions being highly dependent on the goodwill and personal commitment of their participants, especially their leaders, and with a charismatic and personalistic form of authority still quite prevalent in both of these institutions, it is not surprising that the relationships between them are heavily influenced by how the particular actors in each get along with one another. Second, we believe that the specific behavior and actual activities in which rescue groups engage have a bearing on their relationships with shelters or humane societies. Lastly, it matters greatly on behalf of which breed the rescue group operates. The bottom line is that the texture of the relationship between rescue groups and shelters or humane societies has a dramatic impact on the quality and quantity of dogs that the former attains from the latter.

In our research, an overwhelming majority of rescue groups reported experiencing positive relationships with local shelters, as only six of the sixty individuals we interviewed gauged their experiences with local shelters to be negative. Beryl Board in Minnesota argues that the key to cultivating positive relationships with local shelters is to build trust with them and to make it crystal clear to them that they can depend on the rescues' commitment and responsibility. Board stated her views on this topic:

> We always check in with the shelters. We respect that they have Goldens that they are going to adopt out. We help them. They will call us if they have a Golden that they're going to have to euthanize because it has a broken leg.... If they need help, we will be there for them, like if they're out of food, we will try to get it for them. I don't know how we do this, but somehow we can and always will. So those sorts of relationships are cultivated. We do what we say we're going to do. Like [if] we say we're going to be there Saturday at one o'clock to pick up the dogs, we make sure we're there on Saturday at a quarter to one to pick up the dogs. You have to build that trust, especially with large organizations.[8]

This is very much seconded by Robin Adams in Pennsylvania:

> Over the years ... we built relationships with shelters. They know that if they have a Golden they want to relinquish to us, we will show up immediately and we will take the dog regardless of the dog's condition.... So we will get dogs from shelters that they may not be able to afford to treat, that will require expensive and extensive medical care, and we also get a lot of dogs from them whose adoption prospects in shelters are very slim, old dogs in particular.... On the whole, I think we have great relationships with many shelters.[9]

Atlanta-based Lauren Genkinger confirms this:

> Our relationships with shelters are very good. There are twenty-five
> to thirty shelters in this area and we're registered with all of them.
> We learned early on when we first started how to build relation-
> ships. The key to having a good relationship with the shelters down
> here is if you say you're going to come get the dog, you actually go
> get the dog. The shelters just want to know for certain that you're
> going to be there when you say you're going to be there.[10]

Shelters value the effort that these rescues show when cultivating relationships with them, and the mutual respect that such effort can build is vital to
ensuring positive relationships between shelters and rescues.

The emphasis for rescue then is on consistency and respecting the
boundaries of local shelters with regard to their particular needs and
wishes such as which dogs will require assistance, which dogs shelters
will want to adopt out themselves, and which dogs a shelter would like
the rescue group to take. Sometimes, the relationship develops to the
point where the shelter will call the rescue group for any dogs of the
group's breed that are surrendered to the shelter, regardless of the dogs'
condition, as has been the case with the Tidelands Poodle Club Rescue
and its founder Jane Carroll. Amy Compton, a member of the rescue,
states:

> Jane has been doing this for many years in this area and has a good
> relationship with many of the local jurisdictions who just automat-
> ically call her when they get a Poodle in, like the litter of Standard
> [Poodle] puppies that were dropped off at their facility and to which
> they don't want to hang on for some reason and do not want to try
> to adopt them out of their own facility.[11]

Phil Fisher commented on shelters calling rescues: "Most shelters
appreciate us and will call us if they have a Golden that they know is going
to be hard to have adopted because he's been neglected or abused or in bad
shape."[12] On the whole, it seems that as long as rescue groups do not tread
on the shelters' prerogatives and make it clear to them that they do not
intend to be the shelters' rivals but their helpers instead, the likelihood of
relationships between rescue groups and shelters being cooperative, if not
necessarily cordial, is quite high.

However, not all relationships between rescue groups and shelters are
positive, with some becoming quite contentious. There are multiple reasons

for such a tense relationship, apart from personality clashes between the two leadership groups. We discerned three in particular: a shelter's negative experience with a previous rescue group, hoarding concerns, and, perhaps most importantly, the shelters' views of rescues as elitist entities engaged in cherry-picking the most adoptable dogs, thus constituting a direct rivalry with the shelters and undermining them in their very own mission and identity. Beyond the issue of subscribing to a different view as to what constitutes the optimal form of animal and canine welfare, the last point represents, of course, a very simple contestation over desperately needed finances as to which of the two mostly poor organizations will benefit from a particular dog's adoption. In other words, relationships between shelters and rescues will forever remain inherently tense and contested precisely because the boundaries between them remain murky in good part due to the deep complementarity that binds these different organizational structures.

Following a shelter's negative experience with a rescue group, some of the former make the decision never to deal with the latter again. Possible negative experiences that shelters can have with rescue groups include a group slandering a shelter publically for being high-kill (a shelter that euthanizes many of the animals that are brought to it), an individual posing as a representative of a rescue group but actually selling dogs to research facilities, or even personal disputes between shelter directors and leaders of rescue groups that escalate to the point where the shelter refuses to work with that particular rescue or possibly any rescue at all. The refusal to work with rescues then becomes the shelter's official policy, meaning that there is next to nothing that any rescue group can do to commence collaborative relationships with this shelter. Of course, blame and fault finding can flow in the opposite direction as well in that a particular rescue might choose not to collaborate with a shelter.

The fear that a rescue group might actually be a hoarder is another possible reason for local shelters to be leery of involvement with rescue groups. After all, dog hoarding not only results in horrible conditions for the dogs but also sullies the shelter's reputation and jeopardizes one of its core assets, namely, being an entity that reliably provides needy dogs with good forever homes. The shelter's fear of a rescue group being a front for a hoarder typically applies to groups that have yet to get their 501(c)(3) status. But it also pertains to small rescues that do not have the visibility—thus the reputation—of their larger counterparts. The bottom line is that shelters remain wary of rescues they do not know because the overall quality control and general standard of rescues remains undefined. Julie Jones in Southern California addressed this topic:

> The shelters are just so overrun right now, they simply don't have time. It's very frustrating, even from a rescue standpoint. A lot of shelters are not necessarily rescue friendly but I think they're not because there are some bad rescues out there. There are some people who give rescue a bad name because they're hoarders or just do things wrong. We just had two incidents in this area, and the rescue that took these dogs from the hoarders and ended up taking them to the shelters gave the rest of us a bad name. And that's kind of why you have to stay self-contained. We either work by ourselves or work with rescues that have our philosophy.[13]

Hoarders masquerading as rescues damage the reputation of all rescues and can contribute to negative feelings toward or an outright refusal to work with rescues on the part of shelters. Most shelters want to know with the greatest possible certainty that their dogs are going to good homes and not worry whether a rescue is actually a hoarder.

A further factor responsible for a negative relationship between a rescue group and a shelter pertains to the latter viewing the former as inherently elitist, as it "cherry-picks" the most desirable—and thus adoptable—dogs while leaving the shelter with the most problematic ones that might require a long time to be adopted or in fact may never be. Shelters that obtain few dogs belonging to desirable and popular breeds, like Golden Retrievers, Labrador Retrievers, or Poodles, and are swamped by dogs that are much harder to place, such as mixed-breed dogs and a bevy of Pit Bull Terrier variants, often view dogs of the former category as welcome assets for the shelter. Shelters use these desirable dogs to attract potential adopters to the facility who—so the shelters hope—then fall in love with the less desirable breeds that prior to their visit these people would never have wanted to adopt because of the breed's poor reputation or other negative preconceptions. A scenario ensues in which the first eligible candidate adopts the desirable dog, but the subsequent adopters who appear to see the dog can be introduced to other dogs that have wonderful personalities but are of less popular breeds and thus much harder to adopt out. Some shelters therefore view breed rescue groups that arrive at their doorstep solely to take away the dogs belonging to their breed as inherently elitist. And as we have encountered in this book many times, few attributes possess a more negative connotation than the term *elitist*.

On the one hand, shelters categorize the rescues' selection process as intrusive and arrogant because their selection is by definition based purely on exclusive breed specific criteria to define these dogs' fate. Because the

rescue groups' very existence and identity centers on a breed-based exclusivity and entails a clear selectivity based solely on ascriptive categories,
it would not be that far-fetched to categorize some shelters' view of the
rescue groups' elitism as explicit "breedism," a preferential differentiation
based on immutably particularistic physical criteria. At least in its conceptual content if not its volitional intent, this whole construct possesses
some parallels to racism. On the other hand, shelters very much welcome
any of their dogs' adoption and happy departure from their almost-always
overburdened facilities for two reasons: first, the obvious one, namely, that
there now exists at least the prospect, if not always the certainty, that the
departing dogs will face a better life; and second, that upon their departure
these dogs open up desperately needed space for more needy dogs arriving
at the shelters every day.

This type of potentially negative relationship is very difficult to change
because it rests on two profoundly different views as to what best constitutes the most optimal manner of helping dogs. Just as certain shelters
will remain convinced that their universalistic approach to saving dogs is
not only the very best but also the most ethical method; so, too, will rescue groups stand by their particularistic approach featuring the rescue of
dogs belonging to their beloved breed, which, to these groups, represents
an optimal and morally responsible manner to help needy dogs. Many of
our respondents addressed this inherently contested relationship. Here are
some in their own words.

> Phil Fisher: Most shelters will appreciate us. . . . Other shelters will
> say, "Hey, this is a Golden, we know Goldens are great attractions,
> so don't call the rescue group because we want to advertise this and
> get people to come to our place to see the Golden. We want the
> benefits that having a Golden means to us.[14]

> Mary Jane Shervais: The local shelters would always call us when a
> Golden came in. . . . Because if they could get us to foster a Golden,
> this would open up a place for another dog that might not have a
> fostering situation, because the shelters were always limited in the
> number of dogs that they could take and the ones that had been
> there the longest would run the greatest risk of being euthanized to
> make room for new arrivals.[15]

> Debbie Lukasik: A lot of the local humane societies and shelters
> don't give up Goldens because Goldens are gold to them. If they
> get a Golden that doesn't have an issue, medical or behavioral, these
> organizations will not surrender him to the rescue. . . . They just

adore to have Goldens because they can turn them in and out of their door very quickly, so we do not get a lot of these dogs from shelters, and if we do, it's a dog that has severe separation anxiety . . . dogs with behavior issues, or dogs that are too sick for the shelters to handle or need medical care.[16]

Robin Adams: I think we have a great relationship with many of the shelters. . . . Most shelters see a Golden as pretty much bread and butter, it won't take long for Goldens to go out of the shelters. So we never force the issue with them because Goldens get people into the shelter. Goldens are a valuable resource for them. . . . But shelters also know that if they have a Golden that they want to relinquish to us, that we will come pick up the dog regardless of the condition the dog is in. . . . So we will get dogs from them that they may not be able to afford to treat, that will require expensive and extensive medical care, and get a lot of old dogs from them as well, dogs whose adoption prospect in shelters are very, very slim.[17]

Gene Fitzpatrick: Some shelters say: "Well, you only take Goldens," and I say, "well, what do you want us to take? That's our breed, that's what they are." Then they say, "Well, you don't give the other dogs any chance," and I say "Listen, we're taking these off your hands, and you are complaining?" So they are few and far between, but there are some people in shelters that think we're snobs because all we do is rescue Goldens. But we're actually not an all-breed rescue.[18]

Burt Augst: We have one volunteer who does nothing but foster relations with shelters, just stays in touch with them, helps them be rescue-friendly . . . different shelters in different places react to rescue differently. Some are more rescue-friendly than others. . . . I mean they don't dislike us, but they want to do their own thing and they do a good job at that . . . we try to maintain good relationships with shelters for the most part.[19]

Joy Viola: Some shelters say, "OK, great, rescue's taking a dog frees up a run and now we can bring in another dog," but others feel that this is an elitist approach and they resent rescue because they're in the trenches there day-to-day handling lots of needy dogs regardless of pedigree.[20]

Whether or not a rescue's activities are seen as cherry-picking is entirely dependent on the breed of dog in question. Desirable dogs such as Golden Retrievers are immensely attractive commodities for shelters, while rescue groups that take less desirable dogs, such as Pit Bulls, are less likely to be accused of cherry-picking simply by virtue of their specializing in the rescue of dogs belonging to a less desirable, even vilified, breed.

Perhaps Beryl Board's recommendation, that rescue groups accept a situation in which some shelters will only call rescue groups when the dog in question is not very adoptable, would seem to lead to the most practical and cooperative solution. Given the nearly irreconcilable views held by some shelters or humane societies and rescue groups as to what constitutes the best method to help needy dogs, it is a testimony to the power of the larger issue at hand that unites them in common purpose—namely the improvement of the situation of all needy dogs and animals—that positive relationships between these two very different worlds far outweigh the negative ones.

One thing seems indisputable: Positive relationships between the two parties result in an efficient rescuing process in which most, if not all, dogs become adopted. Dogs that are represented by a breed rescue group are pulled from local shelters and thus make room for dogs that do not have a local rescue group as their advocate and thus run the realistic risk of being turned away from the shelter for space reasons. Shelters can keep desirable dogs to attempt to increase traffic for dog adoptions, knowing that rescue groups are willing to handle the less adoptable dogs of their breed that may arrive at their facilities. In a situation with positive relationships, both parties—the rescue groups and the local shelters—win.

However, when rescue groups and local shelters have negative relationships with each other, both sides lose. The rescue groups are unable to help dogs that they could place without individual members of the group resorting to taking dogs out by falsifying the adoption application and pretending not to be affiliated with a rescue group,[21] an action that has the potential to hurt the reputation of the rescue group if the truth were discovered. The worst-case scenario entails dogs that rescue groups could adopt but that languish in shelters with the realistic possibility of their being euthanized there for lack of space or for having the dog develop symptoms of aggression and hostility due to the long duration of its confinement, which render the dog unadoptable. This leads to the doubly troubling scenario in which a perfectly adoptable dog fails to be adopted, resulting in a downward spiral that might result in the dog's euthanasia. Whatever the undesirable outcome of this situation might be, this dog ends up occupying sorely needed space that other homeless dogs deserve but whom the shelter cannot accept due to space limitations. The potentially unnecessary euthanasia of a dog that the rescue could have helped hurts the rescue group from a morale standpoint because a dog belonging to "its" breed had been killed unnecessarily; but it also hurts the shelter in that any unnecessary euthanasia is deemed the worst-case scenario and basically unacceptable to members of both of these organizations. Negative relationships between rescue groups and local shelters damage the efficacy of each organization and lead to harming the only clientele that ultimately matters to both: needy dogs.

Far and away the optimal situation emerges when all concerned parties committed to the dogs' welfare not only get along but also form actual organizational coalitions and genuine synergy to maximize the efficacy of the work in pursuit of their passion. Beryl Board stated:

> RAGOM [Retrieve a Golden of Minnesota] is a founding member of the newly formed coalition of Minnesotan rescues. It's called Minnesota Partnership for Animal Welfare . . . it's a true coalition. . . . It includes large animal humane societies, it has little tiny kitty rescues, it has local Pit Bull organizations, it includes Animal Control offices, local businesses, spay and neuter initiatives . . . it's a genuine cross-section of everyone involved in animal welfare.[22]

When these organizations are able to pool resources and cooperate with purpose and dedication, they enhance their separate as well as collective abilities to rescue the greatest possible number of dogs.

Rescue Groups and Local AKC Clubs

The relationships between rescue groups and local AKC clubs tend to have a greater variety than those of rescue groups and shelters. The purpose of an AKC club is to support the ethical breeding of the dogs whose breed the club represents and to show these dogs regionally and nationally at competitions for conformation and breed specific activities such as hunting and agility. This logic, which is so essential to most AKC clubs and, more or less defines the very core of their existence and identity, can cause friction with some rescue groups, as many, though far from all, of these reject and disdain any breeding of dogs as unethical while dogs continue to languish and perish in shelters. In our research of rescue groups, we noticed the preponderance of what we would categorize as neutral relationships between rescue groups and the local AKC clubs. But we also encountered instances in which there existed virtually no relationship between these two entities. Moreover, we witnessed relationships that were very positive, close, and cordial, but also others that one would have to categorize as extremely negative and outright hostile.

The majority of rescue groups do not have a regular relationship with their local AKC club, as Burt Augst pointedly summarized when he stated, "we don't have any bad relationship with them [the local AKC club], we just don't really have any relationship with them. We'll communicate with them from time to time, but really it's no ongoing relationship."[23] The prevailing attitude and modus operandi in this scenario appears to be mutually benign disinterest—not to say neglect—on the part of both the rescue group and the local AKC club, with the latter often wishing that the former not exist because the unmentioned elephant in the room still remains a pervasive view among clubs that rescues somehow and in some unspecified but still tangible manner diminish the value of the breed. Claire Kontos stated:

> My sense is that clubs don't want to see rescue. I think that on the whole clubs don't like to think that there is a need for rescue and that, in fact, rescues might be contributing to that need. . . . Club folks often think that only poorly bred dogs or dogs with bad temperaments end up in rescue. In other words, if a club does its job right, there will be no dogs with any problems and therefore no need for rescue. And clubs do not want to think, and certainly not admit, that they are producing deficient dogs that end up in rescue. Also, clubs often think that they are better at finding proper homes for the dogs than rescues.[24]

Although club and rescue love the breed, these organizations' priorities diverge in terms of how best to express their appreciation for the breed and how to maximize their support for it.

Positive relationships between rescue groups and local AKC clubs are not as common as neutral—or nonexistent—ones, but they tend to be the result of long-term interactions either by the rescue group's birth emanating from the AKC club or from the two organizations' specific coexistence and actual collaboration in a particular area for an extended period of time. Carol Allen's Golden Retriever Rescue of Central New York exemplifies the former, as her group started as a committee of the club and to this day "the club has remained very attentive to the rescue and very generous to it. We share advertisements in catalogs for example, some expenses at shows. . . . And it doesn't hurt that I've been able to carry the banner as the president of the club."[25] Because the rescue group was originally part of the club, the founding members of the rescue group were individuals that supported the AKC club's mission of ethical breeding. They continue to do so to this day, thus allowing the two parties to have a cordial and mutually beneficial relationship. Debbie Lukasik of Golden Retriever Rescue of Wisconsin stated that "we have a pretty decent relationship with them [the local AKC club]. It's taken a long time to have established this relationship, you know, and it's something that's always a work in progress."[26] Though featuring people with different perspectives and representing different organizational views and priorities, the two entities do—according to Lukasik—agree wholeheartedly on a bottom line, which is to set all differences aside and cooperate for the benefit of the dogs. This common denominator creates a basis of mutual respect that bridges any philosophical differences in the approaches to the dogs' overall welfare. To be sure, such readiness for cooperation still involves a solid, often lengthy, learning process on the club's part to come to tolerate, perhaps even appreciate, the rescue. Joan Puglia gave her thoughts on this very issue:

> In the early days of our existence, it was a standing joke. When we went to one of our national specialties, which is a big thing for the Golden Retriever Club of America, we asked for booth space and they said, "no, no, no, we don't do that type of stuff." We basically had no credibility and the club did not want us, they placed us between the Port-a-Potties and where the bull was serving the cows. . . . We were viewed as marginal and worse—a nuisance even, something to be ashamed of almost, certainly an unnecessary burden. This has changed big time over the years. Now we are treated with respect and welcomed, if not loved.[27]

This rapprochement between club and rescue in New England that Puglia described seems to have reached a sufficiently successful state to have garnered national attention as attested to by Jody Jones's praising comments from across the continent at Homeward Bound, the California-based rescue that Jones has led: "The New England situation has a fabulous relationship between club and rescue. The club has been extremely supportive in terms of its individual members and their attitude towards rescue, and their attendance at auctions and fundraisers for rescue; and both gave us financial support when we were doing our capital campaign."[28] Positive relationships between rescues and local AKC clubs are mutually beneficial; rescues gain resources and connections in their larger breed world, and local clubs benefit from the positive public image they attain when they cooperate with rescue groups devoted to their breed.

Negative relationships between rescue groups and local AKC clubs can develop for many reasons. First, one can never underestimate the damage that personal rivalries and animosities, which have virtually no role in the matter at hand, often create. But much more frequently, the hostilities emanate from different preferences and philosophies concerning the very role of breed specific canine rescue in general and the breed at hand in particular. Some groups have developed negative relationships with their local AKC clubs because "there were some people on the board of the club that thought that rescue wasn't necessary, that there wasn't really a problem at all, that rescue was just grandstanding by some people."[29] The dismissal of rescue as a superfluous imposition in the eyes of the local AKC club understandably hampers any development of a positive relationship between the two organizations. Needless to say, such a negative attitude is clearly not to the rescue organization's liking and is met with equal antipathy toward the club. The infelicitous upshot, of course, is that any meaningful cooperation between the two has been all but impossible.

Another potential source of friction can emanate from rescue group members' comments and references about breeders involved in the local AKC club. If a rescue group speaks negatively about the quality of dogs emerging from a particular breeder and recommends that adopters seeking puppies look at other breeders, it can cause the local AKC club to which the maligned breeder belongs to feel that the rescue group is speaking negatively about the local AKC club as a whole and not just one of its particular members who happens to be a breeder. Conflict between rescue groups and AKC clubs can also develop when the latter openly oppose the creation of the former for fear that the rescue groups will accept and place dogs of "lower" quality, thereby reducing the overall value of the dogs that the clubs so meticulously aim to uphold with their breeding. One rescue stated that "the folks in this breed club were actually opposed to the idea of our starting a rescue and have never really gotten on board with our project. . . . There's an elitist attitude in the club that essentially says: 'We breed quality dogs and you people with your rescue dogs aren't really dealing with good quality dogs.'"[30] Apropos clubs' elitist attitudes toward rescues, Bob Tillay, when asked about his organization's relationship with the local Golden Retriever Club, stated: "When we are at the same event, they, what do you call it, poo-poo us. The Golden Retriever Club has nothing to do with me or 'Love a Golden' [another rescue in the St. Louis area]."[31] Rescuers sense this dismissive attitude on the part of breeders toward the entire rescue project, which needless to say does not endear the latter to the former. Thus the statement by Joan Puglia makes sense: "When you talk to a lot of rescue people, you're going to find a lot of anger towards breed clubs."[32] Differences of opinion with respect to how unwanted dogs should be treated often create negative relationships between rescue groups and local AKC clubs.

This harkens back to the purpose of the AKC clubs, which promote breeding for conformation and want the best dogs to represent the breed, not dogs that might have the slightest physical or temperamental irregularities that would disqualify them from being shown. It is largely over this often massive divergence of views regarding what constitutes the quality of a dog, indeed whether such criteria are even legitimate or ethical mechanisms to measure a dog's very worth, that the conflict between AKC clubs and rescue groups attains a degree of acerbity and acrimony that at times renders their cooperation impossible. Just as shelters and humane societies have often regarded breed specific rescues as elitists and have thus chosen not to deal with them, so, too, have rescue groups regarded AKC clubs and their breeders as elitists because they define the essence of a dog by the alleged purity of its pedigree and the quality of its conformation and breeding. In both cases of these conflict lines, the all-too-dominant and ubiquitous human desire for credentialing and differentiation serves as a major source of antagonism and friction. And once again, as has so often been the case throughout our study, the assignation "elitist" denotes nothing of worth, invoking derision and contempt instead.

The quality of relationships between breed rescues and local AKC clubs can determine the availability of needed resources for both organizations. When positive relationships exist, rescue groups can count on the welcome support of fellow breed enthusiasts who are willing to donate time and money to the rescue organization to help it in its mission of rescuing needy dogs. Rescue groups, in turn, offer breeders who are involved in local AKC clubs the option for humane placement of dogs "that need to vanish out of the litter, because the breeders know that rescues will take such dogs and mum's the word."[33] In other words, in the world of good relationships, rescue groups gain a generous ally in AKC clubs that help these groups in the taxing task of rescue, whereas AKC clubs avail themselves of rescue groups in the safe and reliable placement of dogs that do not fit conformation standards. Although actually not damaging either to the rescue groups or the local AKC clubs, neutral or nonexistent relationships between the two do in fact have a negative bearing in that potential cooperation between the two parties remains absent, and thus leaving valuable resources that could be helpful to both parties fallow. Openly negative relationships, however, are clearly detrimental to both. Mutual denunciations that often accompany such negative relationships bear costs to both in terms of financial losses and—more important still—diminution in stature and reputation, which remain these organizations' most cherished asset. Acrimony and its accompanying tensions and denunciations can lead to a general atmosphere of negativity in which the rescue groups lose donations, and breeders belonging to the AKC clubs may well have fewer potential buyers for their puppies. Above all, negative relations also imply that valuable human energy that could be put to the purpose of helping dogs is needlessly drained by internecine fights that harm the larger common cause in many ways, from a hurt reputation to diminished material support.

Rescue Groups and Their Relationships with Other Local Rescues

Rescue groups and their interactions with other local rescue groups provide numerous opportunities for mutually beneficial relationships and constructive cooperation. These relationships can be intrabreed (cooperation between two or more rescues representing the same breed) or interbreed (cooperation between each rescue representing a different breed). Each has its own advantages. Intrabreed rescue relationships usually occur through the solidarity of rescuing the same breed and by virtue of a large regional need for rescue that no one breed rescue could fulfill. Bob Tillay of Dirk's Fund illustrates this intrabreed rescue relationship: "Love a Golden jumps all over to get a dog. If they can't get it, they will call me immediately or I will call them and say, 'Can you get this dog?' We are as passionate about helping each other as we are about helping the dogs."[34] Relationships with other local rescue groups can be hugely beneficial to rescue groups that are willing and able to participate in such relationships. Through their appreciation of the same breed and their desire to cooperate with one another in the quest of helping this breed's needy dogs, these rescue organizations ensure that they save as many dogs as possible, providing one another with invaluable resources that include transportation, home visits, and even sharing physical resources such as food and space.

Interbreed rescue relationships are typically formed in a specific geographic area, such as the Coalition of All Breed Rescues of Arizona (CABRA), of which Rescue a Golden of Arizona (RAGAZ) is a participating member. Barbara Elk, a member of RAGAZ, describes the benefits of belonging to CABRA:

One of the things they do is hold spay and neuter clinics, so we have joined that, and we help them once every other month with doing that. The county is there, and they're licensing dogs, and another thing that they have been very helpful with is keeping a pulse on the various grants that are out there, and putting us in touch with the organizations that we were not familiar with before.[35]

These groups provide a slightly different support for one another than those shared by intrabreed rescues. By virtue of not having the shared bond of particular affection for a specific breed, interaction among interbreed rescues rests a bit more on practical and instrumental rather than emotional dimensions. Thus, for example, home visits and transportation arrangements are created among interbreed rescues just as they are among their intrabreed counterparts. With the organizational growth and increasing legitimacy of breed specific rescue as an integral institution of the larger human–animal world in the contemporary United States, the differences between inter- and intrabreed cooperation have consistently been diminished.

Neutral relationships between rescue groups, whether intra- or interbreed in nature, largely arise for the same reasons as neutral relationships between rescue groups and local AKC clubs. Benign disinterest seems to be the overwhelming cause for such de facto nonexistent relationships, where rescue groups wish one another well and hope each is successful, but they do not feel any reason or urge to interact with one another. Particularly in the absence of intrabreed relationships, rescue groups obviously neglect potentially valuable resources that any active cooperation would inevitably provide each participant and the cause as a whole.

Negative relationships between rescue groups are almost always the consequence of split-offs of one group from the other. When intrabreed rescue groups split over matters of policy or personality, rather than for geographic reasons, the resulting relationship is almost always negative. This negative intrabreed relationship can sometimes manifest itself as a bitter and active rivalry between the groups or it can also result in a simple refusal to cooperate or coordinate with each other on any level.

A rescue group's relationship with another rescue group can have a strong effect on the behavior and efficacy of both groups. Positive relationships make the job of rescuing dogs easier and ensure that, through resource sharing, more dogs are rescued. This is true of both intra- and interbreed relationships. Neutral relationships, when present between same-breed groups, represent untapped potential for further rescue.

Particularly absent the availability of any large coalitions, neutral inter-breed relationships are not very likely to occur and do not represent the same level of untapped potential as is the case with neutral intrabreed relationships, as the former can only share tangible resources, rather than the networks of adopters, donors, and volunteers that intrabreed relationships have almost by definition.

When the relationship between rescues of the same breed is negative, these groups are not only failing to capitalize on the resources that each could offer the other, but they are also harming their goal of rescuing as many dogs as possible because bickering and competition for dogs and resources harms both groups involved.

Rescue Groups and National Breed Club Organizations

National breed club organizations, such as the parent clubs of local AKC clubs, can have a profound effect on the behavior of local AKC clubs and thus these clubs' relationships with local rescue groups. In addition to their power over the policies of local AKC clubs, the national breed club organizations represent influential potential allies in their own right to rescues, as their national presence can help coordinate local rescue groups in their efforts. This section will discuss the Golden Retriever and Labrador Retriever national AKC parent groups for illustrative purposes with respect to the power of the national breed club organization in relation to rescue.

The majority of Golden Retriever rescue groups have a positive relationship with the Golden Retriever Club of America (GRCA) and its National Rescue Committee (NRC). The GRCA-NRC communicates with many of the Golden Retriever rescue groups; this communication can be as minimal as the annual survey sent out by the GRCA-NRC to which the rescue may or may not respond; but it can also involve the rescue's active participation in the variety of Yahoo! lists that the GRCA-NRC maintains, including a president's list, a list for beginning rescues, and a list for groups working with puppy mill rescues.[36] The GRCA-NRC also works closely with the Golden Retriever Foundation (GRF), an organization that helps to fund rescues in need of assistance.[37] To be sure, we encountered Golden Retriever rescue groups that had not heard of the GRCA-NRC and its main figure, Carol Allen. Tellingly, most of these groups were among the first cohort of such rescues, had thus likely attained and then maintained solid self-sufficiency before the advent of the GRCA-NRC, and therefore saw no reason to seek its assistance.

However, the majority of Golden Retriever rescues that have maintained contact with the GRCA-NRC have reaped important benefits from this relationship, ranging from financial support and helpful information to much-needed coordination in times of natural disasters, as happened with Hurricane Katrina in 2005. The GRCA-NRC maintained a page on their website updating rescue groups on the situation in New Orleans after Hurricane Katrina and coordinated efforts among Golden Retriever rescue groups in addition to communicating with shelters in the New Orleans area to facilitate the rescue of Golden Retrievers.[38] In summary, there is no doubt that the Golden Retriever rescue groups benefit solidly from their relationship with the GRCA, the GRCA-NRC, and the GRF.

This contrasts sharply with the situation of the Labrador Retriever rescue groups and their national breed club organization, the AKC Parent Club of the Labrador Retriever (PCLR). Of the Labrador Retriever rescue groups we interviewed, none knew of or had ever been contacted by the PCLR or its rescue committee. This appears to indicate that, in juxtaposition to the keen interest displayed by the GRCA in rescuing its breed, the PCLR—for whatever reasons—appears to be less involved in rescuing its breed. This seeming inactivity or lack of presence has further ramifications in that the Labrador Retriever rescue groups are much less able to network at the same level as their Golden Retriever counterparts because the PCLR's low profile negatively affects the abilities of Labrador Retriever rescue groups to network with one another and capture the benefits of intrabreed relationships, as mentioned above. At a minimum, Labrador Retriever rescue groups have, without the PCLR's involvement, fewer resources available to assist them in rescuing dogs, thus placing these rescue groups at a decided disadvantage when compared with breed rescues that have more involved national breed club organizations, of which the GRCA is decidedly one.

A Quantitative Comparison

In order to shed more light on the important facet of rescue groups' relationships with outside organizations, which we deem to be crucial for the overall efficacy of breed specific canine rescue, we devised a quantitative measure of the quality of relationships that rescues cultivate with all outside organizations, which has been highlighted in this chapter. Although we are fully aware of the limits of such measures and do not regard quantitative approaches as inherently superior to qualitative ones, we deem them yet another valued piece of data in helping us understand and explain the world of breed specific canine rescue.

Thus, we devised a scoring system for all Golden Retriever rescues and Labrador Retriever rescues that were studied in our research. We culled from all our interviews the respondents' description of their perceptions of their groups' relationships with the five types of external relationships we identified and discussed in this chapter. We assigned each group five relationship scores corresponding to their relationships with the national breed club, the local breed club, local rescue groups, local shelters, and the general public. The possible values ranged from –1 (entirely negative relationship) to +1 (entirely positive relationship), with 0 as neutral or unmentioned and +/–0.5 depending on whether a general statement about relationships was made, but with a counterexample as well. Table 6.1, representing merely an illustrative ideal type, gives examples of hypothetical situations for each possible relationship score.

We then added the five discrete relationship scores for a particular rescue group with the result yielding a networking score that could range

TABLE 6.1. Characterization of the Quality of Relationships that Golden Retriever Rescues and Labrador Retrievers Rescues Maintain with Outside Organizations

Relationship Score	Description	Example
–1	100% of external relationships with a particular type of organization are negative.	A particular rescue group has negative relationships with all local AKC clubs.
–0.5	The rescue group has more negative relationships with a particular type of organization than positive relationships with that type of organization.	A particular rescue group has largely negative relationships with local shelters, but has some positive shelter relationships.
0	The group has a neutral/nonexistent relationship with a particular type of organization or does not mention the organization in the interview.	A particular rescue group has no relationship with the national breed club.
0.5	The rescue group has more positive relationships with a particular type of organization than negative relationships with that type of organization.	A particular rescue group has largely positive relationships with local rescues, but has a few negative relationships with particular local rescues.
1	100% of external relationships with a particular type of organization are positive.	A particular rescue group has an entirely positive relationship with the general public.

from −5 (the group has entirely negative relationships with all external organizations) to +5 (the group has entirely positive relationships with all external organizations). Concretely, our networking scores ranged from a low of 1.5 (one entirely positive relationship score and one mixed relationship score, all other relationship scores being neutral) to a high of 5 (all relationship scores positive). For the twenty-four Golden Retriever rescue groups we interviewed, the average networking score was 3.5, while the eighteen Labrador Retriever rescue groups we interviewed had an average networking score of 2.78. This difference is due to the involvement of the GRCA-NRC in the world of Golden Retriever rescue and the lack of involvement of the PCLR in the Labrador Retriever rescue world; 79 percent of the Golden Retriever rescues we interviewed reported positive interactions with the national club, while none of the Labrador Retriever rescues reported *any* relationship with the national club, many stating they had never been contacted by the national club at all. When compared with the apparent nonexistence of PCLR involvement, the GRCA-NRC's engagement in Golden Retriever rescue represents a large advantage that Golden Retriever rescue groups possess over Labrador Retriever rescues. As presented above, Golden Retriever rescues benefit from positive relationships with the GRCA-NRC, while Labrador Retriever rescues, much to their detriment, appear not to benefit from relationships with the PCLR.

The results of these scores show the remarkable differences between the rescue organizations representing the two breeds and the way they pursue external relationships. The most critical difference appears in each of the rescue groups' relationship with its respective national club. Of the Golden Retriever rescues we interviewed, our measures reveal that 79.17 percent enjoyed positive interactions with the Golden Retriever national club, while, according to our measures, none of the Labrador Retriever rescues had any relationship with the Labrador Retriever national club.[39] Golden Retriever rescues were also twice as likely to have contact with their local clubs, with 62.5 percent of Golden Retriever rescues maintaining some form of contact (positive or negative) with their local club. Only 27.78 percent of Labrador Retriever rescues do the same. These data are supported by our examinations of levels of local breed club involvement in rescue, as 82.54 percent of Golden Retriever clubs had some involvement in rescue (passive [a page on their website listing local rescue groups, for example], active [assisted in rescue or has a rescue committee], or some combination of the two), while only 61.36 percent of Labrador Retriever clubs had some level of involvement in rescue; more Golden Retriever rescues started in local clubs (15.84 percent) than Labrador Retriever rescues (3.41 percent).

Both breeds' rescue groups that had their origins in local breed clubs typically sustain networking advantages both with the local breed club, with whom they are likely to maintain positive contacts, and with other breed rescues, as the networking that occurs as a club's special efforts and characteristics encompasses regional clubs and rescues as well. Both breeds' rescue organizations had similar levels of contact with other local rescue groups and local shelters.

What do these measures mean for the purposes of our comparison? We learn from them that Golden Retriever rescues are much more likely to be in contact with the external entities that they rely on for resources, and the interactions they have are more likely to be positive than in the comparable case with Labrador Retriever rescues. This gives the former a distinct advantage when it comes to cultivating the relationships necessary to procure resources for their rescues, the core of their activity and their very identity. The high level of contact with the national club is particularly important, as the GRCA-NRC works as an organizational hub for the Golden Retriever rescue community, providing it with a reliable infrastructure for communication among groups and allowing them to exchange information and goods speedily and efficiently. The names of early and prominent figures in Golden Retriever rescue such as Joan Puglia and Susan Foster of Yankee Golden Retriever Rescue and Carol Allen of the GRCA-NRC were known to most Golden Retriever rescues that we studied. At least to our knowledge and gauging from our extensive interviews, comparable founding figures and nationally known and respected leaders do not seem to exist in the Labrador Retriever rescue world. The fact that none of the Labrador Retriever rescues we interviewed had contact with the national club suggests that the Labrador Retriever national club does not serve the same function in the rescue world of its breed as the GRCA has in its rescue world.

Conclusion

Rescue groups interact with other organizations on a daily basis. In a world where every ounce of capital—financial, social, cultural—counts, their ability to rescue needy dogs effectively depends on their skill in navigating the relationships they form with the general public, local shelters, local AKC clubs, local rescue groups, and the national breed club organizations that represent their breed. Whether these relationships are positive depends on a variety of factors, many of which are beyond the groups' control. Those that make the effort to have positive relationships with the organizations with which they interact are rewarded by having access to an array of resources that groups with primarily negative relationships to the outside world do not have. Although fostering good relationships with the outside world is not a necessary condition for rescue groups' survival and flourishing, it most certainly provides benefits that no group should ever spurn.

The next chapter will focus on the all-important aspect of communication. It would not be wrong to say that—possibly next to their reputational capital—it is these organizations' communicative abilities that define the level of their efficacy and ultimate success. In particular, we will concentrate on the rise of the use of the Internet, which—we will argue—has completely altered the modus operandi for dog rescue.

Notes

1. Maureen Distler. Interviewed by Katherine Crosby. Telephone Interview. July 28, 2010.

2. Edith Bryan. Interviewed by Katherine Crosby. Telephone Interview. August 12, 2010.

3. Debbie Lukasik. Interviewed by Katherine Crosby. Telephone Interview. August 12, 2010.

4. Phil Fisher. Interviewed by Andrei Markovits. Telephone Interview. July 30, 2009.

5. Susan Wells. Interviewed by Katherine Crosby. Telephone Interview. August 10, 2010.

6. Allie Medendorp. Interviewed by Katherine Crosby. Telephone Interview. August 10, 2010.

7. Tami Stanley. Interviewed by Katherine Crosby. Telephone Interview. July 29, 2010.

8. Beryl Board. Interviewed by Andrei Markovits. Telephone Interview. July 29, 2009.

9. Robin Adams. Interviewed by Andrei Markovits. Telephone Interview. July 7, 2009.

10. Lauren Genkinger. Interviewed by Katherine Crosby. Telephone Interview. August 18, 2010.

11. Amy Compton. Interviewed by Andrei Markovits. Telephone Interview. August 17, 2009.

12. Fisher interview.

13. Julie Jones. Interviewed by Katherine Crosby. Telephone Interview. July 29, 2010.

14. Fisher interview.

15. Mary Jane Shervais. Interviewed by Andrei Markovits. Telephone Interview. August 17, 2009.

16. Lukasik interview.

17. Adams interview.

18. Gene Fitzpatrick. Interviewed by Andrei Markovits. Telephone Interview. August 17, 2010.

19. Burt Augst. Interviewed by Andrei Markovits. Telephone Interview. July 28, 2009.

20. Joy Viola. Interviewed by Andrei Markovits. Telephone Interview. July 16, 2009.

21. The interview subject who provided this material to us requested to remain anonymous because of the information's sensitive nature.

22. Board interview.

23. August interview.

24. Claire Kontos. Interviewed by Andrei Markovits. Telephone Interview. August 3, 2009.

25. Carol Allen. Interviewed by Andrei Markovits. Telephone Interview. July 7, 2009.

26. Lukasik interview.

27. Joan Puglia. Interviewed by Andrei Markovits. Telephone Interview. June 30, 2009.

28. Jody Jones. Interviewed by Andrei Markovits. Personal Interview. Elverta, California. August 20, 2009.

29. Because of the nature of this quote, we decided to allow this interviewee to remain anonymous.

30. Because of the nature of this quote, we decided to allow this interviewee to remain anonymous.

31. Bob Tillay. Interviewed by Andrei Markovits. Telephone Interview. August 18, 2010.

32. Puglia interview.

33. Because of the nature of this quote, we decided to allow this interviewee to remain anonymous.

34. Tillay interview.

35. Barbara Elk. Interviewed by Andrei Markovits. Telephone Interview. August 19, 2010.

36. Bob Bornstein. Interviewed by Andrei Markovits. Telephone Interview. August 12, 2010.

37. Allen interview.

38. Internet Archive, "Coordinated Effort Launched for Golden Retriever Victims of Hurricane Katrina." http://web.archive.org/web/20051230064510/http://www.grca-nrc.org/HurricaneKatrina.htm (accessed on April 27, 2014).

39. Two Labrador Retriever rescues casually mentioned that they were listed on the AKC Parent Club of the Labrador Retrievers' rescue referral website, but stated that they otherwise had no contact with the parent club whatsoever.

CHAPTER 7

Communication, Networking, and Sustenance

I don't think any rescue at any level is really able to operate without the Internet today.

—Burt Augst
Middle Tennessee Golden Retriever Rescue

As far as getting the dogs out there, and for all our communications actually, the web is absolutely critical.

—Kevin Wilcox
Peppertree Rescue

The power of the Internet is totally amazing.... We need it for every aspect of our operation. But like I said, if a rescue does something it shouldn't do, it will be all over the Internet forever.

—Renee Riegel
Greater Dayton Labrador Retriever Rescue

The previous chapter discussed the relationships rescue groups can have with external organizations. This chapter will analyze the mechanisms by which rescue groups engage in these relationships. In particular, we explore answers to the following questions: How do rescue groups communicate and network with external organizations? What are the advantages and disadvantages of these methods of communication? How do rescue groups receive sustenance from these external organizations? Why must rescue groups engage in such activities? In short, this chapter will look at the all-important external networks and overall organizational context that comprise the life world of canine rescue. After all, rescue groups must harness the resources they need for their very survival from structures that are extraneous to them: whether it is the necessity a rescue group encounters involving the transportation of a dog from another rescue group; or attaining a grant from a national breed club; or the ever-present need to garner donations from the general public. Rescue groups greatly depend on their ability to harness the support of an array of disparate organizations, institutions, and people. Thus, the art of communication and networking constitutes one of the most essential ingredients in the survival and success of any canine breed rescue.

Methods of Communication

Newsletters are perhaps the most basic and widespread means of communication that rescue groups have come to adopt as a regular channel to reach the outside world. Newsletters contain a variety of information, depending on the interests and needs of the rescue group at the time of publication. Thus, for example, they can provide updates on dogs the rescue group has acquired or placed as well as listings of future group events. In addition to such factual information, newsletters regularly feature advice concerning the maintenance and improvement of the dogs' health. They also provide tips concerning canine behavior and, of course, include pleas for assistance with regard to specific dogs. The topics covered in newsletters have vastly expanded over the past two decades in which rescue organizations have proliferated across the United States. Indeed, virtually any subject relating to dogs can appear as a matter of course in these publications.

Newsletters can be monthly, bimonthly, or quarterly and usually contain updates on the rescue group's progress, information about upcoming events, dogs in need of specialized assistance (such as an expensive surgery), and even public service announcements about canine health generally. Newsletters highlight the activities of the group since the newsletters' previous issue and maintain connections to individuals and organizations with whom a relationship has already been developed.

Newsletters can be disseminated by one of two methods: via the U.S. Postal Service (USPS) or electronically. Printed newsletters have the advantage of being more user friendly, especially for recipients who are uncomfortable using computers or do not have one. (Yes, these folks still exist.)

Printed newsletters also furnish the most conventional form of published communication of which rescue groups have availed themselves over the years. Moreover, the printed newsletter's more traditional format lends it an air of legitimacy that rescue groups crave and need. Although this means of communication has been on a steep decline over the past few years, it is unlikely to disappear completely in the foreseeable future. Gene Fitzpatrick's words depict the situation quite well: "Yes, we still have a newsletter, believe it or not. We've changed it to once every four months from once per quarter, but we needed to cut down on expenses and we never knew what to put on the front page, so we changed it to every four months."[1]

However, Fitzpatrick's response affirming the continued, though diminished, presence of his organization's printed newsletters constituted a clear minority among our interviewees, most of whom informed us about their organizations' publication of an electronic newsletter in conjunction with a printed one in which the former had assumed a steady ascendance over the past years with the latter clearly fading or, in some cases, becoming extinct. "Basically, we do almost all of our communication by e-mail," said Mary Vanderbloomen. She continued: "Besides our website, we don't do a printed newsletter at all anymore."[2] Added Lauren Genkinger: "We have an electronic newsletter that we send out once a month and sometimes we will send out e-blasts in addition. People sign up for our newsletter on our website, and we also have a Facebook page, and we have a blog. We have 3,000 names on our newsletter list and anyone who adopts a dog is automatically placed on our newsletter."[3] But tellingly, the printed copy will most likely continue its existence as long as the Boomer generation, which, after all, created canine rescue in the first place, remains active in this worthy endeavor. Jacky Eckard added interesting statements on this generational issue informing canine rescue:

> We have a monthly newsletter that we send out electronically and that goes to all our adopters, a large group of people, and anybody that's given us money. And we just tried a new thing, we identified our top one hundred donors and we mailed out a paper newsletter to them thinking that these folks tend to be more like Boomer kind of people that still read mail that comes from the Post Office. We just gave this a try, the printed newsletter just went out this week, so we'll see how that will work.[4]

Printed newsletters allow rescue groups to maintain contact with their volunteers and adopters in a more traditional manner than electronic versions. They bespeak constancy and establishment rather than speed. Additionally, printed newsletters somehow still embody a certain institutional gravitas that their electronic counterparts have yet to attain. Often sent through programs like Constant Contact, electronic newsletters, in contrast to their printed version, allow rescue groups to reach large numbers of people instantaneously and without incurring significant printing and mailing costs. Although each type of newsletter has its advantages and disadvantages, both can point to attaining similar, if not identical, results in terms of the group's operational efficacy. If financially feasible to the groups, the two newsletter formats provide them with much complementarity rather than any redundancy in their communication needs.

After all, a newsletter's main purpose is to establish and maintain contact with individuals who, while not always members of the group, have indicated an interest in the group in some way, typically as a previous donor or adopter. Regardless of the newsletter's format, its regular appearance ensures that individuals who are organizationally peripheral to the group but sympathetic to its cause and supportive of its existence remain updated on the group's affairs and activities. This is particularly effective and important when the newsletter mentions the group's needs, be they for financial donations or volunteers—or often both. Essentially, it is the circle of individuals who have indicated their interest in the breed and have expressed their support of the group's causes but have not joined its ranks of activists whom the rescue group can appeal to when in need and from whom it is likely to receive support. Indeed, such hope is very well placed and frequently crowned by success precisely because this circle of sympathizers represents people who are almost identical to the group's members with the, albeit important, exception of not quite having made the commitment of becoming full-fledged group members. Such people comprise the group's outer circle though not its core. Joan Puglia put it best:

> I like to think of the newsletter as the blood of the organization because it will get out there into every nook and cranny like a circulatory system, and spread the word about rescue to people who are well predisposed towards it but know little or nothing about it. We try to stress the importance of developing and maintaining a newsletter with all the different groups that we work with.[5]

The imagery of the circulatory system is a very apt one for capturing the essence of newsletters, both in their original printed version as well as their subsequent electronic variant, for the rescue groups' operational existence.

Newsletters' major drawback as a tool for communicating with the general public pertains to their not being effective in expanding the readership and thus the group's scope. In order to receive a newsletter, the recipient must provide the group with either an actual (i.e., snail mail) or e-mail address, meaning that such a person will have had to contact the group first as opposed to vice versa, thus placing the burden of initiative squarely on the shoulders of the potentially interested party. This means that newsletters are an ineffective form of first contact because they preach to the choir as it were and only reach the already interested and involved. In short, newsletters do not provide the best means to expand the networks' reach.

Another form of communication that exists between rescue groups and the general public is that of the public outreach or educational events. These modes of communication occur in public spaces, are announced in the community in advance through devices such as posted flyers, and are used to recruit volunteers and educate the public about the breed and responsible dog ownership. These events happen in venues as small as pet stores and their parking lots or as large as city parks. Regardless of their scope and size, these events typically focus on five main topics: details about the breed; spaying and neutering; responsible dog ownership or obedience training; children and dog safety; and canine health issues. Groups often have members present at such public outreach or educational events where they provide demonstrations about the groups' activities and related matters, as well as distribute informational packets groups' make available, featuring topics that they deem especially salient for the particular event.

Public outreach or education events present different advantages and disadvantages than do newsletters. Events held in public venues like pet stores and parks allow any individual who happens to be in such a venue at that particular time to participate in the event, even if he or she was totally unaware of the event's occurrence, let alone its purpose and organizer. This medium therefore presents an opportunity for groups to expand their network to include individuals with whom they had absolutely no previous contact. It also allows groups to recruit such unsuspecting individuals who most likely had never heard of rescue, let alone the particular organizations, but are sympathetic to their cause as future donors, volunteers, adopters, or any or all of these. Public outreach or education events also provide positive public relations for a rescue group, in that by presenting its work and commitment to a less knowledgeable public, the latter attains a greater awareness not only about this particular group's work with its specific breed, but also about many issues salient to any responsible human guardianship of dogs, and indeed other animals. This is particularly true when rescues enter schools to educate children about dog safety and responsible dog owner-ship. Not only are these rescues helping to ensure that children and dogs have safer interactions, but they also instill in the young students the major tenets of responsible dog ownership, both of which enhance the group's positive reputation in the community as a whole. Such events harness the sympathetic public's attention for the rescue's activities and its very exis-tence. They broaden the rescue's appeal and, most important, they mobilize the attention and affect that a large number of well-meaning but ignorant sympathizers might now choose to bestow on the rescue.

The main disadvantages of public outreach or education events are twofold: they are time-consuming to plan and execute, and they are con-strained by geography. These events require that rescue groups plan and coordinate with their membership to ensure that an adequate number of members be present at such events and that all be fully apprised of their tasks and duties. Such preparations and planning take time and exact resources that could easily be spent on arguably more salient rescue-related issues, which already tax most of these groups' meager capabilities. On the client or consumer side as well, these events have drawbacks mainly because they require that all people whom the group is trying to reach appear in a cer-tain place at a certain time or the group's informational efforts may be for naught. Although these events of public outreach, education, or fundrais-ing allow groups to search for new membership, their effectiveness remains confined to the particular venue's purview. At its core, this medium remains totally local. It does not help rescue groups network with the general pub-lic on a regional let alone national level. Its effect remains highly confined and conscribed both spatially and temporally.

The final mechanism for rescue groups to reach the general public is, of course, through the use of the Internet. Although we will cover extensively the various communication tools that are available for rescue groups online in the section devoted to social media later in this chapter, here we will focus on the advantages and disadvantages of the Internet as a mechanism for communication between rescue groups and the general public. The advantages are compelling and powerful: the world's population is accessi-ble to rescue groups via Facebook, Twitter, Petfinder, and the groups' own websites, rendering communication vast in reach, instantaneous in time, and inexpensive, if not free, in cost. Rescue groups can recruit volunteers, adopters, and donors from areas far beyond their actual geographic pur-view, thereby expanding the groups' reach in every imaginable way, which, in turn, enhances their opportunities to save dogs. Via the Internet, res-cue groups can also ensure that their existence and cause are sufficiently promoted in their own region, as searches on search engines for their breeds' rescue in their location can easily lead potential volunteers and adopters straight to them.

Nothing has been a more powerful instrument in terms of modernizing rescue organizations in their internal operations and external relations than the Internet. We present three relevant voices confirming this assessment. First, Edith Bryan on adoption:

> If somebody wants to adopt through us, they go to the Seattle Purebred Dog Rescue website which is spdrdogs.org. They then fill out an adoption application online and when they click submit, they get a copy back, with one going to the Seattle Purebred Dog Rescue and another that comes to us and me. We then contact the applicant. Since we cover a very wide geographic area, we do not make home visits to applicants, unless there's some particular reason to do so. But with Google Earth we can look at people's fences and glean other important information about their homes that we need to know via the Internet.[6]

Then, Becky Hildebrand on the Internet's modernizing the complex web of foster volunteers:

> We do Gmail, so we have Gmail spreadsheets of all our foster homes with all relevant data such as, for example, how many dogs they have and what kinds of dogs they want. So we can tell when a foster family only wants to take a male dog because they have a female dog and their dog only gets along with males, for example. Now the intake coordinator who gets all the new dogs that reach us will coordinate foster homes and know which homes are open, which ones take only male dogs, which female dogs, which accept puppies and which won't do puppies. You know, whatever it is, we can now work closely together with very little time in deciding how to help these rescue dogs.[7]

Lastly, Nina Palmo on the Internet's power in the interaction between foster and the public:

> We have profiles of every dog so that foster parents can go online and update the dogs' status and post pictures and videos of the dogs. And then we have our entire application system on our website, so

when people fill out an application, it goes into the database and we click through the applications there, and when we go in to do the phone interview, we have our own form that we fill out; so everything from every angle happens right on our website. We know everything that we want to know about the dogs and the people who want to adopt them.[8]

The development of the Internet has revolutionized the most basic aspects of how dog rescue functions in that it has come to permit and facilitate the manner by which interested adopters come into contact with the rescue groups and select their dogs.

Groups also use the Internet to educate the public about rescue in general, and the specific group and its breed in particular. Gene Fitzpatrick spoke about this topic: "We tell them about the care of a Golden, what to do for this and for that. Why you should get a Golden, why you should not get a Golden. Why you should not get a puppy. So we try to educate the public and the consumers via the Internet besides using it to get our dogs adopted."[9]

Above all, the Internet's lasting influence might occur in something crucial, though prima facie completely unexpected, for rescues: their institutionalization and routinization. This could not have been more emphatically stated than by Bob Tillay's wonderfully descriptive words: "The Internet and the web have depersonalized—I mean de-Bob'ed—Dirk's Fund, which is exactly what I want. I want the mission to be the thing, not Bob. When people think of Dirk's Fund, I don't want them to think of Bob Tillay but only of what this organization does, its mission, which is to take good care of critters, not Bob."[10] Rescue groups have utilized their websites to their benefit with respect to their ability to educate the general public and to institutionalize their group's organization.

The major disadvantage of using the Internet as a tool for communication with the general public pertains to the effective management of this potentially overwhelming medium. To our question, "Does your group use social media such as Facebook or Twitter?" Alan Jordano from Grey-Save Rescue gave us a completely unexpected but all the more emphatically worded answer, the content of which surely few, if any, rescues share: "NO! While they may have value, they are also time sucking monsters and potential personal security threats."[11] As one rescuer told us:

The only downfall I've found about the Internet is that people tend to really get worked up on it, they get overly demanding and emotional, they voice demands and opinions that they would never have done in person or on the phone or in letters. Too much raw emotion, posting pleas that nobody can fulfill and are unreasonable and are often hurtful and insulting and not helpful to the only task at hand, namely to help our dogs.[12]

Instantaneous communication means that members of the general public who want to adopt or foster a dog apply to do so on a whim, then later change their minds, a process that, if repeated often enough, wastes the time of intake and volunteer coordinators for the groups and makes the process of adoption more cumbersome. It is precisely the spontaneity of the Internet that, on the one hand, lends it such communicative power, yet, on the other hand, requires some way to create a system of accountability that eliminates whimsical actions that are inimical to the project of dog rescue. Groups have to devise all kinds of safeguards and boundaries because shipping a dog from a rescue in California to an adopter in Maine is a major project entailing responsibility, commitment, never mind considerable expenses in money and time. Whims can be most costly in every imaginable way, not least to the only subject that matters in this whole endeavor and is the cause for the entire enterprise: the dog. Thus, the Internet has forced rescue groups to establish screening mechanisms that check the suitability of applicants from across the country that prior to the Internet's reach was performed by one of the group's members via a home visit to the prospective adopter. Needless to say, such screening mechanisms take time (occasionally even money) from the group's overcommitted volunteers, a cherished resource in any canine rescue organization.

Although we briefly discussed in the previous chapter the methods of communication that rescue groups use with external organizations, we will do so more fully here. Rescue groups have a variety of tools at their disposal for communicating with the general public, local shelters or humane societies, local American Kennel Club (AKC) breed clubs, other rescue groups, and national breed clubs. Each of the ways in which rescue groups choose to communicate with these external organizations has distinct advantages and disadvantages, and, when combined properly, can effectively secure as many resources as are available. When communicating with external organizations, groups must decide what constitutes the appropriate level of personalization for the purpose of their communication. For example, handwriting personalized notes to all potential donors in a region is logistically infeasible, yet sending a form letter to an important donor or group with which one is trying to develop a relationship might prove inappropriate and infelicitous in terms of garnering the financial support that the group desperately wants and needs. Whatever the case may be, it is imperative for the efficacy of a rescue group's outreach, especially when it wants to procure funds, to establish a golden mean between efficiently utilizing the paucity of its available resources in time and help, on the one hand, and setting the right tone and texture of the communication, on the other hand. We have therefore decided to categorize methods of communication by the following levels of personalization: highly personalized, semipersonalized, and untargeted. Each level of personalization has distinct advantages and disadvantages, which we will now discuss.

Highly Personalized Communication

Highly personalized forms of communication include personal visits, phone calls, and direct e-mails and letters to individuals and external organizations. These forms of communication are one-on-one contacts between a member of a breed rescue group and a specific individual in an external organization or the general public. The purpose of highly personalized communication is to establish and nurture a strong relationship with a person or organization of interest to the rescue group, such as the president of another local breed rescue group or a wealthy donor. The advantage of highly personalized communication is that it demonstrates the rescue group's clear commitment to the relationship, as highly personalized communication, by its very nature, is time and labor intensive and taxes the rescue group's limited resources. Of course, precisely therein lies the main disadvantage of this form of communication.

Highly personalized communication must be used strategically in order to be effective; sending a personalized, time-consuming letter to an individual who is unlikely to agree to donate to the group wastes the group's time and other precious resources that could have been spent elsewhere. Highly personalized communication is reserved for the relationships that are the most critical to the function of the rescue group and that—at least potentially—provide a substantial portion of the rescue group's resources, like a veterinarian who gives the group a discount for his or her services or a wealthy and generous donor who might bestow major financial support on the group. Because, with some soon-to-be-mentioned exceptions, only a few rescue groups have any genuine expertise in the art of fundraising, the highly personalized communication, though potentially immensely rewarding, remains an underutilized method by many rescues. Although understandable, the rarity of this method of communication is to the rescues' detriment because the possible benefits of highly personalized communication might be so substantial that the time and effort it exacts might often constitute a worthwhile investment. No one has been a more emphatic proponent of the high value this form of communication adds to rescue than Joy Viola:

> When somebody responds back with a personal note, I have taught Yankee Golden Retriever Rescue as well as the Golden Retriever Foundation to always pen something in your own hand at the bottom of any letter or circular, even if it's just "Many thanks for your help," but something personal needs to appear. It's good etiquette but it is an even better investment. I know a lot of others have picked up on this. I see this personalized communication as crucial for rescue's well-being. It goes way beyond just getting much-needed money. It shows a personal commitment that, quite frankly, is priceless.[13]

The personal touch necessary for highly personalized communication demonstrates a rescue group's investment in relationships that it deems special. Few things convey specialness and distinction more than a personal touch, which might indeed prove instrumental in the group's flourishing, or even survival.

Semipersonalized Communication

Semipersonalized forms of communication include e-mail lists, Yahoo! Groups, and newsletters (print and electronic) and are typically used after the rescue group has already approached the individual or organization with which it now seeks contact. E-mail lists (such as through Constant Contact) can be used to send quick bursts of information from the rescue group to its members but also to its circle of sympathizers and friends who are not formally associated with the group. An example of the use of this communication venue might be a group notifying its members that a local puppy mill has closed and that all hands on deck are needed to help with the ensuing crisis in terms of rescuing as many of these abused creatures as possible. Rescues use Yahoo! Groups as a method of intergroup communication, as has been the case, for example, with Golden Retriever Club of America's National Rescue Committee (GRCA-NRC), which maintains several Yahoo! Groups for a variety of subjects, including one Yahoo!

Group used by the presidents of rescue groups countrywide to share ideas and resources quickly and efficiently. Newsletters, of both the electronic and print variety, are typically sent to members of the rescue group, former adopters, and interested parties who contact the rescue group and request copies of the newsletter.

The advantage of semipersonalized communication is that it provides the group with a means of maintaining positive relationships with individuals and external organizations, while clearly not costing the group as much in time and resources as the use of highly personalized communication. The disadvantage of semipersonal communication is that it can only be used for the maintenance rather than the initiation of relationships. Targeted relationship initiation is the provenance of highly personalized communication, and broad relationship initiation is the result of untargeted communication. Semipersonalized communication is therefore an excellent means of relationship maintenance and a necessary tool for the continued receipt of resources from established relationships with external organizations and individuals.

Untargeted Communication

Untargeted communication methods feature means that are designed to reach a broad and undifferentiated audience. Among the most common items are flyers, brochures, or posters (often left at veterinary offices, animal shelters, pet stores, and rescue-friendly businesses); public events such as adoption days; meet-the-breed days; booths at breed shows; and social media (rescue group websites, with Facebook, Twitter, and Petfinder.com being among the most popular).

Flyers, brochures, and posters can be useful ways to catch many people's attention in public spaces. These items of communication reach a large audience and can invite helpful interest. Above all, they are quite cost-effective in that they require only the time and expense to design, print, and distribute to various strategic locations. Although demanding a higher time and resource commitment than flyers, brochures, and posters, public events offer rescue groups the chance to have their membership interact with the general public for the purposes of recruitment, donation, and distribution of information. Members of the general public can attend the event (deliberately or accidentally), ask questions, donate funds, begin the process of adopting a dog through the group, or possibly even join the rescue group as a volunteer.

Social media, which we will discuss in some detail in the next section, offer a form of untargeted communication to rescue groups with unprecedented access to numbers that were simply unimaginable two decades ago. With an estimated 2.267 billion people having access to the Internet on a worldwide basis (as of December 31, 2011), rescue groups essentially have one-third of this globe's population as their target.[14] The Internet has created the phenomenon of social media. These resources have been typically free or could be accessed at very low cost. They have provided a speedy medium that can reach a global audience and have thus become a true game-changer for many institutions, not only canine rescue groups. In short, untargeted communication in its pre- and post-Internet incarnation has offered rescue groups an excellent and cost-effective means for creating relationships with new individuals from a large population.

The advantages of utilizing untargeted methods of communication are their low requirements for resource investment (namely time and money), their speed (particularly in the case of the Internet), and their ability to recruit new members, donors, and adopters to the group. The disadvantages of untargeted methods include the lower level of intimacy when compared with the other two types of communication and the difficulty in gauging the seriousness of interest on the part of would-be volunteers. Lastly, the impersonal nature of this means of communication can easily lead to the unwanted realm of harassment, which can shed a negative light on the rescue group's otherwise positive intentions. Once such dimensions arise, they are often difficult to control or alleviate.

Social Media and Rescue Group Communication

The growth and commercialization of the Internet in the mid-1990s has completely altered the playing field for canine breed rescue groups. In particular, the creation of social media as part of the Internet revolution has shifted the ways in which rescue groups exist and behave. But what exactly constitutes social media? *Merriam-Webster's Dictionary* defines social media as "forms of electronic communication (as Web sites for social networking and micro-blogging) through which users create online communities to share information, ideas, personal messages, and other content (as videos)."[15] The development of social media represents a defining moment in the world of breed specific canine rescue; electronic communication has made the world a smaller place and one that has been easier to navigate for rescues, as well as potential volunteers and donors. Beginning with rescue

websites and culminating in Facebook and Twitter, social media have significantly improved the channels of communication for all rescue groups.

Rescue group websites were the first forms of electronic communication
in which groups could engage. Prior to the Internet boom, groups relied
on a variety of methods for disseminating information, as we discussed
earlier. By making themselves a home on the web, these groups increased
the number of potential adopters, volunteers, and donors that now could
become familiar not only with the specific activities in which these groups
engaged but also with the very world of canine rescue in particular. Above
all, a new medium emerged that featured these groups' raison d'être in the
liveliest possible manner: photographs and videos of *their dogs* in need of
adoption. Groups now attained a new, completely universal method for
spreading information, as the Internet is accessible from any location at
any time, as opposed to hoping individuals stumble upon the groups' flyers
while taking their dogs to the local veterinarian. Rescue groups have come
to use websites for a variety of reasons that include sharing information
about the rescue group. A few among the most common usages have been
the displaying of pictures and descriptions of the dogs available for adoption; publicizing meetings and events; and soliciting assistance from the
community through volunteering and donations.

With the creation of PayPal in 1998, rescue groups gained a valuable
resource: By displaying their PayPal account logo, rescue groups could
solicit donations electronically, making all-important donations a mere
mouse click on the computer, rather than having a check written and
mailed at a later date.[16] This new payment system has greatly expedited
the donation process by lowering the barrier of entry for busy people who
had the inclination to support such groups and appreciated their work and
predicament but who simply would not make a donation due to the steps
that it required. Since the advent and proliferation of the Internet, typical
impulse donors no longer disappear due to the exigencies of a busy day.
Instead, they effortlessly and spontaneously support rescue groups with a
click of their mouse in their living room or via their hand-held devices in
virtually any location on earth.

The development of animal rescue specific websites created greater
opportunities for rescue groups than websites alone could provide. To use
these rescue specific websites—Petfinder and Adopt a Pet being the two
most popular—rescue groups created a profile and homepage, where they
could then post photographs and descriptions about the dogs under their
care. What makes these sites uniquely advantageous is the search function they have at their disposal; visitors to the site can search for specific
dog breeds in their local shelters and rescue groups, with those closest to

their location listed first and dogs farther away listed lower on the page. An individual searching, for example, for a Golden Retriever near Ann Arbor, Michigan, will find dogs listed in a variety of shelters and rescue groups in southeast Michigan. This person then has the option of clicking on the dog's individual page and learning more about both this particular dog and the rescue group that posted its photograph and relevant information. Groups can even post links to their own websites on their profiles, leading to increased traffic on their site. In short, animal and dog rescue specific websites aggregate all shelters and rescue groups, allowing individuals to find groups based on the specific type of dog preferred and their location, rather than having the searchers rely on finding the group through general web searches, which have a realistic likelihood of missing the group entirely.

The most recent evolution of rescue group Internet use is that of social networking sites, such as Facebook and Twitter. These sites rely on profiles or pages created by users, who can then, through a variety of processes including posting on walls, direct messaging, and tweeting, communicate with other members of the social network. Facebook is certainly the most influential and popular of the sites in terms of rescue group use. Via this medium, the current trend is for groups to create pages rather than profiles, as pages can be "liked" by users, who then receive updates from the page via their newsfeeds. Profiles require that the rescue group extend and accept friend requests, a time-consuming process when rescue groups can have hundreds, if not thousands, of individuals interested in them.[17]

Our interviewees mentioned Facebook much more than any of the other social media outlets. Maureen Distler shared her enthusiasm about this medium:

> We love it because we put out a plea . . . and we have maybe 1,300 friends on Facebook . . . so I had one dog who was a Labrador and mountain dog mix and he was big and tall, a lot taller than I was used to, and I needed a raised feeder for him so I put out a plea on Facebook and said, "hey guys, I need a raised feeder, drop it off where I work by noon tomorrow." I mean, I had a reply in less than ten minutes saying, "OK, I can drop one off."[18]

Elena Pesavento seconds this by saying:

> We put dogs on Facebook and we encourage our adopting families to get on Facebook and just stay in contact with us and show and tell us how their new family member is doing. We also post all pleas for

help on Facebook, like an urgent need for a foster home. We have fundraising stuff on Facebook. We do a little bit of everything on it.[19]

Certainly, Facebook's immediacy also has its downside. Colleen Wyatt talked about her painful associations with Facebook:

Of course we are on Facebook. Facebook for me has been a really painful experience because I have 688 friends—it was that many, at least, when I last looked a couple of weeks ago—and what do I find on my wall but dogs that are going to be put to sleep. It's very rough to look through a day's worth of stuff and see that, like, 250 dogs . . . and you know that if you open that up there will be fifty more dogs that are going to appear from shelter pictures—all dogs that are going to be put to sleep. So yes, we are on Facebook which we, of course, also use to work with our volunteers and our adopters though we do not use it to work with the rescue community.[20]

But nothing emphasized the generational importance of Facebook better than this response from Gene Fitzpatrick, who made it emphatically clear that rescue's full adoption of this medium does not represent a choice and a luxury but a clear necessity for its survival in years to come:

We're trying to find a younger volunteer who is really into Facebook because I would say that most of our volunteers are probably over fifty, over forty for sure. And this generation, as a rule, is not so much into Facebook. But the younger generation most definitely is. And we need younger volunteers that we can only reach via Facebook.[21]

Facebook has provided innumerable opportunities for rescue groups to broaden their volunteer base and increase volunteer participation, making it a vital tool for rescue group survival and proliferation in the new millennium.

Rescue groups use social media sites for a variety of purposes, which comprise, among others, attracting potential adopters; recruiting volunteers; requesting donations; increasing public awareness about an array of issues crucial to the group and rescue's overall mission, which include pet homelessness and the necessity of spaying and neutering; and sharing success stories of dogs adopted out by the group. By participating in social networking sites, rescue groups increase the potential resources they can garner to improve and augment their most essential activity—that of rescuing needy dogs and placing them in loving forever homes.

Measuring Social Media Participation

Measuring rescue groups' social media participation entails both quantitative and qualitative approaches. Some measurements, such as whether groups possess Petfinder or Facebook accounts, are purely quantitative; groups either have them or they do not. However, measuring the quality of a group's website, in contrast, is a much more complex matter that involves subjective assessment in addition to objective data. Most, if not all, of the groups that we analyzed in our work have websites. However, they vary immensely in the quality of their designs and thus, we would argue, in the effectiveness of having their message conveyed to a large public that, as a rule, knows little, if anything, about breed specific canine rescue. Thus, some groups have single-page websites with little to no information available as to who they are, what they do, and the dogs available for rescue; while other groups feature elegant, user-friendly websites that display a wealth of information about the organization and its larger mission. Studying rescue group websites is a more complex task than simply ascertaining whether a website exists. Therefore, availing ourselves of the expertise of some professional website designers, we proceeded to construct and utilize a ten-point grading scale for website quality with the clear assumption that the higher the quality, the greater the likelihood that this group's message will reach the public. We assigned the score of 0 to a group that had no website at all; and we accorded a 10 to websites that we deemed perfect or nearly so, with their quality being on par with professionally designed websites used by major corporations. Below is the scale by which we rated each website.

0: No website present.
1: Typically a Petfinder stock profile page or extremely basic html document with very little customization. Important information was missing, incomplete, or had clearly not been updated in a significant period of time. (We deemed such information to include at a minimum the group's contact information, its adoption policies, its current dogs available, and a basic description of the group.) The website did not have an online donation option and was not useful or attractive.
2: Typically a Petfinder stock profile page or extremely basic html document with more information than found in score 1. Html websites tended to have poor execution and were obviously amateur in design and implementation, with automatic music players,

poorly edited photographs, trite and low quality .gif graphics, all giving an impression of a group that lacked professionalism. Color choices were often jarring, with rainbow themes and neon font use prevalent. These websites also did not have provisions to make online donations.

3: A. A complete Petfinder stock profile page, containing all the information necessary for adopting a dog. The emphasis here was on the site being a stock page, as opposed to those groups that created their own custom Petfinder profile pages, which scored higher.

   B. Amateurish html websites, but with a higher level of sophistication than those with a score of 2, tending to have fewer .gifs and better photograph editing.

   C. Websites of higher quality that had consistent loading errors (checked with multiple browsers and on multiple days), indicating that they were not maintained as well as they should be. None of these options included mechanisms to make online donations.

4: Typically resembling websites with scores of 3, but with online donation buttons available, as well as links to social media (although this was not always the case). Somewhat cumbersome to navigate and not aesthetically pleasing.

5: Technically sound websites with very basic, dull designs lacking in visual interest that tended to be outdated but still functioned well. These had online donation options available, but not on the homepage, which was either poorly organized or did not contain sufficient information. Websites tended not to have any information beyond adoption policies, available dogs, contact information, and donations available for the public. They often possessed homepages that required extensive scrolling to find important information, rather than having such all readily visible when first arriving at the site.

6: Similar to websites with scores of 5, but with slightly better organization and more information available to the website visitors, including options to purchase merchandise online. Websites still required scrolling on homepages, but not to the extent that those with a score of 5 did.

7: Score of 6, but with cleaner organization, aesthetically more pleasing from either a proportional or color choice standpoint, sometimes both.

8: Score of 7, with improvements in style and cleanliness of homepage and more information available to visitors, such as advice about dog food, grooming, and treatments for behavioral problems.

9: Professional quality website, obviously designed and maintained by a professional webmaster. Typically one visible error in design (cumbersome homepage, poorly edited photographs, unprofessional color choice being the most common drawbacks).

10: Highly professional website, obviously designed and maintained by a professional webmaster. The website had few, if any, design problems. It was simple and intuitive to navigate, provided a vast amount of information to users in an organized, user-friendly manner. On par with the quality of professional websites featured by A-list corporations such as PepsiCo or Johnson & Johnson.

After establishing this scale, we analyzed each rescue group for the following criteria: website quality, online donations, Petfinder profile, Adopt a Pet profile, Facebook profile, Myspace profile, and Twitter profile.

Social Media and the Top-Ten Breeds

For comparative purposes, we elected to examine rescue websites belonging to organizations representing the top-ten canine breeds in the United States because their high populations mean that they presumably also have the greatest number of rescues, with the exception of Pit Bulls, which represent an exceptional case in the disparity between breed population and AKC popularity. According to AKC registration data, the top-ten breeds in the United States in 2011 were: Labrador Retrievers, German Shepherds, Yorkshire Terriers, Beagles, Golden Retrievers, Bulldogs, Boxers, Dachshunds, Poodles, and Shih Tzus.[22] When examining the quality and quantity of the social media use exhibited by the rescue groups representing these breeds, we discerned several common trends among many substantial differences as to how these organizations utilized social media. We will briefly present the variations we detected in each breed rescue's social media participation. In addition to this intergroup comparison, we will also present one intragroup analysis of the use of social media by highlighting the world of Golden Retriever rescues.

Website quality is an important factor for measuring a rescue group's social media presence and awareness. A well-designed professional website lends legitimacy to the group and ensures that the rescue is viewed as a serious organization. A poorly designed, amateurish website that is difficult to use or contains incorrect or incomplete information signals that the rescue group might not be well organized, which would negatively affect volunteer recruitment, donations, and the impression of potential adopters regarding their desire to donate to or adopt from the group. By our measurements, Bulldog rescue groups attained the highest website quality with an average rating of 6.58. With an average quality score of 3.87, Poodle rescue groups came in last. With standard deviations of 1 to 2.5 points, all of the rescues representing the top-ten breeds were consistent in their scores. Golden Retriever rescue groups had an average website quality rating of 5.99, thus making this breed's rescue groups second only to Bulldogs in this use of social media.

The presence of online donation options on rescue group websites constitutes a critical component of effective fundraising. Thus, it also merits a brief analysis. Websites that have online donation options allow rescues to capitalize on fundraising opportunities present on the Internet and to take advantage of online donors who otherwise might not donate to the rescue group. Bulldog rescue groups had the highest percentage of websites with online donation options, with 84.85 percent of their websites featuring a button for donating. Only 26.32 percent of Poodle rescue group websites had an online donation option, thus making them the least likely among our top-ten list of breed rescues to benefit from this crucial resource. Golden Retriever rescue group websites had online donation options 71.29 percent of the time.

Petfinder accounts help rescue groups spread information about their organization and their dogs to potential adopters, thereby making this device a powerful tool to increase adoptions. Being completely cost free enhances the attractiveness of Petfinder accounts. Labrador Retriever rescue groups had the highest concentration of Petfinder users, with 95.45 percent of their organizations using Petfinder. Poodles, on the other hand, were far less likely to avail themselves of this resource, with only 48.01 percent of Poodle rescue groups using a Petfinder account. The proportion of Golden Retriever rescue groups using Petfinder was 79.21 percent, putting them in eighth place overall.

Adopt a Pet, like Petfinder, is a pet adoption website that rescue groups can use to spread information about their dogs. Although Petfinder is the older and more popular of the two, Adopt a Pet has steadily gained in popularity, particularly as it has come to feature celebrity sponsors such as Drew Barrymore and Kelsey Grammer.[23] German Shepherd rescue groups were the most likely to use Adopt a Pet, with 77.68 percent of them opting to do so. The majority of Poodle rescue groups chose not to use Adopt a Pet, with only 28.21 percent signing up for an Adopt a Pet account, making them the least likely to do so. Golden Retrievers, at 66.34 percent participation in Adopt a Pet, were ranked sixth in participation with regard to Adopt a Pet accounts.

With over 1 billion users worldwide as of December 2011, Facebook has in recent years been the most popular social networking site. It clearly represents a major resource for all rescues, especially because Facebook use provides distinct advantages over other forms of social media, mainly, of course, because more than 50 percent of active users log in daily, as opposed to websites like Petfinder or Adopt a Pet, which do not receive nearly the same level of repeat traffic.[24] The frequency of usage alone renders Facebook an immensely effective communication tool for rescues in terms of reaching a broader audience, including individuals who may not be actively looking for a dog but who have the potential to be mobilized as volunteers for the group. Golden Retriever rescue groups are the most likely to use Facebook, as 83.17 percent of this breed's rescue groups have an account in the form of either a profile, group, or page on this powerful medium. Poodle rescue groups, at a rate of only 41.03 percent of groups using Facebook, were the least likely to do so.

Twitter, second only to Facebook with 100 million active global users and counting, represents another valuable asset to rescue groups.[25] Twitter's different style of communication, tweeting burst communications of 140 characters or fewer to all followers as opposed to posting on every individual's wall, ensures that all followers receive the same message from the rescue group at the same time, which is a vital tool for quickly mobilizing volunteers to assist with events and emergencies. Beagle rescue groups were the most likely to use Twitter, with 26.67 percent choosing to do so, while Poodle rescue groups were the least likely to engage in Twitter, as only 6.41 percent of Poodle rescue groups had a Twitter account at the time of this writing. Golden Retriever rescue groups, exhibiting an 18.81 percent participation rate in Twitter, ranked sixth among the top-ten breeds.

Rescue group use of Myspace demonstrates that these organizations are quite reality savvy and adapt to changing circumstances. Myspace was the premier social media website in the early 2000s but was then massively surpassed by Facebook. Myspace had 31 million users in 2011 when Facebook's user base reached 800 million,[26] which then ballooned to over 1 billion a year later. The global trend of choosing Facebook over Myspace is also reflected in the number of rescue groups that featured Myspace accounts. Of the 667 groups that we analyzed at the outset of our study in the fall of 2010, only 106 (16 percent) had a Myspace account. When we reexamined these 106 groups in January 2012, thirty-one of them no longer showed any evidence of possessing a Myspace account, which we took to mean that they had abandoned this social media platform. Of the remaining seventy-five groups, only one had updated its Myspace account in the course of this time span, with the average time elapsed from the previous update for all rescue groups being 2.5 years (fourteen groups had Myspace accounts but no indication of when they had last been updated). The refusal on the part of rescue groups to continue spending time on a social media site that is on the decline is indicative of their ability to adapt to new strategies to secure resources. The rescue world had arrived at the correct conclusion that Myspace, as a smaller and declining market, was less advantageous in terms of the groups' investment of precious resources such as time, manpower, and money, particularly when compared with the benefits derived from participating in booming sites like Facebook. It is evident that as Myspace's user base shrinks, fewer groups consider it to be a useful tool for social media interaction with potential donors and as an effective means of communication for their overall mission.

Clearly, we were intrigued as to the reasons for the markedly smaller involvement in social media on the part of Poodle rescue groups when compared with the other nine breeds. We believe that the answer to this puzzle lies in the origins of Poodle rescue groups. Club starts account for 54.67 percent of Poodle rescue groups' origins, a number that contrasts sharply with the 15.84 percent in terms of the comparable data pertaining to Golden Retriever rescue groups that commenced as part of a breed club. Although still requiring communication tools with the outside world, clubs do not do so nearly to the degree that rescue groups need to. In other words, clubs constitute a much more enclosed and self-sufficient environment in contrast to rescue groups, whose very being depends on the organizations' largest possible outreach. We believe that the Poodle rescue groups' institutional proximity to Poodle clubs accounts for the paucity of the former's usage of social media when compared with their counterparts in the other nine breed specific canine rescues.

Golden Retriever Rescues and Social Media: The Financial Dimension

The Internal Revenue Service (IRS) contracts with a website, GuideStar .org, to display 501(c)(3) registered charity information including financial data.[27] It is from this website that we obtained the financial data for the top-ten rescue groups. Unfortunately, we were unable to cull a statistically significant sample size of rescue group financial data for any of the breeds in the top ten. This shortcoming was most likely due to a combination of factors; in particular, we believe this is mainly a consequence of the $25,000 income reporting cutoff, as groups reporting an income below this amount need only send an e-postcard, available online but not posted to the Guide Star.org website, to the IRS, rather than complete the much more detailed form that features many of the financial data that would have been helpful for our analysis. However, as fortune would have it, we were able to examine the relationship between social media use and income in the case of Golden Retriever rescue groups. By obtaining detailed financial information for 72 of the 101 Golden Retriever rescue groups in the United States, we believe that we came close to the minimum of 81 such groups that would have been required to bestow our findings with proper statistical significance. Although we cannot claim such impeccable quantitative robustness for our data, we feel reasonably confident to present them here as trends that allow us to draw valid conclusions.

We detected an interesting correlation between website quality and income for Golden Retriever rescues. All of the groups earning over $100,000 annually had website quality ratings of 5 or more. This is likely related to rescues having a sufficiently large income to accord them the luxury not to have to worry about their organization's day-to-day survival and being able to afford the services of a professional web designer at a full or discounted rate. In turn, the professionalism and online donation options that are typically included on high-quality websites enhance the group's monetary intake, as individuals are more likely to donate to groups they perceive as being reliable and revealing competence rather than to those whose appearance conveys an air of amateurism and questionable qualifications. Variations in contributions due to the quality of the website are unlikely to be the driving force behind rescue group incomes exceeding more than $100,000 annually. Groups with annual incomes between $0 and $100,000 have a modest upward trend in website quality as income increases, but there is too much variation to be able to say definitively that this trend constitutes a rule. Thus, although website quality is an important indicator of rescue group wealth, it most definitely cannot be used to gauge a rescue group's annual income.

Comparisons of online donation availability and income reveal that the wealthiest groups tend to have an option for online donations available for the public to use. Of the thirty-three groups earning $100,000 or more annually, only three groups did not have the availability of online donations, meaning that 91 percent of the wealthiest Golden Retriever rescue groups had the ability to solicit donations via the Internet as well as through more conventional methods. Rescue groups can utilize their facilities for online donations to create fund drives for large purchases or expensive surgeries and can mobilize potential donors through linking to their online donation page. This gives websites with online donations a powerful tool for fundraising. This mechanism also appears to have a significant effect on the rescue group's income.

Use of Petfinder, when compared with income, results in a similar correlation to those listed above. Only three of the thirty-three groups with incomes above $100,000 did not use Petfinder. These three groups, Yankee Golden Retriever Rescue (YGRR), Golden Retriever Rescue Education and Training, and NORCAL Golden Retriever Rescue, were all formed in the earliest years of Golden Retriever rescue, with YGRR, founded in 1985, being the oldest. This suggests that when Petfinder emerged and became a relevant resource to other, more recently formed rescue groups, the three aforementioned organizations did not feel the need to join Petfinder and post their dogs there. Instead, these three rescues had established their regional reputations and networks sufficiently early and thoroughly not to see the need for and benefit of having to join Petfinder, as all three groups came to enjoy a high and steady level of success without it. However, it seems that in the case of the other thirty groups, their joining Petfinder proved beneficial in terms of enhancing their exposure that comes with a Petfinder account as was evident in the increasing donations these groups attained and the (accompanying and resultant) growing number of adoptions they successfully completed.

Although less popular than Petfinder, Adopt a Pet tells a similar story when examined in conjunction with group income. Only six of the Golden Retriever groups with incomes above $100,000 did not have an Adopt a Pet account. Although we could not discern any apparent reason for this account's absence in the case of these six organizations, one plausible explanation might be that the groups in this high-income bracket derive the same benefits from Adopt a Pet as they do from Petfinder, thus making an engagement with both sites a bit redundant, especially because the popularity of Adopt a Pet is a bit more modest than that of Petfinder.

Our Golden Retriever rescue groups' use of Facebook provides the most concrete relationship between social media use and rescue group income. Not only do all of the rescue groups with incomes above $100,000 have and use Facebook accounts, but only four of the fifty-five groups with incomes above $50,000 do not have a Facebook account. This strongly indicates that successful groups consider Facebook to be a powerful tool for communication with volunteers and donors. Facebook gives rescue groups the ability to create events and invite individuals to them, to publicize their dogs, and to recruit new volunteers from local citizens.

Twitter presents an interesting case when compared with group income. Although only nineteen Golden Retriever rescue groups used Twitter, thirteen of those nineteen had annual incomes of $100,000 or more. This suggests that while the larger groups, who benefit from being well known and established in the community, find Twitter to be a useful communication tool, their smaller counterparts tend not to see this medium as an asset and might even regard it as a potential drain on their volunteers' limited temporal resources. This at least is our tentative explanation for an immensely fluid situation that in a matter of months might well have changed based on the rapidity with which things develop in the world of the Internet.

Still, in 2012, there was a clear trend indicating that the wealthiest Golden Retriever rescue groups overwhelmingly participated in and utilized social media to their own benefit. These groups harness the power of websites such as Petfinder and Facebook, using them to increase the efficacy of their organizations, which, in its very essence, leads to a constantly improving rescue operation for an ever-increasing clientele of Golden Retrievers in search of loving forever homes. Although we lack the data to state conclusively that we have discovered an irreversible fact, we are reasonably certain that we observed a solid trend in the increasingly central development of social media to Golden Retriever rescues nationwide and the direct linkage of such development to an organization's financial resources. In the same vein, while we failed to obtain the requisite data to examine the financial situations of rescue groups for breeds besides Golden Retrievers, we feel certain that the underlying logic of social media use that we observed with Golden Retriever rescues is in no way breed specific and exists in the rescue world of other breeds as well. Poodle rescues might be a possible exception, because, as noted above, they appear to be real outliers in terms of the caution, if not reluctance, with which they have come to adopt these path-breaking innovations in the communication regimes of the past decade or so. But this, too, might very well change in the course of the next few years.

In concluding our presentation on the Internet's and social media's massive impact on the world of canine rescue, the following overarching themes appear salient: Rescue groups that used to be solely reliant on physical forms of communication (such as flyers, letters, telephone calls, personal meetings, to name but a few) to get all the grueling steps of their dogs' adoption process completed, have had a whole new vista opened to them that has not only increased the potential contacts that rescue groups can now make and cultivate, but also reduced the cost in doing so in terms of time, money, and effort. A rescue group's website has in the meantime advanced from the organization's communicative margins as a kind of gimmick, to the hub of its life and activities, to the core of its very being. In the time before the Internet, rescue groups were forced to limit the amount of information they could disperse because of the cost of printing flyers, which escalated rapidly with the increasing quantity of paper. Now, groups post pictures and descriptions of dogs, explain their adoption policies, solicit donations and volunteers, help adopters with behavioral problems, and share information about a variety of topics from spaying and neutering to picking the appropriate dog food. And they can do all of this—and then some—instantaneously and at very little cost to the organization. One could hardly imagine a more decisive innovation in the world of canine rescue than the Internet's myriad applications.

Fundraising: A Crucial Purpose of Communication

Fundraising constitutes an absolutely vital component to the successful functioning of any rescue group. Apart from adoption fees and the sale of merchandise or other kinds of items that, in effect, are really part of fundraising, the majority of the group's revenue comes from fundraising. Mary Vanderbloomen made this explicit in our interview with her: "Our three sources of income are donations; our adoption fees; and the sale of merchandise."[28] Without fundraising, rescue groups would have to rely solely on the financial generosity of their own members, who are usually not particularly wealthy and who exhibit their generosity with their time, unremunerated labor, and commitment to the well-being of the dogs belonging to their favored breed. Without adequate funds, rescue groups would essentially not be able to fulfill any of the steps essential to their operation, be it proper transportation of the dogs to their homing, veterinary care, and proper nutrition.

At its core, fundraising represents a type of communication in which a rescue group solicits donations of money or other resources (items for auction, dog food, dog beds, the expertise of licensed professionals such as lawyers, accountants, computer programmers, Internet experts, and, of course, veterinarians, among many others) from the general public or from specifically targeted potential donors. To fundraise successfully, groups must communicate effectively with both of these overlapping yet also distinct entities. Effectiveness in this communication demands a delicate mixture of detached professionalism and emotive appeal. Large rescue groups may have specialized volunteers whose primary task within the group is that of fundraising to which they dedicate an extensive amount of time and other resources. This endeavor is quite frequently rewarded by garnering large sums of money for the group. Smaller rescue groups, however, cannot rely on such fundraising specialists. Rather, they depend on multitasking and often overextended volunteers for the group's fundraising needs. Lacking the professional resources of the larger groups, these smaller organizations' fundraising strategies entail low-investment methods that are typically local in their scope and do not require much in the way of organizational and personal resources. Of course, they are also unlikely to result in donations that amass large amounts of money. We discerned three levels of fundraising that rescue groups employ: simple, midlevel, and complex. Each of these has its distinct advantages and disadvantages for the groups that choose to employ them.

Simple fundraisers are characterized by the relative paucity of time and resources that an organization accords to this activity, as well as to the relatively low level of expertise in the art of fundraising that the volunteers bring to the table. Moreover, they are always local in scope. Examples of simple fundraisers include dog washes; can drives; raffles; donation boxes left at supportive businesses; and online donation buttons on websites such as PayPal. Maureen Distler, for example, mentioned the meet and greets that she and her group organize regularly where "we put the little donation jar out and we get maybe a hundred dollars per event . . . but these add up and all of it goes to pay the vet bills."[29] These types of fundraisers are inexpensive to set up and easy to implement and manage. Moreover, many, if not most, of the materials used in these procedures often hail from individual group members, thus sparing the group the costs of purchasing such items. Simple fundraisers do not require a large investment of time or necessitate extensive advanced planning as they are, with the exception of online donations and donation boxes,[30] single bounded events that are completed in a matter of hours. Although the benefit of simple fundraisers lies in their low cost for the group, their obvious disadvantage is that they rarely, if ever, earn the group a substantial amount of money. Because these measures are short term and, in all cases but that of online donations, fixed to a particular location, they do not cover a wide population base from which to draw donations. The simple fundraiser's physical location becomes a limiting factor to the fundraising effort's success. Whereas all sizes of rescues utilize simple fundraisers, they comprise the primary means of fundraising for microgroups, a moderate source of income for mid-level groups, and a relatively small proportion of income for megagroups. Megagroups are able to use more sophisticated forms of fundraising, such as midlevel and complex fundraisers, to increase the efficiency and efficacy of their revenue generation.

We define midlevel fundraising efforts as those that are more com-plex and costly for groups to implement than are simple fundraisers, but that do not demand the expertise and long-term investment that complex fundraisers require. Among many types of midlevel fundraisers, we include silent auctions, benefit 5K races, trivia nights, plant sales, golf outings, hol-iday parties, pub crawls, store catalog sales, calendar creation and sales, and mass letters soliciting donations. These fundraisers require signifi-cantly more time and effort from volunteers than simple fundraisers in good part because events such as 5K races and silent auctions involve a much larger public than the measures we mentioned as representative of simple fundraisers. The midlevel variety often entails multi day activities to which volunteers must devote full-time attention to ensure their suc-cess. Take, for example, the widespread measure of calendar development and sale: the production of such an item requires that a volunteer solicit photographs and donations from interested individuals (often adopters of the group's dogs now happily featured in their forever homes), design and print the calendar, and then manage its sale and delivery. None of these are easy tasks; all of them require some technical skill, much patience, and even more time. The resource costs of midlevel fundraisers also tend to be higher than those of simple fundraisers, as the former might very well require rental fees (e.g., golf outings and pub crawls) or large donations from either group members or sponsors (e.g., objects for silent auctions or food and beverages for dinner benefits).

On the whole, most of the groups whose members we interviewed seemed to engage in what we have categorized as midlevel fundraising, which in its content often featured local and ad hoc characteristics more akin to what we labeled the simple type of fundraising but that in its modus operandi required a degree of organizational exertion and perseverance that we feel fit the complexity of the midlevel variant. As to the various groups' exact choices and concrete options, the sky appeared to be the limit. "The biggest fundraiser is our annual golf tournament," said Gene Fitzpatrick, adding:

> We do that once a year and we also have coming up this October a tennis ball raffle. What we do is that we sell chances and those numbers are placed on a tennis ball. All the tennis balls are then placed in the middle of a field and we send a dog to retrieve one. Whichever ball he brings back will win the first prize, and the second prize, third, fourth, fifth prize.[31]

Fitzpatrick also talked about his organization's trivia night on Saturday and the Valentine's Day appeal. And Joe Maringo told us that "a couple of years ago we set something up on a regular basis where the people on the Labrador forum who could sew would sew a square for a quilt and then we'd send it to someone to sew it all together and then we'd raffle off the handmade quilt with a Labrador theme every year."[32] Debbie Lukasik mentioned that "our largest fundraiser is our annual dog walk." She also informed us of this event's immense labor intensity in that it apparently takes "nine months to pull it off." But the results appear to be very rewarding because "we bring in a huge amount of money with it. We're very fortunate to have a matching funds sponsor, who dangles a carrot in front of our volunteers to get pledges and to get donations for the dog walk, by matching dollar for dollar up to $10,000."[33] Priscilla Skare's organization has had huge yard sales in addition to a local restaurant throwing "a monster golf tournament for us where we didn't have to do anything."[34] Jacky Eckard explained to us the operations in which her Labrador Retriever rescue engages year in year out for its fundraising:

> We have an annual Lab Fest which includes a silent auction among other things. Then we have a Yappy Hour where you can come and pay $15 and your dog can swim in the pool and you can drink beer and eat hot dogs. Then we have an event called Canvas and Cocktails where people come to this place and paint a picture of a dog and then the organization awards prizes. . . . We have an annual calendar which is a big thing. We have photo contests where we judge the pictures and the best ones make it into the calendar and we sell the calendar which is a big deal.[35]

And the late Bob Bornstein's group sold t-shirts featuring the artwork of some of the group's artistically inclined and talented volunteers.

Rescue groups that seek to use midlevel fundraisers require a higher level of commitment from volunteers than those rescues that employ only simple fundraisers; volunteers engaged in the former must be willing to devote significantly more time to fundraising activities than to dog rescue proper, which, of course, is the sole reason most of these people join the rescue group in the first place. Although microgroups will occasionally engage in midlevel fundraising, they often lack the resources in money, time, and manpower to do so on a regular basis. Midlevel and megagroups have the volunteer resources necessary to make midlevel fundraising efforts possible on a regular basis, increasing the funds that these larger groups can earn without investing an even larger proportion of resources exacted by complex fundraisers.

Complex fundraisers are by far the most difficult to organize and implement successfully. They require volunteers with professional (or quasi-professional) fundraising skills who are willing and able to devote a significant amount of their personal time and resources to the successful completion of such a complex fundraising effort. Examples of complex fundraisers include participating in capital campaigns, securing grants, major donor cultivation, and the development of partnerships with organizations such as the United Way. These types of fundraisers are capable of raising amounts necessary to purchase land and to build rescue facilities, as well as create a healthy nest egg for emergencies. In order to achieve these impressive results, rescue groups must be capable of investing the time and resources necessary to make such fundraisers possible; groups engaging in these types of fundraising activities typically have volunteers whose sole task in the organization is fundraising. Indeed, such individuals are not expected to participate in the group's other rescue activities on a regular basis. The high degree of commitment, professionalism, and experience necessary to initiate, implement, and complete complex fundraisers generally means that only megagroups can avail themselves of such operations. Occasionally, complex fundraisers can be used to transition from a midlevel group to a megagroup, as Delaware Valley Golden Retriever Rescue did when this organization successfully completed a capital campaign to raise funds for its current facility. Moreover, it is certainly not by chance that Yankee Golden Retriever Rescue was among the very first rescues to engage in fundraising in a systematic and ambitious manner, recognizing this activity's centrality to the organization's scope and viability. Led by Joy Viola, who had accumulated immense relevant experience as a development officer in a number of nonprofit organizations, Tufts University among them, YGRR approached fundraising quite professionally from the very beginning. Joy Viola shared her thoughts on the subject:

Yankee has, since day one, done a really great job in fundraising with many methods such as getting the dog registration lists from all area towns so we knew where the Golden Retriever owners are, and then we were able to send these people information about Yankee.... The organization has been updating these lists for over twenty years now and that's where it had the basis for a major mailing list when we started our capital campaign [to build Riverview, the organization's permanent facility west of Boston].... Riverview was a tremendous help in bringing in revenue, because it gave a sense of permanence, because people who had large amounts of money could look at it and see that this would not be some sort of here-today-gone-tomorrow kind of thing.... If somebody wants to invest $200,000, they really don't want to leave this up to the whim of a few people. And when they can go to a place like that and see the organization and its facility, they feel much more comfortable about their money going to support dogs.... Now I realize that all of this is very labor intensive, but this is how you build a solid base.... There are, of course, a hundred and one ways to fundraise for your Golden rescue, that I gleaned from the other rescues, but they're all small-event type things. Another dimension of complex fundraising pertains to various estate and inheritance issues in which people devoted to the particular rescue organization and the breed will parts of their estate to the rescue. A parallel phenomenon relates to the receipt of large donations from people whose dogs passed away and who obtained them from the rescue.[36]

Priscilla Skare confirmed to us that:

We received really big donations from people whose dogs passed away. We've also had extreme special needs dogs where we sent out pleas via e-mails with the stories and pictures of these dogs.... It's incredible.... We raised over $3,000 in no time for this dog that had one lung and needed hip surgery.[37]

Viola and Skare demonstrate the major power of complex fundraisers when utilized frequently and effectively to build resources for rescue groups. But they also acknowledged the high volunteer cost in time, skill, and commitment necessary for the successful implementation of complex fundraisers.

By and large, however, complex fundraisers require more from volunteers than micro- and midlevel groups are able to provide. However, precisely because of the pervasive nature of these rather ad hoc, local, and unprofessional fundraising operations performed by albeit enthusiastic and committed but essentially underqualified volunteers in a world in which rescue has grown in its organizational complexity and thus demands greater professional expertise on the part of its participants, we encountered quite often in our interviews the sentiment expressed by Barb Demetrick: "We want and need to get a professional fundraiser on board with us as soon as possible, so we can do even more."[38]

Bespeaking the rescue world's increasingly attractive social capital, accepted stature, and coveted reputation, important organizations and companies, both local and national, have become eager to associate their names and brands with rescues by partnering with them in various fundraising activities, which usually fall in the complex category but often also exist on less ambitious scales that are more akin to what we have categorized as midlevel. Thus, for example, Gene Fitzpatrick informed us that "we wrap gifts at Borders bookstores to raise money . . . and we are partnering with the United Way in organizing some of our donations."[39] Although such cooperative measures did not keep Borders from avoiding bankruptcy and folding completely, they had become quite regular in the rescue world, involving equally well-known and perhaps more successful national brands. Here is Elena Pesavento's confirming comment on this subject: "We have partnered with Starbucks and they make coffee where they put our logo on their cups and products and these things are sold at actually a pretty competitive price, and here is a thing where Facebook really helps, because we ship coffee all over the United States with our logo."[40] Beyond companies producing dog-related items and veterinarians who have increasingly come to attach their names to rescue-related activities and fundraisers, supporting rescues has become good public relations for companies that prima facie have nothing to do with the welfare of animals. Just think about how dog rescue has become the new corporate charity, literally unimaginable prior to the cultural institutionalization of the discourse of compassion on a broad basis. Thus, for example, on October 20, 2013, a full-page Ralph Lauren advertisement appeared depicting an attractive female model holding a Pit Bull on a leash under the accompanying text "The Dog Walk," stating that "for the first time, rescue dogs take the runway to present Ralph Lauren's fall 2013 accessories collection in collaboration with the ASPCA." At the bottom of the page, the Ralph Lauren Company informs us that this partnership with the American Society for the Prevention of Cruelty to Animals (ASPCA) has been entered "in honor of national Adopt-A-Shelter-Dog month." Just a few weeks later, Macy's in San Francisco encouraged the public to "press your nose up against Macy's Holiday Windows featuring adoptable animals from the San Francisco SPCA this holiday season." The text continues to inform us that "over the past nine years, the Holiday Windows have helped the SF SPCA raise over $400,000 and find homes for over 2,300 animals. Thank you to our friends at Macy's for their commitment to helping us find loving homes for San Francisco's cats and dogs."[41] And back East, the New York Mets teamed up with the North Shore Animal League America for a Bark in the Park event where "prior to the first pitch at two September games, dogs and their owners marched around the track at Citi Field, soaking in the appreciative applause of the Mets fans gathered in the stadium. 'The Mets organization is a great supporter of our life-saving mission,' says Byron Logan, our Director of Corporate & National Shelter Relationships. 'They've hosted us many times at Citi Field, and each event is exciting for all involved.' The entire profit of the dog ticket and a portion of the human ticket go to support Animal League America's work."[42]

As can be expected, rescue group size often dictates the type of fundraiser a rescue group will pursue. Microgroups will mainly select simple fundraisers, with an occasional (often annual) midlevel fundraiser. Midlevel groups employ a mix of fundraiser types, drawing largely from simple and midlevel fundraisers, but occasionally also attempting complex varieties. These, capable of earning sums in the tens or even hundreds of thousands of dollars, are usually, though not exclusively, the domain of megagroups. Groups of all sizes select which types of fundraisers they will attempt based on group resources and individual volunteers' willingness to dedicate their time to the fundraising effort of choice. Simple and midlevel fundraisers are critical to funding the day-to-day function of rescue groups, while complex fundraisers are used by megagroups to ensure long-term group survival via the purchase of permanent facilities, the establishment of trusts for the rescue, and even creation of salaried positions within the organization. Regardless of its variant, fundraising constitutes the lifeblood of any rescue. Its importance can simply not be overstated.

Conclusion

Rescue groups must communicate in order to survive. This basic fact drives rescue groups to engage in relationships with external organizations and individuals. By and large, they do so by employing three types of communication, which we have categorized as highly personalized, semipersonalized, and untargeted. In combination or on their own, these methods of communication must exist to help the group recruit, develop, and maintain the relationships that are necessary for it to receive the resources it needs to function and that external organizations provide. A rescue group's main purpose of developing external relationships is to encourage and solicit the donation of resources that are, of course, primarily financial, but that also include other tangible items as well as services that are most valuable to the group's properly fulfilling its mission of helping needy dogs. Rescue groups engage in fundraising efforts according to their needs and abilities, with rescue group size being the most reliable predictor as to the kind of fundraising the group will pursue on a regular basis. Generally, as the size of a rescue grows, the complexity and sophistication of the fundraising methods that the group uses will increase as well. Without developed communication skills and effective fundraising efforts, rescue groups cannot survive long term and will never outgrow the microgroup stage.

In addition to a rescue group's communication resources and other factors discussed in this book—such as its geographic location—we also delved into how the characteristics of particular dog breeds might influence the organizational shape, institutional culture, and overall success of rescues. In particular, we compared the world of Golden Retriever rescues to that of Labrador retriever rescues guided by our hypothesis that the great similarity of these two breeds on many important dimensions would reveal parallel similarities in their respective rescue organizations. We now turn to an account of our surprising findings on this matter in Chapter 8.

Notes

1. Gene Fitzpatrick. Interviewed by Andrei Markovits. Telephone Interview. August 17, 2010.

2. Mary Vanderbloomen. Interviewed by Katherine Crosby. Telephone Interview. August 9, 2010.

3. Lauren Genkinger. Interviewed by Katherine Crosby. Telephone Interview. August 18, 2010.

4. Jacky Eckard. Interviewed by Katherine Crosby. Telephone Interview. July 29, 2010.

5. Joan Puglia. Interviewed by Andrei Markovits. Telephone Interview. June 30, 2009.

6. Edith Bryan. Interviewed by Katherine Crosby. Telephone Interview. August 12, 2010.

7. Becky Hildebrand. Interviewed by Katherine Crosby. Telephone Interview. July 29, 2010.

8. Nina Palmo. Interviewed by Katherine Crosby. Telephone Interview. July 29, 2010.

9. Fitzpatrick interview.

10. Bob Tillay. Interviewed by Andrei Markovits. Telephone Interview. August 18, 2010.

11. Alan Jordano. Interviewed by Katherine Crosby. E-mail Interview. June 30, 2013.

12. Maureen Distler. Interviewed by Katherine Crosby. Telephone Interview. July 28, 2010.

13. Joy Viola. Interviewed by Andrei Markovits. Telephone Interview. July 16, 2009.

14. Internet World Statistics. "World Internet Usage and Population Statistics." Miniwatts Marketing Group, 2012. http://www.internetworldstats.com/stats.htm (accessed on July 25, 2012).

15. "Social Media." *Merriam-Webster Collegiate Dictionary.* 11th ed. 2011.

16. PayPal. "About PayPal." 2011. https://www.paypal-media.com/about.

17. As an example, the Humane Society of Huron Valley, located in Ann Arbor, was "liked" by 4,955 people on December 1, 2011, the date we first drafted this part of our manuscript.

18. Distler interview.

19. Elena Pesavento. Interviewed by Katherine Crosby. Telephone Interview. August 8, 2010.

20. Colleen Wyatt. Interviewed by Katherine Crosby. Telephone Interview. August 4, 2010.

21. Fitzpatrick interview.

22. American Kennel Club. "AKC Dog Registration Statistics." January 2011. http://www.akc.org/reg/dogreg_stats.cfm (accessed on May 13, 2014).

23. AdoptAPet.com. "The Save-A-Pet Show—Learn More About Planned Pet Adoption : Adopt-a-Pet.com." http://www.adoptapet.com/save-a-pet-show/ (accessed on July 21, 2013).

24. Facebook. "Statistics." December 2011. http://www.facebook.com/press/info .php?statistics.

25. Nick Bilton, "Twitter Reaches 100 Million Active Users." *New York Times Bits.* September 8, 2011. http://bits.blogs.nytimes.com/2011/09/08/twitter-reaches-100 -million-active-users/ (accessed on April 28, 2014).

26. Nathan Olivarez-Giles. "Facebook F8: Redesigning and hitting 800 million users." *Los Angeles Times Blogs.* September 22, 2011. http://latimesblogs.latimes.com /technology/2011/09/facebook-f8-media-features.html (accessed on April 28, 2014).

27. GuideStar.com. "About Us." http://www.guidestar.org/rxg/about-us/index .aspx (accessed on July 21, 2013).

28. Vanderbloomen interview.

29. Distler interview.

30. Online donation buttons and donation boxes are long-term processes that only require an initial setup and the occasional collection process, making them low maintenance and easy for small groups to do successfully.

31. Fitzpatrick interview.

32. Joe Maringo. Interviewed by Katherine Crosby. Telephone Interview. July 30, 2010.

33. Debbie Lukasik. Interviewed by Katherine Crosby. Telephone Interview. August 12, 2010.

34. Priscilla Skare. Interviewed by Andrei Markovits. Telephone Interview. August 19, 2010.

35. Eckard interview.

36. Viola interview.

37. Skare interview.

38. Barb Demetrick. Interviewed by Andrei Markovits. Telephone Interview. June 23, 2009.

39. Fitzpatrick interview.

40. Pesavento interview.

41. San Francisco Society for the Prevention of Cruelty to Animals, "SF SPCA Holiday Windows at Macy's," http://www.sfspca.org/support/events/macys-holiday -windows (accessed on May 13, 2014).

42. "Mets Host 'Pup Rallies.'" *PAWPRINTS: A Newsletter of Animal League America*, Issue 4 (2013), p. 7.

CHAPTER 8

The Golden/Labrador Retriever Comparison

Goldens, Labs, they are both wonderful and totally interchangeable and really identical. Goldens have longer hair, Labs have more variety, but other than that there is no difference between them at all. You will love either if and when you decide to get one. But did you say that you wanted an adult dog and not a puppy? If so, there is this new organization called Yankee Golden Retriever Rescue that sent me a flyer in the mail a few weeks ago hanging on the bulletin board in the waiting room at my clinic. I had already heard about them here and there and know of their existence but I really do not know any details. Come by my office soon and take a look at the flyer for all the info. I know nothing similar for Labs.

—Paraphrasing the late Dr. Sidney Mael's, veterinarian
at Oak Hill Veterinary Hospital in Newton, Massachusetts,
advice to Andrei Markovits in 1989, who was then teaching
at Boston University, spent many Jewish holidays with Dr. Mael
and his family, and wanted to adopt an adult Golden Retriever
or Labrador Retriever, which, following Dr. Mael's informed
suggestion, he did by contacting Yankee Golden Retriever
Rescue and eventually adopting its 548th successfully placed
dog, Dovi, as a beloved member of the Markovits family.

The information presented in the previous chapters demonstrate the large diversity of breed rescues. They come in all sizes, from very large thoroughly professionalized organizations to small operations often run by just a few persons, even, on occasion, merely one committed individual. Rescues vary in their organizational philosophies as well as approaches on how best to serve their needy clientele; they pursue different strategies in terms of their relations with outside organizations that also populate the human world devoted to dogs, from American Kennel Club (AKC) groups and clubs to shelters and humane societies. This chapter analyzes how the devotion and commitment to different breeds has had a major influence on the form and content of rescue organizations. Briefly put, human commitment to some breeds appears to spawn more successful rescue groups than to other breeds. For the purposes of argument, we define rescue success as being financially solvent, able to help the most dogs of their breed in their area, and maintaining the positive external relationships necessary to facilitate financial solvency and rescue operations. Moreover, we also include what could best be called visibility, meaning a group's overall presence in the community. If the rescue groups of breed X are substantially better at rescuing than those of breed Y, and if we assume—correctly, we believe—that there exist no differences whatsoever in the rescuers' affection for and commitment to their preferred breeds, then there must be other reasons for this discrepancy in effectiveness. In order to explain these extant inter-breed differences in the efficacy of their respective rescues' work, we must compare breed rescue groups and attempt to discern differences that may be present as well as assign meaning to them. But how can we compare rescues for different breeds?

Any appropriate comparison would require that we analyze breeds with similar characteristics, owner demographics, and popularity. Our intent was to compare two breeds that are as similar as possible, therefore attributing most of the differences in the respective rescues' efficacy to the human side of the equation and not to the dogs' breed. Thus, for example, comparing Yorkshire Terrier rescues with Boxer rescues would not be very helpful or advisable for solving this puzzle, as the two breeds are physically and behaviorally quite dissimilar, thus attracting human advocates and aficionados belonging to rather different demographics. In spite of the remarkable breed similarities between German Shepherds and Belgian Malinois as dogs, a comparison of their respective rescues would also be conceptually and methodologically inappropriate, as German Shepherds are the second most popular breed in the United States, while Belgian Malinois are the seventy-sixth, thus resulting in a significantly larger number of German Shepherds in need of rescue than Belgian Malinois.[1] The top-ten AKC breeds are likely to be the most populous nationally and therefore in need of more rescue groups than less popular breeds. Just to reiterate, the top-ten AKC-registered breeds in 2012 were, in order, Labrador Retrievers, German Shepherds, Beagles, Golden Retrievers, Yorkshire Terriers, Bulldogs, Boxers, Poodles, Dachshunds, and Rottweilers. Of these, the most similar by any measure are Labrador Retrievers and Golden Retrievers. Thus, it is between the rescues of these two breeds that we decided to construct our comparison of their respective organizational and operational efficacy.

Labrador Retrievers and Golden Retrievers have similar physical and behavioral traits. Both are medium-sized dogs, with their sizes being nearly identical. Golden Retriever males are 'expected to be 23 to 24 inches in height at the withers and 65 to 75 pounds, and females should be 21.5 to 22.5 inches tall and weigh 55 to 65 pounds.[2] Labrador Retrievers are slightly larger, with males at 22.5 to 24.5 inches tall and 65 to 85 pounds, and females at 21.5 to 23.5 inches tall and 55 to 70 pounds.[3] The differences between the two breeds is at most half an inch and ten pounds in favor of Labrador Retrievers, but this is so slight as to be practically negligible. Behaviorally, both breeds are described and widely perceived as being friendly, intelligent, energetic, and trainable. Moreover, both are waterfowl-retrieving members of the working dog class. The main difference between the two breeds manifests itself in their coats; Golden Retriever coats are long, silky, and vary in color from light cream to a dark gold, while Labrador Retrievers have shorter, coarser fur and can be yellow (light cream to fox red), chocolate (light to dark chocolate), or black in color. This means that Labrador Retrievers have a greater variety in appearance than Golden Retrievers, but not to a significant amount.[4]

The similarities in physical and behavioral characteristics between Golden Retrievers and Labrador Retrievers mean that they appeal to people sharing many demographic characteristics. Golden Retrievers and Labrador Retrievers were both bred to retrieve waterfowl and thus are favorites for hunters. However, Labrador Retrievers tend to be the most preferred dog for hunters with all but four AKC National Retrieving Champions being Labrador Retrievers; the last time a dog from a breed other than a Labrador Retriever won was when a Golden Retriever prevailed in 1951.[5] Both breeds have excellent reputations as family dogs, particularly because they are characteristically good natured; aggressiveness toward humans or other animals is considered aberrant and undesirable. Furthermore, both breeds furnish a large percentage of assistance dogs because of their featured behavioral traits that are crucial in such work. People exhibiting the demographic characteristics that find

Golden Retrievers to be attractive pets are the same ones that find Labrador Retrievers attractive as well. Apart from avid hunters, both breeds appeal to people who do not perceive their dog(s) as portraying power, let alone aggression. Both of these retrievers are "softies," and it is precisely humans with such personality traits that find both retrievers attractive. Lauren Genkinger put it this way: "When we look for foster homes for a Golden Retriever, we do not want alpha people. We find people that want to babysit a dog, not dominate it. Folks that have fostered German Shepherds and Rottweilers know how to be alpha. What we found is that people that are attracted to Golden Retrievers really are wussies."[6] Lastly, both breeds have enjoyed a high level of national popularity since the late 1980s and early 1990s, thus coinciding temporally with the nationwide proliferation of rescue.

The similar characteristics and demographic appeal of Golden Retrievers and Labrador Retrievers would lead us to believe that the rescue groups for these dogs shared many similarities to the point of being almost identical just as the two retriever breeds and their human fans have been. To our initial surprise and subsequent understanding, we realized that this most certainly has not been the case. Instead, Golden Retriever rescues are much more successful than their Labrador Retriever counterparts, a finding that appeared to have no clear explanation. Our hypothesis as to why this might be the case hinged on two factors affecting rescues of Labrador Retrievers and Golden Retrievers: first, the significantly larger number of Labrador Retrievers compared with Golden Retrievers had to have an important effect in terms of the respective rescues' operation and efficacy; and second, Golden Retriever rescues might have been the beneficiaries of sheer chance in that a critical mass of especially motivated and talented individuals, such as Carol Allen, Joan Puglia, Susan Foster, Jane Nygaard, and Robin Adams, to name just a few, greatly influenced the development and direction of Golden Retriever rescue nationally. In other words, in the all-important stage of initial institutionalization, Golden Retriever rescues were randomly blessed by impressive and effective charismatic authority that the Labrador Receiver rescues seemed to have in much smaller quantities. The true picture, as it turns out, is more complex. Indeed, several factors, including dog population, group histories, regional distributions, financial matters, social media, external relationships, and the power of individuals, contribute to the disparate levels of success between Golden Retriever rescues and Labrador Retriever rescues.

Populations

The single largest factor affecting the success of a group is the proportion of needy dogs it serves. If, as is the case with many of the rarer breeds, only one or two dogs a year require placement, then the rescue groups for these breeds are likely to be very successful in placing needy dogs belonging to these breeds into new homes. As the number of dogs in search of homes grows, however, it becomes increasingly difficult to find such safety and succor for all of them, making it challenging to rescue the large quantity of dogs belonging to the most popular breeds because of the sheer number of dogs involved. With this in mind, it is critical to know how many dogs of a particular breed are in shelters at a given time, thereby defining the number of homeless dogs that need to be helped by a breed rescue. It is tempting to use AKC registration data to generate data on the relative population sizes of Golden Retrievers and Labrador Retrievers. But we rejected the validity of this metric for our purposes for a number of reasons. First, not all dogs are AKC registered; the Humane Society of the United States estimates that only 25 percent of dogs entering animal shelters every year are purebred,[7] and not all of these are registered with the AKC. Second, owners who choose to register their dogs with the AKC are not representative of all dog owners, as these owners tend to be more involved in showing dogs and participating in local breed club events than other owners who may simply be interested in a good family pet, assistance dog, or hunting partner. Third, as we demonstrated amply in Chapter 3, AKC registration trends have been decreasing steadily, with data from 2002 stating that there were 154,616 registered Labrador Retrievers that year while, by 2006, the number had declined to 123,760 registered Labrador Retrievers, which represents a 20 percent decrease in a four-year period. We argue that this numeric decline does not reflect an actual decrease in the number of Labrador Retrievers as much as it indicates a noticeably reduced interest on the part of dog owners to have their companion animals registered with the AKC. Indeed, this represents a problem of which the AKC is aware and which it has been attempting to change.[8] With AKC registration statistics rendered unusable for the purposes of determining the populations of Labrador Retrievers and Golden Retrievers in animal shelters, we were obliged to create a study of our own to obtain the information we sought.

We designed and implemented a project wherein we randomly sampled animal shelters and rescues nationally to calculate the national averages of Golden Retrievers, Labrador Retrievers, and Pit Bulls found in such organizations. First, we combined the lists of animal shelters and rescues that we found at Petfinder.com and AnimalShelter.org to create a master list of animal shelters in the United States. Eliminating duplicates and rescue groups dedicated exclusively to breeds other than the three we were seeking,[9] we arrived at a total of 14,098 animal shelters to sample. We randomly selected 400 shelters or rescues from this group and tracked the number of Labrador Retrievers, Golden Retrievers, and Pit Bulls over a ten-week period.[10] We then averaged the number of dogs of each breed for each shelter over that period and found that nationally the average number of Golden Retrievers per shelter was 0.18, and the average number of Labrador Retrievers per shelter was 2.97.[11] This means that in the period spanning our study, there were more than sixteen times as many Labrador Retrievers in shelters as there were Golden Retrievers. The ramifications of this disparity in population cannot be overstated, as it means that as a matter of course and at the starting line Labrador Retriever rescues require significantly higher resources than their Golden Retriever counterparts to be able to approach an equal level of efficacy in their rescue efforts. Differently put, for every dollar that Golden Retriever rescues spend on dogs, Labrador Retriever rescues must spend $16 to equal the productivity and the output of Golden Retriever rescues. The necessity of increased financial resources to approach Golden Retriever rescue group levels of efficacy is particularly important in the case of veterinary spending and likely offers one reason why Labrador Retriever rescues tend to be more selective in the dogs they choose to assist than Golden Retriever rescues. Quite simply, most Labrador Retriever rescues (although certainly not all) struggle to remain financially solvent and are inundated with dogs to the point of becoming overwhelmed by their sheer numbers, thus rendering the rescue impotent, which, in turn, adds to low morale on the part of rescuers, occasionally resulting in hopelessness and possible abandonment of the very project they set out to accomplish. Labrador Retriever rescues must therefore prioritize dogs that are healthier and therefore less expensive and easier to adopt, as opposed to sick or injured Labrador Retrievers, which may require resources groups do not have and are unlikely to be able to procure.

The vast discrepancy in the sheer quantity of Labrador Retrievers and Golden Retrievers was mentioned by virtually every one of our interviewees as the most significant reason impeding the proper quality of rescue in the case of the former in marked contrast to the latter. Tami Stanley told us: "Labradors are a huge breed here in Texas and there are four Labrador rescues in the Dallas–Fort Worth area alone but we simply cannot keep up with the amount of Labradors that are in shelters every day."[12] Bob Tillay informed us that "the Lab rescue here in St. Louis quit because it just could not handle the numbers. There is a Lab rescue in Illinois, there's one in Granite City here across the river, there's one up in Chicago, they all are just absolutely swamped.... They cannot keep up with the numbers, there's just too many Labs."[13] Nina Palmo stated that "one of the hardest things is that the need is so overwhelming that we can only take in a fraction of the dogs that we hear about."[14] Cathy Mahle shared this sad information with us: "Every day I probably get at least a hundred e-mails from shelters all over the United States that have Labs that are going to be put to sleep that very day."[15] Barbara Elk said: "I can tell you, it breaks my heart that when our shelter coordinator gives me her monthly report, the number of Labs that are being euthanized is huge because the Lab rescue is small, they don't have much money, and they don't have much participation."[16] This was seconded by Priscilla Skare: "I think there is only one Lab rescue in all of North Carolina and they are very hard to reach. I'm sure that they are totally inundated with dogs but they don't return calls and it is therefore very hard to refer a dog to them."[17] In other words, the huge number of needy Labrador Retrievers constitutes a crippling factor that burdens, if not impedes, the creation of state-of-the-art rescues that might somewhat ease the problem if not alleviate it completely.

Histories of Breed Rescue Development

The timeline of development for Labrador Retriever rescues and Golden Retriever rescues is significantly different. The earliest Golden Retriever rescues were formed in 1980, while the earliest Labrador Retriever rescue was not created until 1986. Joan Puglia, one of the two cofounders of Yankee Golden Retriever Rescue in 1985, had this to say about the situation in her area:

> For whatever reason, certainly here in New England but I believe also nationally, the Golden Retriever community started the process of rescue much earlier than did the Labrador Retriever community. I think we acknowledged earlier that there was a real need for rescue and we just went out and did it. We got the necessary 501(c)(3) organizations established, we separated from the clubs but still remained in touch with them so that they would send us people if we needed something or help us in other ways.[18]

The average start year for Golden Retriever rescue groups currently in existence is 1999, while the corresponding Labrador Retriever data begin in 2003. The same can be said for the median start year, where the Golden Retriever value is 2000 and that for the Labrador Retriever is 2004.

What does this all mean? First, the Labrador Retriever rescue movement is younger than its Golden Retriever counterpart. Thus, the former's knowledge base has not been as well developed as the Golden Retriever rescues'. Moreover, the Labrador Retriever rescues have not had as much time as a movement to network with one another as have the Golden Retriever rescues. Second, the earlier temporal development of the Golden Retriever rescues also had substantive ramifications in that the emergence of early groups such as Yankee Golden Retriever Rescue and Retrieve a Golden of Minnesota, with their heavy influence in the development of the world of Golden Retriever rescue, set the stage for a high level of intergroup networking and cooperation among Golden Retriever rescues. These developments happened later and more meekly and tenuously with the Labrador Retriever rescues, a factor that decidedly contributes to the differences in the levels of success between the rescues of the two breeds.

Regionalism

As was demonstrated in Chapter 5, regional variations have a substantial effect on rescues' very existence and efficacy, so comparing Golden Retriever rescues and Labrador Retriever rescues illustrates the importance of taking regional factors into account when assessing their effectiveness. In order to understand fully the regional dimension of the Labrador Retriever rescue versus Golden Retriever rescue comparison, we must analyze the distribution of the two breed populations and the regional distribution of their respective rescues.

We reiterate at this point a comparison in the existence of these two related breeds that serves as a baseline for the argument at hand: The average number of Golden Retrievers in shelters nationally is 0.18 per shelter, whereas the average number of Labrador Retrievers in shelters nationally is 2.97; this means that nationally, on average, there are sixteen times as many Labrador Retrievers in shelters as there are Golden Retrievers. To get a clearer picture of how this affects individual rescues, however, it is important to disaggregate these national averages into their regional components. Table 8.1 provides the average number of Labrador Retrievers and Golden Retrievers per shelter in each region and the proportion describing the

TABLE 8.1. The Average Number of Labrador Retrievers and Golden Retrievers per Shelter in Each of the Ten Regions of the United States

Region	# Labrador Retrievers per shelter	# Golden Retrievers per shelter	Proportions (Labrador Retrievers to Golden Retrievers)
R1	1.3435	0.0217	61.912
R2	1.5384	0.1019	15.097
R3	2.4805	0.3024	8.203
R4	3.6252	0.103	35.196
R5	2.8859	0.1648	17.512
R6	4.3691	0.2904	15.045
R7	4.0472	0.1389	29.138
R8	1.67	0.64	2.609
R9	2.7173	0.1429	19.015
R10	2.5363	0.0363	69.871
Average	2.9745	0.18225	16.32

number of Labrador Retrievers in a shelter for every Golden Retriever in a shelter for each region. These regions are the same as those presented in Chapter 5. The table illustrates that the distributions are not uniform for all regions, and that there are large disparities among regions for each breed. (Please consult pages 155 and 156 for the ten regions of the U.S.)

Region 1 has an average of 1.34 Labrador Retrievers and 0.02 Golden Retrievers per shelter. The 62 to 1 Labrador Retriever to Golden Retriever ratio characterizing this region is approximately four times larger than the national proportion of Labrador Retrievers to Golden Retrievers. This means that while rescues for both breeds located in region 1 generally have fewer dogs to support than the rescues in other regions, there are still significantly more Labrador Retrievers in this region than Golden Retrievers. Although rescue for both breeds in this region is likely to be less expensive than in any other region, Labrador Retriever rescues still need significantly more financial resources than Golden Retriever rescues located within the region. Region 2 also has low concentrations of Labrador Retrievers and Golden Retrievers per shelter; on average there are 1.53 Labrador Retrievers and 0.10 Golden Retrievers per shelter. The ratio of Labrador Retrievers to Golden Retrievers in shelters in this region is 15 to 1, placing it near the national average. Region 3 has a high concentration of Golden Retrievers, with 0.30 Golden Retrievers to 2.48 Labrador Retrievers per shelter, producing a Labrador Retriever to Golden Retriever ratio of 8 to 1, or half of the national average. Region 4 has a high concentration of Labrador

Retrievers, with 3.63 Labrador Retrievers and 0.10 Golden Retrievers per shelter, producing a 35 to 1 ratio of Labrador Retrievers to Golden Retrievers. Region 5 has a near national average number of both Labrador Retrievers and Golden Retrievers per shelter, with 2.89 Labrador Retrievers and 0.16 Golden Retrievers per shelter, a ratio of 17 to 1. With high concentrations of both Labrador Retrievers (4.37 per shelter) and Golden Retrievers (0.29 per shelter), region 6 has a ratio at 15 to 1 that, too, is near the national average. Region 7 has a high concentration of Labrador Retrievers (4.04 per shelter), which when combined with the Golden Retriever average of 0.14 per shelter produces a ratio of 29 to 1. An extremely high concentration of Golden Retrievers in region 8 (0.64 per shelter), combined with a low concentration of Labrador Retrievers in the region (1.67 per shelter) produces, at 2.6 to 1, the most equitable ratio between Labrador Retrievers and Golden Retrievers in the country. Region 9, with 2.71 Labrador Retrievers per shelter and 0.14 Golden Retrievers per shelter, produces a ratio of 19 to 1. Finally, region 10, with its extremely low concentration of Golden Retrievers (0.04 per shelter) and near average number of Labrador Retrievers (2.54 per shelter) yields a 70 to 1 ratio of Labrador Retrievers to Golden Retrievers.

It is critical to note that even when there is a relatively low number of Labrador Retrievers and a relatively high number of Golden Retrievers in the same region, as in region 8, Labrador Retrievers still outnumber Golden Retrievers 2.6 to 1. This means that at best Labrador Retriever rescues have to spend $2.61 for every dollar Golden Retriever rescues spend in order to attain the same level of care per dog. This makes it very clear that at an absolute minimum Labrador Retriever rescues need to be nearly three times richer than their Golden Retriever counterparts to accord a level of care for their dogs that is comparable to what the Golden Retriever rescues offer theirs.

Looking at the distribution of rescues per region gives us a different lens through which we can examine how regional dynamics evolve in a comparison between Labrador Retriever and Golden Retriever rescues. We compared three variables for each region: human population density, average number of breed dogs per shelter, and number of rescues for both Labrador Retrievers and Golden Retrievers. We then characterized each value as low (bottom three values), medium (middle four values), or high (top three values) for each variable. When we compared the human population density with the average breed dog per shelter, we found that the relationship between the two predicted the number of rescues that existed in the region, as illustrated in Table 8.2 (outliers are highlighted by the

TABLE 8.2. The Relationship between Human Population Density and the Average Labrador Retriever and Golden Retriever per Shelter

Human Pop. Density	Average Breed Dog/ Shelter	# Rescues	Total Occurrences
Low	Low	Low	2
Low	Med	Low	1
Low	Med	Med	1
Low	High	Low	2
Med	Low		0
Med	Med	Med	1
Med	Med	High	4
Med	High	Med	1
Med	High	High	2
High	Low	Low	1
High	Low	Med	3
High	Med	Med	1
High	High	Med	1

four "total occurrences" in which the digit "1" appears in a box encased by dotted lines and will be explained in greater detail below).

Regions with a low human population density produce a low number of breed rescues in five of six occurrences as is evident in the "Total Occurrences" column. This indicates that if the human population density is too low, it does not matter how high the average breed per dog per shelter value is, as there are not enough people in the area to increase the number of breed rescues. Low human population densities mean that there are fewer potential volunteers and adopters for groups to recruit, regardless of the number of breed dogs in shelters. As is evident in the first outlier, the single exception was region 7 for Golden Retrievers, which had a low human population density, a medium number of breed dogs per shelter, and a medium number of breed rescues. But this is best explained by the fact that the human population density for region 7 is on the cusp between medium and low values, making this region exhibit characteristics that are more akin to a medium human population density region than a low one.

Regions with a medium human population density produce either a medium or high number of rescues depending on the average number of breed dogs per shelter. If a region with a medium population density has a medium number of breed dogs per shelter, it will yield either a medium or high number of breed rescues, depending on whether the human population density and number of breed dogs per shelter are higher or lower. If a higher medium human population density occurs in the same region where a higher medium number of breed dogs per shelter occurs, those regions will produce a high number of breed rescues. Regions with medium human population densities and high numbers of breed dogs per shelter create a high number of breed rescues. The exception to this rule is region 6 for Golden Retrievers (the second outlier), which has a human population density that is on the cusp between a medium and low human population density value and a number of breed dogs per shelter value that is on the cusp of being a medium breed dog per shelter value, lending the region features that are more commensurate with a medium human population density and a medium number of breed dogs per shelter region, resulting in a medium number of breed rescues.

Regions with a high human population density yield a medium number of rescues in five of six cases. The exception is region 1 for Golden Retrievers (the third outlier), but this is due to the average number of breed dogs per shelter being the lowest of any region. The other unique region with a high human population density is region 3 for the Golden Retrievers (the fourth outlier), as it has a high human population density, a high number of breed dogs per shelter, but a medium number of rescues. However, the number of breed rescues in this region is actually on the cusp between a medium and high number of rescues, so this finding is not as unique as it would seem at first glance.

It is interesting to note that Golden Retriever rescues constitute all of our outliers in that the number of rescues deviates from the amount we would have predicted based on the human population density and dogs per shelter in that region. Three of these regions had lower numbers of breed rescues than we would have predicted based on the human population density and average number of breed dogs per shelter, and one had a higher number of breed rescues than we would have predicted. The three regions with lower numbers of rescues are likely due to the relatively low number of Golden Retrievers in the regions' shelters, as Golden Retrievers are not as common as other breeds in these shelters. Extant rescue groups in these regions led by Yankee Golden Retriever Rescue in region 1 and Delaware Valley Golden Retriever Rescue in region 3 may be able to accommodate enough Golden Retrievers to meet any new demand for rescue services without necessitating the creation of new rescue organizations. The higher than expected number of Golden Retriever rescues in region 7 is likely due to the fact that three rescue groups are located in St. Louis, Missouri, alone, a higher number than would be expected for the population of such a city as a result of developments discussed in Chapter 4.

Financial Matters

As noted in Chapter 7, the only financial information regarding breed rescues that we have approaching any statistical significance is that of the Golden Retrievers. And even this does not have a large enough sample size to be considered statistically significant by conventional measures because from an eighty-one group minimum needed to attain such statistical significance we received data from only seventy-six rescues. For Labrador Retriever rescues, the response rate was lower still, as we obtained the financial information of only forty-four rescue groups, when we needed at least seventy-five to achieve statistical significance. Our methods for obtaining financial information and the functional requirements of the Internal Revenue Service (IRS) for 501(c)(3) tax reporting are the reasons for our inability to obtain statistically significant sample sizes. When rescue groups attain their 501(c)(3) status, they are required to report their income to the IRS annually. When their income is above $25,000 in a calendar year, groups are required, by law, to complete Form 990, which gives detailed information about their group's income, expenditures, and assets. However, when a group's annual revenue falls under $25,000, it is only required to fill out an IRS e-postcard detailing its finances. The critical difference between these two modalities is that the IRS posts copies of Form 990 on its GuideStar.org website, but not copies of the e-postcards it receives from rescues. After obtaining all available copies of Form 990 for both breeds from the IRS, we contacted all Golden Retriever and Labrador Retriever rescue groups for which we had the necessary information,

requesting that they respond by filling out and returning a simple form
with the five financial data points in which we were interested (income,
assets at the beginning of the year, expenses, net gain or loss, and assets
at the end of the year). This is information, which, as a condition of their
501(c)(3) status, is required to be given by all rescues when it is requested
of them by the authorities. Although we had some responses from rescue
groups, the overwhelming majority did not reply to our request, forcing us
to accept that we would not be able to obtain further financial data from
the groups in question. The $25,000 cutoff for filling out a Form 990 leads
us to believe that the vast majority of groups that did not respond to us,
and had no information posted on GuideStar.org, were organizations that
made less than $25,000 in fiscal year 2009.

The groups with the largest incomes belonging to both breeds were
required to fill out a Form 990. Thus, it is virtually certain that we obtained
all relevant financial information from these organizations. This means that
our financial information for both Golden Retriever and Labrador Retriever
rescues represents the highest possible values that these data points could
have; additional financial information from groups with incomes of less
than $25,000 a year would decrease both the average and median values
for all data points. Table 8.3 presents the financial information we obtained
for Golden Retriever rescues and Labrador Retriever rescues as probable
maximum values, with the true averages and medians for all the data likely
to be at a lower value. When we compare the average financial information
for Golden Retriever rescues and their Labrador Retriever counterparts,
the former are substantially wealthier than the latter.

What is particularly striking is that Golden Retriever rescues have,
on average, about 4.3 times as many assets as Labrador Retriever rescue
groups and possessed net gains that were nearly double those of the Labrador Retriever rescues. Also of interest are the median values for both
breeds, as presented in Table 8.4, although they paint a slightly different
picture of the resource dynamic between the two breeds' rescues.

The median income for Labrador Retriever rescues is actually $17,000
higher than that of the Golden Retriever rescues, but the former's median

TABLE 8.3. Sundry Financial Data for Labrador Retriever and Golden Retriever Rescue
Groups

Breed	Income	Assets (Start)	Expenses	Net Gain/Loss	Assets (End)
Labradors	122,650.72	29,645.33	117,606.65	5,692.21	34,554.88
Goldens	131,013.46	130,512.23	124,088.95	8,777.76	149,333.96

TABLE 8.4. Median Values of These Financial Data for Labrador Retriever and Golden Retriever Rescue Groups

Breed	Income	Assets (Start)	Expenses	Net Gain/Loss	Assets (End)
Labradors	100,504.00	15,634.00	94,044.00	1,752.00	18,669.00
Goldens	83,401.50	33,009.70	72,877.00	5,117.00	38,561.00

expenses, which are $22,000 higher than the latter's, complicate the picture. The Golden Retriever rescues had a median net gain that was $3,365 larger than that of the Labrador Retriever rescues, which indicates that the former were able to save more of their money than did the latter. This is borne out in a comparison of the assets for both groups, where Golden Retriever rescues have median assets that are more than double those of the Labrador Retriever rescues. This pattern indicates that although Labrador Retriever rescues need to spend nearly all of their income for the most basic needs of their daily operations, Golden Retriever rescues are able to save some of their income, giving them an important financial cushion in case their donations dropped unexpectedly for some reason or a particularly needy dog taxed the organization's resources by incurring major medical expenses. It also means that Golden Retriever rescues are more likely to be in a position to rent or purchase a kennel or facility of their own and thus move to a more stable and elaborate level of rescue than Labrador Retriever rescue groups.

External Relationships

Through mechanisms highlighted in Chapter 6, a rescue group's relationships with external entities can shape the resources that are available to the organization. To quantify the quality of relationships that rescues cultivate, we devised a scoring system for Golden Retriever rescues and Labrador Retriever rescues whose members we had interviewed. Each group was given a value in five categories based on its relationships with the national breed club, the local breed club, local rescue groups, local shelters, and the general public. The possible values ranged from –1 (entirely negative relationship) to +1 (entirely positive relationship), with 0 as neutral or unmentioned and +/– 0.5 depending on whether a general statement about relationships was made but with a counterexample as well.[19] We then added up the value for each category to give each rescue group a relationship score, with a possible range of –5 (all negative relationships) to +5 (all positive relationships). Golden Retriever rescues attained an average score of 3.5, while the Labrador Retriever Rescues' equivalent was 2.78.

The results of these scores show the remarkable differences pertaining to the perceived quality in external relations these two retriever breeds' rescues entertain, with key players shaping their environment. The most critical difference appears in the relationship with the respective national clubs. Of the Golden Retriever rescues we interviewed, 79.17 percent reported positive interactions with the Golden Retriever national club, while none of the Labrador Retriever rescues had any relationship with the Labrador Retriever national club.[20] Golden Retriever rescues were also twice as likely to have contact with their local clubs, with 62.5 percent of Golden Retriever rescues having some form of contact (positive or negative) with their local club, while only 27.78 percent of Labrador Retriever rescues mentioned any form of contact with their local club. These data are supported by our examination of levels of local breed club involvement in rescue, as 82.54 percent of Golden Retriever clubs had some involvement in rescue (passive, active, or some combination of the two), whereas only 61.36 percent of Labrador Retriever clubs had any level of involvement in rescue. Additionally, more Golden Retriever rescues started in local clubs (15.84 percent) than Labrador Retriever rescues (3.41 percent). Groups that had their origins in local breed clubs feature networking advantages both with the local breed club, with which they are likely to maintain positive contact, and with other breed rescues, as the networking that occurs at club specialties encompasses regional clubs and rescues. Both breeds had similar levels of contact with local rescue groups and local shelters.

These findings highlight that Golden Retriever rescues are much more likely to be in contact with the external entities upon which they rely for resources than their Labrador Retriever counterparts. Moreover, the interactions that the Golden Retriever groups have with these outside organizations are more likely to be positive, giving them a distinct advantage in the procurement of valued resources and overall efficacy of their operations over Labrador Retriever rescues. Of particular importance is the Golden Retriever rescues' high level of contact with the national club, as the Golden Retriever Club of America's National Rescue Committee (GRCA-NRC) functions as an organizational hub for the Golden Retriever rescue community, providing a reliable infrastructure for communication among groups allowing them to exchange information and goods rapidly and efficiently. The names of early and prominent figures in Golden Retriever rescue such as Joan Puglia and Susan Foster of Yankee Golden Retriever Rescue and Carol Allen of the GRCA-NRC are known to most Golden

Retriever rescues. At least to our knowledge and gauging from our extensive interviews, comparable founding figures and nationally known and respected leaders do not seem to exist in the Labrador Retriever rescue world. The fact that none of the persons active in Labrador Retriever rescues whom we interviewed had contact with the national club suggests that the Labrador Retriever national club does not embody the same role for its rescue community as the GRCA does for Golden Retriever rescue, and that the lack of such a vertical resource for Labrador Retriever rescues limits their horizontal communication with one another on a national level.

Conclusion

Several factors contribute to the higher level of success that Golden Retriever rescues achieve, on average, when compared with their Labrador Retriever rescue counterparts, but none is more influential than the difference in the sheer number of Labrador Retrievers in need of rescue compared with Golden Retrievers. With a national average of 16.32 times as many Labrador Retrievers as Golden Retrievers in shelters, the effects of population size on rescue behavior cannot be overstated. Labrador Retriever rescues would have to have incomes sixteen times as high as those of Golden Retriever rescues to be able to spend the same amount of money per dog in shelters, and, as was evident in our presentation of financial matters, it is extremely unlikely that this will be the actual case. The effect that the quantity of dogs in need of rescue has on a rescue is partially determined by the rescue's location and the regional population of dogs in shelters, such that in some regions the ratio of Labrador Retrievers to Golden Retrievers is as low as 2.6 to 1, and in others it is as high as 70 to 1. Given the overwhelming population of needy Labrador Retrievers at all levels, it comes as no surprise that Labrador Retriever rescues remain bogged down in the most essential activities of saving dogs and are simply unable to find the necessary time and resources to create more sophisticated organizational structures that allow for better communication and ultimately enhance efficiency leading to better results, the way the Golden Retriever rescues have. This contributes to the other critical distinction between Golden Retriever and Labrador Retriever rescues: their intergroup networking. Golden Retriever rescue groups possess the services of the GRCA-NRC with its annual surveys, informational e-mail lists, rescue startup assistance, and coordinating capacity in disasters such as Hurricane Katrina; Labrador Retriever rescues do not have any of these. Joy Viola confirmed our finding: "When dogs came out of the South after Katrina by the thousands, there was no Labrador network to step in, and here they are, the number one breed on the AKC list."[21] The contributions of early, successful Golden Retriever rescues such as Yankee Golden Retriever Rescue and Retrieve a Golden of Minnesota are unparalleled in the world of Labrador Retriever rescue. Such groups provided promising models for others to emulate. Also, these pioneering organizations actively assisted beginning Golden Retriever rescue groups, while early Labrador Retriever rescues did not engage in similar outreach activities.

The sheer number of Labrador Retrievers, coupled with their rescues' minimal intergroup networking, does not allow the Labrador Retriever rescue world to enjoy the successes that have become a staple of its Golden Retriever counterpart. In addition to the vast difference in the quantity of dogs between Labrador Retrievers and Golden Retrievers that clearly burden the proper institutionalization of an effective Labrador Retriever rescue network, this breed also suffers from an unclear product differentiation or the lack of a singularly recognizable profile that Golden Retrievers in all their shadings clearly have. Briefly put, the variety of the Labrador Retriever, yellow, chocolate, and black, renders its distinct visual profile murky and thus weakens its immediate recognition by the public, both of which contribute to the dog's "ordinariness" and worse. The public has a clear vision of what a Golden Retriever is. This is much less evident in the case of Labrador Retrievers, further aggravating the breed's easy desirability and thus adoptability, particularly in the case of black labs. After all, black Labrador Retrievers are often the victims of so-called black dog syndrome, the bane of many a shelter whose volunteers and workers know only too well how difficult and, alas, frequently well-nigh impossible it is to have such dogs adopted by a wary public. Just think of all the visual tricks that shelters employ to render black dogs more attractive to potential adopters, from putting red or pink or brightly colored ribbons around their necks to placing extra colorful toys into their kennels. It is all the more important and welcoming to have Fred Levy's and Alexandra Zaslow's truly beautiful, even moving, photo series published by the *Huffington Post* highlighting the beauty of black dogs that are often overlooked in adoption.[22] Lastly, the level of institutionalized difference between Golden Retriever and Labrador Retriever rescues might also be attributable to mere chance in that the all-important founding generation of the breed specific rescue movement happened to be overrepresented among those particularly devoted to Golden Retrievers.

The next chapter will shed light on a very special case in the canine rescue world that—like all others presented thus far—is deeply anchored in the discourse of compassion yet also exhibits characteristics all its own that we found not only interesting but also immensely illustrative of this book's overall argument—rescues devoted to Greyhounds.

Notes

1. American Kennel Club. "AKC Dog Registration Statistics." 2012. http://www.akc.org/reg/dogreg_stats.cfm (accessed on April 12, 2012).

2. American Kennel Club. "AKC Meet the Breeds: Golden Retriever." 1990. http://www.akc.org/breeds/golden_retriever/ (accessed on April 12, 2012).

3. American Kennel Club. "American Kennel Club." AKC meet the breeds: Labrador retriever. 2011. http://www.akc.org/breeds/labrador_retriever/ (accessed on April 12, 2012).

4. There is also a distinction in Labrador Retrievers between dogs bred for Field/American dogs and Show/British dogs, with slightly different head shapes and body builds, but it is nowhere near the difference between Miniature Poodles and Standard Poodles, for example.

5. American Kennel Club. "Past NRC Champions." 2012. http://www.akc.org/events/field_trials/retrievers/past_nrc_champions.cfm (accessed on April 12, 2012).

6. Lauren Genkinger. Interviewed by Katherine Crosby. Telephone Interview. August 8, 2010.

7. The Humane Society of the United States. "HSUS Pet Overpopulations Facts." 2009. http://www.humanesociety.org/issues/pet_overpopulation/facts/overpopulation_estimates.html (accessed on April 12, 2012).

8. Robert H. Menaker, "American Kennel Club—July 2007 Chairman's report." American Kennel Club, July 2007. http://www.akc.org/about/chairmans_report/2007.cfm?page=7 (accessed on April 12, 2012).

9. We chose to exclude rescue groups dedicated to other breeds and animals (cats only, birds only, etc.) as the number of individuals meeting our criteria would be so low as to be effectively nonexistent.

10. For comparative purposes we also included Pit Bulls in the gathering of these data. We will present in greater detail our findings for Pit Bulls in Chapter 10, which is devoted in its entirety to a discussion of this breed's rescue.

11. These numbers are national averages that give us the relative proportions of Labrador Retrievers to Golden Retrievers and do not reflect the average number of dogs of a particular breed in breed rescues, as that number is sure to be higher due to the dog selection behavior inherent in breed rescue.

12. Tami Stanley. Interviewed by Katherine Crosby. Telephone Interview. July 29, 2010.

13. Bob Tillay. Interviewed by Andrei Markovits. Telephone Interview. August 18, 2010.

14. Nina Palmo. Interviewed by Katherine Crosby. Telephone Interview. July 29, 2010.

15. Cathy Mahle. Interviewed by Katherine Crosby. Telephone Interview. August 3, 2010.

16. Barbara Elk. Interviewed by Andrei Markovits. Telephone Interview. August 19, 2010.

17. Priscilla Skare. Interviewed by Andrei Markovits. Telephone Interview. August 19, 2010.

18. Joan Puglia. Interviewed by Andrei Markovits. Telephone Interview. June 30, 2009.

19. A hypothetical example of a +0.5-type relationship: Group X has largely positive relationships with area shelters, but one shelter in particular accuses the group of cherry-picking and refuses to deal with it.

20. Two Labrador Retriever rescues casually mentioned that they were listed on the AKC Parent Club of the Labrador Retrievers' rescue referral website, but stated that they otherwise had no contact with the club whatsoever.

21. Joy Viola. Interviewed by Andrei Markovits. Telephone Interview. July 16, 2009.

22. Alexandra Zaslow, "Stunning Photo Series Highlights the Beauty of Black Dogs That Are Often Overlooked in Adoption," *Huffington Post*, March 27, 2014, http://www.huffingtonpost.com/2014/03/27/black-dogs-project_n_5037181.html (accessed on March 28, 2014). This story highlights Fred Levy's Black Dogs Project.

CHAPTER 9

The Unique Case of Greyhound Rescue

We do programs in our local libraries where we talk about the history of the Greyhound, how they train for racing, what their racing careers are like, and how they transition to being a family pet.

—Cindy Bauer
Greyhound Adoption of Greater Rochester, New York

In the previous chapters on breed specific dog rescues, we omitted mention of Greyhound rescue. But the influence of Greyhound racing on Greyhound rescue dictates that a separate and additional presentation be given this topic because Greyhound rescue represents a phenomenon that is quite different in its origins and logic from the breed rescues featured in previous chapters. To be sure, here, too, the purpose of rescue remains identical in that it focuses solely on giving these much-abused creatures a semblance of succor, dignity, security, and affection for the remainder of their lives. Just like virtually all other breed specific rescues, Greyhound rescue, too, emerged in the wake of what we have termed the discourse of compassion. As to this rescue's organizational manifestations, here, too, we can date its origin in the United States to the late 1970s and the early 1980s. However, in contrast to all other breed specific dog rescues, Greyhound rescue hails from a very concrete institution and a particular phenomenon: the industry of Greyhound racing.

The Greyhound is a type of sight hound, a dog breed that uses sight and speed, rather than scent, to hunt and capture its prey. Sight hound owners have availed themselves of this hunting style, called coursing, for thousands of years.[1] Modern and systematically organized Greyhound racing, however, did not start until the early twentieth century, when O. P. Smith introduced it in Emeryville, California, in 1919. The system he devised had "the racing of greyhounds around an enclosed track in pursuit of an electrically controlled and propelled mechanical hare,"[2] rather than a live lure. Subsequently, this form of racing was introduced in England in 1926, where it became much more popular than it was in the United States.

Greyhound racing mutated from its beginnings in the early twentieth century as an informal and mainly local contest into a highly regulated and lucrative global industry. Greyhound racing is currently practiced in Australia, India, Ireland, Macau, Mexico, New Zealand, the United Kingdom, the United States, and Vietnam.[3] The industry works by breeding Greyhounds on farms, then selecting dogs that show racing promise and transferring them to onsite kennels at tracks where they are raced. The outcomes of races are much-valued objects of gambling using a pari-mutuel betting system, which will be discussed later in this chapter. The racing industry has developed along these lines since its inception in order to maximize profit and minimize cost.

Greyhounds begin their lives on farms and are bred to become the fastest dogs possible. To that end, farms produce thousands of dogs in excess of those that will ever be raced, thus ensuring the largest possible pool from which to select the few that will perform competitively at the track. Dogs that are considered unsuccessful are culled, either by outright destruction or by sale to laboratories.[4] Those that are not culled are trained to race on tracks. This training included the use of live lures, such as hares and cats, until the 1980s, although instances of continued live lure training have occurred after the ban on its use.[5] Greyhounds trained to race are tattooed in both ears to make the identification and tracking of the dog easier for the owner and as part of industry regulations to help prevent fraud in Greyhound racing.

Dogs that show racing potential are moved to kennels at racetracks, where they proceed through a series of grades, from maiden/juvenile (first race or early race) to A or AA (placing in the top three in a succession of races). The tracks are typically sand and loam, one-quarter mile long, with races usually five-sixteenths or three-eighths of a mile; there are eight dogs used per race in the United States and there are usually ten or eleven races per program.[6] The dogs are kept confined for the majority of the day, in kennels stacked two high or small enclosures, and are only occasionally allowed to interact with humans.[7] They are fed raw U.S. Department of Agriculture grade 4D meat (diseased, debilitated, dying, and dead) that is unsuitable for human consumption and contaminated with pathogens like *Salmonella*. One study published in the *Journal of Veterinary Diagnostic Investigation* stated that "outbreaks of *Salmonella enteritis* ('kennel sickness,' 'blowout') and of systemic salmonellosis are common among greyhounds in kennels."[8] Dogs typically end their racing careers at three and a half to four years of age, after which they are retained for breeding purposes, sold to laboratories, euthanized, or rescued.

Greyhound racing in the United States is a business. Thus, its main goal is to maximize profit, which it tries to attain by any means necessary. The Greyhound industry generates revenue through gambling at racetracks, which is performed in a pari-mutuel betting system. Gamblers bet against one another, rather than the house, on a particular event (a dog winning the race, the first three finishers, and other outcomes) and the odds (and payout) are calculated after betting on a particular race is closed. After the race, the house takes its cut, a fixed percentage of the pool, off the top before distributing the winnings. The house's cut is usually sufficiently large to cover state taxes levied on the track while still containing a healthy profit margin. Indeed, there are few instances where the house loses. In recent years, however, the financial viability of the Greyhound racing industry has come into question. Faced with the dwindling returns and mounting costs of Greyhound racing, many racetrack owners have started lobbying for changes that would allow them to expand their in-house casinos and decrease the number of races they are required to hold.[9] These casinos were initially added to supplement racetrack income, but they are now the major source of funds for the racetracks and in some cases even subsidize the costs incurred by operating the racetrack that cannot be covered by the revenue earned through racing itself. Racing is becoming less lucrative for the tracks that operate it; of the forty-nine tracks that were open nationwide in 1997, only twenty-two tracks remained so in 2012.[10] One reason for this decrease in Greyhound racing is the public's greater awareness of the brutality that this "sport" inflicts on the dogs and can thus be directly attributed to the societal growth of the discourse of compassion. In a parallel development, the breeding of Greyhounds has decreased to keep pace with the reduced demand for racing such dogs. Still, following their racing days on the track, life for the surviving animals remains uncertain and often brutal. Thus, rescue groups continue to have a large role in the betterment of the conditions of these exploited and abused creatures.

Who Are the Players in Greyhound Rescue?

The racing industry has polarized Greyhound rescue efforts in a way unknown to any other breed specific rescue movement. Organizations in the racing industry have a profound effect on rescue, and groups that are willing or unwilling to work with the industry each face their own challenges. To that effect, a brief description of each of the major parties that influence the racing industry and Greyhound rescue is in order.

The Greyhound racing industry in the United States includes a variety of organizations representing the interests of all parties involved in the racing business, from dog breeders and owners to racetrack proprietors and operators. Each organization, in its own way, furthers the continuation of the Greyhound racing industry and has a vested interest in seeing its uninterrupted and perpetual existence. The National Greyhound Association (NGA) was founded in 1906 and is "officially recognized by the entire Greyhound racing industry—namely, all Greyhound racetracks and individual racing jurisdictions, as well as foreign Greyhound registries and governing bodies—as the sole registry for racing Greyhounds on the North American continent."[11] It is the organization that runs the stud book for the entire Greyhound racing industry. Dogs that are not registered with the NGA cannot compete on U.S. racetracks. The American Greyhound Track Operators Association (AGTOA), founded in 1946, is "a nonprofit corporation composed of the owners and operators of 36 greyhound tracks located throughout the United States. Membership is open to all lawfully licensed greyhound racetracks, whether they be individuals, partnerships or corporations."[12] AGTOA was a founding member of the World Greyhound Racing Federation (WGRF), which was formed in 1969 and "acts as an international forum for the interchange of information, new technology and other developments to improve greyhound racing globally, and has adopted the preceding statement as its international charter."[13] These organizations, founded prior to the evolution of the discourse of compassion, work together to further the interests of the Greyhound racing industry, most notably its popularity and profitability.

When confronted by the shifting public opinion on Greyhound racing and animal cruelty in the 1980s as a direct consequence of the discourse of compassion that commenced a decade or so earlier, the NGA and the AGTOA jointly created the American Greyhound Council (AGC) in 1987 to "fund and manage greyhound welfare, research and adoption programs for the racing community."[14] The AGC offers grants to Greyhound rescue groups but places strict requirements on organizations that would like to be recipients of such funds, stating in its directives to all applicants that they can "make no false or negative statements about the racing industry (applicant should provide statement on this issue with application, along with any evidence of position)."[15] Also in 1987, Greyhound Pets of America (GPA) was founded by a coalition of preexisting Greyhound rescues, all of which had ties and contacts with the Greyhound racing industry.[16] Finally, the Greyhound Racing Association of America (GRAA) was created in 2002 to

> promote, protect and enhance the sport of greyhound racing and the greyhound industry through education, example and media for the benefit of its members, fans, supporters and the greyhound racing dogs that make this great sport possible. GRA/America plays a leading role in educating the public about Greyhound Racing and attracting new fans. The Association encourages responsible greyhound ownership and the best treatment of the dogs. Fans of a sport want to be proud of it and Greyhound racing has the best fans in America![17]

The pro-racing associations listed above all work for the betterment of the Greyhound racing industry, placing the GPA in a complicated position. Although the GPA's rescue efforts toward racing Greyhounds are commendable, its acceptance of annual donations from the industry that constitutes the very reason for Greyhound rescue's necessary existence in the first place highlights the conflict of interest this organization faces.

Anti-racing organizations' paramount priority is to end the Greyhound racing industry in the United States. The National Greyhound Adoption Program (NGAP) was founded in 1989 as a rescue group for retired Greyhounds and considers itself a strong advocate for Greyhound welfare, refusing to be affiliated with any Greyhound racetrack whatsoever.[18] The Greyhound Protection League (GPL) was created in 1991 and was the first pure Greyhound advocacy group in the United States. However, this organization has never engaged in any rescue activity. Rather, it opposes the Greyhound racing industry by seeking to educate the public about the animal rights issues inherent in commercial dog racing.[19]

GREY2K USA, founded in 2001, is another anti-racing organization, and like GPL, it does not actively rescue Greyhounds, as it maintains a 501(c)(4) status and is considered a social welfare organization, rather than an animal shelter. Its sole mission is to end Greyhound racing in the United States and to pass stronger legislation protecting the welfare of the

Greyhound breed.[20] The Greyhound Welfare Foundation, like GREY2K USA, sees ending Greyhound racing as the only viable solution to the animal cruelty inherent in the Greyhound racing industry. It advocates for that end via legislative measures while also educating the public and rescuing ex-racing Greyhounds.[21] The American Society for the Prevention of Cruelty to Animals (ASPCA)[22] and the Humane Society of the United States (HSUS)[23] also oppose the continuation of the Greyhound racing industry on the grounds that the overbreeding and mass euthanasia encouraged by the industry constitute animal cruelty. These organizations are joined by a number of Greyhound rescue groups that advocate for the end of Greyhound racing and work to ensure that retired racing Greyhounds are adopted, rather than euthanized, at the end of their racing careers.

Some rescue groups seek a neutral identity by maintaining a stance that neither condones nor condemns the Greyhound racing industry. These groups attempt to negate the extremely politicized and highly charged nature of having an opinion about Greyhound racing precisely to maximize their effectiveness of rescuing as many members of this breed as they possibly can. Needless to say, this very neutrality has itself become deeply controversial. These neutral Greyhound rescue groups are attempting to behave like the rescue groups of other canine breeds, hoping that by ignoring the controversy of Greyhound racing, they will simply be able to rescue the largest quantity of dogs that require assistance, rather than allowing themselves to be embroiled in a deeply divisive issue, which, so these groups worry, might sap their much-needed energy and commitment—not to mention their meager resources—needed to rescue abused Greyhounds.

The complexity of this issue is enhanced by the profound disagreement as to how groups perceive racing. On the one hand, there are pro-racing groups like GRA; while on the other hand, there are groups that see the ills afflicting the breed anchored solely in the racing industry. Pro-racing organizations exhibit either positive attitudes toward the racing industry or, at their most daring posture, maintain neutrality toward it. They perceive such a compliant position as vital in order to cooperate with the largest number of groups, regardless of their stance on racing. These organizations see such an inclusive big-tent policy to be the most effective strategy to help Greyhounds. The GRAA encourages owners to place dogs at pro-racing or racing-neutral rescues before resorting to anti-racing groups and contends that anti-racing rescue groups spend more time and effort attempting to "brainwash"[24] the general public than rescuing dogs and, in the words of the GRAA, "what [these organizations] can't seem to fathom is that they have made themselves enemies of the very people from whom they expect to get dogs. Why would owners, breeders and trainers deal with someone who wants to take away their livelihoods? Many will not."[25] In essence, the Greyhound racing industry prefers to work with rescue groups that are either pro-racing or—worst-case scenario—racing neutral. Conversely, the industry is much less likely to cooperate or engage in relationships with anti-racing rescue groups.

Anti-racing organizations, however, contend that it is impossible to be racing neutral and claim this is, at least by omission and default, condoning the racing industry's actions and legitimating its existence. Michigan Retired Greyhounds as Pets (Michigan REGAP in Plymouth, Michigan) hosts a frequently posted article written by Melani Nardone of the Greyhound Welfare Foundation that states the following: "The ethical consequences of a neutral position are far reaching and inevitably contribute to the continued suffering and destruction of this gentle, wonderful dog."[26] Greyhound rescue groups that seek to claim or maintain a neutral racing stance must therefore perform a delicate balancing act to have any hope of remaining relevant and effective in their mission of rescuing needy Greyhounds.

It is interesting to examine the positions of the American Kennel Club (AKC) and the Greyhound Club of America (GCA) with regard to the Greyhound racing industry. The AKC information page about Greyhounds makes no mention whatsoever of the fact that Greyhound racing is a well-established commercial entity, which involves the majority of Greyhounds in the United States and has been operating since the early twentieth century.[27] The Greyhound Club of America (GCA), the parent club of AKC-affiliated regional Greyhound clubs, only makes a limited reference to Greyhound racing in its rescue page, where it states that the GCA's rescue committee primarily assists those rescues adopting AKC Greyhounds, and that it offers assistance grants to those rescues adopting NGA (track) Greyhounds. The GCA also lists several organizations for rescuing ex-racing Greyhounds, all of which characterize themselves as either racing neutral or anti-racing.[28]

In the early 2000s, the GCA petitioned the AKC to allow the GCA to close the GCA's stud book to NGA-registered Greyhounds, an action that the GCA justified as a move to protect the AKC Greyhound type, which is bred for conformation to the breed standard, from the NGA type, which is bred to create the fastest dog possible, regardless of standard. The club was ultimately unable to close its stud book and owners of NGA Greyhounds can still register their dogs as AKC Greyhounds.[29] These facts suggest that the AKC is attempting to maintain a neutral relationship with the

Greyhound racing industry and that the GCA is assuming a position that is anti-racing in nature, though careful not to emphasize this attitude publicly.

Greyhound Rescue: A Brief History

Greyhound racing necessarily shapes the ways Greyhound rescues function. Thus the process of Greyhound rescue greatly differs from rescues of other breeds. With the puppy mill breeding scenarios common to the top-ten canine breeds in the United States, each puppy is considered a product that eventually needs to be sold. This means that mill breeders have incentives to breed and sell as many puppies as possible and to maximize profit by maintaining large litter sizes and ensuring that puppies are not visibly unhealthy, lest they be viewed as unattractive to potential buyers. Greyhound racing, on the other hand, compels breeders to create the fastest dogs possible to have them be competitive in races across the nation. This means that of the thousands of dogs bred each year, only a few will be sufficiently talented and thus lucrative to be sent to the track, with the rest—the vast majority—becoming essentially burdensome surplus, draining Greyhound breeders' resources without offering them any return on their investment. The essential difference between the typical puppy mill breeders and Greyhound breeders is that all puppies are potentially lucrative to the former and, therefore, need to be kept alive until sold, while only a few puppies will be lucrative to the latter, with all remaining dogs constituting a financial drain that is best expeditiously discarded. This unique challenge confronting Greyhounds has shaped the history of Greyhound rescue, which has thus developed differently from the history of any other breed specific canine rescue.

Greyhound rescue commenced in Great Britain in the 1950s. Ann Shannon, a volunteer for the British Union for the Abolishment of Vivisection (BUAV), started a sanctuary for retired Greyhounds and placed them as pets as early as 1956.[30] In 1976, the Retired Greyhound Trust was created by the National Greyhound Racing Club (a racing industry organization in the United Kingdom) and, with over seventy chapters located throughout Great Britain, has been rehoming rescued dogs since that time.[31] The much greater popularity of Greyhound racing in Great Britain (compared to the U.S.) explains why Greyhound rescue started there, as greater public exposure led to an earlier awareness of the plight of retired racing dogs.

For the American story, Greyhound rescue commenced in 1973 when Eileen McCaughern began rescuing Greyhounds from the Seabrook Greyhound Park in New Hampshire.[32] Quite possibly constituting the first breed specific rescue in the United States at this early date, McCaughern and her group, Retired Greyhounds as Pets of Connecticut (REGAP of CT), started as a "single-dog" type rescue, as she initially adopted a dog for herself directly from the kennel. McCaughern subsequently began placing other dogs in homes. Seabrook Greyhound Park is also believed to be the first Greyhound track to promote the concept of Greyhounds as pets, rather than just racing dogs, as this institution had an article published in 1981 in the track newspaper *Post Time* that encouraged track patrons to consider adopting Greyhounds.[33] The first explicit Greyhound rescue group, however, did not emerge until 1982, thus rendering it temporally congruous with the earliest Golden Retriever, Labrador Retriever, and other breed specific rescues, as discussed in earlier chapters of this book. The organization's name was Retired Greyhounds as Pets (REGAP); its founder was Ron Walsek, a retired Greyhound trainer who saw the pet potential in Greyhounds.[34]

In the beginning of the Greyhound rescue movement in the United States, Greyhounds were thought to be vicious because they raced with muzzles on their faces and exhibited the intense prey drive that made Greyhound racing possible. Pioneering rescue groups like REGAP had to fight hard to reverse this inaccurate but widely held perception of Greyhounds. Throughout the early to mid-1980s, Greyhound rescue began to expand nationally so that in 1987 many of the Greyhound rescue groups in the United States banded together to form the Greyhound Pets of America organization, which continues to rescue Greyhounds to this day. These early groups were all pro-racing or racing neutral and cooperated extensively with the Greyhound racetracks.

In 1989, the solidly anti-racing rescue groups had their first advocate in the National Greyhound Adoption Program (NGAP), which drove Greyhounds from Florida to its base in Pennsylvania throughout the 1990s. This organization has continued to provide an example to fledgling anti-racing groups. In 1992 the group built its own kenneling facility and expanded it in 1995 to include a Greyhound clinic that was in 2013 the only veterinary clinic in the world with two Biolase MD diode lasers (used to clean Greyhounds' teeth that have been damaged by consuming the 4D meat provided to the dogs at racetracks).[35] From the late 1980s to the early 1990s and onward, both the pro-racing and anti-racing movements within Greyhound rescue have expanded to encompass their current organizational level of rescue.

Greyhound rescue in the United States has grown immensely in the years since its inception in 1973 (or 1982). Today, there are approximately 300 Greyhound rescue groups in the United States with philosophies running the gamut from pro-racing to staunchly anti-racing. It is difficult to draw valid conclusions about Greyhound rescue groups because of the variety of attitudes, policies, and behavior they exhibit. Some pro-racing groups will have booths at racing events and will keep in direct contact with tracks on a weekly or monthly basis to discuss dogs needing rehoming. Kari Young of Arizona Adopt a Greyhound informed us that "we only work with retired racing Greyhounds—no mixes or other breeds."[36] This Greyhound rescue is not anti-racing. Indeed, it used to perform its rescue as part of a track before it closed. "Founded in 1990 by a lady who worked as a mutuel teller at Phoenix Greyhound Park (PGP)," according to Young, this rescue became a large organization that, prior to the track's closing in 2010, had five paid staff members in addition to 100 to 150 volunteers.[37] The former disappeared in 2010, the latter remained. There was a parallel decrease in the number of dogs this rescue needed to place after the track's demise. Young stated: "When PGP was still racing, we would adopt out approximately 500 dogs per year. Now we place about 200 to 250 per year."[38] Since its inception in 1990, the group has placed more than 6,000 Greyhounds in forever homes.

On the other side of the spectrum, anti-racing groups refuse to work with tracks for fear of giving the tracks and racing industry the good press and coveted legitimacy associated with Greyhound rescue. Moreover, they actively campaign to educate the public about the need to end Greyhound racing in the United States. Rescuers operating in the anti-racing world are convinced that racing needs to be stopped unconditionally because—as an inherently grave injustice to the dogs—it cannot be reformed or rendered "more humane" no matter how hard one tries. Cindy Siddon from Kindred Spirits Greyhound Adoption, which is anti-racing, stated: "I've always loved dogs ... for as far back as I remember. ... I brought home every stray dog I could find as a kid. ... Labs are actually my first love, but the injustice of Greyhound racing has always bothered me and at a point in my life when I was unemployed I had the opportunity to volunteer with a Greyhound rescue group and got hooked."[39] The injustices of the Greyhound racing world, as perceived by volunteers in anti-racing groups, provide a powerful motivation to those who fight to end dog racing in the United States.

In the middle of the ideological spectrum, there are groups that have conflicting opinions about the place of Greyhound racing within Greyhound rescue and may vacillate on positions or claim neutrality in an attempt to avoid the conflict inherent in picking a side on such a contentious matter. "We are neutral on the issue of racing," said Alan Jordano from Grey-Save Rescue, which was founded in 1995 in northwestern Pennsylvania.[40] "Volunteers or adopters may have their own opinions, but at any Grey-Save event we must remain neutral on the topic."[41] This is also emphasized in the group's official policy statement that "as an adoption group, Grey-Save remains neutral on the issue of greyhound racing. As private individuals, we are free to pursue any agenda we so choose."[42] Sensing the delicacy of the racing issue and its deeply divisive nature in the greater Greyhound community, Grey-Save makes it very clear in its policy statement that "[it] is not a political organization," a statement that we barely, if ever, encountered in the case of other rescues' publications. While pursuing a strictly neutral line on racing as the rescue's official policy, Grey-Save only accepts "retired racers" in its rescue. Jordano stated: "We will take in any retired racer . . . and only retired racers . . . AKC Greys or Greyhounds that have not raced are more unpredictable and through a number of bad experiences we modified our policies to work with only retired racers. Some exceptions are possible under extraordinary circumstances."[43] The emphatically demonstrative declarations of neutrality that racing-neutral Greyhound rescues feel obligated to provide as clear markers of their overall policies and normative orientations demonstrate the precarious position in which they find themselves on this ethically loaded and ideologically controversial topic.

Being racing neutral in no way implies that rescues do not perceive the horrors inflicted on Greyhounds by the racing industry. Cindy Bauer from Greyhound Adoption of Greater Rochester New York stated her thoughts on this:

> I got into Greyhound adoption when in 1997 I went to Florida and learned that 20,000 Greyhounds were bred for the racing industry and only 8,000 were finding homes and the rest were killed. I came back to Rochester and joined the local Greyhound rescue group which was Greyhound Pets of America of Rochester, New York, at that time. . . . I never owned a Greyhound until I got into rescue because of what I stated above. . . . GPA of Rochester, New York, was not doing enough to find homes for retired racing Greyhounds so in 2002 three people broke away from the group to start Greyhound Adoption of Greater Rochester, New York, as we are still known today.[44]

The group has come to assume all the standard characteristics that we have encountered with our typical rescue groups across breeds: establishing a 501(c)(3) status; having potential adopters fill out an application form; requiring home visits by volunteer adoption representatives; organizing various outreach programs such as having information booths at many local festivals and doing interviews on local television stations; engaging in fundraisers such as garage sales, car washes, candy bar sales, flower sales, donation jars at meet and greets; and, of course, strictly enforcing all the health-related steps that protect the dogs, from simple spay and neutering to performing complex surgeries. The group's goals are clear: "We feel that every Greyhound retired from the racing industry deserves a loving home and family, and we work hard to find homes for them in the greater Rochester, New York, area."[45] When we closed our interview with Cindy by asking her our standard question (posed to all our interviewees) as to what she would like to see changed about rescue in general, her answer was unique and very revealing of the Greyhounds' singular predicament among all canine breeds: "Nothing, as we can do nothing to stop the racing industry."[46]

Still, the commonality that unites all these Greyhound rescue groups, regardless of their racing ideologies, is that their primary objective remains the emphatic reduction, possibly total elimination, of the euthanasia inflicted on Greyhounds and the placement of surplus Greyhounds from the racing industry into loving forever homes.

The challenges that accompany breed rescue depend greatly on the breed being rescued, a fact that is evident in the varied forms of behavior unique to Greyhound rescue. The psychology and physiology of Greyhounds profoundly shape the adoption practices and advice that Greyhound rescues utilize. Because of their relatively thick necks and smaller heads, Greyhounds require specialized Martingale rather than normal collars to prevent the Greyhound from slipping out of the collar. Greyhounds also cannot be allowed to run in unsecured areas as their speed makes them significantly more difficult to catch than other breeds and their fixation on chasing can lead them into the path of oncoming traffic.[47] Because most Greyhounds are raised on farms and kept in kennels near tracks, they often do not have experience with stairs or basic dog obedience, thus requiring much devoted extra work by both the rescue group and the adopter in order to transition successfully from kennel to home life.[48]

Track closures have also had an effect on Greyhound rescues that are not present in the world of other breed rescues. Unlike puppy mill closures or hoarding seizures, Greyhound track closures are usually known in advance, as these organizations are public entities that court the media when possible. Racetracks will usually inform Greyhound rescues locally when the racetrack is closing permanently and how many dogs the track may possess at that time. This means that Greyhound rescues are often able to coordinate in advance how many dogs will go to which rescue and can thus be in a position to handle a large number of dogs much more smoothly than the rescue organizations of other breeds, whose efforts on a similar scale are usually reactive and unplanned. Excepting this situation in which Greyhound rescues can actually claim a rare advantage over their counterparts serving other canine breeds, Greyhound rescues, on the whole and as a rule, require much more work and greater detailed knowledge from both the rescue group and the adopter than might normally be expected in other breed rescues. The complexity of Greyhound rescue's work might become greater still by virtue of the diversity of the Greyhounds' situation. Alan Jordano told us: "Please understand that there is a huge difference between adopting a retired racing Greyhound and an AKC Greyhound or any Grey that has not raced. They are all completely different subbreeds within the Greyhound 'general' breed heading."[49]

Greyhound rescues experienced the same changes in popular culture, public opinion, and societal attitudes by virtue of the growing societal proliferation of the discourse of compassion as rescues of other breeds, but with the added element of the racing industry's systematic and inherent cruelty to these animals. The Greyhounds that are in need of being rehomed were not merely homeless. Rather, they lived in a situation of acute and constant danger of being euthanized by the industry that had created them in the first place. Initially the racing industry tried to ignore or minimize the public perception of animal cruelty associated with its business practices. But with increasing awareness of animal cruelty cases, its strategy has changed. The industry has come to promote Greyhound rescues and to use them to provide good public relations for its purposes in that the industry can now claim to support rescue efforts.[50]

This change of attitude and approach did not come about in a vacuum or by virtue of a voluntary change of heart. Rather, several instances of animal cruelty have contributed to the racing industry's current decline and loss of status, perhaps even legitimacy. Due to the general public's increasing sensitivity and compassion, the threshold for acceptance of animal cruelty has consistently shrunk over the past three decades. In particular, events that featured the inhumane destruction of Greyhounds and live lure training contributed to the changed public perception of the racing industry. This noticeable culture turn and shift in public perception compelled the industry to make concerted attempts to appear more caring toward these animals, which includes the acceptance, even active support, of formerly spurned and opposed Greyhound rescues. In 1992, the shot and mutilated bodies of nearly 150 Greyhounds were found in Chandler Heights, Arizona; all ears had been removed from these animals' remains in an attempt to prevent the identification of the dogs.[51] This event prompted an outrage in the Greyhound rescue community and spurred the creation of the Greyhound Network News newsletter, which traces animal cruelty in the Greyhound racing industry. In 2000, a member of the Greyhound National Association (GNA), Dan Shonka, was caught obtaining retired racers from other GNA trainers and owners, claiming to rescue them through his shell rescue, when he was actually selling the dogs (more than 1,200 over the course of three years) to laboratories.[52] A former racetrack security guard for the Pensacola Greyhound Park in Florida was found with the remains of an estimated 3,000 Greyhounds on his property in 2002. Confronted with this case of mass murder, this person claimed that he had been paid by the tracks for years to dispose of the dogs that had been too slow to be profitable as racers.[53] Events such as these have come to shape the ways in which a growing segment of the public views the Greyhound racing industry, Greyhound rescue, and the Greyhounds themselves.

Conclusion

Greyhound rescue is unusual in the world of dog rescue in that its relationship with the Greyhound racing industry adds a complexity to the operations of Greyhound rescue groups that simply is not present in the world of other breed rescues. In these, the relevant parties are typically the AKC clubs, the breeders, the puppy mills, and the rescue groups themselves. In Greyhound rescue, however, these parties are joined by pro-racing organizations like the NGA and the AGTOA and their anti-racing opponents like NGAP and GREY2K USA. This adds a politicized dimension to Greyhound rescue that is absent with all others. The challenges that Greyhound rescues face are unique compared with those of other breed rescues. Greyhound rescues therefore deserve their own presentation that features their distinct world apart from that of other breed rescues. Continuing in the vein of presenting particularly sad cases that—in addition to evoking special degrees of compassion, thus making them worthy of being studied and introduced to a wider readership— actually represent organizational outliers and cultural exceptions in the wider world of breed specific canine rescue, we now turn to a discussion of Pit Bulls in the next chapter.

Notes

1. Evidence of coursing can be found in depictions located in ancient Egyptian tombs over 4,000 years old. American Kennel Club. "History of Lure Coursing." 2010. http://www.akc.org/events/lure_coursing/history.cfm (accessed on June 28, 2012).

2. Encyclopaedia Britannica Online. "Dog racing." 2012. http://www.britannica.com/EBchecked/topic/167885/dog-racing (accessed on June 28, 2012).

3. GREY2K USA. "Take Action Worldwide." 2012. http://grey2kusa.org/action/worldwide.html (accessed on June 28, 2012).

4. American Society for the Prevention of Cruelty to Animals. "Greyhound Racing." 2012. http://www.aspca.org/fight-animal-cruelty/greyhound-racing-faq.aspx (accessed on June 28, 2012).

5. Eric Dexheimer, "Could Texas Greyhound Case Affect WV Governor's Race?" *The Statesman*, 2011. http://www.statesman.com/blogs/content/shared-gen/blogs/austin/investigative/entries/2011/10/04/could_texas_greyhound_case_aff.html/ (accessed on June 28, 2012).

6. Encyclopaedia Britannica. "Dog Racing."

7. The Humane Society of the United States. "The Facts About Greyhound Racing." 2009. http://www.humanesociety.org/issues/greyhound_racing/facts/greyhound_racing_facts.html (accessed on June 28, 2012).

8. M. M. Chengappa, et al., "Prevalence of Salmonella in Raw Meat used in Diets of Racing Greyhounds." *Journal of Veterinary Diagnostic Investigation* 5, no. 3 (1993), pp. 372–377.

9. A. G. Sulzberger, "Greyhound Races Face Extinction at the Hands of Casinos They Fostered." *New York Times*, March 8, 2012. http://www.nytimes.com/2012/03/09/us/greyhound-races-fade-with-many-track-owners-eager-to-get-out.html?_r=0 (accessed on June 28, 2012).

10. Ibid.

11. National Greyhound Association. "About Us." 2012. http://ngagreyhounds.com/page/about-us (accessed on June 28, 2012).

12. American Greyhound Track Operators Association. Home Page. 2007. http://www.agtoa.com/ (accessed on June 29, 2012).

13. World Greyhound Racing Federation. "The History of the WGRF." 2009. http://www.wgrf.org/index.php/history (accessed on June 29, 2012).

14. American Greyhound Council. "American Greyhound Council." 2012. http://www.agcouncil.com/ (accessed on June 29, 2012).

15. American Greyhound Council. "AGC Adoption Grant Guidelines." 2012. http://www.agcouncil.com/sites/default/files/AGC%20ADOPTION%20GRANT%20GUIDELINES.pdf (accessed on June 29, 2012).

16. Greyhound Pets of America. "National FAQs and Contacts." 2012. http://www.greyhoundpets.org/ntlfaq.php (accessed on June 29, 2012).

17. Greyhound Racing Association of America. "Greyhound Racing." 2011. http://www.gra-america.org/ (accessed on June 29, 2012). Needless to say, we deeply object to the usage of the term "sport" to the industry of Greyhound racing that abuses animals solely for the betting pleasure of humans.

18. National Greyhound Adoption Program. "About National Greyhound Adoption Program." 2009. http://www.ngap.org/about-ngap-y283.html (accessed on June 29, 2012).

19. Greyhound Protection League. "Greyhound Protection League." 2003. http://www.greyhounds.org/gpl/contents/entry.html (accessed on June 29, 2012).

20. GREY2K USA. "Who We Are." http://www.grey2kusa.org/who/index.html (accessed on June 29, 2012).

21. Greyhound Welfare Foundation. "About Us." 2002. http://www.greyhound welfarefoundation.org/aboutus.htm (accessed on June 29, 2012).

22. American Society for the Prevention of Cruelty to Animals. "We Are Their Voice." Greyhound racing. 2011. http://www.aspca.org/fight-cruelty/animals-in -entertainment/greyhound-racing-faq (accessed on May 13, 2014).

23. The Humane Society of the United States. "The Facts About Greyhound Racing." 2009. http://www.humanesociety.org/issues/greyhound_racing/facts/grey hound_racing_facts.html (accessed on June 29, 2012).

24. Greyhound Racing Association of America. "Adoption Directory." 2012. http://www.gra-america.org/the_sport/welfare/adoptiondirectory.html (accessed on June 29, 2012).

25. Ibid.

26. Melani Nardone, "The Myth of Neutrality." *REGAP—Rescue Greyhounds.* Greyhound Welfare Foundation, 1998. http://www.rescuedgreyhounds.com/end racing/the_myth.html (accessed on June 29, 2012).

27. American Kennel Club. "Greyhound." *AKC Meet the Breeds®: Greyhound.* 2012. http://www.akc.org/breeds/greyhound/ (accessed on June 29, 2012).

28. Greyhound Club of America. "GCA Rescue." 2010. http://www.greyhound clubofamericainc.org/rescue-gcoa.html (accessed on June 29, 2012).

29. American Kennel Club. "Delegates Quarterly Meeting." 2002. http://www .akc.org/pdfs/about/delegates_meeting/dec02.pdf (accessed on June 29, 2012).

30. Joan Dillon, "Early Adoption Pioneers ~ 1956-98." Greyhound Articles Online. The Greyhound Project, 2010. http://greytarticles.wordpress.com/adoption rescue/early-greyhound-adoption-pioneers/ (accessed on June 29, 2012).

31. Retired Greyhound Trust. "About the RGT." 2011. http://www.retiredgrey hounds.co.uk/About-the-RGT/ (accessed on June 29, 2012).

32. Animal Planet. " Meet Eileen McCaughern, 2008 Hero of the Year." 2008. http://animal.discovery.com/convergence/hero_of_the_year/2008/nominees /eileen-mccaughern.html (accessed on June 29, 2012).

33. Dillon, "Early Adoption Pioneers ~ 1956-98."

34. Jude Camillone, "Retired Greyhounds Dog It." *Sun Sentinel*, April 14, 1987. http://articles.sun-sentinel.com/1987-04-14/news/8701240443_1_regap-grey hounds-dogs (accessed on April 30, 2014).

35. National Greyhound Adoption Program. "About National Greyhound Adoption Program." 2009. http://www.ngap.org/about-ngap-y283.html (accessed on June 29, 2012).

36. Kari Young. Interviewed by Katherine Crosby. E-mail Interview. June 2, 2013.

37. Ibid.

38. Ibid.

39. Cindy Siddon. Interviewed by Katherine Crosby. E-mail Interview. July 11, 2013.

40. Alan Jordano. Interviewed by Katherine Crosby. E-mail Interview. June 30, 2013.

41. Ibid.

42. Ibid.

43. Ibid.

44. Cindy Bauer. Interviewed by Katherine Crosby. E-mail Interview. July 12, 2013.

45. Ibid.

46. Ibid.

47. Greyhound Adoption of Ohio. "About Greyhounds." 2011. http://www.grey houndadoptionofoh.org/aboutgreyhounds.htm (accessed on June 29, 2012).

48. N.E. Ohio Greyhound Rescue. "Home Page." 2012. http://members.pet finder.com/~OH550/index.php (accessed on June 29, 2012).

49. Jordano interview.

50. Bill Finley, "Industry Can Learn from Greyhound Ban." *ESPN*, December 28, 2009. http://sports.espn.go.com/sports/horse/columns/story?columnist=finley_bill &id=4776621 (accessed on April 30, 2014).

51. Keith Berger, "Greyhound Racing: Win or Die." *Examiner*, November 21, 2009. http://www.examiner.com/article/greyhound-racing-win-or-die (accessed on April 30, 2014).

52. Jacque Lynn Schultz, "Saving Retired Racing Greyhounds." Petfinder, 2001. http://www.petfinder.com/how-to-help-pets/saving-retired-racing-greyhounds .html (accessed on June 29, 2012).

53. The Associated Press. "Thousands of Racing Dogs Found Dead." *New York Times*, May 22, 2002. http://www.gulfcoastgreyhounds.org/SpecialNews.htm (accessed on June 29, 2012).

CHAPTER 10

Changing Discourse of Compassion within Breed Specific Rescue in the United States

"Good" Breeds versus "Bad" Breeds:
The Case of Pit Bulls

Pit bulls are misunderstood dogs!
—Jen Watson
Pit Sisters Rescue in
Jacksonville, Florida

Let us begin this chapter with an important clarification of the nomenclature that we employed in the chapter's subtitle and that we will use throughout the text: Nothing can be further from our normative orientation than classifying dogs of any breed as "good" and "bad." As will be clear to the reader, we strongly reject any such categorizations. Using the terms "good" and "bad" in this chapter to describe breeds neither corresponds to our view nor reflects our judgment. Rather we employ these terms merely to delineate how society has come to perceive and classify the breeds being discussed here.

As we presented throughout this book, the rising and steadily growing discourse of compassion in the United States has had a profound effect on the treatment of dogs. Thus, at the beginning of this chapter we find it particularly appropriate to recap briefly some of the developments and main themes in the discourse of compassion as they relate to dogs that have clearly been stigmatized as less desirable than others and vilified as downright evil. In the aftermath of the tumultuous cultural and social upheavals that began in the late 1960s, a new discourse of compassion emerged that featured a concerted effort to treat the disempowered and discriminated not only fairly and humanely, but by doing so, to accord them the dignity they had so sorely missed and render them, at least morally and nominally, but less so in actual reality, equal to the already powerful and privileged. Women and minorities were the first to benefit from this massive shift in discourse, attitude, and representation; but this empowerment did not stop there and was soon extended to animals, dogs in particular. It was in this context that animal rescues arose prolifically across the nation; and in the 1980s, the phenomenon known as breed specific rescue, which is the topic of this book, came into existence. Geared toward saving dogs of a particular breed, these groups attempt to improve the material and overall living conditions of abandoned dogs through rehoming efforts. Concurrent with these rescue organizations' short-term goal of helping the dogs in their purview is their long-term goal of reducing pet overpopulation in the United States, which, so these organizations firmly believe, results primarily from societal carelessness. The breeds represented by these groups have, by and large, been breeds that have been very popular in the United States precisely during the era when the discourse of compassion attained broad social and cultural acceptance in the country, that being the 1980s, 1990s, and the 2000s. It is at this time that Labrador Retrievers, Golden Retrievers, Poodles, Beagles, and other top-ten American Kennel Club (AKC) breeds emerged as the most sought-after dogs in America. Precisely because these breeds attained such broad popularity, demand for them increased dramatically, which in turn allowed puppy mill operations to become more lucrative. These, of course, compounded the overbreeding of the canine population, making the plight of the dogs belonging to these popular breeds more visible. This then led to a greater level of social compassion for the fate of many of the abandoned and abused Goldens, Labs, Poodles, Beagles, and other popular breeds.

In more recent years, the discourse of compassion has reached beyond the popular canine breeds to include much-vilified groups. Not all breeds have the popularity and shining image of Golden Retrievers; dogs bred for fighting and personal protection have historically been persecuted for the very traits for which breeders selected them in the first place. Today, the public's view of these dogs is slowly being changed precisely by allowing the discourse of compassion to reach them as well. Although a large percentage of the public considers dogs belonging to these "bad breeds" to be aggressive, dangerous, and even vicious, there is a rising counter-narrative that contests this negative view and depicts these animals as victims rather than villains. This ever-increasing view holds that these dogs' behavior and inclination have conformed precisely to the very traits for which human beings have bred them, and that therefore it is human effort, and in many cases human cruelty, that has rendered these breeds more violent toward other dogs, small animals, and, of course, humans. In other words, it is not the dog's fault that it is aggressive and violent; rather, humans should bear the blame for having instilled these traits in such an animal, and they should have the decency to own up to this malfeasance by pursuing policies and measures that rectify this situation by punishing the true malefactors (i.e., humans) instead of the victims (i.e., dogs). In this view, bad breeds have become the victims of human cruelty and are far from being the villains that the previous (and still dominant) narrative would have it. Ralph Hawthorne and Laurie Maxwell of the Humane Society of the United States argue that "Violence is a learned behavior, and in many cases these young men and women are taught, subliminally and practically, that pit bulls particularly are animals of violence, and it breeds a culture of violence in the community that's abusive to the animal, and it also desensitizes the youth." They continue: "Dog fighting fuels the breed specific legislation and breed bans. Irresponsible owners are really the problem here, and irresponsible owners are dog fighters."[1] Briefly put, in this counter-hegemonic story, there are no "bad breeds" or "bad dogs," just "bad people." Dahlia Canes, director of the Miami Coalition Against Breed Specific Legislation, emphatically stated: "Go get the two-legged animals on the other side of the leash, and stop picking on the four-legged ones. They're the beasts, they're the animals, not the dogs."[2] The negative reputation of the breed has become a battleground for rescuers who seek to counteract the breed's negative stereotype.

Which Breeds and Why?

The designation of "dangerous" or "bad" for a particular breed does not appear randomly. Instead, the breeds deemed bad attained this character-istic solely by virtue of humans breeding these dogs precisely to feature the socially undesirable traits society then uses to brandish them. In gen-eral, these traits fall into two categories: fighting and guarding. In either case, breeds are deemed bad when they are perceived to be dangerous to people or other dogs and animals. A combination of these dogs' appearance, temperament, and past purpose accords them a widely held negative and violent connotation. The public assumes all dogs of these breeds to be dangerous and capable of attacking people and other dogs without provocation by virtue of possessing a vicious and unpredictable temperament.

Fighting Breeds

Dog fighting is an activity that humans have fostered for centuries, though its current incarnation can be traced back to the ban of bull baiting in England in 1835.[3] Large dogs that had been bred to fight bulls were crossed with fast and scrappy Terrier breeds to create the Bull Terrier breed that dominates much of the dog fighting world today. The most famous dog fighting breeds fall into the category known as Pit Bulls, which has been selectively bred to produce dogs that excel at fighting and will continue to fight at all costs. These dogs are genetically as predisposed to behavior that leads to fighting as other breeds are to hunting or retrieving. True to form and fully congruent with the aim of their breeding, these dogs exhibit a relatively high level of aggression toward strange dogs, while their aggression toward humans has been relatively low.[4] Breeds in this category include American Pit Bull Terriers, Staffordshire Bull Terriers, and American Staffordshire Terriers.

Guarding Breeds

Other dog breeds arose out of a perceived need for guarding humans against attacks by other humans. These dogs were bred to be suspicious of and aggressive toward strangers and have the size and strength to inflict serious bodily harm, should it become necessary for them to do so. They were also bred to exhibit "watchdog" type behavior, such as barking at strangers and guarding their territory. Breeds in these categories typically display low to average levels of aggression toward owners and strange dogs, but relatively high levels of aggression toward strange humans, which conforms to the purpose for which they were bred.[5] These breeds include Rottweilers, Doberman Pinschers, and German Shepherds.

A Brief Comparison

Both types of breeds have similar characteristics: they are large, strong, fierce, fearless, and aggressive dogs capable of causing grave injuries, even death, upon their intended targets. The main difference between these two types of breeds consists in the intended purpose of their respective targets, as fighting breeds are bred to attack other dogs, while guarding breeds are bred to attack humans. For the purpose of comparison, we will examine one breed from each group in detail to showcase the slight differences in the rhetoric and behavior of groups committed to the rescue of fighting versus guarding dogs. We will use the Pit Bull as the example of our fighting dog. For our purposes, we will not delineate or differentiate among the three subcategories that we mentioned above that comprise the assignation "Pit Bull," as these subcategories are infrequently used in the literature pertaining to the breed. We will use the Rottweiler as our example of the guarding dog. We chose these two breeds as they are the most recognized and have the largest numerical presence in the two respective categories in the United States.

Image in Society

The images portrayed of bad dogs differ greatly from those conveyed of good dogs. This is evident via a cursory comparison of media portrayals between breeds that are traditionally seen as good, such as Golden Retrievers, for example, and breeds that are conventionally viewed as bad, such as Pit Bulls and Rottweilers.

Golden Retrievers in Media

Positive portrayals of Golden Retrievers in the media abound. Films such as the *Air Bud* series, *Homeward Bound*, *The Retrievers*, *Fluke*, and most recently Pixar's *Up* all portray Golden Retrievers as dogs that are exceptionally desirable as pets. In these media portrayals, Golden Retrievers are friendly, loyal, loving, and actually incapable of malice. This is particularly evident in Pixar's *Up*, as the Golden Retriever named Dug is the only one to help the heroes and is incapable of acting with malice toward the other dogs, even when they threaten to hurt him and those he loves. Golden Retrievers are therefore characterized as dogs that avoid violence whenever possible; they are dogs that can be trusted and loved. We do not know of any portrayals of Golden Retrievers as bad dogs in the media; a search of "evil Golden Retrievers" on Google returns no frightening pictures or synopses for horror films, but rather a list of facetious anecdotes about

Golden Retrievers that have mildly poor behavior, such as digging or bark-ing. On the whole, therefore, the public image of Golden Retrievers is an overwhelmingly positive one.

Pit Bulls in Media

Pit Bulls have undergone a curious transition in American public opinion during the twentieth century. In the early 1900s, Pit Bulls were known as "nanny dogs" and were considered excellent companions for children, even going so far as having pictures taken of children and Pit Bulls together.[6] During World War I, Pit Bulls actually came to represent the U.S. Army through their positive portrayals on recruitment posters.[7] How then did the reputation of the breed known as the "nanny dog" transition to that of the hardened killer? Dog fighting experienced a resurgence of popu-larity in the United States during the 1980s, and Pit Bulls, having been bred to fight first bears and then other dogs, were the natural choice for individuals seeking to engage in dog fighting.[8] Not known as paragons of canine ownership, dog fighters trained their dogs to be hyperaggressive; it is unsurprising, therefore, that the number and severity of dog attacks perpetrated by Pit Bulls increased immensely in the wake of this dog fight-ing revival. News of Pit Bull attacks flooded the media, and as a result, the public image of the Pit Bull shifted from family friend to feared foe.

Current media portrayals of Pit Bulls as good dogs are far fewer than that of Golden Retrievers. The most famous example of a Pit Bull as a good dog is that of Petey from the 1994 *Little Rascals* film, which, in turn, was based on the "Our Gang" comedy shorts produced from the 1920s to the 1940s. Otherwise, the portrayals of Pit Bulls in the media tend to be neg-ative: *No Country for Old Men* features a Pit Bull trained to attack; Pixar's *Up* contains a host of bad Pit Bulls that attack the protagonists; *All Dogs Go to Heaven* has a diabolical Bulldog/Pit Bull mix as the film's antagonist; *Garfield* includes a Pit Bull character that is unable to understand why a cat would rescue a dog (proving that it is not empathic); and World Wrestling Entertainment wrestler John Cena stirred controversy when a t-shirt with the image of him holding two vicious-looking Pit Bulls was made avail-able for sale. News outlets also have a bias against Pit Bulls: the ASPCA analyzed reports of dog bite attacks, noting that attacks by Pit Bulls are much more likely to be reported and have a wider scope of receptivity than attacks by other breeds.[9] Pit Bulls are therefore publically characterized as vicious, aggressive, and overall "bad" dogs that cannot be trusted to behave well around people or other dogs and animals. In short, Pit Bulls have come to represent danger and evil.

In a documentary about Pit Bulls and Pit Bull rescues in which the participants discussed many topics relevant to Pit Bulls, they also delineated the deeply negative and sensationalized manner in which the media portray Pit Bulls when compared with other dogs. Dawn Capp, founder of Chako Pit Bull Rescue, said:

> I guarantee you that, if, say, I made a call on this phone right now to a news station and I said, "Oh my God, a pit bull just bit a child!" we would have a news van come immediately to arrive right outside this building to do the story. But if I said, "Oh my God, a Lab or a Cocker Spaniel just bit a child," do you think there would be a news van here? No.[10]

Carl Friedman, former director of Animal Care & Control in San Francisco, concurred by stating: "When a pit bull, let's say, mauls somebody or bites somebody, chances are you're going to see that on the first or second page of the newspaper, and probably in the five o'clock news, six o'clock news. If another dog bites somebody, a different breed bites somebody, chances are it won't be reported."[11] According to data gathered by the Independent Data Collection Center and reported in the documentary film *Beyond the Myth*, 92 percent of people believe that Pit Bulls are portrayed negatively by the media.[12] Moreover, "60 percent of people with negative opinions of Pit Bulls say that the media contributed to their opinion. Only 15 percent said their personal experiences contributed to thinking Pit Bulls were bad."[13]

However, in the wake of the 2007 Michael Vick trial, the public image of Pit Bulls has begun to change ever so slightly. The unspeakably brutal victimization of the Pit Bulls in Michael Vick's kennel created a situation in which Pit Bulls have become somewhat sympathetic figures that need to be rescued rather than vilified. This change of heart and attitude has given rise to two television shows centered on Pit Bull rescue: *Pit Boss* and *Pit Bulls and Parolees*. These shows follow the rescue of victimized Pit Bulls and refute prima facie the violent stereotype that has characterized these dogs for decades. The public view of Pit Bulls has started to change in light of the Michael Vick case; although tragic, this case has helped the overall perception of the breed by forcing the public to engage with the plight of this breed as a victim of human cruelty rather than a perpetrator of canine brutality and violence.

Rottweilers in Media

Rottweilers also have a negative image in the media. In films such as *The Omen*, *Rottweiler*, and Pixar's *Up*, they are characterized as attack dogs that intend to harm humans. Rottweilers have become almost iconic embodiments of canine evil, but they are also characterized as the companion animals of violent people, such as drug dealers and neo-Nazis, as exemplified by the film *Corky Romano*. To be sure, there also exist positive depictions of Rottweilers in films such as *Lethal Weapon III* and in television shows such as *Entourage* and *Human Target*, where these dogs are portrayed as loving and loyal companions that adore their human partners. Rottweilers have a more mixed representation in the media than Pit Bulls, which is an interesting phenomenon considering that the intentions for which Rottweilers have been bred is to guard against and attack humans, whereas the purpose for the breeding of Pit Bulls has been to fight other dogs. One would assume that the former would be depicted much more negatively, but clearly Pit Bulls have so much become the incarnation of all canine danger and evil that they have crowded out Rottweilers as the most recognized representatives of "bad" dogs.

Discrimination against "Vicious" Breeds in the United States

Pit Bulls and Rottweilers suffer from active discrimination in the United States in a variety of situations. Unlike the breeds considered good, characterized by Golden Retrievers, Labrador Retrievers, and other popular breeds, Pit Bulls and Rottweilers are feared by the general public. This fear leads to a variety of concrete steps that are designed to protect the public from these dogs, which, almost by definition, involves stigmatizing and discriminatory measures against them. Among the most evident areas in which such measures occur are breed selective legislation and home insurance.

Breed Selective Legislation

Breed selective legislation (BSL) entails an effort on the part of legislators to decrease the number and severity of dog attacks within their constituencies. BSL's declared goal has been to eliminate—or at least decrease—dog attacks through actively legislating against breeds that have been considered violent by the community. The vast majority of BSL specifically targets

Pit Bulls and Pit Bull mixes, although other breeds such as Rottweilers, German Shepherds, Doberman Pinschers, American Bulldogs, Akitas, and Mastiffs have also been included in such legislation in specific municipalities.[14] These laws ban the presence of "bad" breeds in their locality and fine owners who have dogs belonging to such breeds. Such laws act under the premise that if the authorities have the legal power to ban dog breeds that are considered dangerous, the rate of dog-related violence will decrease in the community. However, studies by the Centers for Disease Control and Prevention (CDC) and the American Society for the Prevention of Cruelty to Animals (ASPCA) have shown that these laws have not been as effective at preventing dog attacks as the legislators would hope.[15] In fact, BSL has had negative effects and unintended consequences in their communities, including the failure to enact more reliable methods of reducing dog bites as a result of the overreliance on efforts to create breed bans.[16] However one rates the success of BSL, there is no question that the very existence of such measures has increased the negative perception of and consequent discrimination against breeds that have been traditionally bred for violent purposes. The point here is not to contest the fact that dogs in present-day America belonging to such breeds are in fact disproportionately more likely to be dangerous than dogs belonging to other breeds. Rather, we emphasize that these legislative efforts center on the dogs as culprits and perpetrators rather than on the humans who victimize them. Moreover, these measures enhance these breeds' already negative reputation while hardly focusing on owner responsibility and malfeasance, factors much more likely to influence the potential for dog aggression and biting than breed.

Home Insurance

Housing is another area where breed discrimination has occurred. The owners of large breed dogs, as well as breeds deemed to be "bad," are frequently charged higher insurance rates, if companies agree to insure such owners at all. The cause for these punitive insurance rates hails from the perception that these dogs are more difficult to control and are thus more likely to be violent. Therefore, the premises on which such dogs exist should be more expensive to insure. Indeed, some companies refuse outright to insure any property featuring such dogs under any circumstances as they are perceived to be extreme liabilities.[17] This discrimination is also present in leasing situations, where it has become increasingly difficult to find rental housing options that will accept tenants owning "bad" breeds. The plight of owners or guardians, therefore, is one of finding a living situation that will accept their "bad" breed dogs. However, in good part due to the proliferation of the discourse of compassion, steps have occurred toward changing the shape of this discrimination, with insurance agencies like Nationwide offering coverage to owners of "bad" breeds when the dogs have passed a Canine Good Citizenship test. This concrete policy shift is likely attributable to a clearly palpable change in the public discourse toward and perception of these dogs, especially in the wake of the Michael Vick trial. When "bad" breeds were perceived purely as villains, it was easy to discriminate against them with little, if any, qualifications. But with an increase in the discourse of compassion reaching the realm of "bad" breed dogs as well, dogs belonging to such breeds have gradually come to be viewed by a growing percentage of the public as victims of society (while still regarded with suspicion and fear), which has made it harder to deny housing insurance to a person by virtue of having a "bad" breed dog as her or his companion.

Fear the Dog, Fear the Human?

Complicating the successful rehabilitation and rescue of "bad" breeds is their disproportionate association with bad people. Three studies examined the ownership of high-risk or vicious dogs as indicators of antisocial or deviant human behavior. One study used court convictions, ownership style (licensed vs. unlicensed dogs), and breed type (high-risk/vicious vs. low-risk/docile) to assess the risk of child endangerment in a home environment. This study's findings suggest that high-risk dog ownership is an indicator of deviant human behavior and needs to be examined as such in order to understand the true risk of child endangerment in such an environment.[18] In other words, the focus needs to be on the humans having such dogs rather than on the dogs and their breed.

Another study analyzed the personality differences of three different types of dog owners (high-risk dogs, large dogs, and small dogs) and one control group. The authors found that owners of high-risk dogs were significantly more likely to exhibit criminal behavior than individuals in the other three groups, with noticeably higher instances of primary psychopathy and sensation seeking.[19]

Lastly, a third study examined the criminal thinking, callousness, and personality styles of high-risk dog owners. These people exhibited a higher number of incidents of criminal thinking, arrest, and physical altercations than the other individuals in the study.[20]

In short, the results of these studies indicate that the owners of high-risk breeds have higher incidences of criminal activity and psychopathy than owners of lower-risk breeds. This does not mean that all owners of "bad" breeds are psychopaths or criminals, but rather that individuals who are criminals or have deviant personalities tend to prefer dogs that belong to "bad" breeds if and when such people decide to own a dog. Individuals utilize the bad breeds that have the connotation of being vicious, aggressive, and territorial as a way of signaling to the world that the owner needs to be feared. A gang leader with a show-groomed Poodle would have a harder time establishing fear, intimidation, respect, and authority than one with a Pit Bull or a Rottweiler. Enhanced precisely by these "bad" breeds' reputation and fear by general society, their attractiveness to the criminal world only grows. This, of course, reinforces the difficulty of rehabilitating these breeds' damaged image. Criminal owners who flaunt their bad breeds strongly compound the public relations problem that these breeds face, as the general public views both the dog and the owner as untrustworthy and dangerous. This vicious circle of "bad" dogs and bad owners places an added burden on "bad" breed rescue groups that their sister organizations of other breed specific rescues confront much less systematically, and often not at all. To wit, "bad" breed rescue groups must screen applicants carefully to ensure that the dogs they put up for adoption will not go to individuals who will mistreat them or use them for nefarious purposes, which would not only harm the dog but further damage the breed's reputation by reinforcing the general image that such dogs engage in vicious behavior toward other animals and humans.

Breed Population: A Potentially Complicating Factor

Census data on the exact breakdown of breeds by human "ownership" in the United States have not been available and are unlikely to become so in the near future. As we presented in some detail in Chapter 3, AKC registration data indicate that Labrador Retrievers are the most popular dogs in America. But this only tells one side of the story. AKC registration does not provide an accurate sample of the overall canine population and its human companionship, as individuals who choose to register their dogs with the AKC are far from random but fall within special, predictable categories. This is particularly true with the case of owner income, as dog owners falling in the middle and upper classes are significantly more likely than their lower-class counterparts to choose dogs that can be registered to the

AKC and then subsequently opt to do so. We hypothesize then that the ranking of the top-ten AKC registered breeds is not an accurate representation of the actual dog breed populations in the United States and that Pit Bulls, instead of being ranked the seventy-sixth (Staffordshire Bull Terriers) or even seventy-second (American Staffordshire Terriers) most popular breed, belong somewhere in the top-ten most populous breeds in the United States. Indeed, our own survey of U.S. shelters, humane societies, and rescue groups in 2011 showed that, on average, a U.S. shelter will have 2.97 Labrador Retrievers and 2.54 Pit Bulls; there were only 0.18 Golden Retrievers per shelter, and Golden Retrievers appeared as the fourth most popular dog of the AKC registration data in 2011.

To illustrate this point, we present the example of our local humane society branch in Ann Arbor, Michigan. Throughout 2012, on average over 60 percent of the Humane Society of Huron Valley's dogs were listed as either Pit Bulls or Pit Bull mixes, which we deem pretty much the norm for many such institutions across the country. There could be a variety of reasons to explain this situation, among which would be the undoubtedly negative image that continues to burden this breed's reputation, despite a certain sense of compassion that has emerged in the past few years, as already mentioned; the breed's popularity with populations that either cannot afford to or do not choose to have their dogs spayed or neutered, therefore creating a self-perpetuating overpopulation problem; the relatively small number of breed rescues that exist for Pit Bulls (as compared with those for Labrador Retrievers, Golden Retrievers, and German Shepherds); and the difficulty in gaining public support for such rescues once they have been established due to the continued fear and disdain that the public continues to have for Pit Bulls. Simply put, in spite of being one of the more populous breeds in the United States, Pit Bulls do not have the same level of rescue support as less populous breeds do, largely due to the Pit Bull's negative public image. Pit Bulls are populous but certainly not popular in the conventional sense of that term.

How Are Rescues Affected?

The perceived and purported difference between "good" and "bad" dog breeds is not only in the realm of reputation and depiction by the media. Instead, this phenomenon bears concrete effects on how rescue organizations dedicated to such maligned breeds operate on a daily basis. Concretely, these organizations cannot ignore the widely held social perceptions about the breeds to whose rescue they have come to devote much of their physical and emotional energy. It would not serve these groups' purpose were they simply to dismiss the negative image and infelicitous reputation that these dogs have in contemporary U.S. society. Instead, they have to work within these parameters and must devise strategies to help their dogs precisely in such an adversarial atmosphere. While trying to confront such views head on and challenge their veracity or validity, "bad" breed rescues have to devise concrete actions and policies that help their breeds in the here and now and not wait until these societal views might abate or disappear at some uncertain point in the distant future. Thus, the efforts of "bad" breed rescues are by necessity substantially different from those defining the world of rescues representing breeds that society considers "good," which have constituted the vast majority of our study.

Of course, on many outward dimensions—their organizational structures, their operational procedures, and their relation to other institutions such as shelters and humane societies—Pit Bull rescues are virtually identical to rescues dedicated to "good" breeds. In Jake Schramm's responses to our standard questions, the reader would not notice any difference between his comments on Minnesota-based Pit Bull rescue Save-A-Bull and Jane Nygaard's Retrieve a Golden of Minnesota (RAGOM), to use rescue organizations from the same state. The same words appear constantly and steadily, from how applications are processed, all the way to adoption procedures; from the establishment of 501(c)(3) status to the use of Petfinder and the organization of volunteers. But when we asked the question as to what the organization's ultimate goals were, Schramm responded solely: "To change perceptions of 'Pit Bull' type dogs—and to show them as family dogs,"[21] while RAGOM respondents Jane Nygaard and Beryl Board wanted to rescue and rehome as many Goldens as they possibly could. They did not express any desire to change society's perceptions of Golden Retrievers as a prerequisite for the eventual success of their mission. Golden Retrievers do not face the cultural obstacles in the quest of their welfare that Pit Bulls routinely do. To the question as to what the biggest obstacles and problems for rescue were and what made rescuing dogs difficult, Schramm informed us, "Accurate temperament testing in a shelter environment—we have no 'safety net' so we have to only take dogs that we think are the best of the best."[22] Precisely the point: Pit Bull rescues have a zero margin for error. In response to our question as to what the most pronounced challenges were for the specific breed, Schramm stated "one hundred percent negative perception of the breed."[23] Jen Watson, from Pit Sisters Rescue in Jacksonville, Florida, seconded this with virtually identical words in her response to the same question: "Negative perception of 'Pit Bulls' and breed discrimination policies—restrictions on housing, etc."[24] The only way to overcome this, Schramm believed was "by having well mannered, obedient dogs out in public, either at events or via our adoptive families."[25] Few, if any, Golden Retriever or Labrador Retriever rescues had to worry about any ill perceptions of their breed and any detrimental consequences from such for their organizations' rescue efforts. Jane Nygaard of RAGOM confirms this phenomenon when she states that Golden Retrievers are "adaptable, you can come to my house and my guy will go with you in your car and he will show you where his cookie jar is. . . . They're easy, outgoing animals."[26] The differences between the reputations of breeds like Pit Bulls and Golden Retrievers have profound effects on how each breed's rescue has to approach its mission to be successful.

Rescue Rhetoric

Rescue groups dedicated to breeds like Pit Bulls and Rottweilers need to shape their public image differently from groups representing "good" dogs. A visit to the website of any Labrador Retriever or Golden Retriever rescue group will show pictures of puppies and happy, healthy dogs playing with their owners. The rhetoric focuses on human carelessness and irresponsibility and how these factors have adversely affected the breed whose baseline nature is that of a loving, caring, cuddly companion. Never is there even a hint that something character-based or inherent might be amiss with the dogs. Instead, fault lies solely with the irresponsibility, cruelty, or negligence on the part of humans. In essence, "good" dog rescues use their breeds' positive public image to make rescue dogs desirable, to enhance their innate virtue, to emphasize their goodness, and to show that these flawless dogs have in some ways been harmed by fickle and irresponsible owners who have abandoned or neglected the particular dog that thus now needs and deserves a loving forever home. Rarely, if ever, does one encounter on these websites pictures of brutally abused dogs. Pity, compassion, and solidarity with them on the part of prospective adopters and thus helpers are invoked by these dogs' beauty and innocence, not their deformities and bodily harm.

Precisely such deformities and injuries, however, are preponderantly—often solely—featured on the websites of Pit Bull or Rottweiler rescue groups. These websites are peppered with pictures and stories of horribly abused dogs, including dogs with cases of mange so severe that they have virtually no hair remaining, dogs that have been used in fighting rings, and dogs that have been the victims of violent cases of abuse at the hands of their owners. The text used by these rescue groups focuses almost exclusively on human cruelty and society's misperception of these animals; it aims to convey that these dogs are not the monsters that society paints them to be, and that they should not be the victims of abuse because of their bad reputation. The websites then proceed to feature pictures of "reformed" dogs, or dogs that have had horrible pasts but now make excellent pets, as a way of demonstrating that "bad" breed dogs are not bad at all, but only victims of a reputation that has led them to be severely misunderstood and misrepresented. These rescue groups therefore focus in their message and narrative on a much more guilt-based and accusatory approach than "good" dog rescues. In the case of the latter, the dogs' predicament does in fact also involve human error and irresponsibility, but these are almost always the errant ways of a particular individual who, often not through a fault of her or his own but due to circumstances such as a divorce or a move to a new area, has come to harm the dog even if there was never physical abuse of any sort. The point is that rarely, if ever, does the narrative in such cases invoke the evils of society or humanity's cruelty as a collective culprit instead of blaming the misdeeds of a nameless individual.

Not so in the case of the website texts used by "bad" breed rescues. Here, the blame lies clearly with society's erroneous but all the more powerful misconception and misrepresentation of these dogs, which furnishes the prime cause of their constant brutalization that in turn leads to the self-fulfilling prophecy of some of these dogs becoming brutal and thus fully conforming to society's expectations. In the message and narrative of the "bad" breed rescues there is no question that the ultimate responsibility and ethical duty to sever this vicious circle and correct this travesty and tragedy lies solely with society as a whole and not aberrant situations or morally faulty individuals.

Postadoptive Advice and Involvement

Postadoptive advice and involvement represents another area where the actions of "good" breed rescues and their "bad" breed counterparts are tellingly different. We never encountered the former dispensing with advice as to how adopters should act with their dogs in public as the dogs' "good" breed status assures at least their acceptance, if not necessarily outright affection, by the public. Of course there are many tutorials and detailed materials on proper corrective measures for a dog who is a digger or when a dog suffers from separation anxiety, as well as other potential, relatively benign problems that an adopted dog might pose for its new family. But on the whole there appears to be very little, if any, concern on the part of "good" breed rescues that their dogs will misbehave in public or create adverse situations that will give the specific breed a bad name. Above all, there appears to be no worry whatsoever that the dogs might somehow suffer on account of the public's antipathy toward them.

The exact opposite pertains to "bad" breed dogs. Thus, for example, Pit Bull rescues feature detailed instructions on a variety of aspects of daily life affecting the adopted dog and its new family. This includes learning how to introduce a Pit Bull to another dog, why Pit Bulls should avoid using dog parks, how to react to people who fear a Pit Bull, and even how to respond to legislative action against a Pit Bull.[27] These instructions are remarkably sophisticated and nuanced in form and content, bespeaking a tremendous amount of work and care that went into their creation. And all this work is predicated on these animals' poor public reputation. There exists a constant emphasis on separating each dog from its breed, of individualizing it apart from its collective, as a crucial way to understand the particular dog in question and to ensure his or her successful integration into the adopter's milieu. There is a steady exculpatory tone accompanying these documents, in the vein of "Pit Bulls, through no fault of their own, can have behavioral problems (particularly dog aggression) that might not make them appropriate for every home, but Fido is so wonderful, so sweet, so unlike the Pit Bulls portrayed in the media, that you will fall in love with him despite all your apprehensions, which he will allay and the two of you will be happy ever after." Additionally, many of these groups offer free or low-cost obedience training programs, including Canine Good Citizenship tests, to their adopters as a way of encouraging responsible ownership and promoting a positive image of the breed. Dawn Capp knows full well what she is up against in terms of the breed's negative image: "So when I'm out in public and someone sees Tara or Sammy and they say, 'Oh my God, that's such a cute dog and he is so well behaved! What kind of dog is it?' I look at them and I say, 'this is a pit bull'," she is met by stunned silence and incredulous looks.[28] "Bad" breed rescues are deeply concerned with the public image of the breed and how the level of responsibility on the part of each adopter will contribute to the altered and improved image of the breed or—conversely—maintain its negative depiction. Thus, not surprisingly Jen Watson believes that only through major efforts in "education" about the breed (in her case Pit Bulls) and "advocacy" for it can the strong breed specific prejudices that are currently widespread among the American public be overcome.

Acceptable Dog Behavior

The most extreme difference between "good" breed rescues and "bad" breed rescues emerges in their attitudes toward acceptable dog behavior. A crucial mantra of the former holds that dogs with any form of aggression are not to be tolerated. Thus, dogs exhibiting such behavior will, in most cases, not be accepted by these organizations. "Good" breed rescues will attribute dog aggression to poor breeding or mistreatment in the dog's past, thus making aberrant human individuals fully and solely responsible for the animal's adverse behavior and the ensuing disadvantages afflicting the animal. As a rule, "good" breed rescues avoid the inclusion of aggressive dogs in their rescue programs in favor of dogs that do not have aggression issues. This is not to say that "good" breed rescues shy away from helping dogs with a variety of problems and that they only assist perfect dogs with no flaws whatsoever. Far from it; these rescues very much include in their programs dogs that suffer from horrible separation anxiety, are insatiable diggers, are poorly housetrained, and exhibit a variety of other behavioral problems—not to mention suffer from myriad illnesses. "Good" breed rescues emphatically and expertly help dogs with major problems. But as a rule, they draw a firm line concerning one specific character flaw in terms of dogs they put up for adoption: aggression. That is perhaps the sole trait in a dog that will prevent it from having a "good" breed rescue do everything in its power to have the animal adopted into a forever home.

By necessity, "bad" breed rescues have a different attitude toward aggression. Because of the nature and history of the breeds involved, which were often bred for aggression against a variety of targets, "bad" breed groups tend to be more flexible on the issue of aggression. Although aggression against humans remains unacceptable, as it is dangerous to owner and dog alike, Pit Bull rescues and those of other "bad" breeds tolerate some level of aggression against dogs. These rescues do not consider this trait desirable by any means, but dogs with histories of dog aggression are not automatically excluded from their rescue attempts. The acceptance of dog aggression is particularly evident in the case of dogs used for fighting, such as the Michael Vick dogs. Some of these dogs had the scars of prize fighters, others the signs of being bait dogs used for training; in all cases where the dogs showed no aggression toward humans, they were safely placed in homes or welcomed by rescue groups, none more prominent than Best Friends Animal Society in Kanab, Utah, where twenty-two dogs arrived in January 2008. Collectively known as the "Vicktory dogs," these frightfully abused animals received succor, care, and compassion for the first time in their lives, leading to the rehabilitation of some to the point where they were adopted as loving and grateful pets. By the summer of 2013, ten of the twenty-two dogs had been adopted. "Not only are they thriving, they've brought a group of strangers together to form a new kind of family," writes Jamie K. Mulhall in a detailed article about the fate of these dogs.[29] Perhaps none became more famous than Georgia, a dog who was especially abused by Vick and his dog-fighting entourage, who became a television star on the National Geographic Channel series *Dogtown*, featuring this particularly valiant rehabilitation effort among many that have come to characterize Best Friends Animal Society. Georgia also appeared on the *Ellen DeGeneres Show* and *Larry King Live*. But better still than this well-earned fame was that Georgia got to enjoy two happy and loving years with her adopter Amy before losing her battle with kidney failure in early 2014.[30] Vicktory dogs deemed beyond rehabilitation have found a wonderfully nurturing forever home on Best Friends Animal Society's beautiful grounds in the mountains of southern Utah. These dogs—and others like them—were deemed worthy of rescue in spite of their violent pasts, because their rescuers perceived these dogs as victims of cruel human intentions such as dog fighting and, of course, because the rescuers mustered the compassion, patience, and expertise necessary to have these dogs fully rehabilitated to become the companion animals they could—and should—have been had humans not abused them.

Prison Involvement

Prison involvement is a particularly interesting phenomenon as it appears that "good" breed rescues do not often engage in activities with prisons, while "bad" breed rescues and municipal shelters do participate in prison training programs. Thus, for example, the Villalobos Rescue Center for Pit Bulls has both an adult and juvenile offender program that works with parolees to help them reintegrate themselves into society. The linkage here between "bad" breeds and "bad" people is obvious; there is a growing belief among individuals involved in "bad" breed rescues that, just as dogs with violent pasts can be rehabilitated, so too can human beings with similar histories.

These programs attempt to foster positive interactions between parolees and dogs with unhappy pasts, as parolees have a unique insight into being judged based on a generalizing negative label, without being accorded the chance to be assessed on an individual basis apart from a common stigma. The rescue groups therefore attempt to rehabilitate the dogs while giving parolees work that lets them interact with dogs who do not prejudge their new partners the way people can and regularly do. Thus, dogs and parolees often benefit from such interaction, leading to the frequent rehabilitation of both.[31]

Conclusion

What might these issues mean for the future of the rescue world as a whole? One possible development could witness an increasing divergence in the methods and rhetoric of "good" breed and "bad" breed rescues. "Bad" breed rescues will likely try to increase their involvement on the community level in order to fight the bad reputation of their breed and to push for greater spay and neuter responsibility. Legislatively, it seems likely that "bad" breed rescues, particularly ones devoted to Pit Bulls, will push for more stringent dog fighting laws that increase the severity of punishments for engaging in such horrible activities. Concomitantly, such rescues will devote much energy to abolish BSL where it occurs and have it replaced with laws that do not discriminate against entire breeds but instead punish irresponsible owners. BSL is a lingering artifact of the times prior to the culture turn introduced by the discourse of compassion, as it treats dogs as property rather than as family members. As the discourse of compassion continues to spread, it will likely reduce the use of BSL in the United States. Eventually, we believe that as information about "bad" breeds becomes more readily available and education programs about responsible dog ownership increase—in other words, as the beneficial effects of the increasingly powerful discourse of compassion raise the level of human awareness and caring—society will gradually come to view these breeds less negatively. The nature of these breeds is not inherently evil, and as society is exposed to more good dogs of the "bad" breed variety, this step should combat the negative stereotypes from which these breeds currently suffer. It is our hope—and belief—that the discourse of compassion has already begun a successful process of these dogs' destigmatization as villains and has come to portray them as victims of human wantonness, cruelty, ignorance, and arrogance. After all, these dogs did not choose their own history. The broader societal knowledge and growing public awareness of this simple fact represents the first step on the long road to giving these dogs the proper dignity that they so richly deserve.

Notes

1. Cited in Libby Sherrill's documentary film *Beyond the Myth* (Screen Media, 2012).

2. Cited in ibid.

3. American Society for the Prevention of Cruelty to Animals. "History of Dog Fighting." 1997. http://www.aspca.org/fight-animal-cruelty/dog-fighting/history -of-dog-fighting.aspx (accessed on April 25, 2011).

4. Deborah L. Duffy, Yuying Hsu, James A. Serpell, "Breed Differences in Canine Aggression." *Applied Animal Behavioral Science* 114 (2008), pp. 441–460.

5. Ibid.

6. Y. Grossman, "The Cruelest Trick Ever Played on a Breed of Dog." ywgrossman.com. May 4, 2011. http://www.ywgrossman.com/photoblog/?p=676 (accessed on July 26, 2012).

7. J. Bastian, "How Did Pit Bulls Get Such a Bad Rap?" Cesar's Way, 2012. http://www.cesarsway.com/dogbehavior/basics/How-Did-Pit-Bulls-Get-a-Bad -Rap (accessed on April 30, 2014).

8. Ibid.

9. American Society for the Prevention of Cruelty to Animals. "Pit Bull Bias in the Media." 2007. http://www.aspca.org/fight-animal-cruelty/advocacy-center /animal-laws-about-the-issues/pit-bull-bias-in-the-media.aspx (accessed on April 25, 2011).

10. Sherrill, *Beyond the Myth*.

11. Ibid.

12. Ibid.

13. Ibid.

14. American Society for the Prevention of Cruelty to Animals. "Breed Selective Legislation." 2011. http://www.aspca.org/fight-animal-cruelty/dog-fighting/breed -specific-legislation.aspx (accessed on April 25, 2011).

15. Ibid.

16. American Society for the Prevention of Cruelty to Animals. "Are Breed-Specific Laws Effective?" 2003. http://ricp.uis.edu/ASPCA%5CaspcaBSL0707 final.pdf (accessed on April 30, 2014).

17. Einhorn Insurance Agency. "Dog Liability Insurance." 2011. http://einhorn insurance.com/dangerous-dog-liability-insurance/ (accessed on April 25, 2011).

18. J. E. Barnes, B. W. Boat, F. W. Putnam, H. F. Dates, and A. R. Mahlman, "Ownership of High-Risk ("Vicious") Dogs as a Marker for Deviant Behaviors: Implications for Risk Assessment." *Journal of Interpersonal Violence* 21, no. 12 (2006), pp. 1616–1634. http://jiv.sagepub.com/content/21/12/1616 (accessed on July 26, 2012).

19. L. Ragatz, W. Fremouw, T. Thomas, and K. McCoy, "Vicious Dogs: The Antisocial Behaviors and Psychological Characteristics of Owners." *Journal of Forensic Sciences* 54 (2009), pp. 699–703.

20. A. M. Schenk, L. L. Ragatz, and W. J. Fremouw, "Vicious Dogs Part 2: Criminal Thinking, Callousness, and Personality Styles of Their Owners." *Journal of Forensic Sciences* 57 (2012), pp. 152–159.

21. Jake Schramm. Interviewed by Katherine Crosby. E-mail Interview. July 10, 2013.

22. Ibid.

23. Ibid.

24. Jen Watson. Interviewed by Katherine Crosby. E-mail Interview. June 16, 2013.

25. Schramm interview.

26. Jane Nygaard. Interviewed by Andrei Markovits. Telephone Interview. August 6, 2009.

27. Bay Area Doglovers Responsible About Pit Bulls (BAD RAP). "Pros and Cons of Owning a Pit Bull." 2007. http://www.badrap.org/rescue/owning.html (accessed on April 25, 2011).

28. Cited in Sherrill, *Beyond the Myth*.

29. Jamie K. Mulhall, "The Blossoming of Wallflowers: Catching Up with the Vicktory Dogs Five Years Later." *Best Friends* (July/August 2013), p. 35.

30. "Vicktory Dog Georgia Says Goodbye," *Best Friends* (March/April 2014), p. 49. The cover of that issue of the magazine depicts Georgia's beautiful face over the caption "Georgia on our minds."

31. "Woman Rescues Pit Bulls and Parolees." TODAY.com. http://www.today.com/id/32406259/ns/today-today_pets/t/woman-rescues-pit-bulls-parolees/ (accessed on April 30, 2014).

Conclusion

The notion of animal selfhood gives us profound obligations, as individuals and as a society. I do not profess to have the answers to all the questions it raises. However, I am certain of one thing that must underlie the search, and that is the intrinsic value of animal lives. Their influence on human identity has been inestimable. It is time to reciprocate by undertaking the difficult and often uncomfortable task of wrestling with the moral dimensions of our relationship with them.

—Leslie Irvine, *If You Tame Me: Understanding Our Connection with Animals*[1]

Way beyond the rescuing of breed specific dogs, which has been the topic of this study, the discourse of compassion is reaching new, previously unimaginable levels with respect to the animals it affects. Of course, there have been thousands of cat rescues for many years, and in our research we encountered the beginning proliferation of bunny rescues.[2] We all know about the global campaigns to save the dolphins, seal pups, and elephants. The point here is that humans' commitment to the rescue of animals from human encroachment and destruction has far exceeded the world of pets as conventionally construed in Western culture of the past few centuries.

Indeed, the discourse of compassion now includes animals that are dangerous and frightening to humans. Here, too, we can see hitherto unprecedented changes. Thus, for example, mammals such as big cats, bears, and wolves are dangerous to human beings, but their beauty, and the attraction and affection we have for them, makes it easier for humans to feel compassion for them and therefore to want to rescue them when they are in danger. The droves of visitors that zoos come to expect when they have new baby tigers, wolves, or bears, for example, highlights the interest in these animals that humans find "cute" and "cuddly," in spite of the danger they pose to people. The discourse of compassion, however, is moving beyond such wild animals that we see as dangerous yet cute and beautiful and is beginning to encompass animals that humans perceive not only as perilous and frightening but also those for which we are filled with aversion, even disgust. The *Animal Planet* show "Gator Boys" exemplifies this cultural transition, as the show's protagonists rescue nuisance alligators in south Florida and release them into the wild, rather than killing them for their skin and meat.³ The show's emphasis on the ethical treatment of animals like alligators, which are dangerous to humans without enjoying any benefit of being perceived as cute and cuddly, demonstrates the growing importance in American culture of treating all animals ethically, regardless of how we perceive them. Think of the growing movement to save sharks, of which more than 100 million are killed each year just for their fins. Although sharks remain terrifying to humans, exhibiting few, if any, redeeming qualities for their affection—remember Steven Spielberg's classic *Jaws* or the immensely successful recent *Sharknado*, both being movies that thrive on human fear and horror of the shark—"thanks to good public policy and the power of public education and multimedia campaigns featuring stars such as Yao Ming, Jackie Chan and Ang Lee, killing sharks for shark fin soup is no longer cool."⁴ In Montauk, New York, locus of the famed "Monster Fishing" tournaments created by Frank Mundus, who was the model for the macho shark hunter Quint in *Jaws*, the massive killing of sharks and the display of their tails and dorsal fins has been a huge tourist attraction every summer. But in July 2013, new rules came to govern the competition for the very first time: not one shark was killed. "Instead, all of the sharks caught in the contest, being held this weekend, will be photographed and released where they are caught. Fishermen will be asked to use circle hooks, believed to inflict less damage on the fish. . . . It is enough to make some of the old fishermen here wonder what is happening to the world."⁵ Indeed, the culture turn of the late 1960s and the decade of the 1970s and its accompanying animal turn have also reached the tip of Long Island and changed the world there, too, in terms of what now passes for acceptable—indeed socially expected—attitudes and behavior toward animals, sharks included.

This completely revamped view of and approach toward all animals, well beyond the cute and cuddly ones, has reached further than those currently alive. Thus, paleontologist Michael Archer has embarked on two projects to bring back two completely extinct animals: the Thilacine Project to resurrect the Tasmanian tiger, which, despite its name, was a member of the marsupial rather than the feline family; and the Lazarus Project to return to us the gastric brooding frog. Apart from the major scientific significance that has spurred Archer to commit to these projects, he has made it emphatically clear that there is a much greater ethical imperative that drives his endeavor in that he—and a steadily increasing number of people—believes that because it was humans who were the sole reason for these animals' extinction, it is our "moral obligation" (Archer's words) that we bring them back to life and their rightful presence on this earth.[6] Few things better demonstrate how our perception of animals and our treatment of them have changed than Archer's description of how the zookeepers in Hobart, Tasmania, willfully neglected the very last of these tigers on earth, letting him starve and freeze to death in his abysmally small and filthy cage while filming this animal's demise. Adding insult to injury, these men showed their product with zero sense of shame, perhaps even pride in having gotten rid of the last representative of this despised species. What was part of the norm in the 1930s became unthinkable, indeed criminal, in the wake of the animal turn of the late 1960s and 1970s. A recent example is the Symbicort commercial that shows a grandfather who can finally breathe freely thanks to this product's fine asthma-blocking effects and thus can go on a fishing trip with his son and grandson. The commercial distinctly shows the release of the fish into the creek instantly after he has caught it. In other words, the discourse of compassion toward animals of virtually all kinds has reached such social valence and cultural normalcy in the United States of 2013 that a major pharmaceutical giant like AstraZeneca, producer of Symbicort, simply sees the releasing of caught fish back into the water as its own norm or— even if it might not—feels compelled to do so on account of the pressures and expectations of socially accepted attitudes and norms.

To be sure, this wave of compassion and empathy for the weak remains a prerogative of advanced industrial societies governed by liberal democratic polities. Moreover, as we argued in the introduction, in these too, this compassionate approach toward the disempowered hails from a milieu of material security, if not outright abundance and luxury. In the American case, one finds more people in the blue states who have internalized this recent moral code and use it as a compass for their behavior than are found in the red states. Thus, there can be no question that the growth of the discourse of compassion and its deployment into social action bespeaks a material comfort that serves as its necessary though far from sufficient base. One could well argue that the United States and its liberal democratic partners and allies in the advanced industrial world were sufficiently wealthy in decades preceding the late 1960s and the 1970s to have developed this empathetic and compassionate view of the disempowered. But on the whole, they did not. So there is more to the story than material comfort.

Indeed, this also entails the morals of a certain zeitgeist that continues its legacy to this day. Although we do not mean to extol the late 1960s and the decade of the 1970s as being some sort of supernatural force of virtue and good, and although we are fully aware of the ugly sides of this era and the costs that these wrought for many individuals, as well as civil society and the state, we do believe that a kind of democratic wave commenced at this time that not only encompassed many countries, thus forming what has come to be known as the Third Wave of Democracy, but also unleashed a force of inclusion of the hitherto excluded that—at its essence—is profoundly democratic. Thus, fighting for the livelihood, hence the most fundamental rights, of the snail darter—a relatively uncuddly being by any conventional measure of affection and aesthetics—did indeed constitute an act of inclusion and thus a profoundly democratic one. After all, what is the essence of democracy if not the constant struggle for the inclusion of the formerly excluded not only in the formal decision-making structures of politics, but also in their being accorded full equality not just in the formally legal sense of this concept but rather in that of the bestowing of dignity and respect? Snail darters, sharks, alligators, polar bears, and Golden Retrievers do not vote in elections; but they are our full equals in that they, too, are sentient beings deserving—at a minimum—an unthreatened life with no pain. It would not be incorrect to argue that the zeitgeist of the late 1960s and the decade of the 1970s succeeded in implementing—at least partially—the Bentham-based sensitivities that came to view animals as humans' moral equals not by virtue of their being able to reason, speak, read, or write but to suffer.

The growth in this discourse of compassion and empathy directed toward an inclusion of the hitherto disempowered has—not by chance, of course—witnessed the overrepresentation of women as its crucial protagonists. For many reasons, not least the fact that women had been among the excluded for so long and were thus "natural" allies of other excluded groups, the discourse of compassion and empathy toward all disempowered—animals included—has been not only heavily feminized but has come to constitute a "package deal" of a growing counter-narrative that has begun to question, if not downright oppose, the conventional tenets of *man's* (on purpose) relationship to nature. As mentioned in this book, one can perceive the thrust of the entire breed specific rescue project as a taming of men on all levels, not least in their relations to animals. Indeed, plenty of recent research, well summarized by Adam Grant, exists that demonstrates quite convincingly how the presence of women makes men more generous, charitable, understanding, forgiving, and compassionate.[7]

Bill Gates, who spurned establishing charities for a long time, developed into one of the world's most generous philanthropists after his marriage and the birth of his daughter. In a commencement address at Harvard University, Gates openly credited his wife and daughter for being the decisive catalysts of his becoming engaged in philanthropic activities. "Daughters apparently soften fathers and evoke caretaking tendencies. . . . There are even studies showing that American legislators with daughters vote more liberally; this is also true of British male voters. . . . Social scientists believe that the empathetic, nurturing behaviors of sisters rub off on their brothers."[8]

Needless to say, not all men have taken kindly to this softening development. It was not only Huck Finn who wanted to escape Mrs. Douglas's "sivilizing" care. Many men before and since have associated manhood with a clear distancing from women's constraining powers and confining tendencies, essentially from being tamed—emasculated—by women. An example is the thousands upon thousands of almost exclusively male soccer fans every weekend in European stadia that—in a world in which the discourse of compassion has become a major, perhaps even dominant, narrative of official Europe—offer the last safe space of unbridled maleness, of despising compassion, of spurning empathy, of being as politically incorrect as possible, of spewing the worst kinds of racism and anti-Semitic venom that one simply cannot utter anymore in official "sivilized" post-Holocaust Europe with its feminized sensibilities and discourse. In the United States, too, the exact same backlash exists.

One need not see the male challenge to this feminized narrative of compassion and empathy as gloomily as Susan Faludi did in her book *Backlash: The Undeclared War against American Women*. Nor does one have to agree with all of Mariah Burton Nelson's findings in her equally important book *The Stronger Women Get, the More Men Love Football* to understand that any challenges to the power of an existing order will create a backlash and resistance.[9]

Although it was committed feminists who formed the vanguard of the women's movement and although it was animal rights activists who played a parallel agenda-setting role for the vast reforms that have come to improve the lives of many animals in the course of the past four to five decades, and although it has always been the decidedly nonnormal, nonordinary revolutionaries who have instigated any meaningful change, it precisely remains the task of the very normal, the highly ordinary, the most prosaic to convert these massive shifts and bursts of change into regular habits of daily life. There is an inevitable trickle-down process of diffusion that characterizes all social change in that initially radical ideas, almost always advocated by a disliked fringe, mutate into the mainstream and become part of the establishment.

It is the result of this trickle-down process that constitutes the core of this book. Virtually none of the rescue interviewees or any of our survey subjects held anything close to what one could vaguely characterize as radical ideas espoused by animal rights activists. Indeed, as will be recalled, especially from our data in Chapter 2, the typical (mostly female) person forming the backbone of the breed specific canine rescue movement explicitly rejects the world of animal rights advocates and dismisses animal liberation not only as unrealistic in its aims but also, worse still, detrimental to the very constituents it purports to help, namely the animals. One of the most notable characteristics of the canine rescue world's activists has indeed been their ordinariness, their normalcy. These are "regular" middle-of-the-road American women with not an iota of revolutionary ambition in thought or deed within them. And still, we argue, they very much form one strain among many that comprise the discourse of compassion that has changed the way of life in the advanced industrial world over the past four to five decades. These rescuers do not feel any closeness to animal liberationists or animal rights activists and never tire of emphasizing the seemingly unbridgeable gap between the former's vision and their own. And yet, we perceive both of these distinct groups as part of a very similar, perhaps even identical, project: the fundamental alteration of previously encrusted human–animal relations. Our rescuers would never dream of destroying a research laboratory to free the animals on which experiments were being conducted. Nor would they ever spill blood on furs at fashion shows or at the opera. Instead, what we find fascinating and very much part of this book's theme is the virtual absence of such furs in any of the main operas of the contemporary Western world where they were virtually required ornaments and proper dress barely four decades ago.

We also find it fascinating and very much the result of the aforementioned trickle-down mechanism of diffusion that by the late 1970s and throughout the 1980s as well as in all subsequent decades, relatively affluent (mostly female) people with no inclination toward any radicalism started to care enough about the welfare of dogs to go to the inordinate trouble and often considerable expense to organize these new entities called breed specific rescue groups. The way the rescuers and animal rights activists comprise the same world could best be related to an equally powerful revolutionary movement that preceded the current one by almost exactly one century: socialism. Here, too, there emerged completely different interpretations as to what socialism really ought to be; how to conceptualize it; and, most important, how best to attain and implement it. And from the beginning there developed internal rifts in this world that led not only to mutual suspicions and recriminations as well as constant contempt but also to outright hatred, indeed armed conflict, among the different protagonists. This, of course, is not the place to belabor the century-long rivalry and hatred between social democrats and communists. Anybody vaguely familiar with the history of the Old Left in the late nineteenth and throughout the twentieth centuries in virtually all geographic locations of its political existence knows how deep these intra-left conflicts were. Suffice it to say that the gap on every conceivable dimension between Swedish social democracy and any Leninist-style communism, from its expression in the former Soviet Union to its current Cuban incarnation, could not have been any more pronounced. And yet they shared one crucially common component: the possible transformation of capitalism; barring that, most certainly the taming of its worst excesses.

The same pertains to the deep divisions of the New Left, which, as we argued in the introduction, became the progenitor of this book's topic. Just think of the deep hatred and ultimately irreconcilable differences that pitted the Fundamentalists and the Realists against each other in the early days of the German Green Party, leading to the expulsion of the former by the latter. Similar inimical differences have existed in the civil rights movement, the women's movement, and the environmental movement, so why should the movement concerned with animals be different? At first glance it appears that a woman engaged in rescuing Labrador Retrievers by homing some before their adoption to forever homes has absolutely nothing in common with an activist engaged with People for the Ethical Treatment of Animals (PETA). They most likely never speak to one another. Indeed, they probably share nothing but contempt for one another's activities and commitments, about which neither knows much beyond hearsay and generalizations that simply reinforce their already considerable mutual antipathy. But just as in the case of the Swedish social democrat and the Cuban communist, here, too, our protagonists do in fact share a common bond, goal, and commitment: the improvement of the lives of animals (we purposely refrained from using the term "welfare" here precisely because it is so ideologically fraught, thus exhibiting the very differences between these two people that we just described) by taming the wantonness of *man*-kind.

One could even argue that the mechanism of ideological diffusion reaches way beyond the targeted circle of activists, however broadly defined. In other words, what may matter more than preaching to a motley group of converts inhabiting a big unifying tent but exhibiting great diversity in temperament and strategic preferences is to have an effect on people who are far from this tent, however large, and might not even know of its existence. Thus, the more appropriate analogy for many of our rescuers might not so much be the moderation and gradualism of Swedish social democracy (in contrast to the radicalness of communism) and the realist wing of the German Greens (in contrast to the extremism of the fundamentalist), but rather the normal, "apolitical" Swedish housewife who has come to embrace all dimensions of the welfare state as the daily normalcy of her life or her German counterpart who has become a vehement opponent of nuclear power as well as of any kind of plastic packaging that she sees as detrimental to the environment. Needless to say, this diffusional success always entails the original cause's ideological dilution as well as a substantial moderation in the movement's passion and behavior. We believe emphatically that it is precisely breed specific dog rescue's complete ordinariness in contemporary American life that testifies to its tremendous success.

But success need not be permanent. Indeed, it must be earned every day, and it always encounters obstacles. We see two obstacles in particular confronting the rescue movement: the first hails precisely from its very origin, namely, the creation of a particular generation and a very special zeitgeist. The writings of Karl Mannheim, among others, have emphasized the staying power of generations, or—put differently—how a particular generation creates a set of norms and values with which it remains identified for the entirety of its members' physical existence. Being impregnated by particularly poignant political, social, and cultural experiences in one's early adulthood (late teens, early twenties) creates a kind of path dependence, a sort of solid track, from which one is not likely to deviate too much throughout one's life. The lasting commonalities particular to a generation will remain especially potent if they were forged in a period of great systemic changes, which the late 1960s and the decade of the 1970s most assuredly were. As we argued in the introduction, it was at this juncture that what came to be called the culture turn connoted nothing less than the end of the mores and values that so dominated middle-class life since the Victorian era. Little has remained the same since: not the way we dress, speak, relate to people, form families, think and treat the disempowered— and relate to animals, dogs in particular. Simply put, canine rescue is one of the '68-er generation's contributions to the civilizing process, thus making the whole project immensely generation specific. But these boomers are getting on in years and, of course, the question is becoming increasingly urgent whether people belonging to completely different generations will share the same passion for rescue as its founders did. Thus, for example, in a number of interviews we heard the repeated worry that finding quality volunteers who are committed to the cause for the long run was becoming increasingly difficult. Plenty of people seem to be willing to give money to rescues, but getting folks to foster, run errands, go to shelters, organize home visits—in short perform the daily tasks that make the whole rescue project function—has become harder. Every founding generation faces the challenge of passing along its commitment and mission to its successors.

This leads us to the second obstacle, which we discussed under Max Weber's rubric of the routinization of charisma, in other words the mutation of formally personalistic rule and authority into institutions beholden to a legal-rational—and decidedly nonpersonal—authority structure that guarantees continuity of operations and existence regardless of the individual officeholder's personal attributes, qualifications, and commitment. As we argued repeatedly in this book, many rescues have yet to undergo the transformation from the impressive verve of founding individuals who have given their all for these dogs to a more bureaucratic modus operandi of a well-functioning large organization. Given the very nature of breed specific rescue that at its core rests first and foremost in its virtually ubiquitous volunteerism, can this endeavor ever exist based on an impersonal organizational structure? Doesn't rescue rise and fall purely with the commitment of dedicated individuals whose sole reward lies in their realization that their work contributed to the welfare of needy dogs?

We conclude this book on an optimistic note for one simple reason: the nature of democracy and the process of democratization. It is outbursts (like we witnessed in the late 1960s and throughout the decade of the 1970s) that create the hope toward which people strive. But it is the mundane nature of their steps that truly liberates them. Democracy is a chimera whose approximation in daily life is what truly matters. The end (democracy) may never be fully attainable, but it is the means to reach this end that leads to an actually lived democracy. There can be no more influential commentator on precisely this interaction than Max Weber's contemporary Robert Michels, whose work on democracy and the democratic process's daily difficulties and challenges remains as relevant today as it was exactly 100 years ago when he created his masterpiece *Political Parties: A Sociological Study of the Oligarchical Tendencies of Modern Democracy*. Michels wrote: "Democracy is a treasure which no one will ever discover by deliberate search. But in continuing our search, in laboring indefatigably to discover the undiscoverable, we shall perform a work which will have fertile results in the democratic sense."[10] As a small part of a much larger movement, breed specific canine rescue has labored indefatigably to discover the undiscoverable: the complete and lasting eradication of any and all animal abuse. But until such lofty goals become reality, the only thing that matters is the process taking us toward them, which features the granting of succor, safety, and—most important—dignity to needy creatures whom humans can help. The movement that we present in this book deserves high praise for having done just that, and we remain optimistic about its continued contributions to *Tikkun Olam*, Hebrew for "repairing" or "healing the world."

Notes

1. Leslie Irvine, *If You Tame Me: Understanding Our Connection with Animals* (Philadelphia: Temple University Press, 2004), p. 184.

2. The Daily Bunny. "Buy a Shirt, Save a Bun!" June 12, 2013. http://daily bunny.org/2013/06/12/buy-a-shirt-save-a-bun/ (accessed on July 16, 2013).

3. Animal Planet. "About Gator Boys: Animal Planet." http://animal.discovery .com/tv-shows/gator-boys/about-this-show/about-gator-boys.htm (accessed on July 15, 2013).

4. CNN. "How the World Is Saving the Shark." July 15, 2013. http://www.cnn .com/2013/07/15/opinion/sonenshine-sharks/index.html (accessed on July 16, 2013).

5. Jim Rutenberg, "Rethinking Tournaments Where Sharks Always Lose," *New York Times*, July 22, 2013. http://www.nytimes.com/2013/07/23/nyregion /rethinking-tournaments-where-sharks-always-lose.html?_r=0 (accessed on May 1, 2014).

6. TED. "Michael Archer: How We'll Resurrect the Gastric Brooding Frog, the Tasmanian Tiger." http://www.ted.com/talks/michael_archer_how_we_ll _resurrect_the_gastric_brooding_frog_the_tasmanian_tiger.html (accessed on July 19, 2013).

7. Adam Grant, "Why Men Need Women." *New York Times*, July 21, 2013. http://www.nytimes.com/2013/07/21/opinion/sunday/why-men-need-women .html?pagewanted=all (accessed on May 1, 2014).

8. Cited in ibid.

9. Susan Faludi, *Backlash: The Undeclared War against American Women* (New York: Broadway Books, 2006); Mariah Burton Nelson, *The Stronger Women Get, the More Men Love Football: Sexism and the American Culture of Sports* (New York: Harcourt Brace, 1994).

10. Robert Michels, *Political Parties: A Sociological Study of the Oligarchical Tendencies of Modern Democracy* (New York: Free Press, 1962), p. 38.

Appendix A: Data From Our Survey of Michigan Rescues

Table I. Demographic characteristics of survey respondents.

Demographic category	N (Relative frequency)	Total*
Sex		255
Female	235 (92%)	
Male	20 (8%)	
Sexual orientation		251 (98%)
Heterosexual	241 (96%)	
Gay/Lesbian	6 (2%)	
Bisexual	4 (2%)	
Age		255
18–35	63 (25%)	
36–55	127 (50%)	
56–75	64 (25%)	
Over 75	1 (>1%)	
Education level		246 (96%)
High school or equiv.	19 (8%)	
Some college	47 (19%)	
Associate's degree	25 (10%)	
Bachelor's degree	78 (32%)	
Postbachelor/professional degree	77 (31%)	
Employment		219 (86%)
Full-time	152 (69%)	
Part-time	32 (15%)	
Work in the home	15 (7%)	
Retired	20 (9%)	
Household income		255
$0–50,000	72 (28%)	
$50,001–100,000	117 (46%)	
Over $100,001	66 (26%)	
Children in the home		254 (99%)
No	206 (81%)	
Yes	48 (19%)	

Table I. (continued)

Demographic category	N (Relative frequency)	Total*
Type of community		254 (99%)
Urban	74 (29%)	
Suburban	92 (36%)	
Small town/rural	88 (35%)	
Marital status		251 (98%)
Married or living with partner, never divorced	125 (50%)	
Married or living with partner, previously divorced	48 (19%)	
Single	71 (28%)	
Widowed	7 (3%)	

* Differences in the totals arise because of respondents who entered their own category for the questions or who did not answer the question. Some categories used in our statistical model were collapsed for the purposes of this table.

Andrei S. Markovits and Robin Queen, "Women and the World of Dog Rescue: A Case Study of the State of Michigan," *Society and Animals* 17 (2009): 325–342.

Table 2. Demographic characteristics of the respondents we contacted for interviews and of those we actually interviewed.

Demographic category	Contacted	Actually interviewed (percentage of those contacted)
Sex		
Female	56	36 (64%)
Male	4	1 (25%)
Age		
18–35	9	5 (55%)
36–55	27	18 (67%)
56–75	24	14 (58%)
Education level		
High school or equiv.	5	2 (40%)
Some college	12	6 (50%)
Associate's degree	6	2 (33%)
Bachelor's degree	20	14 (70%)
Postbachelor/professional degree	15	11 (73%)
Other	2	2 (100%)
Employment		
Full-time	32	19 (59%)
Part-time	8	8 (100%)
Work in the home	3	1 (33%)
Retired	5	2 (40%)
Other	12	7 (58%)
Leadership		
Yes	26	16 (62%)
No	34	21 (62%)
Household income		
$0–50,000	18	10 (56%)
$50,001–100,000	23	16 (70%)
Over $100,001	17	11 (65%)

Andrei S. Markovits and Robin Queen, "Women and the World of Dog Rescue: A Case Study of the State of Michigan," *Society and Animals* 17 (2009): 325–342.

Table 3. Relative agreement, by sex of respondent, with the statements "Animals have the same basic rights as people"; "I would rather spend time with my dog than my spouse/significant other"; "I have friends who spend as much time with their dogs as I do with mine." Agreement was based on a 7-point Likert Scale.

	Mean	Standard dev.	Mean difference	t	Sig.
Basic rights for animals (N)			1.01	2.166	.04*
Female (229)	5.26	1.638			
Male (20)	4.25	2.023			
Spend time with dog rather than spouse			.68	1.878	.07
Female (224)	4.00	1.508			
Male (20)	3.32	1.600			
Friends who spend time with dogs			.65	1.909	.06
Female (226)	4.35	1.460			
Male (20)	3.70	1.559			

Andrei S. Markovits and Robin Queen, "Women and the World of Dog Rescue: A Case Study of the State of Michigan," *Society and Animals* 17 (2009): 325–342.

Table 4. Relative agreement, by sex of respondent, with the following costs of rescue work: "I don't have enough time for other things I want to do"; "I can't get any paid work done"; "I spend too much time on the computer." Agreement was based on a 7-point Likert Scale.

	Mean	Standard dev.	Mean difference	t	Sig.
Not enough time (N)			.82	2.147	.04*
Female (227)	2.77	1.989			
Male (20)	1.95	1.605			
Paid work not getting done			.55	4.613	.000*
Female (226)	1.65	1.448			
Male (20)	1.10	0.308			
Too much time on the computer			.73	2.661	.01*
Female (227)	2.33	1.868			
Male (20)	1.60	1.095			

Andrei S. Markovits and Robin Queen, "Women and the World of Dog Rescue: A Case Study of the State of Michigan," *Society and Animals* 17 (2009): 325–342.

Table 5. Relative agreement, by sex of respondent, with the following statements concerning why more women than men are involved in rescue work: "Women have more time"; "Women have fewer responsibilities"; "Women are more caring and nurturing"; "Women are more interested in animal well-being"; "Women are more willing to deal with problems." Agreement was based on a 7-point Likert Scale.

	Mean	Standard dev.	Mean difference	t	Sig.
More time (N)			−1.08	2.910	.004*
Female (232)	2.22	1.586			
Male (20)	3.30	1.750			
Fewer responsibilities			−1.02	2.485	.02*
Female (230)	1.43	0.972			
Male (20)	2.45	1.820			
Caring and Nurturing			1.36	3.534	.000*
Female (232)	5.41	1.625			
Male (20)	4.05	1.932			
Animal well-being			1.28	3.285	.001*
Female (231)	5.08	1.656			
Male (20)	3.80	1.824			
Willing to deal with problems			1.21	2.756	.006*
Female (232)	4.71	1.877			
Male (20)	3.50	1.906			

Andrei S. Markovits and Robin Queen, "Women and the World of Dog Rescue: A Case Study of the State of Michigan," *Society and Animals* 17 (2009): 325–342.

Appendix B: Breed Specific Canine Rescue Survey

Part I: About You

1. Choose your age.
    18–25 years old
    26–35 years old
    36–45 years old
    46–55 years old
    56–65 years old
    66–75 years old
    Over 75 years old
2. What is your sex?
    Female
    Male
    Transgender/Other
3. What is your primary race/ethnicity? (Select all that apply.)
    Caucasian/White
    African American/Black
    Hispanic/Latina/o
    Asian or Asian American/Pacific Islander
    Native American/Indian
    Other (Please explain.): _____
4. What is your highest attained education level?
    Less than 12th grade, no diploma
    High school diploma/equivalent

Some college, no degree
Associate's degree
Bachelor's degree
Master's degree
Professional degree
Doctoral degree
Other (Please explain.): _____

5. What is your sexual orientation? (Select which best describes you.)
   Gay/Lesbian
   Bisexual
   Heterosexual
   Unknown
   Other (Please explain.): _____

6. What is your marital status? (Select your current status.)
   Living with partner
   Single, never divorced
   Single, previously divorced
   Married, never divorced
   Married, previously divorced
   Widowed
   Other (Please explain.): _____

7. How many people under 18 currently live in your household?
   0 people
   1–3 people
   4–6 people
   6 or more people

8. How many people 18 years old or older currently live in your household?
   1 person
   2 people
   3–5 people
   6 or more people

9. Do you share your living expenses with a roommate or housemate who is not your spouse or partner?
   Yes
   No
   Unsure

10. How many bedrooms does your home have?
    0–1 bedroom
    2–3 bedrooms

4–5 bedrooms

More than 6 bedrooms

11. How many full or partial bathrooms does your home have?

1 bathroom

2 bathrooms

3–5 bathrooms

More than 6 bathrooms

12. Do you have a formal dining room?

Yes

No

Unsure

13. Do you have a recreation room?

Yes

No

Unsure

14. Which of the following best describes the structure of the house where you live?

Multiunit/apartment building

Duplex

Attached single family (e.g., condominium, row house)

Detached single family, with foundation

Manufactured/mobile

Other (Please explain.): _____

15. Which of the following best describes your living situation?

Own home

Rent home

Other (Please explain.): _____

16. Which of the following best describes the setting where you live?

Large urban (population over 250,000)

Small urban (population under 250,000)

Suburb

Small town

Rural

17. Which of the following best describes your lot/yard?

Fully fenced back and/or front yard

Partially fenced back and/or front yard

Unfenced

No yard

Other (Please explain.): _____

18. How many acres is your property (give best estimate if unknown)?
    Less than 1/4 acre
    1/4 acre
    1/2 acre
    1 acre
    2 acres
    3–5 acres
    6–10 acres
    11–20 acres
    More than 20 acres

19. Estimate your yearly household income from all sources.
    Under $10,000
    $10,000–$30,000
    $30,000–$50,000
    $50,000–$70,000
    $70,000–$100,000
    $100,000–$200,000
    $200,000–$300,000
    More than $300,000

20. What is your employment status?
    Employed full time
    Employed part time
    Full-time homemaker
    Not employed and looking for work
    Not employed and in school
    Not employed
    Retired
    Other (Please explain.): _____

21. If you are employed for pay, what is your occupation?

22. If you are not employed for pay, but have been, what is your usual
    occupation?

23. How many hours a week do you work away from the home (either
    for pay or as a volunteer)?
    0 hours
    1–10 hours
    11–20 hours
    21–30 hours
    31–40 hours
    41–50 hours
    More than 50 hours

24. What is your primary political preference? (Select the one that best describes you.)

   None, not political
   Independent
   Democrat
   Republican
   Green/Rainbow
   Libertarian
   Other (Please explain.): _____

25. On a scale of 1–7, how relevant are politics to your life?

   Very relevant → Not relevant
   1   2   3   4   5   6   7

26. What is your primary religious preference? (Select the one that best describes you.)

   Protestant
   Catholic
   Do not follow organized religion or have no religious preference
   Jewish
   Muslim
   Buddhist
   Hindu
   Unitarian Universalist
   Neo-pagan
   Other (Please explain.): _____

27. On a scale of 1–7, do you consider yourself theologically more conservative or more liberal?

   Very conservative → Very liberal
   1   2   3   4   5   6   7

28. On a scale of 1–7, how relevant is religion to your life?

   Very relevant → Not relevant
   1   2   3   4   5   6   7

29. Which of the following best describes your primary diet?

   I eat most types of foods at least occasionally
   I eat no red meat
   I am primarily vegetarian, but I eat fish/seafood
   I am vegetarian or vegan
   Other (Please explain.): _____

30. On a scale of 1–7, what is your general physical fitness level?

   Very unfit → Very fit
   1   2   3   4   5   6   7

31. On a scale of 1–7, what is your general physical activity level?
    Very inactive → Very active
    1 2 3 4 5 6 7
32. For what organizations, other than dog rescue, do you volunteer
    (list up to 5)? Please list the organization, the type of volunteer
    work you do, and the estimated number of hours per month.

Part 2: About You and Your Dogs

1. On average, how many hours a week do you spend reading books/
   magazines/journals that focus on dogs?
   0 hours
   1–3 hours
   4–6 hours
   7–10 hours
   More than 10 hours
2. How many magazines or journals do you subscribe to that are
   focused primarily on dogs?
   0 magazines
   1–2 magazines
   3–5 magazines
   6–8 magazines
   More than 8 magazines
3. Which of the following is closest to the rough percentage of your
   non-work Internet time per week that is devoted to dog issues?
   0–5%
   15%
   25%
   40%
   60%
   80%
   100%
4. On a scale of 1–7, do you consider yourself a "dog person"?
   Not at all → Absolutely
   1 2 3 4 5 6 7

5. On a scale of 1–7, what do you believe about the statement "There are no bad dogs, only bad dog owners?"

 Completely disagree → Completely agree

 1 2 3 4 5 6 7

6. On a scale of 1–7, would you say you generally prefer people or dogs?

 People → Dogs

 1 2 3 4 5 6 7

7. On a scale of 1–7, how often do you feel like people don't understand your relationship with your dog(s)?

 Never → Always

 1 2 3 4 5 6 7

8. On a scale of 1–7, do you agree or disagree that animals have the same basic rights that people do?

 Completely disagree → Completely agree

 1 2 3 4 5 6 7

9. On a scale of 1–7, how often do you choose to spend time with your dog(s) rather than your spouse, significant other, or best friend?

 Never → Always

 1 2 3 4 5 6 7

10. On a scale of 1–7, how many of your friends spend as much time or more with their dog(s) as you do with yours?

 None of them → All of them

 1 2 3 4 5 6 7

11. Do you think you would have more friends or fewer friends if you didn't have a dog?

 More friends

 Fewer friends

 About the same number of friends

12. Among the people you know who spend as much time or more with their dogs as you do with yours, what rough percentage are women?

 0%

 10%

 25%

 40%

 60%

 80%

 100%

13. How many dogs currently live in your household?

 0 dogs

 1 dog

 2 dogs

 3 dogs

 4 dogs

 5 dogs

 More than 5 dogs

14. How many cats currently live in your household?

 0 cats

 1 cat

 2 cats

 3 cats

 4 cats

 5 cats

 More than 5 cats

15. How many animals other than cats and dogs currently live in your household?

 0 animals

 1 animal

 2 animals

 3 animals

 4 animals

 5 animals

 More than 5 animals

16. Please list the breed, age, and sex of each dog in your household (up to 10).

17. Which of the following comes closest to describing where your dog(s) normally sleep(s) at night?

 In bed with me or another member of the household

 In a bedroom, but not allowed on the bed

 Wherever he/she/they want to

 Outside

 Contained in a room other than a bedroom, such as a bathroom, laundry room or family room

 In a crate in my bedroom (or someone else's bedroom)

18. On a scale of 1–7, how important do you believe it is for dogs to live primarily in the house?

 Not important at all → Very important

 1   2   3   4   5   6   7

19. For any dog in your household who spends time alone, how many hours a day does he/she spend on average without the availability of human companionship?

    o hours

    1–4 hours

    5–8 hours

    9–12 hours

    More than 12 hours

20. Would you leave your dog(s) unattended in the house overnight?

    Yes

    No

    Maybe

    Don't know

21. Which of the following arrangements have you used in the last year for a trip of more than one night without your dog(s)? (Select all that apply.)

    Boarding facility

    Bring dog(s) to friend's home

    Have a friend stay in home with dog(s)

    Have friend/neighbor care for dog(s) but not stay in your home

    Hire pet sitter to care for dog(s) but not stay in your home

    Hire pet sitter to stay in your home with dog(s)

    Have not traveled without dog(s)

    Other (Please explain.): _____

22. Which of the following have you fed your adult dog(s) in the last month? (Select all that apply.)

    Raw food diet (Example: B.A.R.F.)

    Home cooked diet

    Vegetarian diet, either prepared or home made

    Regular dry dog food (Examples: Old Roy, Purina Dog Chow)

    Premium dry dog food (Examples: Science Diet, Iams, Eukanuba)

    Super premium dry dog food (Examples: Wellness, Canidae, Wysong)

    Regular canned food

    Premium or super-premium canned food

    Semimoist food

    Mix of regular canned and dry

    Mix of premium or super premium canned and dry

    Other (Please explain.): _____

23. How many days of the week does your dog do each of the following?

    Walk for at least 10 minutes on a leash

    0   1   2   3   4   5   6   7

    Run/Play in a fenced backyard

    0   1   2   3   4   5   6   7

    Run/Play in an unfenced backyard

    0   1   2   3   4   5   6   7

    Run/Play off leash in a large unfenced area such as a field, school yard, or park

    0   1   2   3   4   5   6   7

    Run/Play off leash in a large fenced area such as a field, school yard, or dog park

    0   1   2   3   4   5   6   7

    Work (e.g., farm work, service work, herding, protection work)

    0   1   2   3   4   5   6   7

    Activities training (e.g., agility, flyball, rally, formal obedience)

    0   1   2   3   4   5   6   7

24. What is your primary type of veterinary care?

    Free/reduced fee clinic, such as the Humane Society

    Emergency clinic

    Self-administered

    Mobile vet (e.g., a vet who makes house calls)

    Traditional veterinary clinic

    None

    Other (Please explain.): _____

25. Do you have expertise as a veterinarian, veterinarian assistant, or veterinarian technician?

    Yes

    No

    Unsure

26. Have you ever used holistic/natural/alternative veterinary care (e.g., herbs and medicinal plants; acupuncture)?

    Yes

    No

    Unsure

27. If you only had time to teach your dog(s) two commands, what would they be and why?

28. On a scale of 1–7, how likely are you to use a choke collar for your dog?

    Not at all likely → Extremely likely

    1   2   3   4   5   6   7

29. On a scale of 1–7, how likely are you to use food treats as a training tool for your dog?

    Not at all likely → Extremely likely

    1   2   3   4   5   6   7

30. On a scale of 1–7, how likely are you to roll a dog on its back to show you are the boss?

    Not at all likely → Extremely likely

    1   2   3   4   5   6   7

31. On a scale of 1–7, how likely are you to pop or jerk the leash as a training strategy?

    Not at all likely → Extremely likely

    1   2   3   4   5   6   7

32. Do any of your dogs compete/train in any of the following dog activities? (Select all that apply.)

    Agility
    Frisbee
    Formal obedience
    Rally
    Flyball
    Tracking
    Earthdog
    Dock diving
    Lure coursing
    Racing
    Dog freestyle (e.g., dancing)
    Other (Please explain.): _____

33. Do any of your dogs work/train in any of the following dog activities? (Select all that apply.)

    Search and Rescue
    Herding
    Guard work
    Therapy work
    Service work (e.g., seizure dog, guide-dog)
    Mushing/Sledding
    Hunting
    Other (Please explain.): _____

Part 3: About Your Rescue Work

1. How many years have you been involved in rescue work?
   Less than 1 year
   1–4 years
   5–7 years
   8–10 years
   More than 10 years
2. How did you learn about the main rescue group with which you are currently involved? (Select all that apply.)
   Adopted a dog from this group
   Heard about them from a friend
   Saw them at a dog event
   Saw them on the Internet
   Heard about them from my veterinarian
   Heard about them through another rescue organization
   Heard about them from my training club/organization
   Other (Please explain.):   _____
3. Roughly how many hours a week do you spend on dog rescue work?
   Less than 2 hours
   2–5 hours
   6–10 hours
   11–15 hours
   16–20 hours
   21–30 hours
   More than 30 hours
4. Rate the benefits of rescue work for you.
   I enjoy spending time with the other people in the group
   Not a benefit → An important benefit
   1   2   3   4   5   6   7
   I enjoy e-mailing and talking to people on the phone
   Not a benefit → An important benefit
   1   2   3   4   5   6   7
   I like to solve problems
   Not a benefit → An important benefit
   1   2   3   4   5   6   7
   I feel valued by my work with rescue
   Not a benefit → An important benefit
   1   2   3   4   5   6   7

I feel needed by my work in rescue
Not a benefit → An important benefit
1 2 3 4 5 6 7

5. Rate the benefits of rescue work for you.

I like raising awareness about the breed I rescue
Not a benefit → An important benefit
1 2 3 4 5 6 7

I like helping people find the dog of their dreams
Not a benefit → An important benefit
1 2 3 4 5 6 7

I get to spend more time with my spouse/loved ones who are also involved in rescue work
Not a benefit → An important benefit
1 2 3 4 5 6 7

It takes my mind off the stresses of life
Not a benefit → An important benefit
1 2 3 4 5 6 7

It relieves me of boredom
Not a benefit → An important benefit
1 2 3 4 5 6 7

6. Rate the benefits of rescue work for you.

It gives me a break from my family
Not a benefit → An important benefit
1 2 3 4 5 6 7

It gives me a break from my work
Not a benefit → An important benefit
1 2 3 4 5 6 7

I get to learn new things and hear about new ideas
Not a benefit → An important benefit
1 2 3 4 5 6 7

I get to meet new people
Not a benefit → An important benefit
1 2 3 4 5 6 7

7. Rate the costs of rescue work for you.

I don't have enough time for other things I want to do
Not a cost → A serious cost
1 2 3 4 5 6 7

My family or social life is suffering
Not a cost → A serious cost
1 2 3 4 5 6 7

I am not getting my paid work (or primary work) done

Not a cost → A serious cost

1   2   3   4   5   6   7

I have to spend too much time on the computer

Not a cost → A serious cost

1   2   3   4   5   6   7

There is too much drama

Not a cost → A serious cost

1   2   3   4   5   6   7

8. Rate the costs of rescue work for you.

I don't feel valued

Not a cost → A serious cost

1   2   3   4   5   6   7

There are too many unpleasant people to deal with

Not a cost → A serious cost

1   2   3   4   5   6   7

I don't have enough say in how the group works

Not a cost → A serious cost

1   2   3   4   5   6   7

I know there are many dogs we can't save

Not a cost → A serious cost

1   2   3   4   5   6   7

I don't spend enough time with my own dogs

Not a cost → A serious cost

1   2   3   4   5   6   7

9. Rate the costs of rescue work for you.

It is too much responsibility

Not a cost → A serious cost

1   2   3   4   5   6   7

10. How many years have you been involved in fostering dogs?

I have never fostered

Less than 1 year

1–4 years

5–7 years

8–10 years

More than 10 years

11. How many dogs have you fostered for the rescue organization(s) you are currently working with?

0 dogs

1–3 dogs

4–7 dogs

8–12 dogs

More than 12 dogs

12. How many dogs are you currently fostering?

    0 dogs

    1 dog

    2 dogs

    3 dogs

    More than 3 dogs

13. On a scale of 1–7, how important do you believe it is to try and save all dogs?

    Not important → Very important

    1 2 3 4 5 6 7

14. On a scale of 1–7, do you believe it is right to spay a pregnant female dog that comes into your rescue group?

    Under no circumstances → Always

    1 2 3 4 5 6 7

15. Does the main rescue organization you currently work with have any paid employees?

    Yes

    No

    Unsure

16. Approximately how many active volunteers does the main rescue organization you work with have currently?

    Fewer than 5 volunteers

    5–10 volunteers

    11–20 volunteers

    21–30 volunteers

    More than 30 volunteers

17. On a scale of 1–7, how difficult do you think it is for someone to adopt a dog from the main rescue organization you currently work with?

    Extremely difficult → Not difficult at all

    1 2 3 4 5 6 7

18. Do you currently hold a position of leadership in the main rescue group you work with?

    Yes

    No

    If yes, select all of the following that apply.

       President/Director

Vice-president
Secretary
Treasurer
Foster Home Coordinator
Intake Coordinator
Board Member
Other (Please explain.): _____
If no, have you held such a position in the past?
Yes
No
If yes, select all of the following that apply.
President/Director
Vice-president
Secretary
Treasurer
Foster Home Coordinator
Intake Coordinator
Board Member
Other (Please explain.): _____

19. In the rescue organization you work for, what rough percentage of the leadership positions are held by women?
0%
10%
30%
50%
70%
90%
100%

20. People have given many reasons for why more women than men seem to be involved in rescue work. Please indicate whether you agree or disagree with the following explanations:
Rescue work is less valued than other types of volunteer work
Strongly disagree → Strongly agree
1   2   3   4   5   6   7
Women have more time
Strongly disagree → Strongly agree
1   2   3   4   5   6   7
Women have fewer responsibilities
Strongly disagree → Strongly agree
1   2   3   4   5   6   7

Women are more caring and nurturing
Strongly disagree → Strongly agree
1 2 3 4 5 6 7
Women are more interested in animal well-being
Strongly disagree → Strongly agree
1 2 3 4 5 6 7

21. People have given many reasons for why more women than men seem to be involved in rescue work. Please indicate whether you agree or disagree with the following explanations.

Women are more interested in looking good by doing good
Strongly disagree → Strongly agree
1 2 3 4 5 6 7
Women are more alienated from other people
Strongly disagree → Strongly agree
1 2 3 4 5 6 7
Women are more willing to deal with problems
Strongly disagree → Strongly agree
1 2 3 4 5 6 7
Women are more likely to get emotional/social support from rescue work
Strongly disagree → Strongly agree
1 2 3 4 5 6 7
Women have less power and control in other parts of their lives
Strongly disagree → Strongly agree
1 2 3 4 5 6 7

22. List any other reasons why you think more women than men seem to be involved in rescue work.

23. On a scale of 1–7, do you think women seem to be better rescue workers than men?
Not at all → Absolutely
1 2 3 4 5 6 7

24. On a scale of 1–7, do you think women seem to care more about their companion animals than men?
Not at all → Absolutely
1 2 3 4 5 6 7

25. We will be conducting a small number of face-to-face interviews concerning dog rescue work. These interviews will last from 30 minutes to an hour on average and you will be compensated for your time with a $20 gift certificate to Amazon.com. Would you

be willing to be interviewed about your rescue work and your life with dogs?

Yes

No

26. If you are willing to be interviewed, please provide an e-mail address where you can be contacted.

Appendix C: Interview Questionnaire

- How did you come to love dogs? (dates when possible)
  - Why your particular breed?
- Why rescue? What was the transition from adoption or ownership to rescue?
- Please tell me about your history within animal rescue.

Organization

- Can you tell me a bit about the group's history, how it was started?
- What sorts of start-up funds did your group have, and where did you get them from?
- Does your group have 501(c)(3) status, and when did it get it?
- What are the rules for your group, and how were they developed? Are they more informal or codified?
- Could you please tell me what your adoption procedures are and why they are the way they are?
  - Does your group use adoption fees?
- What is the structure of your group's leadership?
  - How rigid is the structure?
- How are decisions made?
  - Big decisions
  - Day-to-day decisions

- How does your group delegate?
- How many active members does your group have and what do they do?
  - Are there specific positions within the group and are these positions and their responsibilities clearly codified?
- Does your group have a facility or is it solely foster homes?
- How do your group members communicate with each other?
- How does your group communicate with people who aren't in the group (newsletters, etc.)?
- Does your group network with other local breed rescues (even rescues of other breeds)?
- Does your group network with other breed rescues nationally?
- Does your group do any advertising?
  - What kinds of advertising?
  - What services or messages are in your group's advertisements?
- Does your group actively try to educate the public?
  - What about (breed, rescue, euthanasia)?
- How does your group handle owner surrenders?
- Does your group have a website?
  - What features does the website have?
- Does your group use social media such as Facebook or Twitter?
  - What does your group use these for?
- Does your group do any merchandising?
- What supplies does your group need?
  - How does your group get these supplies?
  - Is there a group credit card for supplies?
- Is your group insured?
  - What does the insurance cover?
- What is your group's operating budget?
  - Typical expenses associated with running the group?
    - Type and amount?
  - Typical income for the group?
    - Type and amount?
- Does your group do fundraising?
- Does your group work with any professionals? Do these professionals volunteer their services for the group or are they paid?
  - Veterinarian
  - Lawyer
  - Advertiser

- Merchandiser
- Webmaster
- Accountant
- Dog Trainer/Obedience Class Instructor
- Professional Groomer
- Other?

Efficacy

- What are your group's goals?
- What is your group's stance on euthanasia? Under what circumstances is it acceptable?
- How many dogs has your group moved to forever homes?
- What is the capacity of your facilities?
- Does your group only accept your particular breed?
  - Do they accept mixes with the breed?
  - Courtesy listings for other breeds?
- How many animals, on average, does your group have?
  - What percentage of these animals are ready for adoption?
  - What percentage are "unadoptable" but are undergoing rehabilitation (medical or behavioral) to be adoptable?
  - What percentage are "unadoptable" and are unlikely to become adoptable?
- What is the average length of time that a dog will spend with you before it is adopted?
- What's the average age of the dogs your group cares for?
  - Rough percentages of dogs by age?
- Does your group have a return clause for dogs?
  - What is the approximate return rate for dogs?
  - What is the re-placement rate for dogs?
- Does the group participate in activities other than rescue, such as showing or agility competitions, and what amount of time does your group spend on them?
- What sort of relationship does your group have with local humane societies and shelters?
- What sort of relationship does your group have with the local AKC club?

- What are some of the obstacles/problems that you have noticed with rescue? Things that make rescuing dogs more difficult?
- What challenges do you feel are specific to rescuing your breed?
  - How do you overcome breed specific challenges?
- What would you change about rescuing in general?

Appendix D: Interview Subjects

1. Adams, Robin. Delaware Valley Golden Retriever Rescue, 7/7/2009
2. Allen, Carol. Golden Retriever Rescue of Central New York, GRCA-NRC, 7/7/2009
3. Angell, Karen. Golden Retriever Rescue of Michigan, 8/8/2008
4. Appling, Toni. Atlanta Dog Squad, 8/3/2010
5. Augst, Burt. Middle Tennessee Golden Retriever Rescue, 7/28/2009
6. Bauer, Cindy. Greyhound Adoption of Greater Rochester, NY, 7/12/2013 (e-mail interview)
7. Board, Beryl. Retrieve a Golden of Minnesota, 7/29/2009
8. Bornstein, Bob. Sooner Golden Retriever Rescue, 8/12/2010
9. Bryan, Edith. Puget Sound Labrador Retriever Association, 8/12/2010
10. Carroll, Jane. Tidelands Poodle Club, 8/17/2009
11. Castleberry, Patti. Lone Star Labrador Retriever Rescue, 9/9/2010 (e-mail interview)
12. Compton, Amy. Tidelands Poodle Club, 8/17/2009
13. Cwiklowski, Craig. Wisconsin Adopt A Golden Rescue, 8/20/2010
14. Davin, Mike and Sharon. With a Golden Spirit, 8/23/2010
15. Demetrick, Barb. Golden Rescue (Canada), 6/23/2009
16. Distler, Maureen. Lowcountry Lab Rescue, 7/28/2010
17. Eckard, Jacky. Safe Harbor Lab Rescue, 7/29/2010

18. Elk, Barbara. Rescue A Golden of Arizona, 8/19/2010
19. Fisher, Phil. NORCAL Golden Retriever Rescue, 7/30/2009
20. Fitzpatrick, Gene. Golden Retriever Rescue Club of Charlotte, 8/17/2010
21. Foss, Gerry. Cocker Spaniel Rescue of New England, 8/17/2009
22. Genkinger, Lauren. Adopt a Golden Atlanta, 8/18/2010
23. Gurinskas, Norma. New Hampshire Doberman Rescue League, 8/17/2009
24. Haggerty, Deb. Homeward Bound Golden Retriever Rescue, 8/20/2009
25. Hildebrand, Becky. Rocky Mountain Labrador Retriever Rescue, 7/29/2010
26. Jones, Jody. Homeward Bound Golden Retriever Rescue, 8/20/2009
27. Jones, Julie. Southern California Labrador Retriever Rescue, 7/29/2010
28. Jordano, Alan. Grey-Save of Northwestern Pennsylvania, 6/30/2013 (e-mail interview)
29. Kassler, Annie. Yankee Golden Retriever Rescue, 7/9/2009
30. Knoche, Jan. Love a Golden Rescue, 8/9/2010
31. Kontos, Claire. Dobermans, 8/3/2009
32. Kruesi, Konrad. Veterinarian, 4/30/2008
33. Lukasik, Debbie. Golden Retriever Rescue of Wisconsin, 8/12/2010
34. Mackie, Rob and Joanna. Golden Rescue (Canada), 6/29/2009
35. Mahle, Cathy. Labs4Rescue, 8/3/2010
36. Maringo, Joe. Southwest PA Retriever Rescue Organization, 7/30/2010
37. Medendorp, Allie. Great Lakes Golden Retriever Rescue, 8/10/2010
38. Muir, Sarah. Labrador Retriever Rescue of the Hudson Valley, 9/6/2010 (e-mail interview)
39. Nygaard, Jane. Retrieve a Golden of Minnesota, 8/6/2009
40. Palmo, Nina. Heart of Texas Lab Rescue, 7/29/2010
41. Pesavento, Elena. Labrador Friends of the South, 8/8/2010
42. Poling, Jeannette. Golden Retriever Club of San Diego Rescue Service, 6/22/2009
43. Puglia, Joan. Yankee Golden Retriever Rescue, 6/30/2009
44. Richardson, Trish. Southwest Virginia Lab Rescue, 8/9/2010

45. Riegel, Renee. Greater Dayton Labrador Retriever Rescue, 8/18/2010
46. Schramm, Jake. Save-A-Bull Rescue, 7/10/2013 (e-mail interview)
47. Shervais, Mary Jane. Golden Retriever Rescue and Education Training, 8/17/2009
48. Siddon, Cindy. Kindred Spirits Greyhound Rescue, 7/11/2013 (e-mail interview)
49. Skare, Priscilla. Cape Fear Golden Retriever Rescue, 8/19/2010
50. Stanley, Tami. Texas Lab Rescue, 7/29/2010
51. Tillay, Bob. Dirk's Fund, 8/18/2010
52. Vanderbloomen, Mary. The Lab Connection, 8/9/2010
53. Viola, Joy. Yankee Golden Retriever Rescue, 7/16/2009
54. Watson, Jen. Pit Sisters, 6/17/2013 (e-mail interview)
55. Wells, Susan. Labrador Retriever Rescue, Inc., 8/10/2010
56. Whitson, Tom. Golden Retriever Rescue of Houston, 8/9/2010
57. Wilcox, Kevin. Peppertree Rescue, 8/18/2010
58. Winter, Lana. Shore Hearts Golden Retriever Rescue, 7/29/2009
59. Wyatt, Colleen. Luvin' Labs, 8/4/2010
60. Young, Kari. Arizona Adopt A Greyhound, 6/2/2013 (e-mail interview)

Index